James Anthony Froude

History of England from the Fall of Wolsey to the Defeat of the Spanish Armada

James Anthony Froude

History of England from the Fall of Wolsey to the Defeat of the Spanish Armada

ISBN/EAN: 9783741135910

Manufactured in Europe, USA, Canada, Australia, Japa

Cover: Foto ©ninafisch / pixelio.de

Manufactured and distributed by brebook publishing software (www.brebook.com)

James Anthony Froude

History of England from the Fall of Wolsey to the Defeat of the Spanish Armada

HISTORY OF ENGLAND

FROM THE FALL OF WOLSEY TO THE DEATH OF ELIZABETH.

REIGN OF ELIZABETH.

VOLUME II.

HISTORY OF ENGLAND

FROM

THE FALL OF WOLSEY

TO

THE DEFEAT OF THE SPANISH ARMADA.

BY

JAMES ANTHONY FROUDE, M.A.

LATE FELLOW OF EXETER COLLEGE, OXFORD

VOLUME VIII.

LONDON:
LONGMANS, GREEN, AND CO.
1870.

CONTENTS OF VOLUME II.

CHAPTER VII.

	PAGE
Ireland under Queen Mary	1
Habits and character of the people	2
The especial wretchedness of the Pale	3
Report of 1559	5
The King of Spain declines the advances of the Irish Chiefs	9
The Scotch in Antrim	10
The O'Neil and his children	11
Election of Shan O'Neil by tanistry	12
Schemes of Shan for the Ulster sovereignty	14
Philip again discourages an Irish rebellion	16
Loyalty of the Earl of Kildare	17
Letter of Shan O'Neil to Elizabeth	18
The English Government proposes to invade Ulster	19
Shan carries off the Countess of Argyle	21
Skirmish at Armagh	22
Defeat of the Earl of Sussex	26
Attempt to procure the assassination of Shan	28
Second invasion of Ulster	29
Shan goes to London	31
Shan at the Court of Elizabeth	32
Murder of the Baron of Dungannon	35
Indentures between Shan and Elizabeth, and return of Shan to Ireland	37
Fresh treachery of Sussex	38
Shan again rebels	40
The Countess	42

vi   *Contents.*

	PAGE
Disagreements between the Irish Council and the Earl of Sussex	43
Campaign in Ulster	44
Irish successes	46
Second attempt to assassinate Shan	49
Triumph of Shan	53
Inquiry into the disorders of the Pale	54
Sir Nicholas Arnold	55
Desolation of Munster	56

CHAPTER VIII.

War with France	58
Negotiations for peace	60
The Peace of Troyes	66
Conspiracies to murder Elizabeth	67
Defences of England	68
The French Embassy at Bekesbourne	69
Improved relations with Spain	71
The Succession	72
Mary Stuart and Lord Robert Dudley	73
The Earl of Bothwell	75
Mary Stuart prefers Darnley	77
Elizabeth urges Lord Robert	78
Book of John Hales on the Succession	80
Objections to Darnley in Scotland	82
Guzman de Silva comes to England	83
Reception of de Silva at the Court	84
A Party at Richmond	87
The Dudley marriage	89
Elizabeth at Cambridge	91
Disorders in the Church	93
Fresh thoughts of the Archduke Charles	94
Sir James Melville	95
Lord Robert Dudley is created Earl of Leicester	99
Delay of Parliament	100
Mary Stuart's friends in England	101

Contents.

	PAGE
Conversation between Elizabeth and de Silva	102
The Scotch succession	105
Instructions to Bedford and Randolph	106
State of feeling in Scotland	109
Conference at Berwick	110
Final demands of the Scots	113
Reply of Cecil	115
David Ritzio	117
Affected compliance of Mary Stuart	118
Proposed marriage between Elizabeth and the King of France	121
Darnley goes to Scotland	127
The settlement of the succession is postponed	129
Discipline of the Church of England	130
Marriage of the Clergy	131
The Queen and the Bishops	132
The Queen insists on the observance of the Act of Uniformity	134
The Queen at Paul's Cross	136
Archbishop Parker remonstrates	137
Ecclesiastical Commission at Lambeth	139
Riots in London	140
Letter of Parker to Cecil	141
Alarm in Scotland	143
Scene at the Market Cross at Edinburgh	144
The Queen of Scots resolves to marry Darnley	145
Approbation of Philip and the Duke of Alva	147
Agitation at the English Court	148
Attitude of Murray	151
Sir Nicholas Throgmorton at Stirling	154
Character of Darnley	157
Probable consequence of the Darnley marriage	159
Resolutions of Council	163
A game at chess	165
The Archduke again	167

CHAPTER IX.

	PAGE
State of parties in Scotland	168
Strength of Mary Stuart's position	170
Lennox and Darnley are ordered to return to England	173
Elizabeth invites the Scotch Protestants to rebel, and promises to assist them	174
Measures in the General Assembly	176
Renewed promises of support from England	178
Randolph expostulates with Mary Stuart	182
Lennox and Darnley throw off their allegiance to Elizabeth	183
Marriage of Mary Stuart and Darnley	184
Mission of Tamworth	186
Irresolution of Elizabeth	189
The Lords of the Congregation in arms	190
Mary Stuart takes the field	191
Retreat of the Lords	192
Elizabeth determines to break her promise	195
The Archduke	197
Marriage of Lady Mary Grey	199
Debate in the English Council	202
Resolution not to interfere in Scotland	205
The Lords of the Congregation at Dumfries	206
Flight of the Lords into England	208
Remonstrance of the Earl of Bedford	209
Murray goes to London	213
Reception of Murray by the Queen	214
Private Protest of Murray	218
Letter of Elizabeth to Mary Stuart	219
Questionable instructions to Randolph	221
Anticipated consequence of Elizabeth's conduct	222
Resentment of Argyle	224
Advice of Sir N. Throgmorton to Mary Stuart	225
Mischievous influence of Ritzio	226
Mary Stuart applies for help to Philip	228
Philip communicates with the Pope	229
Elizabeth begins to recover herself	233

Contents.

	PAGE
Catholic League in Europe	235
Differences between Mary Stuart and her husband	236
The crown matrimonial	237
Mary Stuart and Ritzio	239
Divisions among the Scotch Protestants	240
Conspiracy to murder Ritzio and restore Murray	243
Randolph is expelled from Scotland	244
Sketch of the plot	247
Intended attainder of Murray	249
The Queen's rooms at Holyrood	250
Murder of Ritzio	251
Return of Murray	260
Escape of Mary Stuart to Dunbar	264
Return in form to Edinburgh	266
Flight of the conspirators	267
Letter of Morton and Ruthven to Cecil	268

CHAPTER X.

Popularity of Mary Stuart in England	269
General character of Elizabeth's policy	271
Prospects of the Queen of Scots	272
Treachery of Darnley	276
Argyle threatens to join Shan O'Neil	277
A spy at Holyrood	280
Letter of Elizabeth to the Queen of Scots	282
Birth of James Stuart	284
The Archduke or Leicester	285
Increasing strength of Mary Stuart's party	289
Elizabeth visits Oxford	291
Position of Darnley in Scotland	295
Mary Stuart and Bothwell	296
Intended flight of Darnley to England	299
The Scotch Council at Holyrood	300
Meeting of the English Parliament	302
The Bishops' Bill	303
The Succession	305
The Queen promises to marry	307

Contents.

The Queen and de Silva	309
Parliament resolves to address the Queen on the Succession	311
Presentation of the Address	313
Reply of Elizabeth	314
Irritation of the House of Commons	317
Question of Privilege	319
Remonstrance	320
Speech of Mr. Dalton	322
The Queen yields	323
Subsidy Bill	325
The Thirty-nine Articles	328
De Silva and Elizabeth	329
Proposed covenant between the two Queens	334
Close of the Session	336
Speech of Elizabeth	337
The Queen of Scots at Jedburgh	340
Her dangerous illness	342
Differences with Darnley	343
Consultation at Craigmillar	344
Bond for the destruction of Darnley	347
Baptism of James, and recall of Morton	349
Illness of Darnley at Glasgow	351
Mary Stuart visits him	354
Letter to Bothwell	359
Plan of Kirk-a-Field	362
Darnley is removed thither from Glasgow	363
The last night	367
Murder of Darnley	370
Effect on the Catholics in England	371

CHAPTER XI.

The English army in Ireland	372
Sir T. Stukeley	373
Irish policy of the Tudor Sovereigns	375
Projects for Irish Reform	376

	PAGE
The Primacy	378
Shan O'Neil defeats the Scots	380
Invasion of Connaught	381
Sir Henry Sidney appointed Deputy	383
The Presidency of Munster	386
Sidney lands in Ireland	387
Shan O'Neil at home	390
Sidney demands men and money	391
Anger and hesitation of Elizabeth	393
Alliance between O'Neil and Argyle	395
Shan O'Neil writes for assistance to France	396
Sidney ineffectually demands his recall	397
Plan for a campaign	398
The Ormond and Desmond controversy	401
Troops are sent from England under Col. Edward Randolph	402
Desmond refuses to join Shan	403
The Antrim Scots	404
Sidney invades Ulster	405
Col. Randolph at Derry	407
Success of Sidney	408
Ill-humour of Elizabeth and advice of Cecil	410
Defeat of Shan and death of Col. Randolph	412
The Scots attack Shan	413
Pestilence at Derry	414
Final ruin of the settlement	416
Shan's last battle	418
Death of Shan	419

CHAPTER XII.

English sailors before the Sixteenth Century	423
Voyage of John Cabot	424
England and Spain	425
First expansion of the English Navy	426
The Merchant Adventurers	427
The African slave-trade	428
Foreign trade at the accession of Elizabeth	430

Contents.

	PAGE
Alarms and comments of Cecil	431
Decay of the fisheries	432
Foreign fishermen in the English waters	433
Cecil's fast	434
English gentlemen on the coast	436
The Channel privateers	437
English outrages and Spanish reprisals	439
English sailors and the Inquisition	440
Petition of Dorothy Seeley	441
Englishmen burnt in Spain	444
Illusage of Englishmen in Spanish prisons	446
Exploit of Thomas Cobham	447
Commissions to prey on Papists	450
Privateers and pirates	451
The Channel and the Thames	453
Piracy of English men-of-war	455
Arrest of English ships in Spain	456
The ports of England closed against the Flemings	458
Sufferings of English prisoners	460
Elizabeth attempts to repress piracy	462
The pirates in Ireland	463
Conference at Bruges	465
The negro trade	467
First slaving voyage of John Hawkins	470
Second voyage	473
Profits of the adventure	478
Third voyage	480
Scene in Plymouth harbour and last protest of the Spanish ambassador	482

CHAPTER VII.

THE currency speculations of the Government of Edward the Sixth had not recommended to the Irish the morals of the Reformation; the plays of Bishop Bale had failed to convert them to its theology. On the accession of Mary the Protestant missionaries had fled from their duties, being unambitious of martyrdom, and the English service which had been forced into the churches disappeared without sound or effort. The monasteries of the four shires, wherever the estates had remained with the crown, were rebuilt and reinhabited; beyond the border of the Pale the Irish chieftains followed the example, wherever piety or superstition were stronger than avarice. In the south the religious houses had been protected from spoliation by the Earl of Desmond, and the monks had been secretly supported; with the change of government they were reinstated in their homes, and the country reverted to its natural condition. The English garrisons ceased and pillaged the farmers of Meath and Dublin; the chiefs made forays upon each other, killing, robbing, and burning. When the war broke out between England and France there were the usual conspiracies and uprisings of nationality; the young Earl of Kildare, in reward to the Queen who had restored him to his rank, appearing as the natural leader of the patriots.

Ireland was thus happy in the gratification of all its natural tendencies. The Brehon law readvanced upon the narrow limits to which by the exertions of Henry the Eighth the circuits of the Judges had been extended; and with the Brehon law came anarchy as its inseparable attendant. 'The Lords and Gentiles of the Irish Pale that were not governed under the Queen's laws were compelled to keep and maintain a great number of idle men of war to rule their people at home, and exact from their neighbours abroad—working every one his own wilful will for a law—to the spoil of his country and decay and waste of the common weal of the same.' 'The idle men of war ate up all together;' the lord and his men took what they pleased, 'destroying their tenants and themselves never the better;' 'the common people having nothing left to lose,' became 'as idle and careless in their behaviour as the rest,' 'stealing by day and robbing by night.' Yet it was a state of things which they seemed all equally to enjoy, and high and low alike 'were always ready to bury their own quarrels to join against the Queen and the English.'[1]

At the time when the crown passed to Elizabeth the good and bad qualities of the people were thus described by a correspondent of the Council.

'The appearance and outward behaviour of the Irish sheweth them to be fruits of no good tree, for they exercise no virtue, and refrain and forbear from no vice, but think it lawful to do every man what him listeth.

'They neither love nor dread God nor yet hate the

---

[1] The disorders of the Irishry, 1559.—*Irish MSS. Rolls House.*

devil. They are worshippers of images and open idolaters. Their common oath they swear is by books, bells, and other ornaments which they do use as holy religion. Their chief and solemnest oath is by their lord's or master's hand, which whoso forsweareth is sure to pay a fine or sustain a worse turn.

'The Sabbath day they rest from all honest exercises, and the week days they are not idle, but worse occupied.

'They do not honour their father or mother so much as they do reverence strangers.

'For every murder they commit they do not so soon repent; for whose blood they once shed, they lightly never cease killing all that name.

'They do not so commonly commit adultery; not for that they profess or keep chastity, but for that they seldom or never marry, and therefore few of them are lawful heirs, by the laws of the realm, to the lands they possess.

'They steal but from the strong, and take by violence from the poor and weak.

'They know not so well who is their neighbour as whom they favour; with him they will witness in right and wrong.

'They covet not their neighbours' goods, but command all that is their neighbours' as their own.

'Thus they live and die, and there is none to teach them better. There are no ministers. Ministers will not take pains where there is no living to be had, neither church nor parish, but all decayed. People will not come to inhabit where there is no defence of law.'[1]

The condition of the Pale was more miserable than

---

[1] The disorders of the Irishry, 1559.—*Irish MSS. Rolls House.*

CHAP VII
1559

The misery of the Pale.

that of the districts purely Irish. The garrison took from the farmers by force whatever they required for their support, paying for it in the brass shillings in which they themselves received their own wages. The soldiers robbed the people; the Government had before robbed the soldiers; and the captains of the different districts in turn robbed the Government by making false returns of the number of men under their command. They had intermarried with the Irish, or had Irish mistresses living in the forts with them, and thus for the most part they were in league with those whom they were maintained to repress; so that choosing one master instead of many, and finding themselves obnoxious to their own countrymen by remaining under a rule from which they derived no protection, the tenantry of Meath flocked by hundreds over the northern border, and took refuge with O'Neil.[1]

Sir Edward Bellingham in 1549, by firmness of hand and integrity of heart, had made the English name respected from the Giant's Causeway to Valentia. Could Bellingham have lived a few years longer—could Somerset or Northumberland or Mary, so zealous each in their way for 'the glory of God,' have remembered that

---

[1] After six years of discipline and improvement, Sir Henry Sidney described the state of the four shires, the Irish inhabitants, and the English garrison, in the following language:—
'The English Pale is overwhelmed with vagabonds—stealth and spoil daily carried out of it; the people miserable—not two gentlemen in the whole of it able to lend twenty pounds. They have neither horse nor armour, nor apparel nor victual. The soldiers be so beggarlike as it would abhor a general to look on them; yet so insolent as to be intolerable to the people, so rooted in idleness as there is no hope by correction to amend them, yet so allied with the Irish I dare not trust them in a fort or in any dangerous service. They have all an Irish w———e or two—never a married wife among them; so that all is known that we intend to do here.'—*Sidney to Leicester, March* 5, 1556. *Irish MSS. Rolls House.*

without common sense and common honesty at the
bottom of them, creeds and systems are as houses built
on quicksands—the order which had taken root might
have grown strong under the shadow of justice, and
Ireland might have had a happier future.

But this was not to be. The labour and expense of a
quarter of a century was thrown idly away. The Irish
army, since the rebellion of Lord Thomas Fitzgerald, had
cost thirteen or fourteen hundred thousand pounds, yet
the Pale was shortened and its revenues decreased; the
moral ruin was more complete than the financial, and the
report of 1559 closed with an earnest exhortation to
Elizabeth to remember that the Irish were her subjects;
that it was her duty as their sovereign 'to bring the
poor ignorant people to better things,' 'and to recover
so many thousand lost souls that were going headlong to
the devil.'[1]

Following close on the first survey, a more detailed
account was furnished to Cecil of the social condition of
the people. The common life of a chief and the relations
between any two adjoining tribes were but too familiar
and intelligible. But there was a general organization
among the people themselves, extending wherever the
Irish language was spoken, with a civilization of an Irish
kind and an intellectual hierarchy. Besides the priests
there were four classes of spiritual leaders and teachers,
each with their subdivisions.

'The first,' wrote Cecil's correspondent, 'is called the
Brehon, which in English is called "the judge;" and
before they give judgment they take pawns of both the
parties, and then they will judge according to their own

[1] *Irish MSS. Rolls House.*

CHAP VII discretion. These men be neuters, and the Irishmen
1559 will not prey them. They have great plenty of cattle,
and they harbour many vagabonds and idle persons; and
if there be any rebels that move rebellion against the
prince, of these people they are chiefly maintained; and
if the English army fortune to travel in that part where
they be, they will flee to the mountains and woods,
because they would not succour them with victuals and
other necessaries.

'The next sort is called the "Shankee." They also
have great plenty of cattle wherewith they do succour
the rebels. They make the ignorant men of the country
believe that they be descended of Alexander the Great, or
of Darius, or of Cæsar, or of some other notable prince,
which makes the ignorant people to run mad and care not
what they do—the which is very hurtful to the realm.

'The third sort is called "Denisdan," which is to say
in English the "Boulde." These people be very hurtful
to the commonwealth, for they chiefly maintain the rebels;
and further they do cause them that would be true, to be
rebellious—thieves, extortioners, murderers, raveners—
yea and worse if it was possible. Their first practice, if
they see any young man descended of the septs of O or
Mac, and have half a dozen about him, then will they
make a rhyme wherein they will commend his father and
his ancestors, numbering how many heads they have cut
off, how many towns they have burned, how many
virgins they have deflowered, how many notable murders
they have done; and in the end they will compare them
to Annibal, or Scipio, or Hercules, or some other famous
person—wherewithal the poor fool runs mad and thinks
indeed it is so. Then will he gather a sort of rascals
to him, and he must get him a prophecier who shall
tell him how he shall speed as he thinks. Then will

he get him lurking to the side of a wood and there keepeth him close till morning; and when it is daylight then will they go to the poor villages, not sparing to destroy young infants and aged people; and if a woman be ever so great with child, her will they kill, burning the houses and corn, and ransacking the poor cots. Then will they drive all the kine and plough horses, with all other cattle, and drive them away. Then must they have a bagpipe blowing before them, and if any of the cattle fortune to wax weary or faint they will kill them rather than it should do the owner good. And if they go by any house of friars or religious house, they will give them two or three beeves; and they will take them and pray for them—yea, and praise their doings, and say " his father was accustomed so to do ;" wherein he will rejoice.

'And when he is in a safe place they will fall to a division of the spoil according to the discretion of the captain. Now comes the rhymer that made the rhyme with his "Rakery." The "Raker" is he that shall utter the rhyme, and the rhymer himself sits by with the captain very proudly. He brings with him also his harper, who plays all the while that the raker sings the rhyme. Also he hath his bard, which is a foolish fellow who must have a horse given him. The harper must have a new saffron shirt and a mantle; and the raker must have two or three kine; and the rhymer himself a horse and harness, with a nag to ride on, a silver goblet, and a pair of bedes of coral with buttons of silver. And this with more they look for to have for the reducing of the people, to the disruption of the commonwealth and blasphemy of God; for this is the best thing the rhymer causeth them to do.

'The fourth sort are those which in England are called

Poets. These men have great store of cattle, and use all the trade of the others with an addition of prophecies. These are maintainers of witches and other vile matters to the blasphemy of God and to the impoverishing of the commonwealth.

'These four septs are divided in all places of the four quarters of Ireland and some of the islands beyond Ireland, as "the Land of the Saints,"[1] the "Innis Buffen," "Innis Turk," "Innis Main," and "Innis Clare." These islands are under the rule of O'Neil, and they are very pleasant and fertile, plenty of wood, water, and arable ground and pastures and fish, and a very temperate air.[2]

'There be many branches belonging to the four septs —as the Gogath, which is to say the glutton, for one of them will eat half a mutton at a sitting; another called the Carrow; he commonly goeth naked and carrieth dice and cards with him, and he will play the hair off his head; and these be maintained by the rhymers.

'There is a set of women called the Goyng women. They be blasphemers of God, and they run from country to country sowing sedition among the people. They are common to all men; and if any of them happen to be with child she will say that it is the great Lord adjoining, whereof the Lords are glad and do appoint them to be nursed.

'There is another two sorts that goeth about with the Bachelo of Jesus,[3] as they call it. These run from country to country; and if they come to any house where a

---

[1] Arran, outside Galway Bay.
[2] At present they are barren heaps of treeless moors and mountains. They yield nothing but scanty oat-crops and potatoes, and though the seas are full of fish as ever, there are no hands to catch them. The change is a singular commentary on modern improvements.
[3] The Baculum Jesus, said to have been brought over by St. Patrick.

woman is with child they will put the same about her, and whether she will or no causeth her to give them money, and they will undertake that she shall have good delivery of her child, to the great disruption of the people concerning their souls' health.

'Others go about with St. Patrick's crosier, and play the like part or worse; and no doubt so long as these be used the word of God can never be known among them, nor the Prince be feared, nor the country prosper.'[1]

So stands the picture of Ireland, vivid because simple, described by some half-Anglicised half-Protestantized Celt who wrote what he had seen around him, careless of political philosophy or of fine phrases with which to embellish his diction. The work of civilisation had again to begin from the foundation. Occupied with Scotland and France and holding her own throne by so precarious a tenure Elizabeth for the first eighteen months of her reign had little leisure to attend to it; and the Irish leaders taking advantage of the opportunity offered themselves and their services to Philip's ambassador in England. The King of Spain who at the beginning desired to spare and strengthen Elizabeth, sent them a cold answer, and against Philip's will the great Norman families were unwilling to stir. The true-bred Celts however, whose sole political creed was hatred of the English, were less willing to remain quiet. To the Celt it was of small moment whether the English sovereign was Protestant or Catholic. The presence of an English deputy in Dublin was the symbol of his servitude and the constant occasion for his rebellion. Had there been no cause of quarrel the mere pleasure of fight-

[1] Report on the State of Ireland, 1559.—*Irish MSS. Rolls House.*

ing would have insured periodical disturbances; and in Ulster there were special causes at work to produce a convulsion of peculiar severity.

The Scottish settlers in Antrim.
Identical in race and scarcely differing in language, the Irish of the north and the Scots of the Western Isles had for two centuries kept up a close and increasing intercourse. Some thousand Scottish families had recently emigrated from Bute, Arran, and Argyleshire, to find settlements on the thinly-peopled coasts of Antrim and Down. The Irish chiefs had sought their friendship, intermarried with them, or made war on them, as the humour of the moment prompted; but their numbers had steadily increased whether welcome or unwelcome, and at Elizabeth's accession they had become objects of alarm both to the native Irish whom they threatened to supplant and to the English whom they refused to obey.

Lord Sussex, who was Mary's last deputy, had made expeditions against them both in the Isles and in Ulster; but even though assisted by the powers of O'Neil had only irritated their hostility. They made alliance with the O'Donnells who were O'Neil's hereditary enemies. James M'Connell and his two brothers, near kinsmen of the House of Argyle, crossed over with two thousand followers to settle in Tyrconnell, while to the Callogh O'Donnell the chief of the clan, the Earl of Argyle himself gave his half-sister for a wife.

With this formidable support the O'Donnells threatened to eclipse their ancient rivals, when there rose up from among the O'Neils one of those remarkable men who in their own persons sum up and represent the energy, intellect, power, and character of the nation to which they belong.

. In the partial settlement of Ireland which had been brought about by Henry the Eighth, the O'Neils among the other noble families surrendered their lands to the crown to receive them again under the usual feudal tenure; and Con O'Neil the Lame had received from Henry for himself and his heirs the title of Earl of Tyrone. For himself and his heirs—but who the heirs of Con O'Neil might be was not so easy to decide. His son Shan in explaining his father's character to Elizabeth said that he was 'a gentleman,'—the interpretation of the word being that 'he never denied any child that was sworn to him, and that he had plenty of them.'[1] The favourite of the family was the offspring of an intrigue with a certain Alyson Kelly, the wife of a blacksmith at Dundalk. This child, a boy named Matthew, grew to be a fine dashing youth such as an Irish father delighted to honour; and although the earl had another younger son Shan or John with some pretensions to legitimacy, Henry the Eighth allowed the father to name at his will the heir of his new honours. Matthew Kelly became Baron of Dungannon when O'Neil received his earldom; and to Matthew Kelly was secured the reversion on his father's death of the earldom itself.

No objection could be raised so long as Shan was a boy; but as the legitimate heir grew to manhood the arrangement became less satisfactory. The other sons whom Con had brought promiscuously into the world were discontented with the preference of a brother whose birth was no better than their own; and Shan with their help, as the simplest solution of the difficulty, at last cut the Baron of Dungannon's throat.

They manage things strangely in Ireland. The old O'Neil instead of being irritated saw in this exploit a proof of commendable energy. He at once took Shan

---

[1] Shan O'Neil to Elizabeth, February 8, 1561.—*Irish MSS. Rolls House.*

into favour, and had he been able would have given him his dead brother's rights; but unfortunately the Baron had left a son behind him, and the son was with the family of his grandmother beyond the reach of steel or poison.

Impatient of uncertainty and to secure himself by possession against future challenge, Shan next conspired against his father, deposed him, and drove him into the Pale where he afterwards died; and throwing over his English title and professing to prefer the name of O'Neil to any patent of nobility held under an English sovereign, he claimed the right of succession by Irish custom, precedent, and law. In barbarous and half-barbarous tribes there is generally some choice exercised among the members of the chief's family, or some rule is followed, by which the older and stronger are preferred to the young and weak. In our own Heptarchy the uncle if able and brave was preferred to the child of an elder brother.

In Tyrone the clan elected their chief from the blood of the ancient kings; and Shan waiving all question of legitimacy received the votes of his people, took the oath with his foot upon the stone, and with the general consent of the north was proclaimed O'Neil.[1]

This proceeding was not only an outrage against order, but it was a defiance of England and the English system. The descent to an earldom could not be regulated by election, and it was obvious that the English Government must either insist upon the rights of the young

---

[1] 'They place him that shall be called their captain upon a stone always reserved for that purpose, and commonly placed on a hill.'—SPENSER's *View of the State of Ireland*. The stone in Westminster Abbey brought from Scone by Edward the First was one of these, and according to legend is the original Lias Fail or thundering stone on which the Irish kings were crowned. The Lias Fail however still stands on Tara Hill, ready for use when Ireland's good time returns.

Baron of Dungannon, or relinquish the hope of feudalizing the Irish chieftains. Knowing therefore that he could not be left long in the enjoyment of his success, Shan O'Neil attempted to compose his feud with the O'Donnells, and his first step was to marry O'Donnell's sister. But the reconciliation was of brief duration; the smaller chiefs of Ulster in loyal preference for greatness attached themselves for the most part to the O'Neils. Shan no longer careful of offence 'misused' his wife; and the Callogh at the time when the notice of the English Government began to be drawn towards the question was preparing with the help of the Scots to revenge her injuries.[1]

Where private and public interests were closely interwoven there was a necessary complication of sides and movements. The English Government in the belief that the sister of the Earl of Argyle might be a means of introducing Protestantism into Ulster made advances to the M'Connells whom before they had treated as enemies; they sent a present to the Countess[2] of some old dresses of Queen Mary's 'for a token of favour,' and they promised to raise the Callogh to a rival earldom on condition of good service.[1]

They were encountered however by an embarrassing

---

[1] A detailed account of these proceedings is found in a letter of Lord Justice Fitzwilliam to the Earl of Sussex, written on the 8th of March, 1560.—*Irish MSS. Rolls House.*

[2] This lady, who was mentioned above as the wife of the Callogh and the half-sister of Macallommore, is always described in the Irish despatches as the Countess of Argyle. There is no difficulty in identifying the person. It is less easy to understand the title.

[3] 'MEMORANDUM.—To send to O'Donnell, with the Queen's thanks for service done, and her promise to make him an Earl on further merit on his part. The gown and kirtle that were Queen Mary's, with some old habiliments, to be sent to the Countess Argyle, O'Donnell's wife, for a token of favour to her good disposition in religion.'—*Irish MSS.*

cross current. The M'Connells affected to reciprocate the English good will, but the Earl of Argyle's connexion with the reforming party in Scotland had not touched the dependencies of his clan. The hearts of ninety-nine out of every hundred persons on the north of Tweed were fixed on securing the English crown either for Arran or for Mary Stuart; and James M'Connell was heard in private to say that the Queen of Scots was rightful Queen of England[1]. Shan O'Neil therefore adroitly availed himself of the occasion to detach from the O'Donnells their formidable northern allies. The 'misused' wife being disposed of by some process of murder or otherwise, he induced M'Connell to give him his daughter. He married or proposed to marry her—for ties of this kind sat with astonishing lightness on him—and the Callogh was outmanœuvred.

Again an interval, and there was another and a bolder change. Either the new lady did not please Shan or his ambition soared to a higher flight. Supposing that the Scots in Ireland would not dare to resent what the Earl of Argyle should approve, and that the clan would welcome his support to Mary Stuart's claims, he had scarcely rid himself of his first wife and married a second than he wrote to the Earl proposing that his sister the Countess should be transferred from O'Donnell to himself. The M'Connells could be got rid of, and the Scotch colony might pass under the protection of the O'Neils. James M'Connell's daughter might be thought a diffi-

---

[1] 'At my kinsman being with him in Kintyre, James M'Connell ministered to him very evil talk against the Queen's Majesty, saying the Queen of England was a bastard, and the Queen of Scotland rightful heir to the crown of England. It was not once nor twice, but divers times; not only by him but by his wife also.'—*John Piers to Sir William Fitzwilliam. Irish MSS. Rolls House.*

culty, 'but we swear to you our kingly oath,' the audacious Shan dared to write, 'that there is no impediment
by reason of any such woman.'[1]

Unprepared to recognize such swift transmutations,
and at that time concerned with the rest of his party in
the scheme for the elevation of the Earl of Arran, Argyle
contented himself with enclosing Shan's letter to the
English Council. He told them briefly that O'Neil was
the most dangerous person in Ireland; and he said that
unless the Queen was prepared to acknowledge him she
had better lose no time in bringing him to reason.

So matters stood in Ireland in the spring of 1560,
when the conspiracy of the Guises and the necessity of
defending her throne forced Elizabeth into the Scotch
war. The deputy Lord Sussex was in England; Sir
William Fitzwilliam was left in command in Dublin,
watching the country with uneasy misgivings; and from
the symptoms reported to him from every quarter he
anticipated, notwithstanding Philip's coldness, a summer
of universal insurrection; the Parliament of the Pale
had given the Catholics a rallying cry by endorsing the
Act of Uniformity; and 'big words,' 'prophecies of the
expulsion of the English within the year,' and rumours of
armies of liberation from France and Spain, filled all the
air. The outward quiet was undisturbed, but 'inwardly
never such fears since the rebellion of Lord Thomas Fitzgerald.' The country was for the most part a wilderness,
but the desolation would be no security. The Irish, Fitzwilliam anxiously reported, could keep the field where the
English would starve; 'no men of war ever lived the
like, nor others of God's making as touching feeding and

---

[1] Notice and letter sent by the Earl of Argyle.—*Irish MSS. Rolls House.*
[2] *Ibid.*

living; they were like beasts and vermin bred from the earth and the filth thereof; but brute and bestial as by their outward life they showed, there was not under the sun a more craftier vipered undermining generation.'[1]

The immediate fear was of the great southern earls. If Kildare and Desmond rose, the whole of Ireland would rise with them, even the Pale itself. They had promised Fitzwilliam to be loyal, but he did not trust them. They had met at Limerick in the winter; they were known to have communicated with Shan, and O'Brien of Inchiquin had gone to Spain and France to solicit assistance. If he brought back a favourable answer, the Geraldines 'would take the English part until such time as the push came, and then the English company should be paid home.'[2]

Philip refuses to encourage a rebellion in Ireland.

Most fortunately for Elizabeth the success of the Queen of Scots was more formidable to Philip than the temporary triumph of heresy. He discouraged all advances to himself; he used his best endeavours to prevent the Irish from looking for assistance in France; and although his advice might have been little attended to had the Guises been at liberty to act, Elizabeth's intrigues with the Huguenots had provided them with sufficient work at home. They could spare no troops for Ireland while they were unable to reinforce their army at Leith.

O'Brien however received promises in abundance. Three French ships accompanied him on his return, and Irish imagination added thirty or forty which were said to be on the way. Kildare called his retainers under arms, and held a Parliament of chiefs at Maynooth which

---

[1] Fitzwilliam to Cecil, March and April, 1560.—*Irish MSS. Rolls House.*
[2] Ibid.

was opened with public mass. In speeches of the time-honoured type the patriotic orators dwelt upon the wrongs of Ireland; they swore that they would be 'slaves' no longer; they protested 'that their kingdom was kept from them by force by such as were aliens in blood;' and Fitzwilliam frightened by the loud words wrote in haste for assistance that 'the English might fight for their lives before they were all dead.'[1]

With the death of Henry the Second, the fall of Leith, and the failure of the French to appear, the Irish courage cooled and the more pressing danger passed off. Kildare's larger knowledge showed him that the opportunity was gone. His father's death on the scaffold and his own long exile had taught him that without support from abroad a successful insurrection was impossible; and having no personal interests to defend he bought his pardon for the treason which he had meditated by loyally returning to his allegiance.

Shan O'Neil was less favourably circumstanced. His rank and his estates were at stake, and he on his part had determined never to submit at all unless he was secured in their possession. But he too thought it prudent to temporize. His father was by this time dead. He was required to appear before Elizabeth in person to explain the grounds on which he challenged his inheritance; and after stipulating for a safe-conduct, and an advance of money for expenses of his journey, he affected a willingness to comply; but he chose to treat with the Government at first hand, and in a characteristic letter to Elizabeth he prepared the way for his reception.

He described his father's miscellaneous habits, and 'gentlemanlike' readiness to acknowledge every child

....

[1] Advertisements out of Ireland, May 28, 1560.—*Irish MSS. Rolls House.*

that was assigned to him; he explained his brother's birth and his own election as the O'Neil; he then proceeded thus:—[1]

Letter of Shan O'Neil to Elizabeth.

'The deputy has much ill-used me your Majesty; and now that I am going over to see you I hope you will consider that I am but rude and uncivil, and do not know my duty to your Highness nor yet your Majesty's laws, but am one brought up in wildness far from all civility. Yet have I a good will to the commonwealth of my country; and please your Majesty to send over two commissioners that you can trust that will take no bribes nor otherwise be imposed on, to observe what I have done to improve the country and to hear what my accusers have to say; and then let them go into the Pale and hear what the people say of your soldiers with their horses and their dogs and their concubines. Within this year and a half three hundred farmers are come from the English Pale to live in my country where they can be safe.

'Please your Majesty, your Majesty's money here is not so good as your money in England, and will not pass current there. Please your Majesty to send me three thousand pounds of English money to pay my expenses in going over to you, and when I come back I will pay your deputy three thousand pounds Irish, such as you are pleased to have current here.

'Also I will ask your Majesty to marry me to some gentlewoman of noble blood meet for my vocation. I will make Ireland all that your Majesty wishes for you. I am very sorry your Majesty is put to such expense. If

---

[1] The voluminousness of the letter renders some abridgement necessary; but the character, substance, and arrangement are preserved.

, you will trust it to me I will undertake that in three years you shall have a revenue where now you have continual loss.

'Also your Majesty's father granted certain lands to my father O'Neil and to his son Matthew. Mat Kelly claims these lands of your Majesty. We have a saying among us Irishmen that "whatsoever bull do chance to bull any cow in any kerragh, notwithstanding, the right owner of the cow shall have the calf and not the owner of the bull." How can it be or how can it stand with natural reason that the said Matthew should inherit my father's lands, and also inherit his own rightful father the smith's, and also his mother's lands which the said Matthew hath peaceably in possession?'[1]

Whether Shan would follow up his letter by really going over was not so certain. It depended on the answer which he received, or on the chances which might offer themselves to him of doing better for himself in some other way.

The English Government had no advantage over him in sincerity. Towards Ireland itself the intentions of Elizabeth were honourable; but she had determined to use her first leisure in restoring order and obedience there; and for Shan the meaning of his summons to England was merely to detain him there 'with gentle talk,' till Sussex could return to his command and the English army be reinforced.

Preparations were made to send men and money in such large quantities that rebellion should have no chance; and so careful was the secrecy which was ob-

---

[1] Shan O'Neil to Queen Elizabeth, February 8, 1561.—*Irish MSS.* Compare Shan O'Neil to Cecil (same date).

served to prevent Shan from taking alarm, that a detachment of troops sent from Portsmouth sailed with sealed orders, and neither men nor officers knew that Ireland was their destination till they had rounded the Land's End.[1]

Notwithstanding these precautions Shan's friends found means to put him on his guard. He was to have sailed from Dublin, but the weeks passed on and he did not make his appearance. At one time his dress was not ready; at another he had no money, and pressed to have his loan of the three thousand pounds sent up for him into Tyrone; and to this last request Fitzwilliam would give no sort of encouragement, 'being,' as he said, 'for his own part unwilling to lend Shan five shillings on his bond, and being certain that he would no sooner have received the money than he would laugh at them all.'

The Government however cared little whether he submitted or stayed away. As yet they had not been forced to recognize Shan's ability, and the troops who were to punish him were on their way. Kildare whom Elizabeth most feared had gone to London on her first invitation. As long as Kildare was loyal Desmond would remain quiet; and no serious rebellion was considered any longer possible. O'Donnell was prepared to join the English army on its advance into Ulster; and the Scots, notwithstanding their predilection for Mary Stuart, were expected to act as Argyle and as his sister 'should direct.'

But Shan had prepared a master stroke which disconcerted this last arrangement. Though his suit found no favour with the Earl of Argyle, he had contrived

---

[1] Matters to be ordered for Ireland, February 25, March 4, March 13.—Irish MSS.

to ingratiate himself with 'the Countess.' The Scots were chiefly anxious to secure their settlements in Antrim and Down; and Shan was a more useful ally for them than Elizabeth or the feeble Callogh. The lady from whom such high hopes had been formed cared less for Protestantism than for the impassioned speeches of a lover; and while Queen Mary's gown and kirtle were on their way to her, Fitzwilliam was surprised with the sudden news that Shan had made a raid into Tyrconnell and had carried off both her and her husband. Her Scotch guard, though fifteen hundred strong, had offered no resistance; and the next news was that the Callogh was a prisoner in Shan's castle, and that the Countess was the willing paramour of the O'Neil. The affront to M'Connell was forgiven, or atoned for by private arrangement; and the sister of the Earl of Argyle—an educated woman for her time, 'not unlearned in Latin,' 'speaking French and Italian,' 'counted sober wise and no less subtle'—had betrayed herself her people and her husband.[1]

The O'Neils by this last manœuvre became supreme in Ulster. Deprived of their head, the O'Donnells sunk into helplessness; the whole force of the province such as it was, with the more serious addition of several thousand Scotch marauders, was at Shan's disposal, and thus provided he thought himself safe in defying England to do its worst.

Both sides prepared for war. Sussex returned to Dublin at the beginning of June; his troops and supplies had arrived before him; and after a debate in 'the Council' the Irish of the Pale were invited to join in a 'general hosting' into Tyrone on the first of July.

---

[1] Fitzwilliam to Cecil, May 30.—*Irish MSS.*

CHAP VII
1561
An English garrison at Armagh.

Sussex himself as a preliminary move made a dash upon Armagh. He seized the cathedral, which he fortified as a depôt for his stores. Leaving a garrison there he fell back into Meath, where in a few days he was joined by Ormond with flying companies of 'galloglasse.'

But Sussex did not yet understand the man with whom he was dealing. He allowed himself to be amused and delayed by negotiations;[1] and while he was making promises to Shan which it is likely that he intended to disregard, Armagh was almost lost again.

Skirmish with the Irish.

Seeing a number of kerne scattered about the town the officer in command sallied out upon them, when Shan himself suddenly appeared, accompanied by the Catholic Archbishop, on a hill outside the walls; and the English had but time to recover their defences when the whole Irish army, led by a procession of monks and 'every man carrying a faggot,' came on to burn the cathedral over their heads. The monks sung a mass; the primate walked three times up and down the lines, 'willing the rebels to go forward, for God was on their side.' Shan swore a great oath not to turn his back while an Englishman was left alive; and with scream and yell his men came on. Fortunately there were no Scots among them. The English though outnumbered ten to one stood steady in the churchyard, and after a sharp hand to hand fight drove back the howling crowd. The Irish retired into the 'friars' houses' outside the cathedral close, set them on fire, and ran for their lives.

So far all was well. After this there was no more talk of treating; and by the 18th Sussex and Ormond were themselves at Armagh, with a force—had there

[1] 'The second of this month we assembled at Baskreagh, and still treated with Shan for his going to your Majesty, making him great offers if he would go quietly.'—*Sussex to the Queen, July* 16. *Irish MSS.*

been skill to direct it—sufficient to have swept Tyrone
from border to border.
The weather however was wet, the rivers were high,
and slight difficulties seemed large to the English commander. He stayed in the town doing nothing till the
end of the month, when his provisions began to run
short, and necessity compelled him to move. Spies
brought him word that in the direction of Cavan there
were certain herds of cows which an active party might
cut off; and cattle-driving being the approved method of
making war in Ireland, the Deputy determined to have
them.

The Earl of Ormond was ill, and Sussex in an evil
hour for his reputation would not leave him. His troops
without their commander set out with Irish guides for
the spot where the cows had been seen.

O'Neil as may be supposed had been playing upon
Saxon credulity; the spies were his own men; and the
object was merely to draw the English among bogs and
rivers where they could be destroyed. They were to
have been attacked at night at their first halting-place;
and they escaped only by the accident of an alteration of
route. Early the following morning they were marching
forward in loose order; Fitzwilliam, with a hundred
horse, was a mile in advance; five hundred men-at-arms
with a few hundred loyal Irish of the Pale struggled
after him; another hundred horse under James Wingfield
brought up the rear.

Weaker in numbers, for his whole force did not
amount to more than six hundred men, O'Neil came up
with them from behind. Wingfield instead of holding
his ground galloped forward upon the men-at-arms, and
as horses and men were struggling in confusion together,
on came the Irish with their wild battle-cry—' Laundarg

CHAP. VII
1591
July

Shan O'Neil defeats the English.

Abo!'—'The bloody hand!'—'Strike for O'Neil.' The cavalry between shame and fear rode down their own men, and extricated themselves only to fly panic-stricken from the field to the crest of an adjoining hill, while Shan's troopers rode through the broken ranks 'cutting down the footmen on all sides.'

Fitzwilliam ignorant of what was passing behind him was riding leisurely forwards, when a horseman was observed galloping wildly in the distance and waving his handkerchief for a signal. The yells and cries were heard through the misty morning air, and Fitzwilliam, followed by a gentleman named Parkinson and ten or twelve of his own servants, hurried back 'in a happy hour.'

Without a moment's delay he flung himself into the mêlée. Sir George Stanley was close behind him with the rest of the advanced horse; 'and Shan receiving such a charge of those few men and seeing more coming after,' ran no further risk, blew a recall note and withdrew unpursued. Fitzwilliam's courage alone had prevented the army from being annihilated. Out of five hundred English, fifty lay dead, and fifty more were badly wounded; the Irish contingent had disappeared; and the survivors of the force fell back to Armagh so 'dismayed' as to be unfit for further service.

In his official report to the Queen the Earl of Sussex made light of his loss, and pretended that after a slight repulse he had won a brilliant victory. The object of the false despatch however was less to deceive Elizabeth than to blind the English world. To Cecil the Deputy was more open, and though professing still that he had escaped defeat, admitted the magnitude of the disaster.

'By the cowardice of some,' Sussex said, 'all was like

to have been lost, and by the worthiness of two men all
was restored and the contrary part overthrown. It was
by cowardice the dreadfullest beginning that ever was
seen in Ireland; and by the valiantness of a few (thanks
be given to God!) brought to a good end. Ah! Mr.
Secretary, what unfortunate star hung over me that day
to draw me, that never could be persuaded to be absent
from the army at any time, to be then absent for a
little disease of another man? The rereward was the
best and picked soldiers in all this land. If I or any
stout man had been that day with them, we had made
an end of Shan, which is now further off than ever it
was. Never before durst Scot or Irishman look on
Englishmen in plain or wood since I was here; and now
Shan, in a plain three miles away from any wood, and
where I would have asked of God to have had him, hath
with a hundred and twenty horse and a few Scots and
galloglasse scarce half in numbers, charged our whole
army, and by the cowardice of one wretch whom I hold
dear to me as my own brother, was like in one hour to
have left not one man of that army alive, and after to
have taken me and the rest at Armagh. The fame of
the English army, so hardly gotten, is now vanquished,
and I wrecked and dishonoured by the vileness of other
men's deeds.'[1]

The answer of Cecil to this sad despatch betrays the
intriguing factiousness which disgraced Elizabeth's court.
Lord Pembroke seemed to be the only nobleman whose
patriotism could be depended on; and in Pembroke's
absence there 'was not a person—no,' Cecil reiterated,
'not one,' who did not either wish so well to Shan

[1] Sussex to Cecil, July 31.—*Irish MSS.*

O'Neil or so ill to the Earl of Sussex as rather to welcome the news than regret the English loss.[1]

The truth was soon known in London notwithstanding 'the varnished tale' with which Sussex had sought to hide it. A letter from Lady Kildare to her husband represented the English army as having been totally defeated; and Elizabeth irritated as usual at the profitless expense in which she had been involved determined in her first vexation to bury no more money in Irish morasses. Kildare undertoook to persuade Shan into conformity if she would leave him in possession of what it appeared she was without power to take from him; the Queen consented to everything which he proposed, and the old method of governing Ireland by the Irish— that is of leaving it to its proper anarchy—was about to be resumed. Most tempting and yet most fatal; for the true desire of the Irish leaders was to cut the links altogether which bound them to England, and England could not play into their hands more effectively than by leaving them to destroy at their leisure the few chiefs who had dared to be loyal.

Kildare returned to Dublin with full powers to act as he should think best; while Sussex leaving a garrison as before in Armagh Cathedral returned with the dispirited remnant of his army into the Pale. Fitzwilliam was despatched to London to explain the disaster to the Queen; and the Irish Council sent a petition by his hands that the troops who had been so long quartered in the four shires should be recalled or disbanded. Useless in the field and tyrannical to the farmer they were a burden on the English exchequer and answered no purpose but to make the English name detested.

---

[1] Cecil to Sussex, August 12.—WRIGHT, vol. i.

The petition corresponded but too well with Elizabeth's private inclination, but Fitzwilliam while he presented it did not approve of its recommendations; he implored her—and he was supported in his entreaties by Cecil—to postpone at least for a short time a measure which would be equivalent to an abandonment of Ireland. The Queen yielded, and in allowing the army to remain permitted it to be reinforced from the trained soldiers of Berwick. Fitzwilliam carried back with him three thousand pounds to pay the arrears of wages; Cecil pressed hard for three thousand besides; but Elizabeth would risk no more till 'she saw some fruit arise from her expenditure.'

To Shan O'Neil she sent a pardon with a safe-conduct for his journey to England if Kildare could prevail on him to come to her; and 'accepting the defeat as the chance of war which she must bear' she expressed to Sussex her general surprise at his remissness, with her regret that an English officer should have disgraced himself by cowardice. She desired that Wingfield might be immediately sent over and that the other offenders should be apprehended and imprisoned.'

Meantime Sussex having failed in the field had attempted to settle his difficulties by other methods. A demand from Shan had followed him into the Pale that the Armagh garrison should be withdrawn. The bearers of the message were Cantwell O'Neil's seneschal, and a certain Neil Grey one of his followers who affected to dislike rebellion and gave the Deputy an opportunity of working on him. Lord Sussex it appeared regarded Shan as a kind of wolf whom having failed to capture

---

Memoranda of Letters from Ireland, August 20 (Cecil's hand).—*Cecil to Sussex, August 21. Elizabeth to Sussex, August 20. Irish MSS. Rolls House.*

in fair chase he might destroy by the first expedient which came to his hand.

The following letter betrays no misgivings either on the propriety of the proceeding which it describes or on the manner in which the intimation of it would be received by the Queen.

THE EARL OF SUSSEX TO QUEEN ELIZABETH.

August 24, 1561.

'May it please your Highness,

'After conference had with Shan O'Neil's seneschal I entered talk with Neil Grey; and perceiving by him that he had little hope of Shan's conformity in anything, and that he therefore desired that he might be received to serve your Highness, for that he would no longer abide with him, and that if I would promise to receive him to your service he would do anything that I would command him, I sware him upon the Bible to keep secret that I should say unto him and assured him if it were ever known during the time I had the government there that besides the breach of his oath it should cost him his life. I used long circumstance in persuading him to serve you to benefit his country and to procure assurance of living to him and his for ever by doing of that which he might easily do. He promised to do what I would. In fine I brake with him to kill Shan; and bound myself by my oath to see him have a hundred marks of land by the year to him and to his heirs for his reward. He seemed desirous to serve your Highness and to have the land, but fearful to do it doubting his own escape after with safety, which he confessed and promised to do by any means he might escaping with his life. What he will do I know not, but I assure your

Highness he may do it without danger if he will. And if he will not do that he may in your service, then be done to him what others may. God send your Highness a good end. CHAP VII
1561
August

'Your Highness's
'Most humble and faithful Subject and Servant,
                                    'T. SUSSEX.[1]
'From Ardbrachan.'

English honour like English coin lost something of its purity in the sister island. Nothing came of this undesirable proposal. Neil Grey however kept his secret, and though he would not risk his life by attempting the murder sought no favour with Shan by betraying Sussex.

Elizabeth's answer—if she sent any answer—is not discoverable. It is most sadly certain however that Sussex was continued in office; and inasmuch as it will be seen that he repeated the experiment a few months later his letter could not have been received with any marked condemnation.

Shortly after Fitzwilliam returned from England with the Berwick troops, and before the season closed and before Kildare commenced his negotiations the Deputy was permitted to make another effort to repair the credit of English arms.

Despatching provisions by sea to Lough Foyle he succeeded this time in marching through Tyrone and in destroying on his way four thousand cattle which he was unable to carry away; and had the vessels arrived in time he might have remained in Ulster long enough to do serious mischief there. But the wind and weather

Sussex again invades Tyrone.

---
[1] *Irish MSS. Rolls House.*

were unfavourable. He had left Shan's cows to rot where he had killed them; and thus being without food and sententiously and characteristically concluding that 'man by his policy might propose but God at his will did dispose,'[1] Lord Sussex fell back by the upper waters of Lough Erne sweeping the country before him.

O'Neil in the interval had been burning villages in Meath; but the Deputy had penetrated his stronghold, had defied him on his own ground, and he had not ventured to meet the English in the field. The defeat of July was partially retrieved and Sussex was in a better position to make terms. Kildare in the middle of October had a conference with Shan at Dundalk, and Shan consented to repair to Elizabeth's presence. In the conditions however which he was allowed to name he implied that he was rather conferring a favour than receiving one, and that he was going to England as a victorious enemy permitting himself to be conciliated. He demanded a safe-conduct so clearly worded that whatever was the result of his visit he should be free to return; he required a complete amnesty for his past misdeeds, and he stipulated that Elizabeth should pay all expenses for himself and his retinue; the Earls of Ormond, Desmond, and Kildare must receive him in state at Dundalk and escort him to Dublin; Kildare must accompany him to England; and most important of all Armagh Cathedral must be evacuated.

On these terms he was ready to go to London; he did not anticipate treachery; and either he would persuade Elizabeth to recognize him and thus prove to the Irish that rebellion was the surest road to prosperity and power, or at worst by venturing into England and return-

---

[1] Sussex to Elizabeth, September 21.—*Irish MSS. Rolls House.*

ing unscathed he would show them that the Government might be defied with more than impunity.

Had Neil Grey revealed to him those dark overtures of Sussex the Irish chief would have relied less boldly on English good faith. When his terms were made known to Elizabeth's Council the propriety of acceding to them was advocated for 'certain secret respects;' and even Sir William Cecil was not ashamed to say 'that in Shan's absence from Ireland something might be cavilled against him or his for non-observing the covenants on his side; and so the pact being infringed the matter might be used as should be thought fit.'[1]

The intention of deliberate dishonour was not persisted in. Elizabeth after some uncertainty whether concessions so ignominious could be safely made wrote to accept them all except the evacuation of the cathedral. Making a merit of his desire to please her, Shan said that although for 'the Earl of Sussex he would not mollify one iota of his agreement,' yet he would consent at the request of her Majesty;[2] and thus at last with the Earl of Kildare in attendance, a train of galloglasse, a thousand pounds in hand and a second thousand waiting for him in London the champion of Irish freedom sailed from Dublin and appeared on the 2nd of January at the English court.

Not wholly knowing how so strange a being might conduct himself, Cecil, Pembroke and Bacon received him privately on his arrival at the Lord Keeper's house. They gave him his promised money and endeavoured to impress upon him the enormity of his misdemeanors. Their success in this respect was indifferent. When Cecil spoke of rebellion Shan answered that two thou-

---

[1] Cecil to Throgmorton, November 4, 1561.—CONWAY MSS.
[2] Kildare to Cecil, December 3.—MS. Ibid.

sand pounds was a poor present from so great a Queen. When Cecil asked if he would be a good subject for the future he was sure their honours would give him a few more hundreds. He agreed however to make a general confession of his sins in Irish and English; and on the 6th of the month Elizabeth received him.

The Council, the Peers, the foreign ambassadors, bishops, aldermen, dignitaries of all kinds were present in state as if at the exhibition of some wild animal of the desert. O'Neil stalked in, his saffron mantle sweeping round and round him, his hair curling on his back and clipped short below the eyes which gleamed from under it with a grey lustre, frowning fierce and cruel. Behind him followed his galloglasse bare-headed and fair-haired with shirts of mail which reached their knees, a wolfskin flung across their shoulders and short broad battle-axes in their hands.

At the foot of the throne the chief paused, bent forward, threw himself on his face upon the ground, and then rising upon his knees spoke aloud in Irish:—

'Oh! my most dread sovereign lady and Queen, like as I Shan O'Noil, your Majesty's subject of your realm of Ireland, have of long time desired to come into the presence of your Majesty to acknowledge my humble and bounden subjection so am I now here upon my knees by your gracious permission, and do most humbly acknowledge your Majesty to be my sovereign lady and Queen of England, France, and Ireland; and I do confess that for lack of civil education I have offended your Majesty and your laws, for the which I have required and obtained your Majesty's pardon. And for that I most humbly from the bottom of my heart thank your Majesty and still do with all humbleness require the continuance of the same; and I faithfully promise here before Almighty God and your Majesty, and in presence of all these your nobles that I intend by God's grace to live hereafter in the obedience of your Majesty as a subject of your land of Ireland.

'And because this my speech being Irish is not well understanded I have caused this my submission to be written in English and Irish, and thereto have set my hand and seal; and to these gentlemen my kinsmen and friends I most humbly beseech your Majesty to be merciful and gracious lady.'[1]

To the hearers the sound of the words was as the howling of a dog.[2] The form which Shan was made to say that he had himself caused to be written, had been drawn for him by Cecil; and the gesture of the culprit was less humble than his language; the English courtiers devised 'a style' for him, as the interpretation of his bearing, 'O'Neil the Great, cousin to St. Patrick, friend to the Queen of England, enemy to all the world besides.'[3]

The submission being disposed of the next object was to turn the visit to account. Shan discovered that notwithstanding his precautions he had been outwitted in the wording of the safe-conduct. Though the Government promised to permit him to return to Ireland, the time of his stay had not been specified. Specious pretexts were invented to detain him; he required to be recognized as his father's heir; the English judges desired the cause to be pleaded before themselves; the young Baron of Dungannon must come over to be heard on the other

---

[1] *Irish MSS. Rolls House.*
[2] 'He confessed his crime and rebellion with howling.'—CAMDEN. So Hotspur says—'I had rather hear Lady my brach howl in Irish.' CAMPION.

CHAP VII
1561
January

Offers of
Shan to
Elizabeth.

side; and while to Shan it was pretended that the Baron had been sent for, Cecil wrote privately to Fitzwilliam to prevent him from leaving Ireland.

At first the caged chieftain felt no alarm, and he used his opportunities in flattering and working upon Elizabeth. He wrote to her from time to time, telling her that she was the sole hope and refuge which he possessed in the world; in coming to England his chief desire had been to see that great person whose fame was spoken of through the world, and to study the wisdom of her Government that he 'might learn how better to order himself in civil polity.' If she would give him his father's earldom, he said, he would maintain her authority in Ulster where she should be undisputed Queen over willing subjects; he would drive away all her enemies; he would expel Mary Stuart's friends the Scots; and with them it seems he was prepared to dismiss his 'countess;' for 'he was most urgent that her Majesty would give him some noble English lady for a wife with augmentation of living suitable;' and he on his part would save the Queen all further expense in Ireland 'with great increase of revenue.' As the chief of the House of O'Neil he claimed undisputed sovereignty over the petty Ulster chiefs. He admitted that he had killed his brother, but he saw nothing in so ordinary an action but what was right and reasonable.[1]

So the winter months passed on. At last when January was gone, and February was gone, and March had come, and 'the young Baron' had not appeared, Shan's mind misgave him. His time had not been wasted; night after night he had been closeted with de Quadra, and the insurrectionary resources of Ireland had

[1] Shan O'Neil to Elizabeth, January.—*Irish MSS.*

been sketched out as a bait to Philip. His soul in the land of heretics had been cared for by holy waters from de Quadra's chapel; but his body he began to think might be in the lion's den, and he pressed for his dismissal.

A cloud of obstacles was immediately raised. The Queen, he was told, was indifferent who had the earldom provided it was given to the lawful heir; and as soon as the Baron arrived the cause should instantly be heard. When Shan was still dissatisfied, he was recommended if he wished for favour 'to change his garments and go like an Englishman.'

He appealed to Elizabeth herself. With an air of ingenuous simplicity he threw himself, his wrongs, and his position on her personal kindness, 'having no refuge nor succour to flee unto but only her Majesty.' His presence was urgently required in Ireland; the Scots were 'evil neighbours;' his kinsmen were fickle: if however her Majesty desired him to stay he was her slave, he would do all which she would have him do; he would only ask in return that 'her Majesty would give him a gentlewoman for a wife such as he and she might agree upon;' and he begged that he might be allowed—the subtle flatterer—to attend on the Lord Robert; 'that he might learn to ride after the English fashion, to run at the tilt, to hawk, to shoot, and use such other good exercises as the said good lord was most apt unto.'[1]

He had touched the Queen where she was most susceptible, yet he lost his labour. She gave him no English lady, she did not let him go. At length the false dealing produced its cruel fruit, the murder of the boy who was used as the pretext for delay. Sent for to England, yet prevented from obeying the command, the

---
[1] Shan O'Neil to Elizabeth, March.—*Irish MSS.*

young Baron of Dungannon was waylaid at the beginning of April in a wood near Carlingford by Tirlogh O'Neil. He fled for his life with the murderers behind him till he reached the bank of a deep river which he could not swim, and there he was killed.[1]

The crime could not be traced to Shan. His rival was gone, and there was no longer any cause to be pleaded; while he could appeal to the wild movements of his clan as an evidence of the necessity of his presence among them.

The Council were frightened. O'Neil promised largely, and Elizabeth persuaded herself to believe him. She durst not imprison him; she could no longer detain him except by open force: she preferred to bribe him into allegiance by granting him all that he desired.

The earldom—a barren title for which he cared little—was left in suspense. On the 20th of April an indenture was signed by Elizabeth and himself, in which Shan bound himself to do military service and to take the oath of allegiance in the presence of the Deputy; while in return he was allowed to remain Captain of Tyrone with feudal jurisdiction over the northern counties. The Pale was to be no shelter to any person whom he might demand as a malefactor. If any Irish lord or chief did him wrong, and the Deputy failed within twenty days to exact reparation, Shan might raise an army and levy war on his private account. One feeble effort only was made to save O'Donnell whose crime against O'Neil had been his devotion to England. O'Neil consented to submit O'Donnell's cause to the arbitration of the Irish earls.[2]

---

[1] Fitzwilliam to Cecil, April 14.—*Irish MSS.*

[2] Indenture between the Queen of England and Shan O'Neil, April 30, 1562.--*Irish MSS.*

A rebel subject treating as an equal with his sovereign for the terms on which he would remain in his allegiance was an inglorious spectacle; and the admission of Shan's pretensions to sovereignty was one more evidence to the small Ulster chiefs that no service was worse requited in Ireland than fidelity to the English crown. The M'Guyres, the O'Reillies, the O'Donnells—all the clans who had stood by Sussex in the preceding summer—were given over to their enemy bound hand and foot. Yet Elizabeth was weary of the expense, and sick of efforts which were profitless as the cultivation of a quicksand.

True it was that she was placing half Ireland in the hands of an adulterous murdering scoundrel; but the Irish liked to have it so, and she forced herself to hope that he would restrain himself for the future within bounds of decency.

Shan therefore with his galloglasse returned in glory, his purse lined with money, and honour wreathed about his brows. On reappearing in Tyrone he summoned the northern chiefs about him; he told them that 'he had not gone to England to lose but to win;' they must submit to his rule henceforth or they should feel his power.

The O'Donnells in vain reliance on the past promises of the Deputy dared to refuse allegiance to him. Without condescending to the form of consulting the Government at Dublin, he called his men to arms and marched into Tyrconnell, killing, robbing, and burning in the old style, through farm and castle.

The Earl of Sussex not knowing how to act could but fall back on treachery. Shan was bound by his engagement to take the oath of allegiance in Dublin. The Lord Deputy desired him to present himself at the first opportunity. The safe-conduct which accompanied the request was ingeniously worded; and enclosing a copy of it to Elizabeth, Sussex inquired whether in the event of Shan's coming to him he might not twist the meaning of the words and make him prisoner.[1] But Shan was too cunning a fish and had been too lately in the meshes, to be caught again in so poor a snare. His duty to the Queen, he replied, forbade him to leave his province in its present disturbed condition. He was making up for his long fast in England from his usual amusements; and when fighting was in the wind neither he nor his troopers, nor as it seemed his clergy, had leisure for other occupations. The Catholic Primate having refused allegiance to Elizabeth, the see of Armagh was vacant, and Sussex sent down a *congé d'élire* for the appointment of 'Mr. Adam Loftus.' He received for answer 'that the chapter there whereof the greater part were Shan O'Neil's horsemen, were so sparkled and out of order that they could by no means be assembled for the election.'[2]

Lord Sussex attempts to catch Shan. Once more Lord Sussex set his trap, and this time he baited it more skilfully. The Scotch countess was not enough for Shan's ambition. His passionate desire for an English wife had survived his return, and Elizabeth in this point had not gratified his wishes. Lord Sussex had a sister with him in Dublin, and Shan sent an intimation that if the Deputy would take him for a

---

[1] The safe conduct was worded thus:—'Plenam protectionem nostram per præsentes dicto Joanni concedimus qua ipse ad præmissa perficienda cum omnibus quibuscunque qui cum illo venerint ad nos venire et a nobis cum voluerint libere recedere valeant et possint absque ulla perturbatione seu molestatione.' The word 'præmissa' referred to the oath of allegiance; it was anticipated that Shan would make a difficulty in doing homage to Sussex as Elizabeth's representative; and Sussex thought he might then lay hands on him for breach of compact. —*Sussex to Elizabeth, August 27. Irish MSS.*

[2] Sussex to Elizabeth, September 2. —*Irish MSS.*

brother-in-law their relations for the future might be improved. The present sovereign of England would perhaps give one of her daughters to the King of Dahomey with more readiness than the Earl of Sussex would have consigned his sister to Shan O'Neil; yet he condescended to reply 'that he could not promise to give her against her will,' but if Shan would visit him 'he could see and speak with her, and if he liked her and she him they should both have his good will.'[1] Shan glanced at the tempting morsel with wistful eyes. Had he trusted himself in the hands of Sussex he would have had a short shrift for a blessing and a rough nuptial knot about his neck. At the last moment a little bird carried the tale to his ear. 'He had advertisement out of the Pale that the lady was brought over only to entrap him, and if he came to the Deputy he should never return.'[2]

After this second failure Sussex told Elizabeth that she must either use force once more or she must be prepared to see first all Ulster and afterwards the whole 'Irishry' of the four provinces accept Shan for their sovereign. There was no sort of uncertainty as to O'Neil's intentions: he scarcely affected to conceal them. He had written to the Pope; he was in correspondence with the Queen of Scots; he had established secret relations with Spain through de Quadra; and Sussex advised war immediate and unsparing. 'No greater danger,' he said, 'had ever been in Ireland;' he implored the Queen not to trifle with it, and with a modest sense of his own failures he recommended her to send a more efficient person than himself to take the command—not,

---

[1] Sussex to the Queen, September 20.—*Irish MSS.*
[2] Sussex to Elizabeth, September 29.—*Irish MSS.*

CHAP VII
1561
September

Shan again rebels.

he protested, 'from any want of will, for he would spend his last penny and his last drop of blood for her Majesty,' but he knew himself to be unequal to the work.

Post after post brought evidence of the fatal consequences of the quasi recognition of Shan's sovereignty. Right and left he was crushing the petty chiefs, who one and all sent to say that they must yield unless England supported them. Sussex wrote to him in useless menace 'that if he followed his foolish pride her Majesty would destroy him at the last.' He 'held a parley' with the Irish Council on Dundalk Bridge on the 17th of September, and bound himself 'to keep peace with the Queen' 'for six months;' but he felt himself discharged of all obligations towards a government which had aimed at his life by deliberate treachery. In the face of his ambiguous dealings the garrison had been still maintained at Armagh; at the beginning of October the hostages for his good behaviour which he had sent in on his return from England escaped from Dublin Castle; and on the 10th in a dark moonless night the guard at the cathedral were alarmed with mysterious lights like blown matches glimmering through the darkness. Had the troops ventured out to reconnoitre, some hundreds of 'harquebusmen' were in ambush to cut them off. Suspecting treason they kept within their walls, and Shan was compelled to content himself with driving their cattle; but had they shown outside not a man of them would have been left alive. The next day the Irish came under the gate and taunted them with 'cowardice,' 'telling them the wolves had eaten their cattle, and that the matches they thought they saw were wolves' eyes.'[1]

[1] Sussex to Elizabeth, October 15.—*Irish MSS.*

Con O'Donnell the Callogh's son wrote piteously to Elizabeth that after carrying off his father and his mother, Shan had now demanded the surrender of his castles; he had refused out of loyalty to England, and his farms were burnt, his herds were destroyed, and he was a ruined man.[1]

A few days later M'Guyre from the banks of Lough Erne wrote that Shan had summoned him to submit; he had answered 'that he would not forsake the English till the English forsook him;' 'wherefore,' he said, 'I know well that within these four days the sayed Shan will come to dystroy me contrey except your Lordshypp will sette some remedy in the matter.'[2] Shan crushes the Ulster chiefs.

Sussex was powerless. Duly as the unlucky chief foretold, Shan came down into Fermanagh 'with a great hoste;' M'Guyre still kept his truth to England; 'wherefore Shan bygan to wax mad and to cawsse his men to bran all his corn and howsses;' he spared neither church nor sanctuary; three hundred women and children were piteously murdered; and M'Guyre himself 'clean banished,' as he described it, took refuge with the remnant of his people in the islands on the lake, whither Shan was making boats to pursue him.

'Help me your lordship,' the hunted wretch cried in his despair to Sussex; 'I promes you, and you doo not sy the rather to Shan O'Nele is besynes, ye ar lyke to make hym the strongest man of all Erlond, for every man wyll take an exampull by me gratto lostys; take

---

[1] Con O'Donnell to Elizabeth, September 30.—*Irish MSS. Rolls House.* Sussex, in forwarding the letter, added—

'This Con is vallant, wise, much disposed of himself to civility, true of his word, speaketh and writeth very good English, and hath natural shamefastness in his face, which few of the wild Irish have, and is assuredly the likeliest plant that can grow in Ulster to graft a good subject on.'

[2] M'Guyre to Sussex, October 9.—Wright's *Elizabeth*, vol. i. p. 93.

hyd to yourself by thrynes for he is lyke to have all the power from this place thill he come to the wallys of Gallway to rysse against you.'[1]

Elizabeth knew not now which way to turn. Force, treachery, conciliation, had been tried successively, and the Irish problem was more hopeless than ever. Sussex had protested from the first against the impolicy of recognizing Shan; the event had proved that he was right, and the Queen now threw herself upon him and the Council of Ireland for advice. In the dense darkness of the prospects of Ulster there was a solitary gleam of light. Grown insolent with prosperity Shan had been dealing too peremptorily with the Scots; his countess, though compelled to live with him and to be the mother of his children, had felt his brutality, repented of her folly, and perhaps attempted to escape. In the day time when he was abroad marauding, she was coupled like a hound to a page or a horse-boy, and only released at night when he returned to his evening orgies.[2] The fierce Campbells were not men to bear tamely these outrages from a drunken savage on the sister of their chief; and Sussex conceived that if the Scots could by any contrivance be separated from Shan they might be used 'as a whip to scourge him.'

Elizabeth bade Sussex do his best. The Irish Council agreed with the Deputy that the position of things 'was the most dangerous that had ever been in Ireland;' and that if the Queen intended to continue to hold the

---

[1] Shan M'Guyre to Sussex, October 20, and November 25.—WRIGHT, vol. I. M'Guyre adds a curious caution to Sussex to write to him in English and not in Latin, because he would not clerks nor other men should know his mind.

[2] 'Shan O'Neil possessth O'Donnell's wife, and by him she is with child. She is all day chained by the arm to a little boy, and at bed and board, when he is present, she is at liberty.'—Randolph to Cecil, Scotch MSS. Rolls House.

country Shan must be crushed at all hazards and at all costs. In desperate acquiescence she consented to supply the means for another invasion; yet with characteristic perversity she refused to accept Sussex's estimate of his own inability to conduct it. In submitting to his opinion she insisted that he should take the responsibility of carrying it into action.

Once more therefore the Deputy prepared for war. Fresh stores were thrown into Armagh, and the troops there increased to a number which could harass Tyrone through the winter. The M'Connells were plied with promises to which they were not unwilling to listen; and among the O'Neils themselves a faction was raised opposed to Shan under Tirlogh, the murderer of the Baron of Dungannon. O'Donnell was encouraged to hold out; M'Guyre defended himself in his islands. By the beginning of February Sussex undertook to relieve them.

Unhappily the Deputy had but too accurately measured his own incapacity. His assassination plots were but the forlorn resources of a man who felt his work too heavy for him; the Irish Council had no confidence in a man who had none in himself; and certain that any enterprise which was left to him to conduct would end in disaster, they were unwilling to waste their men their money or their reputation. The army was disaffected disorganized and mutinous; Sussex lamented its condition to the Home Government, but was powerless to improve it; at length Kildare and Ormond in the name of the other loyal noblemen and gentlemen, declared that they had changed their minds; they declined to supply their promised contingents for the invasion, and requested that it should be no longer thought of. The farmers of the Pale gathered courage from the example.

They too refused to serve. When required to supply provisions, they replied with complaining of the extortion of the soldiers. They swore 'they would rather be hanged at their own doors' than establish such a precedent. 'If the Deputy looked to have provisions from them he would find himself deceived;' and Sussex, distracted and miserable, could only declare that the Irish Council was in a conspiracy 'to keep O'Neil from falling.'[1]

Thus February passed and March, and M'Guyre and O'Donnell were not relieved. At last between threats and entreaty, Sussex wrung from Ormond an unwilling acquiescence; and on the 6th of April, with a mixed force of Irish and English, ill armed, ill supplied, dispirited and almost disloyal, Sussex set out for the north. He took but provision for three weeks with him. A vague hope was held out by the farmers that a second supply should be collected at Dundalk.

The achievements of an army so composed and so commanded scarcely require to be detailed. The sole result of a winter's expensive if worthless preparation was thus summed up in the report from the Deputy to the Queen:—

'*April* 6. The army arrives at Armagh.

'*April* 8. We return to Newry to bring up stores and ammunition which had been left behind.

'*April* 11. We again advance to Armagh, where we remain waiting for the arrival of galloglasse and kerne from the Pale.

'*April* 14. A letter from James M'Connell, which we answer.

---

[1] Sussex to Elizabeth, February 19. Sussex to the English Council, March 1. Sussex to Cecil, March 1.—*Irish MSS. Rolls House.*

'*April* 15. The galloglasse not coming, we go upon Shan's cattle of which we take enough to serve us; we should have taken more if we had had galloglasse.

'*April* 16. We return to Armagh.

'*April* 17, 18, 19. We wait for the galloglasse. At last we send back to Dublin for them, and begin to fortify the churchyard.

'*April* 20. We write to M'Connell, who will not come to us notwithstanding his promise.

'*April* 21. We survey the Trough Mountains, said to be the strongest place in Ireland.

'*April* 22. We return to Armagh with the spoil taken, which would have been much greater if we had had galloglasse, "and because St. George's even forced me her Majesty's lieutenant to return to Divine service that night."

'*April* 23. "Divine service."'

The three weeks had now all but expired; the provisions were consumed; it was necessary to fall back on the Pale, and if the farmers had kept their word, if he could obtain some Irish horse, and if the Scots did not assist Shan which he thought it likely that they would do, Sussex trusted on his next advance that he would accomplish something more. Conscious of failure he threw the blame on others. 'I have been commanded to the field,' he wrote to Cecil, 'and I have not one penny of money; I must lead forth an army and have no commission; I must continue in the field and I see not how I shall be victualled; I must fortify and have no working tools.'[1]

---

[1] Sussex to the Council, April 24. Sussex to Cecil, April 24.—*Irish MSS.*

Such after six months of preparation was the Deputy's hopeless condition; the money in which, if the complaints in England of the expenses of the Irish war were justified he had not been stinted, all gone; and neither food nor even spade and mattock. In the Pale 'he could not get a man to serve the Queen nor a peck of corn to feed the army.'[1] At length with a wild determination to do something, he made a plundering raid towards Clogher feeding his men on the cattle which they could steal, wasted a few miles of country, and having succeeded in proving to the Irish that he could do them no serious harm, relinquished the expedition in despair. He exclaimed loudly that the fault did not rest with him. The Scots had deceived him. 'The Englishry of the Pale' were secretly unwilling that the rebellion should be put down. The Ulster chiefs durst not move because they distrusted his power to protect them. The rupture between England and France had given a stimulus to the rebellion, and 'to expel Shan was but a Sisyphus' labour.'[2]

There may have been some faint foundation for these excuses. The Irish Council, satisfied of the Deputy's incapacity, had failed to exert themselves; while in England the old policy of leaving Ireland to be governed by the Irish had many defenders; and Elizabeth had been urged to maintain an inefficient person against his will in the command, with a hope, unavowed by those who advised her, that he would fail.

Most certainly the English commander had done no injustice to his incompetency. Three hundred horses were reported to have been lost, and Cecil wrote to

---

[1] Sussex to the Council, April 28.— *Irish MSS.*
[2] Sussex to Cecil, May 20.

inquire the meaning of it. Sussex admitted that 'the
loss was true indeed.' Being Easter-time, and he having
travelled the week before and Easter-day till night,
thought fit to give Easter Monday to prayer—and in
this time certain churls stole off with the horses.[1]

The piety which could neglect practical duty for the
outward service of devotion, yet at the same time could
make overtures to Neil Grey to assassinate his master,
requires no very lenient consideration.

The news of the second failure reached Elizabeth at
the crisis of the difficulty at Havre. She was straining
every nerve to supply the waste of an army which the
plague was destroying. She had a war with France
hanging over her head. She was uncertain of Spain and
but half secure of the allegiance of her English subjects.
It was against her own judgment that the last enterprise
had been adventured, and she reverted at once to her
original determination to spend no more money in reforming a country which every effort for its amendment
plunged into deeper anarchy. She would content herself
with a titular sovereignty. She would withdraw or
reorganize on a changed footing the profligate and
worthless soldiers whose valour flinched from an enemy,
and went no further than the plunder of a friend. The
Irish should be left to themselves to realize their own
ideals and govern themselves their own way.

Sir Thomas Cusak a member of the Irish Council
came over with a scheme which, if the Queen consented
to it, would satisfy the people and would ensure the return of Shan O'Neil to a nominal allegiance. The four
provinces should constitute each a separate presidency.
Ulster Connaught and Munster should be governed in

---

[1] Sussex to Cecil, May 26.—*Irish MSS.*

the Queen's name by some Irish chief or nobleman—if not elected by the people, yet chosen in compliance with their wishes. O'Neil would have the north, the O'Briens or the Clanrickards the west. The south would fall to Desmond. On these conditions Cusak would undertake for the quiet of the country and for the undisturbed occupation of the Pale by the English Government.

Prepared as Elizabeth had almost become to abandon Ireland entirely, she welcomed this project as a reprieve. She wrote to Sussex to say that finding his expedition had resulted only in giving fresh strength to Shan O'Neil, 'she had decided to come to an end of the war of Ulster by agreement rather than by force;' and Cusak returned the first week in August empowered to make whatever concessions should be necessary, preparatory to the proposed alteration.

To Shan O'Neil he was allowed to say that the Queen was surprised at his folly in levying war against her; nor could she understand his object. She was aware of his difficulties; she knew 'the barbarity' of the people with whom he had to deal; she had never intended to exact any strict account of him; and if he was dissatisfied with the arrangements to which he had consented when in England, he had but to prove himself a good subject, and he 'should not only have those points reformed, but also any pre-eminence in that country which her Majesty might grant without doing any other person wrong.' If he desired to have a council established at Armagh, he should himself be the president of that council; if he wished to drive the Scots out of Antrim, her own troops should assist in the expulsion; if he was offended with the garrison in the cathedral, she would gladly see peace maintained in a manner less expensive to herself. To the Primacy he might name the person most agreeable to himself; and with the Primacy, as a matter of course, even the form of maintaining the Protestant Church would be abandoned also.

In return for these concessions the Queen demanded only that to save her honour Shan should sue for them as a favour instead of demanding them as a right;[1] the rebel chief consented without difficulty to conditions which cost him nothing; and after an interview with Cusak, O'Neil wrote a formal apology to Elizabeth, and promised for the future to be her Majesty's true and faithful subject. Indentures were drawn on the 17th of December, in which the Ulster sovereignty was transferred to him in everything but the name; and the treaty—such treaty as it was—required only Elizabeth's signature, when a second dark effort was made to cut the knot of the Irish difficulty.

As a first evidence of returning cordiality, a present of wine was sent to Shan from Dublin. It was consumed at his table, but the poison had been unskilfully prepared. It brought him and half his household to the edge of death, but no one actually died. Refined chemical analysis was not required to detect the cause of the illness; and Shan clamoured for redress with the fierceness of a man accustomed rather to do wrong than to suffer it.

The guilt could not be fixed on Sussex. The crime was traced to an English resident in Dublin named Smith; and if Sussex had been the instigator, his instrument was too faithful to betray him. Yet after the fatal letter in which the Earl had revealed to Elizabeth his own personal endeavours to procure O'Neil's murder, the suspicion cannot but cling to him that the second attempt

CHAP VII
1561
August

Poisoned wine is sent from Dublin to Shan.

---
[1] Instructions to Sir Thomas Cusak, August 7.—*Irish MSS.*

ELIZ. II. E

was not made without his connivance. Nor can Elizabeth herself be wholly acquitted of responsibility. She professed the loudest indignation; but she ventured no allusion to his previous communication with her; and no hint transpires of any previous displeasure when the proposal had been made openly to herself.

In its origin and in its close the story is wrapped in mystery. The treachery of an English nobleman, the conduct of the inquiry, and the anomalous termination of it, would have been incredible even in Ireland, were not the original correspondence extant in which the facts are not denied. Elizabeth on the receipt of O'Neil's complaint directed Sir Thomas Cusak to look into the evidence most scrupulously; she begged Shan to produce every proof which he could obtain for the detection 'both of the party himself and of all others that were any wise thereto consenting; to the intent none might escape that were parties thereunto of what condition soever the same should be.'

'We have given commandment,' she wrote to Sussex, 'to show you how much it grieveth us to think that any such horrible attempt should be used as is alleged by Shan O'Neil to have been attempted by Thomas Smith to kill him by poison; we doubt not but you have as reason is committed the said Smith to prison, and proceeded to the just trial thereof; for it behoveth us for all good and honourable respects to have the fault severely punished, and so we will and charge you to do.'[1]

'We assure you,' she wrote to Cusak, 'the indignation which we conceive of this fact, being told with some probability by you, together with certain other causes of suspicion which O'Neil hath gathered, hath wrought

---

[1] The Queen to Sussex, October 15.—*Irish MSS.*

no small effect in us to incline us to bear with divers things unorderly passed, and to trust to that which you have on his behalf promised hereafter in time to come.'[1]

It is in human nature to feel deeper indignation at a crime which has been detected and exposed than at guilt equally great of which the knowledge is confined to the few who might profit by it; yet after the repeated acts of treachery which had been at least meditated towards Shan with Elizabeth's knowledge, she was scarcely justified in assuming a tone of such innocent anger; nor was the result of the investigation more satisfactory. After many contradictions and denials Smith at last confessed his guilt, took the entire responsibility on himself, and declared that his object was to rid his country of a dangerous enemy. The English law in the sixteenth century against crimes of violence has not been suspected of too much leniency; yet it was discovered by some strange interpretation that as the crime had not been completed it was not punishable by death. Notwithstanding Elizabeth's letter there was an evident desire to hush up the inquiry; and strangest of all Sir Thomas Cusak induced O'Neil to drop his complaint. 'I persuaded O'Neil to forget the matter,' Cusak wrote to Cecil, 'whereby no more talk should grow of it; seeing there is no law to punish the offender other than by discretion in imprisonment, which O'Neil would little regard except the party might be executed by death, and that the law doth not suffer. So as the matter being wisely pacified it were well done to leave it.'[2]

Behind the fragments of information preserved in the

---

[1] The Queen to Sir Thomas Cusak.—*Irish MSS.*
[2] Sir Thomas Cusak to Cecil, March 22, 1564.—*Irish MSS.*

CHAP VII
1564

Shan's attempted revenge.

State correspondence, much may remain concealed which if found might explain a conclusion so unexpected. Had Smith been the only offender it might have been expected that he would have been gladly sacrificed as an evidence of Elizabeth's evenhandedness, and Shan perhaps did not care for the punishment of a subordinate if he could not reach the principal.

He used the occasion however to grasp once more at the great object of his ambition, and to obtain with it if possible a refined revenge on Sussex. Seeing Elizabeth anxious, whether honestly or from motives of policy, to atone for the attempt to murder him, he renewed his suit to her for an English wife. The M'Ilams, relations of the Countess of Argyle, had offered him a thousand pounds to let her go; and Elizabeth half promising if the Countess were restored to her friends to consider his prayer, he fixed on Sussex's sister, who had been employed as the bait to catch him; so to humble the haughty English Earl into the very dust and dirt.

Elizabeth's desire to conciliate however stopped short of ignominy. Lord Sussex deserved no better, nor his sister if she had been a party to her brother's plot; but Cecil did not even venture 'to move the matter to the Queen, fearing how she might take it;' and Shan laying by his resentment, contented himself with the substantial results of his many successes. M'Guyre had to fly from his islands; O'Donnell's castles were surrendered; the Armagh garrison was withdrawn at last. Over lake and river, bog and mountain, Shan was undisputed Lord of Ulster—save only on the Antrim shore where the Scots maintained a precarious independence. So absolute was he that with contemptuous pity he opened the doors of the Callogh's prison. The aged and broken chief came to sue for maintenance at the Court to which his fidelity had ruined him; and Cusak consoled Cecil with saying that 'he was but a poor creature without activity or manhood,' and that 'O'Neil continuing in his truth was more worthy to be embraced than three O'Donnells.'[1]

Here then for the present the story will leave Shan, safely planted on the first step of his ambition, in all but the title sole monarch of the north. He built himself a fort on an island in Lough Neagh, which he called 'Foogh-ni-Gall'—or 'Hate of Englishmen;' and grew rich on the spoils of his enemies, 'the only strong man in Ireland.' He administered justice after a paternal fashion, permitting no robbers but himself; when wrong was done he compelled restitution, 'or at his own cost redeemed the harm to the loser's contentation.'[2] Two hundred pipes of wine were stored in his cellars; six hundred men-at-arms fed at his table—'as it were his janissaries;' and daily he feasted the beggars at his gate, 'saying it was meet to serve Christ first.' Half wolf, half fox, he lay couched in his 'Castle of Malepartus,' with his emissaries at Rome, at Paris, and at Edinburgh. In the morning he was the subtle and dexterous pretender to the Irish throne; in the afternoon, 'when the wine was in him,' he was a dissolute savage revelling in sensuality, with his unhappy countess uncoupled from her horse-boy to wait upon his pleasure.

He broke loose from time to time to keep his hand in practice: at Carlingford for instance he swept off one day some two hundred sheep and oxen, while his men violated sixty women in the town.[3] But Elizabeth looked

---
[1] Cusak to Cecil, 1564.—*Irish MSS.*
[2] CAMPION.
[3] Fitzwilliam to Cecil, June 17, 1565.—*Irish MSS.*

away and endeavoured not to see; the English Government had resolved 'to stir no sleeping dogs in Ireland till a staff was provided to chastise them if they would bite.'[1] Terence Daniel, the Dean of those rough-riding canons of Armagh, was installed as Primate; the Earl of Sussex was recalled to England; and the new Archbishop unable to contain his exultation at the blessed day which had dawned upon his country, wrote to Cecil to say how the millennium had come at last—glory be to God!

Meantime Cecil set himself to work at the root of the evil. Relinquishing for the present the hope of extending the English rule in Ireland, he endeavoured to probe the secret of its weakness and to restore some kind of order and justice in the counties where that rule survived. On the return of Sussex to England Sir Thomas Wroth and Sir Nicholas Arnold were sent over as commissioners to inquire into the complaints against the army. The scandals which they brought to light, the recrimination, rage, and bitterness which they provoked, fill a large volume of the State Papers.

Peculation had grown into a custom; the most barefaced frauds had been converted by habit into rights; and 'a captain's' commission was thought 'ill-handled' if it did not yield beyond the pay 500*l.* a year. The companies appeared in the pay books as having their full complement of a hundred men. The actual number rarely exceeded sixty. The soldiers followed the example of their leaders, and robbed and ground the peasantry. Each and all had commenced their evil ways, when the Government itself was the first and worst offender.

A few more years—perhaps months—of such doings

---

[1] Cecil to Sir Nicholas Arnold.—*Irish MSS.*

would have made an end of English dominion. Sir
Thomas Wroth described the Pale on his arrival as a
weltering sea of confusion—'the captains out of credit,'
'the soldiers' mutinous, the English Government hated;
'every man seeking his own, and none that which was
Christ's;' 'few in all the land reserved from bowing the
knee to Baal;' 'the laws for religion mere words.'[1]

Something too much of theological anxiety impaired
Wroth's usefulness. He wished to begin at the outside
with reforming the creed. The thing needful was to
reform the heart and to bring back truth and honesty.
Wroth therefore was found unequal to the work; and
the purification of the Pale was left to Arnold—a hard,
iron, pitiless man, careful of things and careless of phrases,
untroubled with delicacy, and impervious to Irish 'en-
chantments.' The account books were dragged to light;
where iniquity in high places was registered in inexorable
figures. The hands of Sir Henry Ratcliffe the brother of
Sussex were not found clean. Arnold sent him to the
castle with the rest of the offenders. Deep leading drains
were cut through the corrupting mass; the shaking
ground grew firm; and honest healthy human life was
again made possible. With the provinces beyond the
Pale Arnold meddled little, save where taking a rough
view of the necessities of the case he could help the Irish
chiefs to destroy each other. To Cecil he wrote—

'I am with all the wild Irish at the same point I am
at with bears and bandogs; when I see them fight, so
they fight earnestly indeed and tug each other well, I
care not who has the worst.'[2]

Why not indeed? Better so than to hire assassins!

---

[1] Sir Thomas Wroth to Cecil, April 16.—*Irish MSS.*
[2] Sir Nicholas Arnold to Cecil, January 29. 1565.—*Irish MSS.*

Cecil with the modesty of genius confessed his ignorance of the country and his inability to judge; yet in every opinion which he allowed himself to give there was always a certain nobility of tone and sentiment.

'You be of that opinion,' he replied, 'which many wise men are of—from which I do not dissent being an Englishman; but being as I am a Christian man I am not without some perplexity to enjoy of such cruelties.'[1]

Arnold however though perhaps not personally responsible saw the Irish rending each other as he desired. The formal division into presidencies could not be completed on the moment; but English authority having ceased to cast its shadow beyond the Pale, the leading chiefs seized or contended for the rule. In the north O'Neil was without a rival. In the west the O'Briens and the Clanrickards shared without disputing for them the glens and moors of Galway, Clare, and Mayo. The richer counties of Munster were a prize to excite a keener competition; and when the English Government was no longer in a position to interfere, the feud between the Butlers and the Geraldines of the south burst like a volcano in fury, and like a volcano in the havoc which it spread. Even now the picture drawn by Sir Henry Sidney and repeated by Spenser can scarcely be contemplated without emotion. The rich limestone pastures were burnt into a wilderness; through Kilkenny, Tipperary, and Cork, 'a man might ride twenty or thirty miles nor ever find a house standing;' 'and the miserable poor were brought to such wretchedness that any stony heart would have rued the same. Out of every corner of the woods and glens they came creeping forth upon their hands, for their legs

---

[1] Cecil to Sir N. Arnold, February 28.—*Irish MSS.*

could not bear them; they looked like anatomies of
death; they spoke like ghosts crying out of their graves;
they did eat the dead carrions, happy where they could
find them; yea, they did eat one another soon after, insomuch as the very carcasses they spared not to scrape
out of their graves; and if they found a plot of watercresses or shamrocks, there they flocked as to a feast for
a time. Yet were they not all long to continue therewithal, so that in short space there were none almost
left, and a most populous and plentiful country was suddenly left void of man and beast; yet surely in all that
war there perished not many by the sword, but all by
the extremity of famine which they themselves had
wrought.'[1]

---

[1] Compare Spenser's 'State of Ireland' with 'A Description of Munster,' by Sir Henry Sidney, after a journey through it in 1566. The original of Sidney's despatch is in the Record Office. It was printed by Collins.—SIDNEY Papers, vol. i.

CHAPTER VIII.

THE policy of Elizabeth towards the French Protestants had not been successful. Had her assistance been moderately disinterested she would have secured their friendship, and at the close of the eight years fixed by the Treaty of Cambray for the restoration of Calais she would have experienced the effects of their gratitude. By the forcible retention of Havre after the civil war was ended she had rekindled hereditary animosities: she had thrown additional doubt on her sincerity as a friend of the Reformation; she had sacrificed an English army, while she had provided the French Government with a fair pretext for disowning its obligations, and was left with a war upon her hands from which she could hardly extricate herself with honour. A fortnight before Havre surrendered, the Prince of Condé had offered if she would withdraw from it that the clause in the Treaty of Cambray affecting Calais should be reaccepted by the King of France, the Queen-mother, the Council, the noblesse, and the Parliament. She had angrily and contemptuously refused; and now with crippled finances, with trade ruined, with the necessity growing upon her as it had grown upon her sister, of contracting loans at Antwerp, her utmost hope was to extort the terms which she had then rejected.

Unable to maintain a regular fleet at sea she had let loose the privateers, whose exploits hereafter will be more particularly related. In this place it is enough to say that they had found in the ships of Spain, Flanders, or even of their own country, more tempting booty than in the coasting traders of Brittany. English merchants and sailors were arrested in Spanish harbours and imprisoned in Spanish dungeons in retaliation for 'depredations committed by the adventurers;' while a bill was presented by the Madrid Government of two million ducats for injuries inflicted by them on Spanish subjects.[1] In vain Philip struggled to avoid a quarrel with Elizabeth; in vain Elizabeth refused to be the champion of the Reformation: the animosities of their subjects and the necessity of things were driving them forward towards the eventually inevitable breach. Mary Stuart was looking to the King of Spain and the King of Spain to Mary Stuart, each as the ally designed by Providence for the other; and the English Government in this unlucky war with France was quarrelling with the only European power which since the breach of Henry the Eighth with the Papacy had been cordially its friend. The House of Guise was under eclipse. The Queen of Scots' ambitions were no objects of interest to the Queen-mother. The policy of France was again ready to be moderate, national, anti-Spanish, and anti-Papal, to be all which England would most desire to see it. It was imperatively necessary that Elizabeth should make peace, that she should endure as she best might the supposed ingratitude of Condé, and accept the easiest terms to which Catherine de Medici would now consent.[2]

---

[1] Reasons for a peace with France, March 10, 1564.—*French MSS. Rolls House.*

[2] A letter of Sir John Mason to Cecil expresses the sense entertained by English statesmen of the necessity of

CHAP VIII
1564
January

Negotiation for peace.

The diplomatic correspondence which had continued since the summer had so far been unproductive of result. The French pretended that the Treaty of Cambray had been broken by the English in the seizure of Havre, and that Elizabeth's claims on Calais and on the half million crowns which were to be paid if Calais was not restored were alike forfeited. They demanded therefore the release of the hostages which they had given in as their security; and they detained Sir Nicholas Throgmorton on his parole until their countrymen were returned into their hands.

peace:—'My health, I thank God, I have recovered, nothing remaining but an ill cough, which will needs accompany *senectutem meam* to the journey's end; whereof my care is much lessened by the great care of the many sicknesses that I see in our commonwealth, which is to me more dear than is either health or life to be assaulted with; which would God were but infirmities as you do term them, so non potius *καισήθειαι*, seu quod genus morbi sit magis immorigerum et ad sanandum rebellius; and that worse is, cum universæ corporis partes nobis doleant a vertice capitis usque ad plantam pedis, dolorem tamen (for any care that is seen to be had thereof) sentire non videmur, quod mentis ægrotantis est indicium. A great argument whereof is that in tot Reipublicæ difficultatibus editur bibitur luditur altum dormitur privata curantur publica negliguntur ceu rideretur omnia et pax rebus esset altissima. The fear of God, whereby all things were wont to be kept in indifferent order, is in effect gone, and he seemeth to weigh us and to conduct our doings thereafter. The fear of the Prince goeth apace after, whereof we see daily proof both by sea and land. It is high time therefore for her Highness to take some good way with her enemy, and to grow with him to some reasonable end, yielding to necessity cui ne Dii quidem resistunt, et non ponere rumores ante salutem; and to answer our friends in reason, so as rebus foris constitutis, she may wholly attend to see things in better order at home; the looseness whereof is so great, as being not remedied in time, the tempest is not a little to be feared cum tot coactæ nubes nobis minantur, which God of his mercy, by the prayer of decem justi, a nobis longissime avertat.

'The Queen is expected to go north on progress, whereunto no good man will counsel her. There be in this city and about it numbers of men in much necessity, some for lack of work and some for lack of will to work. If these with others that have possessed the highways round about be not by some good means kept in awe, I fear there will be ill dwelling near unto London by such as have anything to take to.'—*Mason to Cecil, March 8.* LANSDOWNE MSS. 7.

The English maintained on the other side that they had acted only in self-defence, that the treaty had been first violated by the French when Francis and Mary assumed Elizabeth's arms and style, that the House of Guise had notoriously conspired against her throne, and that Calais therefore had been already forfeited to themselves.

Between these two positions Paul de Foix the French ambassador in London, Sir Thomas Smith, Elizabeth's ambassador in Paris, and Throgmorton with a special and separate commission, were endeavouring to discover some middle ground of agreement.

The French hostages individually had proved themselves a disagreeable burden on Elizabeth. They had been sent to reside at Eton, where they had amused themselves with misleading the Eton boys into iniquity; they had brought ambiguous damsels into the Fellows' Common Room, and had misconducted themselves in the Fellows' precincts 'in an unseemly manner.' To give them up was to acquiesce in the French interpretation of the Calais question. They were therefore arrested in retaliation for the arrest of Throgmorton, and were thrown into prison.

Yet the exigencies of England required peace, and France knew it; and the negotiations took a form which might without difficulty have been foreseen; Elizabeth made demands on which she durst not insist, and she acquiesced at last in a conclusion which was made humiliating by the reluctance with which it was accepted.

On the 28th of January Sir Thomas Smith reported that the Queen-mother and her ministers were anxious to come to terms, that they desired nothing better than a return to the 'natural love' which had existed 'between old King Francis and King Henry;' but that to speak any more of ' the ratification of the Treaty of Cambray was lost labour.'[1] Elizabeth knew that she must give way, yet she desired to give way with dignity: instead of replying to Smith she wrote to Throgmorton, who was intrusted with powers to negotiate independently of his colleague. She admitted that if the treaty was not to be ratified she could not stand out upon it; yet unwilling to commit herself formally she desired Throgmorton to go 'as of himself' to the Queen-mother and inquire whether she would consent to a general peace with a mutual reservation of rights. She said that she would not part with the hostages. If their restitution was demanded as a right 'she would rather abide the worst that could be done against her.' There might be a private understanding that on the signature of the treaty they should be released from arrest; but even so they must remain in England[2] until the French had either paid the money or had given mercantile security for it. To surrender them otherwise would be an admission that the Treaty of Cambray was no longer binding.

February was consumed in diplomatic fencing over these proposals; and Throgmorton tried in turn the Queen-mother, the Cardinal of Lorraine, the Constable, the Cardinal of Bourbon, and the Chancellor. But if Elizabeth was afraid of doing anything to compromise the treaty the French were equally afraid of doing anything to acknowledge it. They would give no second security to recover the hostages; they would not pay the half million crowns because it was the sum which the

---

[1] Sir Thomas Smith to Elizabeth, January 28.—*French MSS. Rolls House.*

[2] 'We mean not by any our own act to consent that the hostages should depart hence, as persons in whom we had no interest in respect of the Treaty of Cambray, without we may have caution according to the treaty; and though they be not here but for a sum of money, yet if we should let them depart, having neither the money nor other hostages, nor yet caution of merchants, we should thereby to our dishonour consent that the treaty was void.'— *Elizabeth to Throgmorton, February* 3. *MS. Ibid.*

treaty named. Throgmorton said that his mistress would make no objection to six hundred thousand if they were afraid of the stipulated figures; but this way out of the difficulty did not commend itself.

La Halle, a gentleman of the court, aiming at Elizabeth through her weak side, suggested a present of a hundred thousand crowns to Lord Robert. The Queen-mother offered to add to it some rich jewel from the French crown; but Sir Nicholas encouraged this suggestion as little as the French Court had encouraged the other. At last the Cardinal of Lorraine in private told him that a hundred and twenty thousand crowns would be paid for the hostages—so much and no more. The Prince of Condé and those in the French council whom the Queen of England had obliged the most were opposed to making any concessions at all and only wished the war to continue; and the Cardinal hinted as a reason for Elizabeth's consent that it was well known that she could not trust her own subjects.

To this last suggestion Throgmorton answered that 'Although there were some that desired the Roman religion, as he thought there were, yet the former agitations and torments about the change of religion had so wearied each party that the whole were resolved to endure no more changes, for they were so violent; all sorts, of what religion soever they were, did find more ease and surety to serve and obey than to rebel; and for proof the greatest number of those that had lost their lives in the wars at Newhaven and other places were reported to be of the Roman religion: so as surely the diversity of conscience did not in England make diversities of duties or breed new disobedience.'[1]

---

[1] Throgmorton to Elizabeth, February 28.—French MSS. Rolls House.

Some truth there doubtless was in this account of the state of English feeling; yet Throgmorton could scarcely have felt the confidence which he expressed. The disaffection of the Catholics was but too notorious, although Philip had embarrassed their action by forbidding them to look to France for assistance.

The loyalty or disloyalty of the English people however did not touch the immediate question. Beyond the hundred and twenty thousand crowns the French offer would not rise. Throgmorton wrote home for instructions, and the proposal was met in the spirit which usually characterized Elizabeth's money transactions.

The Queen replied with directing the ambassadors to demand four hundred thousand crowns; if the French refused, she said that they might descend to three hundred thousand, and must protest that they had no power to go lower; if there was no hope of obtaining three hundred thousand, 'they must do their uttermost to make the sum not less than two hundred thousand.'

These instructions were delivered in the usual form to the state messenger Somers, and appeared to be an ultimatum; but Somers carried with him a second sealed packet which he was not to deliver except at the last extremity. The ambassadors were to be able to say with a clear conscience that they had no authority to accept less than the two hundred thousand; yet sooner than let the chance of peace escape they were to be allowed at the last extremity to take whatever Catherine de Medici would give.

The French Court was at Troyes when Somers arrived. Smith and Throgmorton who had been employed hitherto as rivals—each informed of but half the truth, and intrusted with information which had been concealed from the other—were united at last in a common humiliation. With the first despatch in his hand Sir Thomas Smith repaired to the Queen-mother, and descended his scale so far as he then knew that his powers extended. Catherine replied shortly that the recovery of Havre had cost France two millions of gold; on the sum to be paid to Elizabeth 'she had not bargained and huckstered and altered her terms as the English had done; she had fixed in her own mind at first what she would give; and she would give that or nothing.' She intended to leave Troyes the following morning. If not accepted in the mean time the offer would be withdrawn.

With this answer Smith returned to his brother ambassador. They were looking blankly in each other's faces when Somers produced his second letter. The seal was broken. They found themselves permitted to consent; and they sent a message to Bourdin, Catherine's secretary, begging him to come to them. Their tempers were not improved by the position in which Elizabeth had placed them; and while waiting for Bourdin's arrival each laid on the other the blame of their bad success. Throgmorton 'chafed and fumed,' 'detested and execrated himself;' and then accused his companion of having betrayed to the Queen-mother the secret of the second commission. Smith protested that he could not have betrayed what he did not know; but five years of 'practice' and conspiracy were ending in shame; and Sir Nicholas could not bear it and was unreasonable.

Sir Thomas Smith himself describes the scene.

'"I tell the Queen-mother!" quoth I. "Why or how should I tell her?"

'"Thou liest!" said Throgmorton, "like a whoreson traitor as thou art!"

'"A whoreson traitor! Nay, thou liest!" quoth I.

CHAP VIII
1564
April

"I am as true to the Queen's majesty as thou, every day in the week, and have done and do her Highness as good service as thou."

'Hereupon Sir Nicholas drew his dagger, and poured out such terms as his malicious and furious rage had in store; and called me "arrant knave," "beggarly knave," "traitor," and other such injuries as came next to hand out of his good store.

'I drew my dagger also. Mr. Somers stepped between us; but as he pressed with his dagger to come near me, I bade him stand back and not come no nearer to me, or I would cause him stand back, and give him such a mark as his Bedlam furious head did deserve.'[1]

To such a pass had two honest men been brought by Elizabeth's bargain-driving. Throgmorton felt the wound most deeply, as the person chiefly answerable for the French policy. He had offered 'to lie in prison for a year rather than the enemy should have their will.' To rouse the Queen to fierceness he had quoted the French proverb, that 'if she made herself a sheep the wolf would devour her;'[2] and it ended in his being compelled at last to haggle like a cheating shopkeeper, and to fail.

The Peace of Troyes.

The ruffled humours cooled at last, and when quiet was restored Smith proposed one more attempt to 'traffic;' but Sir Nicholas would not give Catherine any further triumph; Bourdin came, and the Peace of Troyes was arranged.

The terms were simple. Complicated claims and rights on both sides were reserved; the Treaty of Cambray was neither acknowledged nor declared void; the French

---

[1] Smith to Cecil, April 13.—*French MSS. Rolls House.*
[2] 'Si to te fais ung mouton le loup te mangera.'

hostages were to be released from England; the French Government undertook to pay for them the hundred and twenty thousand crowns; and free trade was to be allowed 'between the subjects of both sovereigns in all parts of their respective dominions.'[1] The unfortunate war was at an end. Elizabeth was obliged to bear graciously with the times; and her bitterness was reserved for the Prince of Condé. From him she charged Smith to demand instant repayment of the loan which she had advanced to him in his hour of difficulty. 'We mean not,' she said, 'to be so deluded as both to forbear our money and to have had at this time no friendship by his means in the conclusion of the peace.'[2]

The peace itself came not an hour too soon. Scarcely was it signed than news came from Italy that the Sacred College had repented of their first honest answer to the English Catholics who had asked leave to attend the established services. It had been decided in secret council to permit Catholics in disguise to hold benefices in England, to take the oaths of allegiance, and to serve Holy Church in the camp of the enemy. 'Remission of sin to them and their heirs—with annuities, honours, and promotions,' was offered 'to any cook, brewer, baker, vintner, physician, grocer, surgeon, or other who would make away with the Queen;' the curse of God and his vicar was threatened against all those 'who would not promote and assist by money or otherwise the pretences of the Queen of Scots to the English crown;'[3] the court of Rome, once illustrious as the citadel of the

---

[1] Peace of Troyes.—Rymer.
[2] Elizabeth to Sir T. Smith, May 2.—*French MSS. Rolls House.*
[3] Report of E. Denaum, April 13, 1564.—Strype's *Annals of Elizabeth*, vol. I., part 2, p. 54.

saints, was given over to Jesuitism and the devil; and the Papal fanatics in England began to weave their endless web of conspiracy—aiming amidst a thousand variations at the heart of Queen Elizabeth.

The ruffle with France sunk speedily into calm. The ratifications were promptly exchanged. Lord Hunsdon went to France, taking with him the Garter for the young King.[1] M. de Gonor and the Bishop of Coutances came to England; and an attempt not very successful was made to show them in their reception that England was better defended than they supposed. In January, when a French invasion was thought likely, Archbishop Parker had reported 'Dover, Walmer, and Deal as forsaken and unregarded for any provision;' 'the people feeble, unarmed, and commonly discomforted towards the feared mischief.' The Lord Warden had gone to his post 'as naked without strength of men.' The Archbishop living at Bekesbourne with the ex-Bishop of Ely and another Catholic at free prison, felt uneasy for his charge; and not sharing Throgmorton's confidence and believing that if the French landed they would carry all before them, wrote to Cecil to warn him of the danger 'which if not looked to he feared would be irreparable.'

'If the enemy have an entry,' he said, 'as by great consideration of our weakness and their strength, of their vigilance and our dormitation and protraction, is like, the Queen's majesty shall never be able to leave to

---

[1] The ceremony was nearly spoilt by an old accident. The Garter, though Hunsdon said it cost her Majesty dear, was a poor and shabby one. It had been made on the common pattern, as if for some burly English nobleman, and would not remain on the puny leg of Charles the Ninth. Hunsdon was obliged to send back in haste for one which had belonged to King Edward or King Philip. 'These things,' he said, 'touch her Majesty's honour.'—*French MSS.*, May 1564. *Rolls House.*

her successors that which she found delivered her by God's favourable hand.'[1]

The peril had passed over; and for fear the French ambassadors might carry back too tempting a report of the defencelessness of the coast, Lord Abergavenny was directed—as if to do them honour—to call under arms the gentlemen of the south-eastern counties. The result not being particularly successful, the Archbishop invited de Gonor and the Bishop of Coutances to Bekesbourne, and 'in a little vain brag, perhaps infirmity,' showed them his well-furnished armoury, hoping that his guests would infer that if a prelate 'had regard of such provisions others had more care thereabout.'[2]

The thin disguise would have availed little had there been a real desire for the continuance of the war. In the unprotected shores, the open breezy downs, the scattered and weakly-armed population, they observed the facility of invasion, and remarked upon it plainly. But Catherine de Medici had no interest in Mary Stuart and no desire to injure Elizabeth. Mary Stuart's friends were rather at Madrid than at Paris; and the French ministers were more curious of the religious condition of England than of its military defences.

Their visit to Bekesbourne therefore gave occasion for the Archbishop and his visitors to compare ecclesiastical notes. The Bishop of Coutances expressed the unexpected pleasure which it had given him to find that 'there was so much reverence about the sacraments,' 'that music was still permitted in the quires,' and that the lands of the suppressed abbeys had been bestowed 'for pious uses.' He wished that as happy a change

---

[1] Parker to Cecil, January 20 and February 6, 1564.—LANSDOWNE MSS.
[2] Parker to Cecil, June 3.—Domestic MSS. Eliz., vol. xxxiii.

could be worked in France; and marvelled that the deposed bishops should have been 'so stiff' in refusing 'to follow the Prince's religion;' he noted and delighted in English mediocrity; charging the Genovans and the Scots with going too far in extremities.' The Archbishop told him that 'there were priests and bishops in England both married and unmarried;' 'he did not disallow thereof, and was contented to hear evil of the Pope.'

The ambassadors proceeded to London, leaving behind them an agreeable impression of themselves, and carrying with them a sunny memory of a pleasant English summer home, with its woods and gardens and cawing rooks and cheery social life; the French pages had been so well schooled in their behaviour that when they were gone the Archbishop was surprised to find 'he could not charge them with purloining the worth of one silver spoon.'[1] On both sides of the Channel, in London and Paris, the peace once made there was the warmest endeavour to obliterate painful recollections; the moderate party was in power at the Court of Catherine, and with it the liberal anti-Spanish foreign policy; the interests of France and England were identical on the great political questions of the day; and Elizabeth was fortunate in having a treaty forced upon her which obliged Philip to look with less favour on the Queen of Scots—which compelled the Spanish ministers to postpone their resentment against English piracies, and drove them rather to dread their own inability to retain their own Low Countries than to seek opportunities for interference abroad.

The King of Spain had intended to send no more

---

[1] Parker to Cecil, June 3.—*Domestic MSS. Eliz*, vol. xxxiii

ambassadors to England till Mary Stuart was on the throne: on the Peace of Troyes he changed his mind and resumed or affected to resume his friendly relations with Elizabeth. Guzman de Silva received his commission as de Quadra's successor; and once more in the old language Louis Romano, the Spanish agent in London, reported to Granvelle 'the affliction and discontent of the English Catholics, who had been encouraged to hope that their trials were at an end, who had rested their entire hopes on Philip, and now knew not where to turn.'[1]

Mary Stuart, as her hopes of the Prince of Spain grew fainter, was pausing over the answer which she should make to Elizabeth's last proposals. She had been in communication throughout the winter with the Netherlands, and was perhaps aware in some degree of the difficulties created by the Prince's character. She had decisively refused the Archduke of Austria whom Philip wished her to take in his son's stead; and although the Spanish Court, waiting probably for some favourable change in Don Carlos, had not yet determined that the marriage must be given up, the Queen of Scots knew enough to prevent her from feeling sanguine of obtaining him. It became necessary for her to consider whether she could make anything out of the English overtures.

Elizabeth's attitude towards her was in the main honourable and statesmanlike. The name of a successor, as she said herself, was like the tolling of her death-bell. In her sister's lifetime she had experienced how an heir

---

[1] 'Los Catolicos del Reyno estan muy afligidos con gran descontento, viendo que todas las esperanças que tenian eran en su Mag^d., y que no veen semblante ninguno para principio de remediar tanta desventura.' —*Louis Romano to Granvelle*, 1564. *MS. Simancas.*

presumptive with an inalienable right became inevitably a rallying point of disaffection. She did not trust the Queen of Scots, and if she allowed her pretensions to be sanctioned by Act of Parliament she anticipated neglect, opposition—perhaps worse. But of assassination she could scarcely be in greater danger than she was already; and if she could induce Mary to meet her half way in some moderate policy, and if the Queen of Scots instead of marrying a Catholic prince and allying herself with the revolutionary Ultramontanes, would accept an English nobleman of whose loyalty to herself she could feel assured, she was ready to sacrifice her personal unwillingness to what she believed to be the interest of her people. There could then be no danger that England would be sacrificed to the Papacy. Some tolerant creed could be established which Catholics might accept without offence to their consciences, and Protestants could live under without persecution; while the resolution of the two factions into neutrality if not into friendship, the union of the crowns, and the confidence which would arise from a secured succession, were objects with which private inclination could not be allowed to interfere. Elizabeth had made the offer in good faith, with a sincere hope that it would be accepted, and with a fair ground of confidence that with the conditions which she had named the objections of the House of Commons to the Queen of Scots would be overcome.

Even in the person whom in her heart she desired Mary to marry, Elizabeth was giving an evidence of the honesty of her intentions. Lord Robert Dudley was perhaps the most worthless of her subjects; but in the loving eyes of his mistress he was the knight *sans peur et sans reproche;* and she took a melancholy pride in offering her sister her choicest jewel, and in raising Dudley, though she could not marry him herself, to the reversion of the English throne.

She had not indeed named Lord Robert formally in Randolph's commission. She had spoken of him to Maitland, but she had spoken also of the Earl of Warwick; and she perhaps retained some hope that if Mary would be contented with the elder brother she might still keep her favourite for herself.[1] But if she entertained any such thought she soon abandoned it; her self-abnegation was to be complete; and in ignorance of the objections of Mary Stuart to the Archduke Charles she had even allowed Cecil at the close of 1563 to re-open negotiations with the Emperor for the transfer of his son to herself. Ferdinand however had returned a cold answer. He had been trifled with once already. Elizabeth had played with him he said for her own purposes with no real intention of marriage; and neither he nor the Archduke should be made ridiculous a second time.[2] Elizabeth accepted the refusal and redoubled her advances to Mary Stuart; relinquishing—if she had ever really entertained the thought of a simultaneous marriage for herself until she had seen how her scheme for Dudley would end.

---

[1] Randolph himself seems to have thought something of the kind. On the 21st of January, before the peace with France, he wrote to Elizabeth: 'The French have heard through M. de Foix of your Majesty's intent, and the Cardinal of Guise is not to hinder it. He writes to the Queen of Scots to beware of your Majesty, that you mean nothing less than good faith with her; and that it proceedeth of finesse to make her believe that you intend her good, or that her honour shall be any way advanced by marriage of anything so base as either my Lord Robert or Earl of Warwick, of which two your Majesty is determined to take the one and to give her the other. Though this whole matter be not true, your Majesty seeth that he hath a shrewd guess at it.'—*Randolph to Elizabeth, January 21. Scotch MSS. Rolls House.*

[2] Christopher Mundt to 'Cecil, December 28. 1563.—BURLEIGH *Papers,* HAINES.

CHAP VIII
1564
March

She was so capable of falsehood that her own expressions would have been an insufficient guarantee for her sincerity; yet it will be seen beyond a doubt that those around her—her ministers, her instruments, Cecil, Randolph, the foreign ambassadors—all believed that she really desired to give Dudley to Mary Stuart and to settle the Scottish difficulty by it. In this as in everything else she was irresolute and changeable; but neither her conduct nor her words can be reconciled with the hypothesis of intentional duplicity; and the weak point of the project was that which she herself regarded with the greatest self-admiration. She was giving in Lord Robert the best treasure which she possessed; and Cecil approved the choice to rid his mistress of a companion whose presence about her person was a disgrace to her.

But no true friend of the Queen of Scots could advise her to accept a husband whom Elizabeth dared not marry for fear of her subjects' resentment. The first two months of the year passed off with verbal fencing; the Queen of Scots was expecting news from Spain, and Murray and Maitland declined to press upon her the wishes of Elizabeth;[1] while Mary herself began to express an anxiety which derives importance from her later history for the return to Scotland of the Earl of Bothwell.

The Earl of Bothwell.
Bothwell it will be remembered had been charged two years before by the Earl of Arran with a design of killing Murray and of carrying off the Queen. He had been imprisoned in Edinburgh Castle and had escaped, not it was supposed without Mary's connivance. He

---
[1] Letters of Randolph to Cecil and Elizabeth, January and February, 1564.—MS. Rolls House.

had attempted to fly to France, but had been driven by foul weather into Berwick, where he was arrested by the English commander. When Randolph informed the Queen of Scots of his capture 'he doubted whether she did give him any thanks for the news;' and a few days after she desired that he should be sent back 'to her keeping.' Her ministers 'suspecting that her mind was more favourable to him than was cause,' and fearing that she wished for him only 'to be reserved in store to be employed in any kind of mischief,' had said that they would rather never see him in Scotland again; and Randolph took the opportunity of giving Cecil his opinion of the Earl of Bothwell.

'One thing I thought not to omit that I know him as mortal an enemy to our whole nation as any man alive; despiteful above measure, false and untrue as a devil. If he could have had his will neither the Queen's Majesty had stood in as good terms with the Queen of Scots as she doth, nor minister left alive that should be a travailer between their Majesties for a continuance of the same. He is an enemy to my country, a blasphemous and irreverent speaker both of his own sovereign and the Queen's Majesty my mistress; and over that the godly of this whole nation hath cause to curse him for ever. Your honour will pardon me thus angrily to write; it is much less than I do think or have cause to think.'[1]

Having an animal of this temper in her hands Elizabeth had not been anxious to let him go. Bothwell was detained for three months at Berwick, and was then

---

[1] Randolph to Cecil, January 22, 1563.—*MS. Rolls House.*

sent for to London. The English Government exasperated at the unexpected support which the Scotch Protestants then were lending to Mary Stuart's claims trusted by keeping him in close confinement and examining him strictly to extract secrets out of him which could be used to reattach them to England—some proof that the Queen intended as soon as occasion served to turn round against them and against the Reformation.[1]

Bothwell was too loyal to his mistress to betray her; but the cage door was not opened. More than a year had passed since his arrest and he was still detained without right or shadow of right a prisoner in the Tower. At length however Mary Stuart pleaded so loudly for him that Elizabeth could not refuse. In the midst of the marriage discussion the Queen of Scots asked as a favour what if she had pleased she could have demanded as a right. Bothwell was let go and made his way into France.

This object secured Mary Stuart addressed herself more seriously to the larger matter. The Emperor supported by the Cardinal of Lorraine was still pressing the Archduke Charles upon her, and to make the offer more welcome he proposed to settle on his son an allowance of two million francs a year. But the Archduke Charles was half a Protestant and was unwelcome to the English Catholics. At the end of February she sent her secretary to Granvelle to explain the reasons which obliged her to refuse the Austrian alliance and to learn conclusively

---

[1] 'La de Inglaterra, deseosa de descubrir alguna cosa que pudiese causar division entre la de Escocia y Milord James y los demas Protestantes, le ha hecho venir aqui, donde sera examinado y bien guardado. Esto es evangelio que aqui se usa.'— *De Quadra to Philip, April 24, 1563. MS. Simancas.*

whether she had anything to hope from Spain.¹ If the Prince of Spain failed her friends in England wished that she should marry Lord Darnley. She now proposed to play with the position, to affect submission, to induce the Queen of England herself if possible to propose Darnley to her; and by accepting him with deferential and seeming reluctance to obtain the long-desired recognition. Once married to Darnley and admitted by Parliament as heir presumptive her course would then be easy. At the bottom of her heart she had determined that she would never cease to be Elizabeth's enemy; never for a moment had she parted with the conviction that the English crown was hers and that Elizabeth was a usurper. But without support from abroad she was obliged to trust to her address; could she win her way to be 'second person' and were she married with Elizabeth's consent to the favourite of the insurrectionary Catholics she could show her colours with diminished danger; she could extort concession after concession, make good her ground inch by inch and yard by yard, and at last when the favourable moment came seize her rival by the throat and roll her from her throne into the dust. Elizabeth had offered her the choice of any English nobleman. Darnley's birth and person marked him out as the one on whom her choice if anywhere might naturally be expected to rest. It was with some expectation of hearing his name at least as one among others that she at last pressed Elizabeth to specify the person whom she had in view for her. It was with some real and much affected surprise that she found the name when it came at last —to be that of Lord Robert Dudley—and of Lord Robert Dudley alone.

---

¹ Mary Stuart to Granvelle.—LABANOFF, vol. i. p. 200.

Randolph conveyed Elizabeth's wishes to her, and with them a distinct promise that as Dudley's wife the Queen of England would have her named as successor.

She commanded herself so far as to listen cautiously. She objected to Dudley's inferiority of rank and said that a marriage with him would impair her honour.

It was honour enough, Randolph replied, to inherit such a kingdom as England.

'She looked not,' she said, 'for the kingdom, for her sister might marry and was likely to live longer than herself; she was obliged to consider her own and her friends' expectations, and she did not think they would agree that she should abase her state so far.'

So far she answered in public; but Mary Stuart's art was to affect a peculiar confidence in the person whom she was addressing. She waited till she was alone and then detaining Randolph when the courtiers were gone she said:

'Now, Mr. Randolph, tell me, does your mistress in good earnest wish me to marry my Lord Robert?'

Randolph assured her that it was so.

'Is that,' she said, 'conform to her promise to use me as a sister or daughter to marry me to her subject?'

Randolph thought it was.

'If I were a sister or a daughter,' she said, 'were it not better to match me where some alliance or friendship might ensue than to marry me where neither could be increased?'

The alliance which his sovereign desired, Randolph answered, was the perpetual union of the two realms in a single monarchy.

'The Queen your mistress,' she said, 'being assured of me might let me marry where it may like me; and I always should remain friend to her; she may marry herself and have children and what shall I have gained?'

Randolph said his mistress must have provided for that chance and would act honourably. But Mary Stuart replied justly that she could take no step of so great consequence without a certainty to rely upon; she bade him tell Elizabeth that the proposal was sudden—she could give no answer without longer thought; she had no objection to Lord Robert's person, but the match was unequal; commissioners on both sides might meet to consider it; more she could not say. She left Randolph with an impression that she had spoken as she felt, and Maitland bade him not be discouraged. If Elizabeth would pay the price she might obtain what she wished. Yet some secret friend advised Randolph to be on his guard in the following remarkable words:— 'Wheresoever she hovers and how many times soever she doubles to fetch the wind I believe she will at length let fall her anchor between Dover and Berwick though perchance not in that fort, haven or road that you wish she should.'[1]

Elizabeth either satisfied from Randolph's report that the Queen of Scots was on the way to compliance or determined to leave her nothing to complain of, at once gave a marked evidence that on her part she would adhere to her engagement. Although the debate in Parliament had gone deeply into the succession question, yet it had been carried on with closed doors; and the turn which it had taken was unknown except by rumour to the public. Lady Catherine Grey was still, though pining in captivity, the hope of the Protestants; and

---

[1] Randolph to Cecil, March 20 and April 13, 1564.—*Scotch MSS. Rolls House.*

CHAP VIII. John Hales, Clerk of the Hanaper—report said with
1564   Cecil's help and connivance—collected the substance of
April   the arguments in her favour; he procured opinions at
John Hales the same time from Italian canonists in support of the
and the
title of the validity of her marriage with Lord Hertford; and out
Lady
Catherine. of these materials he compiled a book in defence of her
title which was secretly put into circulation. The
strongest point in Lady Catherine's favour—the omission of the Scottish line in the will of Henry the
Eighth—could only be touched on vaguely, the will
itself being still concealed; but the case which Hales
contrived to make out, representing as it did not only
the wishes of the ultra-Protestants but the opinions of
Lord Arundel and the Howards, was strong enough to
be dangerous. Elizabeth, who in addition to her political sympathies cherished a vindictive dislike of her
cousin, sent Hales to the Fleet and inflicted on Cecil the
duty of examining and exposing what she chose to regard as conspiracy.[1]

The imprisonment of Hales was accepted as little less
than a defiance of the Protestant party in England and as
equivalent to a public declaration in favour of the Queen
of Scots. The long-talked-of meeting of the Queens was
again expected in the approaching summer, and the recognition of Mary Stuart was anticipated with more certainty than ever as the result of the interview.

The Queen of Scots however was growing impatient
with hopes long deferred. She either disbelieved Elizabeth's honesty or misinterpreted her motives into fears.
As Darnley was not offered to her she more than ever

---

[1] 'In this matter I am by commandment occupied, whereof I could be content to be delivered; but I will go upright, neither ad dextram nec ad sinistram; and yet I am not free from suspicion.'—*Cecil to Sir Thomas Smith, May* 1564. WRIGHT's *Elizabeth*. vol. i.

inclined towards getting possession of him; and antici- CHAP VIII
pating a storm she would not wait to let events work for ―――
her and showed her intentions prematurely in preparing 1564
the way for his acceptance in Scotland.

The Earl of Lennox it will be remembered had lost Objections
his estates in the interests of England. For some years to the Earl
past he had pressed for their restoration, and his petition of Lennox.
had been supported by Elizabeth. So long as Mary had
hopes elsewhere she had replied with words and excuses.
The lands of Lennox had been shared among the friends
of the Hamiltons. The lands of Angus which he claimed
in right of his wife were in the grip of the dark Morton,
whom the Queen of Scots durst not quarrel with. The
law in Scotland was the law of possession, and the sword
alone would have reinstated the exiled earl. The position
of his family had hitherto been among the greatest objections to her thinking seriously of Lord Darnley as a husband. If Elizabeth offered him she would have less to
fear; if to gratify the English Catholics she was to marry
him against Elizabeth's will, she would have in the first
instance to depend on her subjects to maintain her, and
among them the connexion might prove an occasion of
discord.

So long as the Hamiltons were strong the marriage
would have been absolutely impossible. Chatelherault
however was now in his dotage; the Earl of Arran was
a lunatic; the family was enfeebled and scattered; and
Mary Stuart was enabled to feel her way towards her
object by allowing Lennox to return and sue for his
rights. Could the House of Lennox recover its rank in
Scotland the next step would be more easy.

Had she affected to consult Elizabeth—had she openly
admitted her desire to substitute Darnley for Lord Robert
—affecting no disguise and being ready to accept with

him the conditions and securities which the English Parliament would have attached to the marriage—Elizabeth would probably have yielded, or in refusing would have given the Queen of Scots legitimate ground of complaint.

But open and straightforward conduct did not suit the complexion of Mary Stuart's genius: she breathed more freely and she used her abilities with better effect in the uncertain twilight of conspiracy.

Agitation among the Protestants Although both Murray and Maitland consented to the return of Lennox, the Protestants in Scotland instantly divined the purpose of it. 'Her meaning therein is not known,' wrote one of Randolph's correspondents to him on the 31st of April, 'but some suspect she shall at last be persuaded to favour his son; we are presently in quiet, but I fear it shall not be for long, for things begin to grow to a ripeness and there are great practisers who are like to set all aloft.'[1] 'The Lady Margaret and the young earl are looked for soon after,' wrote Knox; 'the Lord Bothwell will follow with power to put in execution whatever is demanded, and Knox and his preaching will be pulled by the ears.'[2]

This last contingency would not have deeply distressed Elizabeth; but she knew Mary Stuart too well to trust her smooth speeches. The Queen of Scots had represented the return of Lennox as a concession to the wishes of her dear sister the Queen of England. The expressions of friendliness were somewhat overdone, and served chiefly to place Elizabeth on her guard.

Randolph sent an earnest entreaty that Lennox should be detained in England; and when the earl ap-

---

[1] —— to Randolph, April 31.—*Scotch MSS. Rolls House.*
[2] Knox to Randolph, May 3.—*Ibid.*

plied for a passport to Scotland, a variety of pretexts were
invented for delay or refusal.

Mary Stuart wanted the self-control for successful
diplomacy. She saw that she was suspected, and the
suspicion was the more irritating because it was just.
Her warmer temper for the moment broke loose. She
sent for Randolph, bade him go to his mistress and tell
her that there could be no interview in the summer:
her council disapproved of it. She wrote violently to
Elizabeth herself, and Maitland accompanied the letter
with another to Cecil, in which he laid on England the
failure of all the attempts to reconcile the two Queens.
Why Lennox should be prevented from returning when
Elizabeth herself had supported his suit he professed
himself unable to understand. The conduct of the English
Court was a mystery to him, and 'he much feared
that God by the ingratitude of both the nations being
provoked to anger would not suffer them to attain so
great worldly felicity as the success of the negotiation'
for the union.[1]

On these terms stood Elizabeth and Mary Stuart in
the beginning of June, when the new Spanish ambassador
Don Diego Guzman de Silva arrived in London.
De Silva though a more honourable specimen of a Castilian
gentleman, was far inferior to de Quadra in ability
for intrigue; yet he was a man who could see clearly
and describe intelligibly the scenes in the midst of which
he lived; and his despatches are more pleasing and under
some aspects more instructive than the darker communications
of his predecessor.

In the following letters he tells the story of his recep-

---

[1] Maitland to Cecil, June 6, June 23, and July 13.—*Scotch MSS. Rolls House.*

CHAP VIII
1564
June

tion at Elizabeth's Court; where the curtain being once more lifted, Lord Robert Dudley is still seen at his old game, professing at home an increasing attachment to the Reformation, abroad maintaining an agent at the Vatican, and declaring himself to Philip the most devoted servant of Rome.

DE SILVA TO PHILIP II.

London, June 27.

De Silva at the English Court.

'I arrived in London the 18th of this month. The day following the Queen sent an officer of the household to welcome me in her name. I had previously received a number of kind messages from the Lord Robert, and in returning him my thanks I had asked him to arrange my audience with her Majesty. She promised to see me on Thursday the 22nd. The court was at Richmond: I went up the river in a barge and landed near the palace. Sir Henry Dudley and a relative of Sir Nicholas Throgmorton met me at the stairs and brought me to the Council Room. There Lord Darnley, Lady Margaret Lennox's son, came to me from the Queen and escorted me into her presence.

'As I entered some one was playing on a harpsichord. Her Majesty rose, advanced three or four steps to meet me, and then giving me her hand said in Italian she did not know in what language to address me. I replied in Latin, and after a few words I gave her your Majesty's letter. She took it, and after first handing it to Cecil to open, she read it through.

'She then spoke to me in Latin also—with easy elegance—expressing the pleasure which she felt at my arrival. Her court she said was incomplete without the presence of a minister from your Majesty; and for herself she was uneasy without hearing from time to time of your Majesty's welfare. Her "ill friends" had told her that your Majesty would never send an ambassador to England again. She was delighted to find they were mistaken. Her obligations to your Majesty were deep and many, and she would show me in her treatment of myself that she had not forgotten them.

'After a few questions about your Majesty she then took me aside and inquired about the Prince, how his health was, and what his character was. She talked at length about this; and then falling back into Italian, which she speaks remarkably well, she began again to talk of your Majesty. Your Majesty she said had known her when she was in trouble and sorrow. She was much altered since that time, and altered she would have me to understand much for the better.'

Some unimportant conversation followed and de Silva took his leave, Lord Darnley again waiting upon him to his barge.

A postscript was added in cipher:—

'An intimate friend of Lord Robert Dudley has just been with me. I understand from him that Lord Robert was on bad terms with Cecil before the late book on the succession appeared, and that now the enmity between them is deeper than ever, because he takes Cecil to have been the author of it.[1] The Queen is furious, but there are so many accomplices in the business that she has been obliged to drop the prosecution. This gentleman, although he desires me to be careful how I mention Lord Robert's name, yet entreats me at the same time to lose no opportunity of urging the Queen to severe measures.

---

[1] Lord Robert hoped that if the Queen of Scots was recognised as heir to the throne after Elizabeth and her children, the country would waive the objection to himself in the desire to see the Queen married.

If Cecil can once be dismissed from the Council, the Catholic religion and your Majesty's interests in England will all be the better for it. Lord Robert who is your Majesty's most faithful friend believes that this book may be the knife with which to cut his throat. If the Queen can be prevailed upon to part with him much good will follow, and I am strongly advised to use Lord Robert's assistance.

'I have said that I shall always welcome Lord Robert's help, that your Majesty I was well aware would wish me to do so, and that in the present matter I will do what I can; but I mean to move cautiously and to see my way before I step.'

DE SILVA TO PHILIP II.

July 2.

Lord Robert professes devotion to Spain and Rome.

'Lord Robert is more pressing than ever in offering his assistance to your Majesty. The gentleman of whom I spoke tells me that Lord Robert has still hopes of the Queen; and that if he succeeds, the Catholic religion will be restored. Again cautioning me to be secret he informed me that Lord Robert was in communication with the Pope about it, and had agents residing continually at the Papal Court. He spoke of his intentions in the warmest terms, especially with reference to the restoration of the truth.

'The interests at stake are so weighty, there are so many pretensions liable to be affected, and such a multitude of considerations on all sides which may not be overlooked, that I must entreat your Majesty to direct me what to do and say. I have not as yet exchanged a word upon the subject with any one except the person I speak of. I suspect the French have been trying to make use of Lord Robert. His father, people tell me, had large French connexions.'

DE SILVA TO PHILIP II.

July 10.

'I have been at Court at Richmond again. The Queen was in the garden with the ladies when I arrived, and she bade the Grand Chamberlain bring me to her. She received me with the most pointed kindness. She had been so anxious to see me, she said, that she could not help giving me the trouble of coming.

'She took me aside and led me into a gallery, where she kept me for an hour, talking the whole time of your Majesty, and alluding often to her embarrassments when she first came to the throne. I need not weary your Majesty with repeating her words; but she spoke with unaffected sincerity, and seemed annoyed when we were interrupted by supper.

'The meal was attended with the usual ceremonies. Nothing could be more handsome than the entertainment. She made the band play the "Battle of Pavia," and declared it was the music that she liked best in the world.

'After supper she had more conversation with me; and as it was then late I thought it time to take my leave: but the Queen said I must not think of going; there was a play to be acted which I must see. She must retire to her room for a few minutes, she said, but she would leave me in the hands of Lord Robert. The Lord Robert snatched the opportunity of her absence to speak of his obligations to your Majesty, and to assure me that he was your most devoted servant. She returned almost immediately,' and we adjourned to the theatre. The piece which was performed was a comedy, of which I should have understood but little had not the Queen herself been my interpreter. The plot as usual turned on marriage. While it was going on the Queen recurred to the Prince of Spain, and asked about his stature. I replied that his Highness was full grown. She was silent a while, and then said—

'"Every one seems to disdain me. I understand you think of marrying him to the Queen of Scots?"

'"Do not believe it your Majesty," I said. "His Highness has been so ill for years past with quartan ague and other disorders that his marriage with any one has been out of the question. Because he is better now the world is full of idle stories about him. Subjects are never weary of talking of their princes."

'"That is true," she answered. "It was reported a few days since in London that the king my brother intended to offer him to me."

'The play was followed by a masque. A number of people in black and white, which the Queen told me were her colours, came in and danced. One of them afterwards stepped forward and recited a sonnet in her praise; and so the spectacle ended. We adjourned to a saloon where a long table was laid out with preserved fruits and sweetmeats. It was two in the morning before I started to return to London. The Queen at the same time stepped into her barge and went down the river to Westminster.'

It is possible that the communications from Lord Robert to the Spanish ambassador were part of a deliberate plot to lead Philip astray after a will-o'-the-wisp; to amuse him with hopes of recovering Elizabeth to the Church, while she was laughing in her sleeve at his credulity. If Lord Robert was too poor a creature to play such a part successfully, it is possible that he too was Elizabeth's dupe. Or again it may have been that Elizabeth was insincere in her offer of Lord Robert to the Queen of Scots, while she was sincere in desiring the recognition of Mary Stuart's title—because she hoped that to escape the succession of a Scottish princess, one party or other would be found in England to tolerate her marriage with the only person whom she would accept. If the Queen was playing a false game it is hard to say which hypothesis is the more probable; yet on the one hand it will be seen that Cecil, Randolph—every one who has left an opinion on record—believed that she was in earnest in desiring Mary Stuart to accept Lord Robert; while on the other hand the readiness with which the Spanish Court listened to Lord Robert's overtures proves that they at least believed that he had a real hold on Elizabeth's affections; and it is unlikely, with the clue to English state secrets which the Spanish ministers undoubtedly possessed, that they would have been deceived a second time by a mere artifice. The least subtle explanations of human things are usually the most true. Elizabeth was most likely acting in good faith when she proposed to sacrifice Dudley to the Queen of Scots. Lord Robert as probably clung to his old hopes, and was sincere—so far as he could be sincere at all—in attempting to bribe Philip to support him in obtaining his object.

That this was Philip's own opinion appears certainly from his answer to de Silva.

PHILIP II. TO DE SILVA.

August 6.

'Your reply to the advances made to you by Lord Robert's friend was wise and cautious. So long as Cecil remains in power you must be careful what you do. If means should offer themselves to overthrow him, every consideration should move you not to neglect the opportunity; but I leave you to your own discretion.

CHAP VIII.
1564
August

'As to Lord Robert's marriage with the Queen; if he will assure you that when he becomes her husband he will restore the true ancient and Catholic faith, and will bring back the realm under the obedience of the Pope and the Holy See, you may promise in our name that we will assist him to the uttermost of our power.

Philip will befriend Lord Robert if Lord Robert will restore the Church.

'The propositions of the Irish Catholics you will cut short, courteously but firmly.[1] The time does not suit to encourage rebellion in that quarter. They have applied to me before and I have answered always in the same tone.

'I have read what you say of the book on the succession; of the Queen's anger; and of the suspicions indicated to you by Lord Robert that Cecil was at the bottom of it. I avail myself of the occasion to tell you my opinion of that Cecil. I am in the highest degree dissatisfied with him. He is a confirmed heretic; and if with Lord Robert's assistance you can so influence the matter as to crush him down and deprive him of all further share in the administration, I shall be delighted to have it done. If you try it and fail, be careful that you are not yourself seen in the matter.'

Over such mines of secret enmity walked Cecil, standing between his mistress and her lover, and never knowing what a day would bring forth.

At the beginning of August the Court broke up from

---

[1] Alluding to something in a letter of de Silva's which is lost. The same letter contained expressions about Lord Robert's agent in Rome, which would have shown more clearly what de Silva himself thought about Lord Robert. Philip answers—'En lo de aquel caballero Ingles que so tuvó en Roma, y platicas que os avisó mi Embajador que habia tenido con su Santidad, sospechamos lo mismo que vos.'

Richmond. Elizabeth went on progress, and for a time had a respite from her troubles. Among other places she paid a visit to Cambridge, where she had an opportunity of showing herself in her most attractive colours. The divisions of opinion, the discrepancies of dress and practices by which Cambridge like all other parts of England was distracted, were kept out of sight by Cecil's industry. He hurried down before her, persuaded the college authorities for once into obeying the Act of Uniformity; ordered the fellows and chaplains to appear in surplices; concealed the dreary communion tables in the college chapels behind decent coverings; and having as it were thrown a whitewash of order over the confusion, surprised the Queen into an expression of pleasure. The Church of England was not after all the miserable chaos which she had believed; and 'contrary to her expectation, she found little or nothing to displease her.'

She was at once thrown into the happiest humour; and she moved about among the dignitaries of the University with combined authority and ease. She exchanged courtesies with them in Latin; when they praised her virtues she exclaimed 'Non est veritas;' when they praised the virgin state she blessed them for their discernment; she attended their sermons; she was present at their disputations; and when a speaker mumbled she shouted 'Loquimini altius.' The public orator addressed her in Greek—she replied in the language of Demosthenes. On the last day of her visit she addressed the University in Latin in the Senate House. In a few well-chosen sentences she complimented the students on their industry; she expressed her admiration of the colleges and chapels—those splendid monuments of the piety of her predecessors. She trusted if God spared her life she might leave her own name not undistinguished by good work done for England.

Not one untoward accident had marred the harmony of the occasion. The Queen remained four days; and left the University with the first sense of pleasure which she had experienced in the ecclesiastical administration. Alas! for the imperfection of human things. The rashness of a few boys marred all.

Elizabeth had been entreated to remain one more evening to witness a play which the students had got up among themselves for her amusement. Having a long journey before her the following day, and desiring to sleep ten miles out of Cambridge to relieve the distance, she had been unwillingly obliged to decline.

The students, too enamoured of their performance to lose the chance of exhibiting it, pursued the Queen to her resting-place. She was tired, but she would not discourage so much devotion, and the play commenced.

An unfortunate play.
The actors entered on the stage in the dress of the imprisoned Catholic bishops. Each of them was distinguished by some symbol suggestive of the persecution. Bonner particularly carried a lamb in his arms at which he rolled his eyes and gnashed his teeth. A dog brought up the rear with the host in his mouth. Elizabeth could have better pardoned the worst insolence to herself: she rose, and with a few indignant words left the room; the lights were extinguished, and the discomfited players had to find their way out of the house in the dark, and to blunder back to Cambridge.[1]

---

[1] De Silva to the Duchess of Parma, August 19.—*MS. Simancas.* De Silva was not present, but described the scene as he heard it from an eye-witness. The story naturally enough is not mentioned by Nicolls, who details with great minuteness the sunny side of the visit to the University.—*Progresses of Elizabeth,* 1564.

It was but a light matter, yet it served to irritate Elizabeth's sensitiveness. It exposed the dead men's bones which lay beneath the whited surface of University good order; and she went back to London with a heart as heavy as she carried away from it. The vast majority of serious Englishmen if they did not believe in transubstantiation yet felt for the sacrament a kind of mysterious awe. Systematic irreverence had intruded into the churches; carelessness and irreligion had formed an unnatural alliance with Puritanism; and in many places the altars were bare boards resting on tressels in the middle of the nave. The communicants knelt, stood, or sat as they pleased; the chalice was the first cup which came to hand; and the clergymen wore surplice, coat, black gown, or their ordinary dress, as they were Lutherans, Calvinists, Puritans, or nothing at all.[1]

The parish churches themselves, those amazing monuments of early piety, built by men who themselves lived in clay hovels while they lavished their taste, their labour, and their wealth on 'the house of God,' were still dissolving into ruin. The roofs were breaking into holes; the stained whitewash was crumbling off the damp walls, revealing the half-effaced remains of the frescoed stories of the saints; the painted glass was gone from the windows; the wind and the rain swept through the dreary aisles; while in the churchyards swine rooted up the graves.

And now once more had come a reaction like that which had welcomed Mary Tudor. In quiet English homes there arose a passionate craving to be rid of all these things; to breathe again the old air of reverence and piety; and Calvinism and profanity were working

---

[1] Varieties used in the administration of the service, 1564.—LANSDOWNE MSS.

hand in hand like twin spirits of evil, making a road for another Mary to reach the English throne.

The progress being over, Elizabeth returned to the weary problems which were thickening round her more and more hopelessly. From France came intelligence that 'a far other marriage was meant for the Queen of Scots than the Lord Robert; with practices to reduce the realm to the old Pope, and to break the love between England and Scotland.'[1] The Earl of Lennox had been allowed to cross the Border at last as a less evil than the detaining him by violence; but Cecil wrote from Cambridge to Maitland, 'making no obscure demonstration of foul weather.' Parliament was expected to meet again in October, and with Parliament would come the succession question, the Queen's marriage question, and their thousand collateral vexations. Either in real uncertainty, or that she might have something with which to pacify her subjects, Elizabeth was again making advances towards the eternal Archduke. His old father Ferdinand, who had refused to be trifled with a second time, was dead. Ferdinand had left the world and its troubles on the 25th of July; but before his death, in a conversation with the Duke of Wirtemburg, he had shown himself less implacable. An opportunity was offered for reopening the suit, and Cecil by the Queen's order sent a message through Mundt the English agent in Germany, to the new Emperor Maximilian, that although for his many excellent qualities the Queen would gladly have married Lord Robert Dudley, yet finding it impossible, she had brought herself to regard Lord Robert as a brother, and for a husband was thinking of the Archduke.[2] On

---

[1] Sir T. Smith to Cecil (cipher), Sept. 1, 1564.—*French MSS. Rolls House.*
[2] Cecil to Mundt, September 8, 1564.—*Jussu Reginæ.* BURLEIGH *Papers,* HAINES, vol. i.

the 12th of September a resolution of Council was taken to send an embassy to Vienna, ostensibly to congratulate Maximilian on his accession—in reality to feel the way towards 'the prince with the large head.'[1] A few days later during an evening stroll through St. James's Park, Elizabeth herself told the secret to de Silva, not as anything certain, but as a point towards which her thoughts were turning.[2]

The Queen of Scots meantime, to whom every uttered thought of Elizabeth was known, began to repent of her precipitate explosion of temper. She had obtained what she immediately desired in the return of Lennox; her chief anxiety was now to prevent the Austrian marriage, and to induce Philip, though she could not marry his son, to continue to watch over her interests. In September the Spanish ambassador in Paris wrote that his steps were haunted by Beton Mary's minister; he had met the advances made to him with coldness and indifference; but Beton had pressed upon him with unwearied assiduity;[3] desiring, as it appeared afterwards, to learn what Philip would do for his mistress in the event of her marriage with Darnley.

At the same time it was necessary to soothe Elizabeth, lest she might withdraw her protection, and allow Parliament to settle the succession unfavourably to the Scot-

---

[1] 'Some one is to be sent with condolences on the death of the Emperor—Sir H. Sidney or Sir N. Throgmorton or I or Lord Robert; which it shall be I think nobody yet knoweth. But to tell you the truth, there is more meant than condolence or congratulation. It may be an intention for the marriage with the Archduke. This may be very strange, and therefore I pray you keep it very close.'—Cecil to Sir T. Smith, September 12, 1564. WRIGHT, vol. I.

[2] De Silva to the Duchess of Parma, Sept. 23.—MS. Simancas. Elizabeth said that the court fool advised her to have nothing to do with Germans, who were a poor heavy-headed set.

[3] Don F. de Alava to Philip II., September 20, 1564.—TEULET, vol. v.

CHAP VIII
1564
September
Character
and story of
Sir James
Melville.

tish claims. Maitland therefore having forfeited Cecil's confidence, the Queen of Scots obtained the services of a man who without the faintest pretensions to statesmanship was as skilled an intriguer as Europe possessed. Sixteen years had passed since Sir James Melville had gone as a boy with Monluc Bishop of Valence to the Irish Castle, where Monluc by his light ways was brought to shame. From the Bishop, Melville had passed to the Constable Montmorency. From Montmorency he had gone to the Elector Palatine, and had worked himself into a backstairs intimacy with European courts and princes. Mary Stuart herself had probably known him in France; and in the spring of 1564 she wrote to request him to return to Scotland to be employed in secret service. So highly she valued his abilities that notwithstanding her poverty she settled on him an annual pension of a thousand marks—twice the income perhaps of the richest nobleman in Scotland.[1] He was already acquainted with Elizabeth, who according to his own account had spoken confidentially with him about the Queen of Scots' marriage.

This Melville it was whom Mary Stuart now selected to be her instrument to pacify and cheat Elizabeth, to strengthen her party at the English Court, and to arrange with Lady Lennox for Darnley's escape to Scotland. She directed him to apologize to Elizabeth for the hasty letter which she had written, and to beg that it might be forgotten. He was to entreat her not to allow his mistress's interests to suffer any prejudice in Parliament; and further, he had secret instructions from Mary's own lips, the nature of which he indicates without explaining

---

[1] So Melville himself says in his *Memoirs*; but Melville's credibility is a very open question.

himself more completely—'to deal with the Spanish ambassador, Lady Margaret Douglas, and sundry friends she had in England of different opinions.'

Melville left Edinburgh towards the end of September,[1] preceded by Randolph, who after communicating with Elizabeth was on the point of returning to Scotland at the time of Melville's arrival. The information which Randolph had brought had been utterly unsatisfactory, and Elizabeth was harassed into illness and was in the last stage of despair. 'I am in such a labyrinth about the Queen of Scots,' she wrote on the 23rd of September to Cecil, 'that what to say to her or how to satisfy her I know not. I have left her letter to me all this time unanswered nor can I tell what to answer now. Invent something kind for me which I can enter in Randolph's commission and give me your opinion about the matter itself.'[2]

In this humour Melville found Elizabeth. She was walking when he was introduced in the garden at Westminster. He was not a stranger and the Queen rarely allowed herself to be long restrained by ceremony. She began immediately to speak of 'the Queen of Scots' despiteful letter' to her. 'She was minded,' she said, 'to answer it with another as despiteful' in turn. She took what she had written out of her pocket, read it aloud

---

[1] The copy of his instructions printed in his *Memoirs* is dated September 28. But Melville was in London on Michaelmas-day, when Lord Robert Dudley was created Earl of Leicester, and was present at the ceremony; 28 is perhaps a misprint for 30.

[2] 'In ejusmodi labyrintho positu sum de responso meo reddendo ad Reginam Scotiæ, ut nesciam quomodo illi satisfaciam, quum neque toto isto tempore illi ullum responsum dederim, nec quid mihi dicendum nunc sciam. Invenias igitur aliquid boni quod in mandatis scriptis Randall dare possim, et in hâc causâ tuam opinionem mihi indica.' Endorsed in Cecil's hand—'The Queen's Majesty's writing, being sick, September 23.'—*Scotch MSS. Rolls House.*

and said that she had refrained from sending it only because it was too gentle.

Melville accustomed to courts and accustomed to Elizabeth explained and protested and promised. With his excuses he mingled flattery, which she could swallow when mixed by a far less skilful hand; in his first interview he so far talked her into good humour that 'she did not send her angry letter;' and although he satisfied himself at the same time that she was dealing insincerely with his mistress he perhaps in this allowed his suspicions to mislead him. Elizabeth was only too happy to believe in promises which it was her interest to find true. Personally she cared as little for the Queen of Scots as the Queen of Scots cared for her; but Mary Stuart's position and Mary Stuart's claims created an intense political difficulty for which there appeared but one happy solution; and Elizabeth so far as can be seen from the surface of the story clutched at any prospect of a reasonable settlement with an eager credulity. Melville might indeed naturally enough believe Elizabeth as insincere as he knew himself to be. At the very moment when he was delivering Mary's smooth messages apologies and regrets he knew himself to be charged with a secret commission to the Catholic conspirators; but Elizabeth's duplicity does not follow from his own and she may at least be credited with having been honest when she had no interest in being otherwise. She saw the Scotch ambassador daily, and the Queen of Scots' marriage was the incessant subject of discussion. Melville said his mistress would refer it to a commission. Murray and Maitland might meet Bedford and Lord Robert at Berwick to talk it over.

'Ah!' she said, 'you make little of Lord Robert, naming him after the Earl of Bedford. I mean to make him a greater earl and you shall see it done. I take him as my brother and my best friend.'

CHAP VIII
1564
September

She went on to say that she would have married Lord Robert herself had she been able. As she might not, she wished her sister to marry him; and 'that done,' 'she would have no suspicion or fear of any usurpation before her death, being assured that Dudley was so loving and trusty that he would never permit anything to be attempted during her time.'[1]

'My Lord Robert's promotion in Scotland is earnestly intended,' Cecil wrote a few days later to Sir Thomas Smith.[2] On Michaelmas-day he was created Earl of Leicester at Westminster in Melville's presence — to qualify him for his higher destiny; while Elizabeth vain of his beauty showed off his fair proportions and dwelt on the charms which she was sacrificing.

Lord Robert Dudley is created Earl of Leicester.

Nor was she unaware of Melville's secret practices or of Mary's secret desires. 'You like better,' she said sadly to the ambassador, 'you like better yonder long lad'—pointing to Darnley, who tall and slim with soft and beardless face bore the sword of state at the ceremony.

To throw her off the scent Melville answered that 'no woman of spirit could choose such an one who more resembled a woman than a man.' 'I had no will,' he said of himself, 'that she should think that I had an eye that way, although I had a secret charge to deal with Lady Lennox to procure liberty for him to go to Scotland.'

Elizabeth was not deceived but she chose to blind herself. Clinging to her favourite scheme she allowed a legal opinion to be drawn out in favour of the Scottish title. She promised Melville that when Parliament met

---

[1] MELVILLE's *Memoirs*. [2] Cecil to Smith, October 4.—WRIGHT, vol. I.

H 2

she would again protect his mistress's interests. The poor Archduke was to be once more cast overboard; she undertook to bind herself never to marry unless 'necessitated by her sister's hard behaviour;' and last of all—as the strongest evidence which she could give that she was acting in good faith—she risked the discontent which would inevitably be provoked and postponed the Parliament till the spring or the following autumn. Randolph who had been detained on Melville's arrival was sent off to tell Mary that 'the tragedy created by her letter had turned into comedy;' the Queen of England would consent with pleasure to the proposed meeting of commissioners; and meanwhile—'contrary to the expectation and desire of her people, contrary to the disposition of no small number of her council and also to some detriment of herself for her own private lucre, by the intention of her people to have gratified her with some subsidy—her Majesty had by proclamation prolonged her Parliament that should have been even now begun in October:' meaning of purpose to have no assembly wherein the interests of her sister might be brought in question until it were better considered that no harm might thereof ensue to her, and that her Majesty and the Queen of Scots might have further proceedings in the establishment of their amity.'[1]

In the delay of the Parliament the Queen of Scots had gained one step of vital moment; she had next to obtain the consent of her own people to her marriage with Darnley; she had to strengthen the Lennox faction that it might be strong enough to support her against the

---

[1] Message sent by Randolph to the Queen of Scots, October 4.—Scotch MSS. Rolls House.

Hamiltons, and when this was done to get the person of Darnley into her hands.

Lennox himself was distributing presents with lavish generosity in the court at Holyrood. Melville when he returned to Scotland carried back with him Lady Margaret's choicest jewels to be bestowed to the best advantage. For the full completion of the scheme it was necessary to delude Elizabeth into the belief that Mary Stuart would give way about Leicester; and having satisfied her that she really had nothing to fear from Darnley's visit to Edinburgh, to obtain leave of absence for him for three months to assist Lennox in the recovery of his property. When the father and son were once on Scottish soil she could then throw off the mask.

The ambassador had employed his time well in England making friends for his mistress and had carried back with him from London profuse promises of service; some from honourable men who looked to Mary Stuart's succession as a security for the peace of the country, some from the courtier race who desired to save their own fortunes should the revolution come.

Among these last was Leicester—that very Leicester in whose affection Elizabeth was blindly confiding, who was to be her own protection when she had named Mary Stuart her heir. The man who thought it no preposterous ambition to aspire to the hand of Elizabeth excused himself to Melville with abject apologies as having been forced to appear as the suitor of a princess whose shoes he was unworthy to loose; he implored the Queen of Scots to pardon him for 'the proud pretences which were set forward for his undoing by Cecil and his secret enemies.'[1]

---

[1] MELVILLE's Memoirs.

CHAP VIII
1564
October

On the position and views of Lord Robert—on the state of feeling at the court—on the Scotch and other questions—additional light is thrown by a letter of de Silva written on the 9th of October.

DE SILVA TO PHILIP.[1]

London, October 9.

'The gentleman sent hither from the court of Scotland has returned, and this Queen has written by him to say that for various reasons there will be no Parliament this year. The succession question therefore will be allowed to rest. She says she is not so old that her death need be so perpetually dragged before her.

Elizabeth intends to check the Protestants.

'Cecil has intimated to the heretical bishops that they must look to their clergy; the Queen is determined to bring them to order and will no longer tolerate their extravagances.

'He desires them too to be careful how they proceed against the Catholics; the Queen will not have her good subjects goaded into sedition by calumnies on their creed or by irritating inquiries into their conduct. I am told that the bishops do not like these cautions. Cecil understands his mistress and says nothing to her but what she likes to hear. He thus keeps her in good humour and maintains his position. Lord Robert is obliged to be on terms with him although at heart he hates him as much as ever. Cecil has more genius than the rest of the Council put together and is therefore envied and hated on all sides.

'The Queen happening to speak to me about the beginning of her reign mentioned that circumstances had at first obliged her to dissemble her real feelings in

---

[1] *MS. Simancas.*

religion; but God knew, she said, that her heart was sound in his service; with more to the same purpose: she wanted to persuade me that she was orthodox, but she was less explicit than I could have wished.

'I told her (she knew it already) that the preachers railed at her in the most insolent language for keeping the cross on the altar of her chapel. She answered that she meant to have crosses generally restored throughout the realm.

'Again and again she has said to me, "I am insulted both in England and abroad for having shown more favour than I ought to have shown to the Lord Robert. I am spoken of as if I were an immodest woman. I ought not to wonder at it: I have favoured him because of his excellent disposition and for his many merits; but I am young and he is young and therefore we have been slandered. God knows they do us grievous wrong and the time will come when the world will know it also. I do not live in a corner—a thousand eyes see all that I do and calumny will not fasten on me for ever."

'She went on to speak of the Queen of Scots, whose beauty she warmly praised.

'"Some tell me," she said, "that my sister will marry your Prince after all."

'I laughed and said that the last story which I had heard was that the Queen of Scots was to marry the King of France.

'She said that could not be, "The Queen-mother and the Queen of Scots were not good friends."

'The Lord Robert whom they now call Earl of Leicester has been with me again repeating his protestations of a desire to be of use to your Majesty. He mentioned particularly the troubles in the Low Countries and the necessity of taking steps to pacify them.

'I assured him of the confidence which your Majesty felt in his integrity and of the desire which you entertained for his advancement. I repeated the words which the Queen had used to me about religion; and I said that now when she was so well disposed there was an opportunity for him which he should not allow to escape. If the Queen could make up her mind to marry him and to reunite England to the Catholic Church your Majesty would stand by him and he should soon experience the effects of your Majesty's good-will towards him; the Queen's safety should be perfectly secured and he should be himself maintained in the reputation and authority which he deserved.

'He answered that the Queen had put it off so long that he had begun to fear she would never marry him at all. He professed himself very grateful for my offer but of religion he said nothing. In fact he is too ill-informed in such matters to take a resolute part on either side unless when he has some other object to gain.

'I told him that the dependence of the Catholics was wholly on the Queen and himself. To him they attributed the preservation of the bishops and of the other prisoners; and I said that by saving their lives he had gained the good-will of all Christian princes abroad and of all the Catholics at home, who as he well knew were far more numerous than those of the new religion. The heretics notoriously hated both him and his mistress, and had not the Catholics been so strong would long ago have given them trouble; the Queen could see what was before her in the book on the succession, which after all it appeared she was afraid to punish.

'His manner was friendly but I know not what he will do. Had the Catholics as much courage as the heretics he would declare for them quickly enough, for he admits that they are far the larger number; things are in such a state that the father does not trust his child.'

To return to the Queen of Scots' marriage. Notwithstanding Lennox's efforts and Lady Margaret's jewels the Scottish noblemen were difficult to manage. Mary Stuart was still unable to act without her brother and Maitland; and the Earl of Murray was a better Protestant than Knox believed him to be, and Maitland's broad statesmanship had little in common with the scheming conspiracies which were hatched in the chambers of priests. Maitland's single object was the union of the realms, where Scotland in compensation for the surrender of its separate independence would have the pride of giving a sovereign to its ancient enemy. While therefore he was zealous for the honour of his mistress he had no interest in those collateral objects of religious revolution and personal revenge of which Mary was in such keen pursuit. With the Darnley connexion, as it appeared afterwards, he had no sympathy, unless Darnley was freely offered by Elizabeth and the choice was freely sanctioned by the two Parliaments.

So far therefore Maitland was ill suited for the Queen of Scots' purposes; on the other hand he was by far the ablest minister that she possessed. He was fanatically eager—so far as a man of so cool and clear an intellect could be fanatical about anything—to secure the English succession for her; and aware of his value she named him with her brother to meet the English commissioners and consider in form Elizabeth's proposals. The conference was to be kept secret from the world. The Queen of Scots would go to Dunbar in the middle of November. The two ministers would leave her as if for a few days' hawking on the Tweed, and the Governor of Berwick would invite them to visit him.

Lord Bedford and Randolph were to represent England; and Elizabeth's instructions to them are a fresh evidence of the feelings with which she regarded Leicester. When Leicester's name was first officially mentioned, Maitland had urged on Cecil the propriety of leaving Mary's choice of a husband as little restricted as possible. If Elizabeth objected to a foreign prince she must at least permit a free selection among the Scotch and English nobility. Besides Darnley there was Norfolk, there was Arundel—each more eligible than the son of the parvenu Northumberland; and Elizabeth had no right to demand more than a marriage which did not threaten herself or the liberty of England.

But Elizabeth's heart was fixed on Leicester, and she could see no merit anywhere but in him. 'Among all English noblemen,' she said in giving her directions to the commissioners, 'she could see none for her own contentation meeter for the purpose than one who for his good gifts she esteemed fit to be placed in the number of kings and princes; for so she thought him worthy: and if he were not born her subject, but had happened with these qualities to be as nobly born under some other prince as he was under herself, the world should have well perceived her estimation of him. The advantage of the marriage to the Earl of Leicester would not be great, but to the Queen of Scots it would be greater than she could have with any other person. The Earl would bring with him no controversy of title to trouble the quietness of the Queen of Scots, and she preferred him to be the partaker of the Queen of Scots' fortunes, whom if it might lie in her power she would make owner and heir of her own kingdom. She had already placed a check on all other pretenders to the succession; and whatever sovereign might do in the direction of the matter for her sister's advantage should not be wanting. If after her recognition the Queen of Scots should desire to reside in England she would herself bear the charge of the family both of her and of the Earl of Leicester, as should be meet for one sister to do for another.'

But Elizabeth admitted that before the recognition could be carried through Parliament the Queen of Scots must first accept the indispensable condition. She should receive the prize which hung before her eyes only when she was Leicester's wife, and till that time she must be contented with a promise that she should not be disappointed. 'If she require to be assured first,' Elizabeth continued with an appearance of mournful sincerity, if she will not marry till an Act of Succession in her favour has been actually passed, 'you may of yourselves say it may work in us some scruple to imagine that in all this friendship nothing is more minded than how to possess that which we have; and that it is but a sorrowful song to pretend more shortness of our life than is cause, or as though if God would change our determination in not desiring to marry, we should not by likelihood have children. We can mean no better than we do to our sister; we doubt not that she shall quietly enjoy all that is due to her, and the more readier we are so to do, because we are so naturally disposed with great affection towards her, as before God we wish her right to be next to us before all other.'¹

Mary Stuart herself meanwhile was in close communication with Lady Lennox, and was receiving from her

---

¹ Elizabeth to Bedford and Randolph, October 7, 1564.—*Scotch MSS. Rolls House.*

more and more assurances of the devotion of the English Catholics. Randolph on his return to Edinburgh from London found Maitland open-mouthed at the suspension of the prosecution of Hales for his book on the succession. The Scotch Court had expected that he would have been 'put to death as a traitor.'

Randolph protested against the word 'traitor' inasmuch as it implied 'the certainty of the Queen of Scots' claim,' 'which many in England did not believe to be certain at all.' 'Hales has not deserved death,' he said, 'and imprisonment was the worst which could be inflicted.'

Maitland spoke menacingly of the disaffection among the Catholics. Randolph 'bade him not make too much account of conspirators;' 'the behaviour of the Scotch Court,' he said 'was so strange that he could only suppose they meant to quarrel with England;' 'and with these words they grew both into further choler than wisdom led them.'[1]

Mary's own language was still smooth, affectionate, and confiding; but Maitland and even Murray protested beforehand that when the commission met they would agree to no conditions and accept no marriage for their mistress unless her title was first fully admitted and confirmed. Darnley's name was not mentioned; but 'it was through the mouths of all men that it was a thing concluded in the Queen's heart;' and Randolph was under the mistaken impression that Maitland was as much in favour of it as his mistress.[2]

'Their object,' Randolph on the 7th of November wrote to Elizabeth, 'is to have the Lord Darnley rather offered by your Majesty than desired of themselves;'

---

[1] Randolph to Cecil, October 24.—*Scotch MSS. Rolls House.*
[2] Randolph to Cecil, October 31.—*MS. Ibid.*

'but your Majesty I am assured will consider the
unfitness of the match for greater causes than I can
think of any—of which not the least will be the loss
of many a godly man's heart that by your Majesty
enjoyeth now the liberty of their country, and know
but in how short a time they shall lose the same if your
Majesty give your consent to match her with such an
one as either by dissention at home or lack of knowledge
of God and his word may persecute them that profess
the same.'[1]

The Scotch Protestants comprehended instinctively
the thousand dangers to which they would be exposed.
The House of Lennox was the hereditary enemy of the
Hamiltons, who had headed the Revolution of 1559.
Darnley was known to be a Catholic; and his marriage
with Mary Stuart was well understood to mean a Catholic
revolution.

'The terrible fear is so entered into their hearts,' continued Randolph, 'that the Queen tendeth only to that,
that some are well willing to leave their country, others
with their force to withstand it, the rest with patience to
endure it and let God work His will.'

Maitland seems to have believed that Mary Stuart
would be moderate and reasonable even if she was
recognized unconditionally and was left to choose her
own husband; he professed to imagine that some
'liberty of religion' could be established in the modern
and at that time impossible sense in which wolf
and dog, Catholic and Protestant, could live in peace
together, neither worried nor worrying each other.
But few of the serious Reformers shared his hope; and
a gap was already opening wide between him and the

---

[1] *Scotch MSS. Rolls House.*

Earl of Murray. Maitland was inclined to press England 'to the uttermost;' Randolph in a private conversation with Murray 'found in that nobleman a marvellous good will' to be guided by Elizabeth, although he was disturbed by the conflict of duties. The Earl, as the meeting of the commissioners approached, in his perplexity sent Elizabeth a message 'that whatever he might say, or however vehement he might seem to be in his mistress's cause, he hoped her Majesty would not take it as if he was in any way wanting in devotion to her.' Both Murray and Randolph were nervously conscious of their incapacity to cope with Maitland in a diplomatic encounter.

'To meet with such a match,' Randolph wrote to Elizabeth, 'your Majesty knoweth what wits had been fit. How far he exceedeth the compass of one or two heads that is able to govern a Queen and guide a whole realm alone, your Majesty may well think. How unfit I am, and how able is he to go beyond me, I would it were not as I know it to be.'[1]

Little time was lost in preparation. On the 18th of November the four commissioners met at Berwick: Bedford, a plain determined man, with the prejudices of a Protestant and the resolution of an English statesman; Randolph, true as Bedford to Elizabeth, but entangled deeply in the intricacies of diplomacy, and moving with more hesitation; Murray, perplexed as we have seen;

---

[1] Randolph to Elizabeth, November 7.—COTTON MSS., CALIG. B. 10. On the same day Randolph wrote to Leicester. 'I would you were to be at Berwick to my somewhat for yourself, for there I assure you somewhat will be said of you that for your lordship may tend to little good. How happy is your life that between these two Queens are tossed to and fro. Your lordship's luck is evil if you light not in some of their laps that love so well to play.'—Scotch MSS. Rolls House.

and Maitland, at home in the element in which he
played with the practised pleasure of a master.

The preliminaries were soon disposed of. Both sides
agreed on the desirableness of the union of the realms;
and the English ministers admitted the propriety of the
recognition of the Queen of Scots, if adequate securities
could be provided for Elizabeth's safety and for the
liberties of the realm.

The main subject was then approached. Lord Bedford
said that his mistress would undertake to favour Mary
Stuart's title if Mary Stuart would marry where the
English Council wished; and he proposed the Earl of
Leicester as a suitable husband for her.

'The Earl of Leicester,' Maitland replied, ' was no fit
marriage for his mistress taken alone; and he desired to
be informed more particularly what the Queen of England
was prepared to do in addition. Indefinite promises
implied merely that she did not wish the Queen of Scots
to make a powerful alliance; his mistress could not
consent to make an inferior marriage while the Queen of
England was left unfettered; the Queen of England
might herself marry and have children.'

'It is not the intention of the Queen of England,'
said Randolph, 'to offer the Lord Robert only as Earl
of Leicester without further advancement. She desires
to deal openly, fairly, and kindly, but neither will her
Majesty say what she will do more, nor ought she to
say, till she knows in some degree how her offer will be
embraced.' 'As you,' he said particularly to Maitland,
'have spoken an earnest word, so I desire without offence
to have another, which is that if you think by finesse,
policy, or practice, or any other means, to wring anything out of her Majesty's hands, you are but abused and
do much deceive yourselves.'

As much as this had probably been foreseen on all

sides. Maitland wished to extort an independent admission of Mary's claims from which Elizabeth would not afterwards be able to recede; the English would admit nothing until Mary had consented generally to conditions which would deprive her of the power of being dangerous. But it seems that they were empowered, if Leicester was unacceptable, to give the Queen of Scots the larger choice which Maitland demanded. Cecil had foreseen that Leicester would be rejected. 'I think,' he said, writing on the 26th of November to Sir Thomas Smith, 'that no marriage is more likely to succeed than ——, *if it may come from them.*'

The name omitted was doubtless Darnley's. De Silva in describing the conference to Philip said that the English commissioners had given the Scots the alternative of Leicester, Norfolk, or Darnley.[1] Of Norfolk at that time there had been little mention or none. Darnley perhaps Elizabeth would have consented to allow if the Queen of Scots would ask for him; for in giving way to Mary Stuart's wishes she could have accompanied her consent with restrictions which would render the marriage innocuous; while the Queen of Scots on the other side would have accepted Darnley had Elizabeth offered him; for Elizabeth would have been unable to shackle her own proposal with troublesome stipulations.

No matter what promises Elizabeth might make, no matter to what engagements she might bind herself, the Queen of Scots had long resolved to agree to nothing which would alienate the Catholics. As Maitland had told the Bishop of Aquila, she could have no confidence that any engagement would be observed unless she was supported by a force independent of Elizabeth; and if she married Darnley it was necessary for her to keep un-

---

[1] De Silva to Philip, December 18.—*MS. Simancas.*

impaired her connexion with the party of insurrection CHAP VIII
and with the foreign Catholic powers.

1564
November

Thus neither side would be the first to mention
Darnley. The arguments played round the mark but
never reached it; and at last, when there was no longer
a hope of a satisfactory end, the commissioners found it
was useless to waste time longer. They parted without
a quarrel, yet without a conclusion, Maitland summing
up his own demands in the following words :—

'That the Queen of England would permit his mistress Final demands of
to marry where she would, saving in those royal houses the Scots.
where she desired her to forbear; that her Majesty
would give her some yearly revenue out of the realm of
England, and by Parliament establish unto her the
crown, if God did his will on her Majesty and left her
without children; in so doing her Majesty might have
the honour to have made the marriage, and be known to
the world to have used the Queen of Scots as a dear and
loving sister.'[1]

Immediately after the breaking up of the conference
Mary Stuart wrote to request that Lord Darnley might
be allowed to join his father in Scotland, and assist him
in the recovery of the Lennox estates. Had Elizabeth
anticipated what would follow she would probably instead of complying have provided Darnley with a lodging in the Tower. But the reports from Scotland were
contradictory; Lennox said openly that 'his son should
marry the Queen;' yet Randolph 'knew of many, by
that which had been spoken of her own mouth, that the
marriage should never take effect if otherwise she might
have her desire.' Lennox had succeeded imperfectly in
making a party amongst the lords; and Darnley's eleva-

---

[1] Report of the Conference at Berwick.—COTTON MSS., CALIG. B. 10.

tion to the Crown of Scotland would wake a thousand sleeping feuds. The requested permission was suspended without being refused; while Elizabeth began again as usual to play with thoughts of the Archduke. Cecil sent to Germany to urge Maximilian to propose in form for her hand;[1] while stranger still, Catherine de Medici meditated an alliance between Elizabeth and her son Charles the Ninth. Elizabeth was twenty-nine and Charles not more than fourteen; but political convenience had overruled more considerable inequalities; and though Elizabeth affected to laugh at the suggestion as absurd, de Silva reminded her that the difference of age was scarcely greater than that between Philip and her sister; while the Queen-mother of France made the proposal, as will presently be seen, in perfect seriousness.[2]

On their return to Edinburgh from Berwick, Maitland and Murray wrote a joint letter to Cecil in which they recapitulated their arguments at the conference and put forward again the demand on behalf of their mistress with which Maitland had concluded. They dwelt on the marriages abroad which were offered to her acceptance—far exceeding in general desirableness that which was proposed by Elizabeth. They expressed themselves however deferentially, and professed a desire which both of them really felt for a happy termination of the difficulty.

Cecil's answer was straightforward consistent and honourable. He was glad to perceive from their letter, he said, that they were beginning to comprehend the Queen of England's real feelings. If they persisted in the tone which they had first assumed they would alienate England altogether. They talked of proposals to marry

---

[1] Roger Strange to Gaspar Preguyar, February 1, 1565.—HAYNES, vol. I.
[2] De Silva to Philip, October 9.—*MS. Simancas.*

their mistress in this place and that; there were pro- CHAP VIII
posals for his own mistress as well, and they would do ⎯⎯⎯
better in confining themselves to the subject which was December
immediately before them. They professed to desire to
know the Queen of England's real wishes. They knew
them already perfectly well. His mistress had never
varied either in her words or in her intentions. She
wished well to the Queen of Scots. She had no objection to the Queen of Scots' recognition as second person
if England could be satisfied that its liberties would not
be in danger.

'And now,' Cecil said, 'in return for this you propose Cecil's
that the Queen's Majesty should permit your Sovereign answer.
to marry where she would, saving in some places prohibited, and in that consideration to give her some yearly
revenue out of the realm of England, and by Parliament
establish the succession of the realm to her; and then
you add that it might be the Queen's Majesty's desire
would take effect. Surely my Lord of Ledington I
see by this—for it was your speech—you can well tell
how to make your bargain. Her Majesty will give the
Earl of Leicester the highest degree that any nobleman
may receive of her hand; but you look for more—you
would have with him the establishment of your Sovereign's title to be declared in the second place to the
Queen's Majesty. The Queen's Majesty will never agree
to so much of this request neither in form nor substance,
as with the noble gentleman already named. If you will
take him she will cause inquisition to be made of your
Sovereign's rights; and as far as shall stand with justice
and her own surety she will abase such titles as shall be
proved unjust and prejudicial to her sister's interest.
You know very well that all the Queen's Majesty

I 2

mindeth to do must be directed by the laws and by the consent of the three Estates; she can promise no more but what she can with their assent do. The Queen of England if trusted as a friend may and will do what she will never contract or bargain to do or submit to be pressed to do. It is a tickle matter to provoke sovereigns to determine their succession.

'Wherefore, good my Lords,' Cecil concluded, 'think hereof, and let not this your negotiation which is full of terms of friendship be converted into a bargain or purchase; so as while in the outward face it appears a design to conciliate these two Queens and countries by a perpetual amity, in the unwrapping thereof there be not found any other intention but to compass at my Sovereign's hands a kingdom and a crown, which if sought for may be sooner lost than gotten, and not being craved may be as soon offered as reason can require. Almighty God assist you with His spirit in your deliberation upon this matter to make choice of that which shall increase his glory and fortify the truth of the gospel in this isle.'[1]

Before this letter reached Scotland Maitland had become disposed to receive it in the spirit in which it was written. He had expressed his regret to Randolph for having 'meddled' with English Catholic conspirators; he was drawing off from the dangerous policy to which he appeared to have committed himself; and Randolph who a month before had been more afraid of him than of any man in Scotland, wrote on the 16th of December, the date of Cecil's despatch, that 'he never thought better of him than at that moment.'[2]

---
[1] Cecil to Maitland and Murray, December 16.—*Scotch MSS. Rolls House.*
[2] Randolph to Cecil, December 16.—*MS. Ibid.*

So anxious Maitland seemed to be to recover the confidence of the English Government, that except for the opposition which he continued to offer—when opposition had become dangerous — to the Darnley marriage, it might have been thought that he was in league with Mary to throw Elizabeth off her guard. His motives must in part remain obscure. He had perhaps become acquainted with Darnley in England, and had foreseen the consequences if a youth of such a temperament came in too close contact with his mistress. Perhaps too he had never meant to do more than play with poisoned tools; and withdrew when he saw that Elizabeth would not be frightened with them. But an obvious reason for Maitland's change of posture was to be found in the new advice and the new advisers that were finding favour with the Queen of Scots. Two years before, M. de Moret the ambassador from Savoy had brought in his suite to Mary Stuart's court an Italian named David Ritzio. The youth—he was about thirty—became a favourite of Mary. Like Châtelar, he was an accomplished musician; he soothed her hours of solitude with love songs, and he had the graceful tastes with which she delighted to amuse her leisure. He had glided gradually into her more serious confidence, as she discovered that he had the genius of his countrymen for intrigue and that his hatred for the Reformers rivalled her own in its intensity.

The adroit diplomacy of statesmen found less favour in Mary's cabinet than the envenomed weapons of deliberate fraud. She shook off the control of the one supremely able minister that she possessed, and she went on with renewed spirit, disembarrassed of a companion who was too honourable for her present schemes. To the change of counsellors may be attributed her sudden advance in the arts of intrigue. On a sudden, none knew why,

Chap. VIII

1565
January

David
Ritzio in
favour with
Mary
Stuart.

Chap VIII
1565 January

Mary Stuart affects a willingness to marry Leicester.

she professed a readiness to yield to Elizabeth's wishes. 'Her mind to the Lord Robert,' she said to Randolph at the end of January, 'was as it ought to be to so noble a gentleman;' 'such a one as his mistress would marry were he not her subject ought to content her;' 'what she would do should depend on the Queen of England, who should wholly guide her and rule her.'[1] She deceived Maitland as she deceived Randolph, and Maitland wrote warmly to Cecil, full of hopes 'that the great work at which they had so long laboured together, the union of the two countries, would be accomplished at last to their perpetual honour.'[2] It appears as if she had persuaded him that she had looked the Darnley marriage in the face and had turned away from it as too full of danger; and even Cecil was so far convinced that he entered in his diary at the date of these letters—'Mr. Randolph writeth at length of the Queen of Scots' allowance of my Lord of Leicester, and giveth great appearance of success in the marriage.'[3]

On the 6th of February Randolph wrote again to Leicester as if there was no longer any doubt that he would be accepted. 'This Queen,' he said, 'is now content to give good ear to her Majesty's suit in your behalf; she judges you worthy to be husband to any Queen.'[4] And though Randolph himself still vaguely anticipated evil, and though other persons who understood the state of things in Scotland shared his misgivings,[5] Elizabeth

---

[1] Randolph to Cecil, Feb. 5.—*Scotch MSS. Rolls House.*
[2] Maitland to Cecil, January 16 and February 1.—*MS. Rolls House.*
[3] Cecil's Diary, Feb. 5.
[4] Randolph to Leicester, Feb. 6.—WRIGHT, vol. I.

[5] Among the CONWAY MSS. there is a remarkable paper, unsigned and unaddressed, on the Lennox question in Scotland, and on the views supposed to be entertained by Lady Lennox and her husband. It shows how remarkably the religious parties were

permitted herself to be persuaded that Mary Stuart was sincere. Cecil and Leicester shared her confidence or were prepared to risk the experiment; and Darnley was allowed leave of absence for three months in the belief that it might be safely conceded.

---

intersected by family feuds; and how disintegrating and dangerous to the Catholic party in Scotland the marriage of Mary Stuart and Darnley must have been.

NOTE OF AFFAIRS IN SCOTLAND.
February 3, 1564-5.

'Enemies to the Earl of Lennox— All the Protestants of that realm in general, and in special the Duke of Chatelherault, with all the Hamiltons in Clydesdale, Linlithgow, and Edinburgh; the Bishop of St. Andrew's; the Abbot of Kilwinning; the Bishop of Glasgow; all the Botons; the allies of the late Cardinal of St. Andrew's; the Laird of Borthwick, and all the Scots. The Earl of Argyle, sister's son to the Duke; all the Campbells; the Earl of Glencairn, whose eldest son is sister's son to the Duke; and all the Cunninghams. The Earl of Eglinton was never good Lennox. The Earl of Cassilis, young, and of small conduct. The remnants of Huntley's house will favour the Duke, and so will James M'Connell, and others of the Isles. The Lord James and Ledington in their hearts have misliked Lennox; unless now, in hope to continue their rule in that realm, they may be changed. The Earl of Morton, being Chancellor; the young Earl of Angus, Drumlanrig, and all the Douglasses, with the Justice Clerk; M'Gill and their alliance, if my Lady Lennox do not relinquish her title to the Earldom of Angus,

which I suppose, in respect of the greater advancement, she hath already promised. The Lords Maxwell and Erskine, allied to Argyle. Livingstone is friend to the Duke, and Fleming likewise. Borthwick will hang with the Douglasses. The Earl of Montrose and the Leslies being Protestants,

'Of these [some] may be won, partly in hope that Darnley will embrace religion, which I doubt will never be, partly by preferment of spiritual lands, partly by money, and partly but in fear by the authority and in respect of other insolent pretences.

'Friends hoped upon it—
'The Humes and the Kers, albeit they will choose the best side.
'The Earl of Bothwell, of no force now.
'The Earl Athol; the Earl Errol; the Lords Ruthven and Seton; the gentlemen of Lennox, and some of the Barony of Renfrew. The Laird of Tullybardine, a young head.
'The Queen being his chief countenance, thinketh from the Duke's overthrow, if she can bring it to pass, to advance Lennox as her heir apparent, failing of her issue. If Darnley can hit the mark, then careth my Lady (Lady Lennox) neither for the Earldom of Lennox, Angus, nor lands in England, having enough that way; and if the Queen can bring it about, division shall follow. The overthrow of religion is pre-

Darnley therefore went his way. Elizabeth herself meanwhile, half-desponding, half hopeful of the result, and perhaps to hold a salutary fear over the Queen of Scots, listened to the proposals of Catherine de Medici for her own marriage with the boy King of France.

On the 24th of January the Queen-mother addressed a letter to Paul de Foix, setting forth that considering the rare excellence of the Queen of England, the position of England and France, separated as they were only by a three hours' passage, and the deep interests of both countries in their mutual prosperity, she would feel herself the happiest mother in the world if either of her sons could convert so charming a sister into a daughter equally dear.[1]

Before Mary Stuart had given signs of an alteration of feeling, and immediately that she was made aware of the ill success of the conference at Berwick, Elizabeth had been again haunted by the nightmare of marriage.

---

tenced; the French to be reconciled; their aid again to be craved; and if they can, they intend to pretend title here in England, where they make account upon friends. Whenas they have Lennox, Darnley, and the mother within their border, whatsoever flourishing words be used for the shift, either here or in Scotland, by Lady Lennox, her son, or husband, their hearts portend enmity to our Sovereign and division to her realm. They are only bent to please and revenge the Queen of Scots' quarrel, and to follow her ways, who remembereth as I am informed, her mother, her uncle Guise, and her own pretences. This realm hath a faction to serve their turn. Betwixt Chatelherault and Lennox, take heed that ye suffer not that Chatelherault be overthrown, and in the end advance him who shall be enemy to this realm. It may fall out the Queen's Majesty's purpose may be followed by them of Scotland, in which case it should be well; but I in my simple opinion am in despair thereof, for they look for her where the Lord preserve her, and therefore betimes seek ways to stop the tide, and fill their hands full at home, which may well be done.'—CONWAY MSS. Rolls House.

[1] ' Me sentirois la plus heureuse mère du monde si un de mes enfans d'une bien aymée sœur m'en avoit faict une très chère fille.'—Catherine de Medici to Paul de Foix. Vie de Marie Stuart.—MIGNET; Appendix.

Again Cecil had communicated with Maximilian, and in writing to Sir Thomas Smith on the 15th of December, he had said:

'This also I see in the Queen's Majesty, a sufficient contentation to be moved to marry abroad; and if it may so please Almighty God to lead by the hand some meet person to come and lay hands on her to her contentation, I could then wish myself more health to endure my years somewhat longer, to enjoy such a world here as I trust will follow; otherwise I assure you as now things hang in desperation I have no comfort to live.'[1]

Cecil's interest was in the Archduke who was a grown man. Elizabeth if she was obliged to marry preferred perhaps a husband with whom her connexion for a time would be a form.

When Paul de Foix read Catherine's letter to her she coloured, expressed herself warmly grateful for an offer of which she felt herself unworthy, and wished that she had been ten years younger. She feared she said that if at her age she married any one so young as the King of France, it would be with her as it had been with her sister and King Philip. In a few years she would find herself a discontented old woman deserted by a husband who was weary of her.

The ambassador politely objected. She might have children to give stability to the throne; virtue never grew old, and her greatness would for ever make her loved.

She said she would sooner die than be a neglected wife, and yet while conscious of its absurdity she allowed the thought to rest before her. She admitted that her subjects desired her to marry. They would perhaps

---

[1] Cecil to Sir T. Smith, December 15.—Wright, vol. I.

prefer an Englishman for her; but she had no subject in England of adequate rank except the Earl of Arundel, and Arundel she could not endure. She could have loved the noble Earl of Leicester, but her subjects objected and she was bound to consult their wishes.

So with a promise to consider the proposal she graciously dismissed de Foix and proceeded to consult Cecil. The careful Cecil with methodical gravity paraded the obvious objections, the inequality of age, the danger should the marriage prove fruitful of the absorption of England into France, the risk of being involved in continental wars, and the innovations which might be attempted upon English liberty and English law.

Elizabeth admitted the force of these considerations, but she would not regard them as decisive. De Foix suggested that the crown of England might be entailed on the second son or the second child; and Catherine de Medici herself excited by Elizabeth's uncertainty became more pressing than ever, and made light of difficulties.

She even tempted Cecil with splendid offers if he would recommend the French alliance and do her a pleasure; but she had mistaken the temperament which she was addressing. Cecil answered like himself 'that he thought neither of how to gratify the Queen of France nor of any gift or recompense which might accrue to himself; his sole care was for the service of God, the weal of his mistress, and the interests of the realm; if the marriage would further these it should have his hearty support, if otherwise no second consideration could move him.'[1]

The Queen-mother was too eager to be daunted. The Queen of Spain was coming in the course of the spring to Bayonne on a visit to her mother. Some marriage in

---

[1] Mignet's *Mary Stuart*; Appendix.

Philip's interest would then probably be proposed for her son; and while de Foix was working on Elizabeth, Catherine herself continued to press upon the English ambassador and to urge the necessity of an immediate resolution.[1]

Elizabeth really thought for the time that unless she could succeed with Mary Stuart her choice lay only between the Archduke and the King of France. She told de Silva in March that she must marry or she could not face another Parliament, whilst she durst not marry Leicester for fear of an insurrection.[2] Catherine de Medici knew the necessity which was bearing upon her, and laboured hard with Sir Thomas Smith to remove the objections raised by Cecil.

Age was nothing she said. If the Queen of England was contented with the age of her son he would find no fault with hers. Elizabeth professed to fear that a marriage with the King of France might oblige her to be often absent from England. Catherine could see no difficulty in governing England by a viceroy; and it was to no purpose that Smith urged that the English people were less easy to govern than the French, and that their princes had trouble enough to manage them though they remained always at home. He told Cathe-

---

[1] Sir Thomas Smith reports a singular Order of Council for the behaviour of the French Court, in preparation for the Queen of Spain's visit:—

'Orders are taken in the Court that no gentleman shall entertain with talk any of the Queen's maids except it be in the Queen's presence, or except he be married. And if any demoiselle do sit upon a form or stool, he may sit by her, but not lie along as the fashion was afore in this Court, with other such restraints, which whether they be made for this time of Lent, or to somewhat imitate the austerity of the Spanish Court, that they should not be offended or think evil of the liberty used in this Court, I cannot tell.'—*Sir T. Smith to Cecil, April* 10. *French MSS. Rolls House.*

[2] De Silva to Philip, March 17.—*MS. Simancas.*

CHAP VIII
1565
April

rine that he thought she was too precipitate; the young people might meet and make acquaintance. 'You are a young man, sir,' he said to Charles himself; 'when you are next in Normandy you should disguise yourself, go lustily over unknown, and see with your own eyes.'

The Queen-mother laughed, but said it could not be. She must have an answer at once; and the match was so advantageous for both parties that she could not believe Elizabeth would refuse. France and England united could rule the world, for French and English soldiers united could conquer the world. 'France had the honour for horsemen, English footmen were taken for invincible.'

The conversation turned on the chances of children, where Catherine was equally confident; and the dialogue which followed was reported by Sir T. Smith in a letter to Elizabeth herself:—

Charles the Ninth and Elizabeth.

'The Queen told me that she was married when King Henry had but fifteen years and she fourteen; and that Mr. Secretary Cecil had a child at fourteen years of age, as her ambassador had written to her; and said she "you see my son, he is not small nor little of growth."

'With that the King stood upright.

'"Why," said she, "you would show yourself bigger than you be," and laughed.

'"But what think you will be the end, M. l'Ambassador," saith she; "I pray you tell me your opinion frankly."

'"By my troth, madame," quoth I, "to say what I think, I think rather it will take effect than no; and yet in my letters I see nothing but deliberation and irresolution and request of delay to consult; but methinks it groweth fast together and cometh on hotlier than I did imagine it would have done; and that maketh me judge rather that at the last it will take effect than otherwise. But methinks on your part and the King's you make too much haste. If the King had three or four more years and had seen the Queen's Majesty and was taken in love with her, then I would not marvel at this haste."

' "Why," said the King, "I do love her indeed."

' "Sir," quoth I, "your age doth not yet bear that you should perfectly know what love meaneth; but you shall shortly understand it, for there is no young man, prince nor other, but he doth pass by it. It is the foolishest thing, the most impatient, most hasty, most without respect that can be."

' With that the King blushed.

' The Queen said this is no foolish love.

' "No, Madame," quoth I, "this is with respect and upon good grounds, and therefore may be done with deliberation." '[1]

' "So your Majesty is to marry the King of France after all," said de Silva to Elizabeth a little after this.

' She half hid her face and laughed. " It is Lent," she said; " and you are a good friend, so I will confess my

---

[1] Sir Thomas Smith to Elizabeth, April 15.—*French MSS. Rolls House.*

Elizabeth had desired the ambassador to describe the young king to her. Smith said he was a pale, thin, sickly, ungainly boy, with large knee and ankle joints. His health had been injured by over-doses of medicine. He seemed amiable, cheerful, and more intelligent than might have been expected, 'seeing he had not been brought up to learning, and spoke no language but his own.'

In a letter to Cecil, the ambassador said—

'The Queen-mother hath a very good opinion of you. She liketh marvellous well that you had a son in your fourteenth or fifteenth year, for she hopeth therefore that her son the King shall have a son as well as you in his sixteenth year, and thinketh you may serve as an example to the Queen's Majesty not to contemn the young years of the King's.'—*Smith to Cecil, MS. Ibid.*

sins to you. My brother the Catholic King wished to marry me, the King of Sweden and Denmark wished to marry me, the King of France wishes to marry me."

'"And the Archduke also," said de Silva.

'"Your Prince," she went on without noticing the interruption, "is the only one who has not been at my feet; I have had all the rest."

'"When the King my master failed," replied de Silva, "he supposed your Majesty would never marry at all."

'"There was no need of so hasty a conclusion," she said; "although it is true that at that time I was very unwilling to marry; and I assure you that if at this moment I could name any fitting person to succeed to my crown I would not marry now; I have always shrunk from it; but my subjects insist, and I suppose I shall be forced to comply unless I can contrive some alternative, which will be very difficult. The world, when a woman remains single, assumes that there must be something wrong about her, and that she has some discreditable reason for it. They said of me that I would not marry because I was in love with the Earl of Leicester, and that I could not marry him because he had a wife already; yet now he has no wife, and for all that I do not marry him, although at one time, the King my brother advised me to do it. But what are we to do? tongues will talk, and for ourselves we can but do our duties and keep our account straight with God. Truth comes out at last, and God knows my heart that I am not what people say I am."'[1]

Meanwhile in Scotland the drama was fast progressing.

---

[1] MIGNET; Appendix 6.

Darnley reached Edinburgh on the 12th of February; and a week later he was introduced to Mary at Wemyss Castle in Fife. As yet he had but few friends: the most powerful of the Catholic nobles looked askance at him; the Cardinal of Lorraine, the Cardinal of Guise, and the widowed Duchess, misunderstanding the feeling of his friends in England, imagined that in accepting a youth who had been brought up at Elizabeth's court the Queen of Scots was throwing up the game.[1] The Archbishop of Glasgow, Mary's minister in Paris—a Beton, and therefore an hereditary enemy of Lennox—sent an estafette to Madrid in the hope that Philip would dissuade her from a step which he regarded as fatal; and though Melville, who was in the confidence of the English Catholics, assured her 'that no marriage was more in her interest, seeing it would render her title to the succession of the crown unquestionable,' although Ritzio, 'the known minion of the Pope,' threw himself into Darnley's intimacy so warmly 'that they would lie sometimes in one bed together,'[2] Mary Stuart either displayed her resolution or delayed the publication of it till Philip's answer should arrive. She had not yet relinquished hope of extracting concessions from Elizabeth by professing a desire to be guided by her; she was afraid of driving Elizabeth by over-precipitancy to accept the advances of France.

In the interval therefore she continued to assure Ran-

---

[1] When Mary's final resolution to marry Darnley was made known in Paris, Sir Thomas Smith wrote to Leicester, 'The Cardinal of Guise, Madame de Guise, and the Scottish ambassador, are in a marvellous agony for the news of the marriage of the Scottish Queen with the Lord Darnley. They have received letters out of Scotland from some friends there, which when they had read, they fell weeping all that night.' —*Smith to Leicester, April* 1565. *French MSS. Rolls House.*

[2] CALDERWOOD.

dolph that she would be guided by 'her sister's' wishes. 'How to be sure that it is her real mind and not words only,' Randolph wrote on the 1st of March, 'is harder than I will take upon me; but so far as words go, to me and others she seems fully determined. I never at any time had better hopes of her than now.'[1]

Yet the smooth words took no shape in action. She pressed Randolph every day to know Elizabeth's resolution, but the conditions on both sides remained as they were left at Berwick. Elizabeth said to Mary Stuart, 'Marry as I wish and then you shall see what I will do for you.' Mary said, 'Recognize me first as your successor and I will then be all that you desire.' Each distrusted the other; but Elizabeth had the most producible reason for declining to be credulous. However affectionate the Queen of Scots' language might be, the Treaty of Edinburgh remained unratified.

The more Mary pressed for recognition therefore, the more Elizabeth determined to withhold what if once conceded could not afterwards be recalled, till by some decisive action her suspicion should have been removed. With the suspense other dangerous symptoms began to show themselves. Soon after Darnley's appearance the Queen of Scots made attempts to reintroduce the mass. Murray told Randolph that 'if she had her way in her "Papistry" things would be worse than ever they were." Argyle said that unless she married as the Queen of England desired 'he and his would have to provide for their own.' The chapel at Holyrood was thrown open to all comers; and while the Queen insisted that her subjects should 'be free to live as they listed,' the Protestants 'offered their lives to be sacrificed before they would

---

[1] Randolph to Cecil, March 1.—*Scotch MSS. Rolls House.*

suffer such an abomination.' Becoming aggressive in turn they threatened to force the Queen into conformity, and they by their violence 'kindled in her a desire to revenge.' Mary Stuart was desiring merely to reconcile the Catholics of the anti-Lennox faction to her marriage with Darnley. There was fighting about the chapel door; the priest was attacked at the altar; and in the daily quarrels at the council-board the Lords of the Congregation told Mary openly that 'if she thought of marrying a Papist it would not be borne with.'[1] Suddenly, unlooked for and uninvited, the evil spirit of the storm, the Earl of Bothwell, reappeared at Mary's Court. She disclaimed all share in his return; he was still attainted; yet there he stood—none daring to lift a hand against him—proud, insolent, and dangerous.

At this crisis Randolph brought Mary a message which she was desired to accept as final; that until Elizabeth had herself married or had made up her mind not to marry, the succession must remain unsettled. The Queen of Scots 'wept her fill;' but tears in those eyes were no sign of happy promise. Randolph so little liked the atmosphere that he petitioned for his own recall. Lennox had gathered about him a knot of wild and desperate youths—Cassilis, Eglinton, Montgomery, and Bothwell—the worst and fiercest of all. Darnley had found a second friend and adviser besides Ritzio in Lord Robert Stuart, the Queen's half-brother, 'a man full of all evil.' The Queen's own marriage with him was now generally spoken of; and Chatelherault, Argyle, and Murray, gave the English ambassador notice that mischief was in the wind, 'and joined themselves in a new bond to defend each other's quarrels.'[2]

[1] Randolph to Cecil, March 15, March 17, and March 20.—*MS. Rolls House.*
[2] Randolph to Cecil, March 20.—COTTON *MSS.* CALIG. B. 10.

CHAP VIII
1565
March

'To help all these unhappy ones,' Randolph wrote to Cecil, 'I doubt not but you will take the best way; and this I can assure you that contrary to my sovereign's will, let them attempt, let them seek, let them send to all the cardinals and devils in hell, it shall exceed their power to bring anything to pass, so that be not refused the Queen of Scots which in reason ought to content her.'[1]

The elements of uncertainty and danger were already too many, when it pleased Elizabeth to introduce another which completed the chaos and shook the three kingdoms. Despising doctrinal Protestantism too keenly to do justice to its professors, Elizabeth had been long growing impatient of excesses like that which had shocked her at Cambridge, and had many times expressed her determination to bring the Church to order. Her own creed was a perplexity to herself and to the world. With no tinge of the meaner forms of superstition, she clung to practices which exasperated the Reformers, while the Catholics laughed at their inconsistency; her crucifixes and candles, if adopted partly from a politic motive of conciliation, were in part also an expression of that half belief with which she regarded the symbols of the faith; and while ruling the clergy with a rod of iron, and refusing as sternly as her father to tolerate their pretensions to independence, she desired to force upon them a special and semi-mysterious character; to dress them up as counterfeits of the Catholic hierarchy; and half in reverence, half in contempt, compel them to assume the name and character of a priesthood which both she and they in their heart of hearts knew to be an illusion and a dream.

Elizabeth determines to restore order in the Church.

---

[1] Randolph to Cecil, March 20.—COTTON MSS. CALIG. B. 10.

Elizabeth's view of this subject cannot be called a fault. It was the result of her peculiar temperament; and in principle was but an anticipation of the eventual attitude into which the minds of the laity would subside. But the theory in itself is suited only to settled times, when it is safe from the shock of external trials: from the first it has been endured with impatience by those nobler minds to whom sincerity is a necessity of existence; and in the first establishment of the English Church, and especially when Elizabeth attempted to insist on conditions which overstrained the position, she tried the patience of the most enduring clergy in the world.

Her first and greatest objection was to their marriage. The holy state of matrimony was one which she could not contemplate without bitterness; and although she could not at the time of her accession prevent the clergy from taking wives, and dared not re-enact the prohibitory laws of her sister, she refused to revive the permissive statutes of Edward. She preferred to leave the archbishops and bishops with their children legally illegitimate and themselves under the imputation of concubinage. Nor did time tend to remove her objections. Cecil alone in 1561 prevented her from making an attempt to enforce celibacy.[1] To the Archbishop of Canterbury himself 'she expressed a repentance that he and the other married bishops were in office, wishing it had been otherwise;' she thought them worse as they were ' than in the glorious shame of a counterfeited chastity;' ' I was

---

[1] 'Her Majesty continues very ill-affected towards the state of matrimony in the clergy; and if I were not therein very stiff, her Majesty would utterly and openly condemn and forbid it.'—*Cecil to Archbishop Parker, August 12, 1561.* STRYPE's *Life of Parker.*

in horror,' the Archbishop wrote after a conversation with her on the subject, 'to hear such words come from her mild nature as she spake concerning God's holy ordinance of matrimony.' 'Princes hitherto had thought it better to cherish their ecclesiastical state as conservators of religion; the English bishops alone were openly brought in hatred, shunned and traduced before the malicious and ignorant people as beasts without knowledge, as men of effrenate intemperancy, without discretion or any godly disposition worthy to serve in their state.'[1]

Quarrel between the Queen and the Bishops.

In the same spirit the Queen attempted to force her crucifixes into the parish churches; and she provoked by it immediate rebellion. The bishops replied with one voice 'that they would give their lives for her; but they would not set a trap for the ignorant and make themselves guilty of the blood of their brethren;' 'if by the Queen's authority they established images they would blemish the fame of their notable fathers who had given their lives for the testimony of God's truth.'

Thus the antagonism went on, irritating Elizabeth on her side into dangerous traffickings with the Bishop of Aquila and his successor; while Parker declared openly that he must obey God rather than man; and that however the Queen might despise him and his brethren 'there were enough of that contemptible flock that would not shrink to offer their blood for the defence of Christ's verity.'[2]

The right however, as has been already pointed out, was not wholly on the Protestant side. The recollections of Protestant ascendancy in the days of Edward were not yet effaced; and the inability of the Reformers to keep in check the coarser forms of irreverence and

---

[1] Parker to Cecil.—STRYPE's *Life of Parker.* [2] Ibid.

irreligion was as visible as before. They were themselves aggressive and tyrannical; and when prebends' wives melted the cathedral organ-pipes into dish-covers and cut the frames into bedsteads, there was something to be said even in favour of clerical celibacy. The bad relations between the Crown and the spiritual estate prevented the clergy from settling down into healthy activity. The Queen insulted her bishops on one side; the Puritans denounced them on the other as imps of Antichrist; and thus without effective authority—with its rulers brought deliberately into contempt—the Church of England sunk deeper day by day into anarchy.

Something no doubt it had become necessary to do; but Elizabeth took a line which however it might be defended in theory was approved of only by the Catholics —and by them in the hope that it would prove the ruin of the institution which they hated.

At the close of 1564, after the return of the Court from Cambridge, an intimation went abroad that the Queen intended to enforce uniformity in the administration of the services and to insist especially on the use of the surplice and cap—the badges which distinguished the priest from the Genevan minister. The Puritan clergy would sooner have walked to the stake in the yellow robes of Sanbenitos. But it was in vain that the Dean of Durham insisted that it was cruel to use force against Protestants while 'so many Papists who had never sworn obedience to the Queen nor yet did any part of their duty to their flocks enjoyed their liberty and livings.' It was in vain that Pilkington and others of the bishops exclaimed against disturbing the peace of the Church at such a time 'about things indifferent.'[1]

---

[1] Pilkington to Leicester, October 25, 1564.—STRYPE's *Parker*, Appendix.

CHAP. VIII
1565

Elizabeth insists on the observance of the Act of Uniformity.

On the 24th of January the Queen addressed a letter to the Archbishop of Canterbury, 'that whereas the ecclesiastical government ought to be the example in its perfection to all others—by the carelessness of him the Archbishop and of the other bishops, differences of opinion, differences of practice, differences in the rites used in the churches, had risen up throughout the realm to the great offence of godly, wise, and obedient persons. She had hoped that the bishops would in time have remembered their duties; but finding her expectation disappointed she had now resolved to use her own authority and suppress and reform all novelties, diversities, and varieties. The Act of Uniformity should be obeyed in all its parts, and the bishops must see to it at their peril.' In the first draft of the letter a clause was added in Cecil's hand, recommending them to act with moderation; but the words were struck through and a menace substituted in their place that 'if the bishops were now remiss, the Queen would provide other remedy by such sharp proceedings as should not be easy to be borne by such as were disordered; and therewith also she would impute to them the cause thereof.'[1]

Much might have been said on the manner of these injunctions. To the matter there was no objection, provided discretion had been observed in limiting the points which were to be insisted on within the bounds which were indispensably necessary, and provided the bishops' powers were equal to the duties imposed upon them. Henry the Eighth had again and again issued similar orders; and on the whole, because he was known to be evenhanded and because the civil authority supported the

---

[1] The Queen to Archbishop Parker, Jan. 24, 1565.—STRYPE's *Life of Parker*.

ecclesiastical, he had held in check the more dangerous excesses both of Catholic and Protestant. But the reformed opinions had now developed far beyond the point at which Henry left them. They had gained a hold on the intellect as well as on the passions of the best and noblest of Elizabeth's subjects; and on the other hand, as the Dean of Durham complained, vast numbers of the Catholic clergy were left undisturbed in their benefices who scarcely cared to conceal their creed. The bishops were rebuked if they attempted to exact the oath of allegiance from Papist recusants; while the Queen's displeasure was reserved for those who were true from the bottom of their hearts to the throne which the Catholics were undermining. The ablest and worthiest of the English clergy were those on whom the injunctions would press most heavily. Elizabeth it seemed had not yet forgiven the good service which they had done her when Amy Robsart died, and when but for them she would have married Lord Robert.

But there was no escape. The surplice should be worn though it scorched like the robe of Nessus. The Archbishop, with the help of the Bishops of London, Ely, Lincoln, and Winchester, drew up a body of articles for 'uniformity of apparel and ritual,' and submitted them to Cecil for approval. Elizabeth meanwhile had supplemented her first orders by a command that 'matters in controversy in religion' should not be discussed in sermons; the clergy while wearing Catholic garments were not to criticise Catholic doctrines. The Archbishop told Cecil that while 'the adversaries' were so busy on the Continent writing against the English Liturgy, this last direction was thought 'too unreasonable;' and implored him 'not to strain the cord too tight;' while he requested an order in writing from the Queen, addressed to himself and the Bishop of London, as their authority for enforcing her first commands.[1]

Neither a letter from herself however, nor assistance in any form from the Government would Elizabeth allow to be given. The bishops should deliver their tale of bricks, but they should have no straw to burn them. They were the appointed authorities, and by them she was determined at once that the work should be done and that the odium of it should be borne.

She did something indeed; but not what Parker desired. As if purposely to affront the Protestants the Court had revived the ceremonies of the Carnival. On Shrove Tuesday Leicester gave a tournament and afterwards a masque, where Juno and Diana held an argument on the respective merits of marriage and celibacy. Jupiter as the umpire gave sentence at last for matrimony; and the Queen who had the Spanish ambassador as usual at her side, whispered to him 'that is meant for me.' A supper followed, but not till past midnight. As Lent had begun the ambassador declined to eat, and Elizabeth laughed at him. The next day being Ash Wednesday, de Silva accompanied her to St. Paul's, where Nowell the Dean was to preach. A vast crowd had assembled—more, the Queen thought, to see her than to hear the sermon. The Dean began, and had not proceeded far when he came on the subject of images—'which he handled roughly.'

'Leave that alone,' Elizabeth called from her seat. The preacher did not hear, and went on with his invectives. 'To your text! Mr. Dean,' she shouted, raising her voice; 'To your text; leave that; we have heard enough of that! To your subject.'

---

[1] Parker to Cecil, March 3, 1565.—LANSDOWNE *MSS.* 8.

The unfortunate Doctor Nowell coloured, stammered out a few incoherent words, and was unable to go on. Elizabeth went off in a rage with her ambassador. The congregation—the Protestant part of it—were in tears.[1]

Archbishop Parker seeing the Dean 'utterly dismayed,' took him 'for pity home to Lambeth to dinner;'[2] and wrote to Cecil a respectful but firm remonstrance. Without the letter for which he had applied he was powerless to move. The bishops without the support of the Queen or Council would only be laughed at. Let Leicester, Bacon, Cecil himself, and the Queen, send for the Protestant ministers if they pleased, and say to them what they pleased. They had begun the trouble, and it was for them to pacify it. 'I can do no good,' he said. 'If the ball shall be tossed unto us, and we have no authority by the Queen's hand, we will sit still; I will no more strive against the stream—fume or chide who will. The Lord be with you!'[3]

Still labouring to do his best, the Archbishop called a meeting of the bishops and invited them either to recommend obedience among the clergy or to abstain from encouraging them in resistance. But the bishops were now as angry as the Queen. They refused in a body to 'discourage good Protestants;' and Parker told Elizabeth plainly that unless she supported him in carrying them out the injunctions must be modified. He had to deal with men 'who would offer themselves to lose all, yea, their bodies to prison, rather than condescend;' while the lawyers told him that he could not deprive incumbents of their livings 'with no more warrant but the Queen's mouth.'

---

[1] De Silva to Philip, March 12.—*MS. Simancas.*
[2] Parker to Cecil, March 8.—LANSDOWNE *MSS.* 8.
[3] Ibid.

While Parker addressed the Queen, the other bishops waited on Cecil with the same protest. The Reforming clergy, they said, refused everywhere 'to wear the apparel of Satan;' 'Christ had no fellowship with Belial;' and 'for themselves they would not be made Papists in disguise.'

Cecil who knew that all appeals to Elizabeth in her present humour would only exasperate her, replied that 'they talked more rhetoric than reason; the Queen must be obeyed or worse would follow.'[1]

Never were human beings in a more cruel position. Elizabeth sat still in malicious enjoyment of the torture which she was inflicting, while Parker and Grindal, after a fresh consultation with the lawyers, undertook at last to summon the London clergy and attempt to extort a promise from them to obey the Act of Uniformity; if the clergy refused the Archbishop supposed that the Court was prepared for the consequences, and that he must proceed to sequestration and deprivation; but while he consented to submit to the Queen's commands he warned Cecil of the inevitable consequences: many churches would be left destitute of service; many ministers would forsake their livings and live at printing, teaching children, or otherwise as they could: 'what tumults would follow, what speeches and talks were like to rise in the realm and in the city, he left it to Cecil's wisdom to consider;' and driven as he was against his will to these unwise extremities, he again entreated that some member of the Council might be joined in commission with him 'to authorise the Queen's commandments.'[2]

---

[1] De Silva to Philip, March 12.
[2] Parker and Grindal to Cecil, March 20.—LANSDOWNE MSS. 8.

On this last point Elizabeth would yield nothing. The clergy were under the charge of the bishops; and the bishops should manage them with law or without. One or two of the most violent of the London preachers were called before the Council and 'foul chidden:' but lay interference with them was limited to remonstrance. The responsibility of punishing them was flung persistently on the Archbishop, who at length after once more ineffectually imploring Cecil 'to pacify the Queen,' opened a commission at Lambeth with the Bishop of London on the 26th of March.

A few hours' experience sufficed to justify the worst alarm. More than a hundred of the London clergy appeared. Sixty-one promised conformity; a few hesitated; thirty-seven distinctly refused and were suspended for three months 'from all manner of ministry.' They were the best preachers in the city; 'they showed reasonable quietness and modesty other than was looked for,' but submit they would not.[1] As an immediate consequence, foreseen by every one but the Queen, the most frequented of the London churches either became the scenes of scandal and riot or were left without service. When the Archbishop sent his chaplains to officiate the congregation forcibly expelled them. The doors of one church were locked, and six hundred citizens 'who came to communion' were left at the doors unable to find entrance; at another, an Anglican priest of high church tendencies who was sent to take the place of the deposed minister, produced a wafer at the sacrament; the parishioners when he was reading the prayer of consecration removed it from the table 'because it was not common bread.' At a third church

---

[1] Parker to Cecil, March 26.—LANSDOWNE MSS. 8.

CHAP VIII
1565
April

the churchwardens refused to provide surplices. The Bishop of London was besieged in his house at St. Paul's by mobs of raging women whom he vainly entreated to go away and send their husbands instead. Unable to escape from the hands of these Amazons he was about 'to pray aid of some magistrate' to deliver him; and was rescued only by one of the suspended clergy who persuaded them to go away quietly—'yet so as with tears they moved at some hands compassion.'[1] Everywhere 'the precise Protestants' 'offered their goods and bodies to prison rather than they would relent.'

Simultaneously and obviously on purpose Elizabeth forced upon the people the most alarming construction of the persecution. On Good Friday, her almoner Guest the high church Bishop of Rochester, preached a sermon in the Chapel Royal on the famous *Hoc est corpus meum*. He assured his congregation again and again 'that the bread at the sacrament was the very body, the very same body which had been crucified,' 'and that the Christian must so take it and so believe of it,' and an enthusiastic Catholic in the audience was so delighted to hear the old doctrine once more in the Sovereign's presence, that he shouted out—'That is true, and he that denies it let him be burnt.'

Elizabeth affects Catholic usages.

On Easter Tuesday Elizabeth in stiff black velvet and with all solemnity and devotion publicly washed the feet of a poor woman; and the washing business over, with slow deliberation she had a large crucifix brought to her which she piously kissed.[2] In part perhaps she was but

---

[1] Parker to Cecil, March 26, March 28, April 3, April 12.—LANSDOWNE *MSS.* Grindal to Cecil, May 4.— *Domestic MSS.*, ELIZ., vol. xxxix., *Rolls House.*

[2] ' Acabando de lavar el pie á la pobre, hacia de mucho espacio una cruz muy larga y bien hecha para besar en ella de que pesaba á muchos de los que alli estaban.'— *De Silva to Philip, April 21. MS. Simancas.*

a politic hypocrite, and desired to deceive de Silva and
Philip; but the world took her at her word and believed
that she was openly making profession of Catholicism
while she was compelling the Protestants to be their own
destroyers.'

Once more Parker poured out to Cecil his despair and
distraction.¹

Lambeth, April 28.

'SIR,—The Queen's Majesty willed my Lord of York to declare her pleasure determinately to have the orders go forward. I trust her Highness hath devised how it may be performed. I utterly despair therein as of myself and therefore must sit still as I have now done, always waiting either for toleration or else further aid. Mr. Secretary, can it be thought that I alone having sun and moon against me can compass this difficulty? If you of her Majesty's Council provide no otherwise for this matter than as it appeareth openly, what the sequel will be *horresco vel reminiscendo cogitare*. In King Edward's days the whole body of the Council travailed in Hooper's attempt; my predecessor Cranmer of blessed memory,² labouring in vain with Bishop Ferrars, the Council took it in hand; and shall I hope to do that which the Queen's Majesty will have done? What I hear and see, what complaints be brought to me, I shall not report, [or] how I am used of many men's hands. I commit all to God. If I die in this cause—malice so far prevailing—I shall commit my soul to God in a good conscience. If the Queen's Majesty be no more considered, I shall not marvel what be done or said to me. If you hear and see so manifestly as may be seen, and will not consult in time to prevent

---

¹ Archbishop Parker to Cecil.—LANSDOWNE *MSS.* 9.
² Parker's words are 'my predecessor D. Cranmer labouring in vain,' &c. D. is *Dirus*, and the expression in the text is its nearest English equivalent.

CHAP VIII
1565
April

so many miseries, I have and do by these presents discharge my duty and conscience to you in such place as ye be. I can promise to do nothing but hold me in silence within my own conscience, and make my complaints to God ut exsurgat Deus et judicet causam istam, ille, ille, qui comprehendit sapientes in astutiâ eorum.[1] God be with your honour.

'Your honour's in Christ,
'MATT. CANTUAR.'

Protest of Adam Loftus.

The alarm produced by Elizabeth's attitude was not confined to the English Protestants. Adam Loftus, titular Archbishop of Armagh, bewailed to Cecil the malice of the crafty 'devil and subtle Satan' who was 'turmoiling and turning things topsy-turvy, bringing in a mingled religion, neither wholly with nor wholly against God's word.' Such a religion was 'the more dangerous,' the Irish primate thought, 'as it was accounted good and comely;' but for himself he would rather see God followed wholly or Baal followed wholly; 'it was dangerous to urge a necessity in things which God's word did set at liberty.'[2]

Alarm of the Scotch Calvinists.

Far worse was the effect in Scotland. The rigid Calvinists who had long watched Elizabeth with jealous eyes clamoured that she was showing herself at last in her true colours. 'Posts and packets flying daily in the air,' brought such news as lost her and lost England 'the hearts of all the godly.' No imagination was too extravagant to receive credit. The two Queens were supposed to be in a secret league for the overthrow of the truth, and Darnley's return was interpreted as part of an

---

[1] 'That God may arise, and may judge in this cause,—He—He—who taketh the wise in their own craftiness.'
[2] The Archbishop of Armagh to Cecil, 1565.—*Irish MSS. Rolls House.*

insidious policy—at once 'to match the Queen of Scots meanly and poorly,' and to confirm her in her evil ways 'by marrying her to a Papist.' The 'godly' exclaimed in anguish 'that no hope was left of any sure establishment of Christ's religion, but all was turned to confusion.' 'The evil effect' on men's minds was described 'as beyond measure infinite;' and Mary Stuart's desire to obtain liberty of conscience for the Catholics and the increasing favour which she showed to Darnley, were alike set down to Elizabeth.

The Leicester scandals were revived with new anecdotes to confirm them.[1] The Protestants goaded into fear and fury swore that the priests at Holyrood should be hanged, and 'idolatry' be no more suffered. Mary Stuart being on a visit at Lundy in Fife, the Laird—'a grave antient man with a white head and a white beard' —led his seven sons before her, all tall and stalwart men. They knelt together at her feet. 'The house,' the laird said, 'was hers and all that was in it, and he and his boys would serve her truly till death;' 'but he prayed that while she remained no mass should be said there.' She asked why. He said it was 'worse than the mickle de'il.'[2]

Remonstrance did not rest in words. A priest in Edinburgh taking courage from the reports which were

---

[1] 'It is in every man's mouth that lately the Duke of Norfolk's Grace and my Lord of Leicester were playing at tennis, the Queen beholding them, and my Lord Robert being very hot and sweating, took the Queen's napkin out of her hand and wiped his face, which the Duke seeing said he was too saucy, and sware he would lay his racket upon his face. Hereupon arose a tumult, and the Queen offended more with the Duke. This tale is told by the Earl of Athol. Whatsoever is most secret among you is sooner at this Queen's ears than some would think it. I would you doings were better, or many of your tattling tongues shorter.' —*Randolph to Throgmorton, March* 31. *Scotch MSS. Rolls House.*

[2] Randolph to Cecil, March 27.— *MS. Ibid.*

in the air, said mass at Easter at a private house. He was denounced, caught, hurried before the town magistrates, and having confessed, was fastened hand and foot to the market cross. There from two o'clock in the afternoon till six he stood exposed, while 'ten thousand eggs' were broken upon his face and body; and the hungry mob howled round his feet and threatened to dash his brains out with their clubs as soon as he was taken down. The Provost who had gone contentedly home to supper was obliged to return with the city guard to bring him off in safety; and the miserable wretch pasted with slime and filth was carried senseless into the Tolbooth and there made fast in irons with two of his congregation at his side.[1]

The Queen of Scots, who was at Stirling when she heard of this cowardly outrage, sent for the Provost and ordered him to release his prisoner; 'not however,' wrote an unknown correspondent in relating the story to Randolph,[2] 'without great offence of the whole people;' 'whereby,' he said, 'I trust whenever the like occurs again, and there be knowledge gotten, execution will be made in another manner of sort without seeking of further justice at the magistrates' hands; I assure you there is greater rage now amongst the faithful nor ever I saw since her Grace came to Scotland.'

Meantime Mary Stuart weary of the mask which she had so long worn, and unable to endure any longer these wild insults to her creed and herself, determined to run the chance of dividing Scotland, to throw herself on the

---

[1] Randolph to Cecil, April, 1565.—Rolls House MS.

[2] One of a number of letters to Randolph, in the Rolls House, written in the same hand, and signed 'You know who.' To this person, whoever he was, Randolph was indebted for much of his secret information. The hand partly resembles that of Kirkaldy of Grange; partly, though not to the same degree, that of Knox.

loyalty of the Catholic party in her own country, in England, and abroad, to marry Darnley and dare the worst which Elizabeth could do. Whether she had received any encouraging answer from Philip before she made up her mind does not appear. It is most likely however that she had learnt from the Government in the Netherlands what the answer would be when it arrived; and the opinions of the Spanish ministers when made known at last were decisively favourable. After a consultation at the Escurial the Duke of Alva and the Count de Feria recommended Philip by all means to support the Queen of Scots in taking a Catholic husband who by blood was so near the English crown; and Philip sent her word and through de Silva sent word to the English Catholics that she and they might rely on him to bear them through.[1]

Tired of waiting, and anticipating with justifiable confidence that Philip would approve, the Queen of Scots in the middle of April came to a fixed resolution. As Darnley was an English subject it was necessary to go through the form of consulting the English sovereign; and Maitland, who to the last moment had believed that he had been successful in dissuading his mistress from so rash a step, was the person chosen to inform Elizabeth that the Queen of Scots had made her choice, and to request her consent.

With but faint hopes of success—for he knew too much to share the illusions of his countrymen—Maitland left Edinburgh on the 15th of April, taking Randolph with him as far as Berwick. Three days later he reached London. Mary Stuart still trusted Maitland with her secrets, in the belief that although he might disapprove of what

[1] *MS. Simancas.*

she was doing he would remain true to her. He carried with him private messages to de Silva and Lady Lennox, and was thoroughly aware of all that she intended. It is certain however from Maitland's subsequent conduct that although ready to go with his mistress to the edge of a rupture with Elizabeth he was not prepared for open defiance. Elizabeth's conduct had been so strange and uncertain that it was possible that she might make no difficulty. Even the Spanish ambassador believed that although she would prefer Leicester, yet sooner than quarrel with the Queen of Scots she would agree to the marriage with Darnley; and with a faint impression that it might be so Maitland had accepted the commission. Yet either Maitland betrayed his trust, or Elizabeth already knew all that he had to tell her: immediately afer his arrival de Silva reported that the Queen of England 'had changed her mind;'[1] while Mary Stuart as soon as she was freed from the restraint of Maitland's presence no longer concealed that she had made up her mind irrevocably whether Elizabeth consented or refused.

Letters from Randolph followed close behind Maitland to say that the marriage was openly declared; Lady Lennox even told de Silva that she believed it had secretly taken place; and amidst the exultation of the Catholics a general expectation spread through England that 'the good time was at hand when the King of Spain and the Queen of Scots would give them back their own again.'[2]

Nor were their hopes without sound foundation. Mary Stuart as soon as her resolution was taken de-

---

[1] 'A lo que he podido entender esta Reyna se ha mucho alterado de este negocio.'—*De Silva to Philip, April 25. MS. Simancas.*
[2] Ibid.

spatched a messenger post haste to Spain to acquaint Philip with it and to tell him that she depended on his support. The messenger met the Duke of Alva at Bayonne, where the Duke answered for his master in terms which corresponded to her warmest hopes.

'I replied,' wrote Alva in a despatch to Philip, 'that I had your Majesty's instructions to inform the Queen of Scots of your Majesty's interest in her welfare; I said that your Majesty earnestly desired to see her in the great position to which she aspired; and you were assured that both for herself and for the realm she could not do better than marry the young Lennox.

'Your Majesty, I continued, recommended her to conduct herself with great caution and dissimulation towards the Queen of England, and for the present especially to refrain from pressing her in the matter of the succession. The Queen of England might in that case do something prejudicial to the Queen of Scots' interests, and either declare war against her or else listen to the proposals of the Queen-mother of France and marry the young King. If the Queen of Scots would follow your Majesty's advice your Majesty would so direct and support her that when she least expected it she would find herself in possession of all that she desired.'[1]

The messenger flung himself at Alva's feet and wept for joy. His mistress, he said, had never in her life received such happy news as these words would convey to her; and he promised that she would act in every particular as the King of Spain advised.

Although this conversation took place two months after Maitland's despatch to England, yet it spoke of a

---

[1] Alva to Philip, June.—TEULET, vol. v.

foregone conclusion which Elizabeth too surely anticipated. In the first flurry of excitement she sent Lady Lennox to the Tower; and uncertain whether she might not be too late, she proposed to send Sir Nicholas Throgmorton on the spot to Scotland, to say that 'if the Queen of Scots would accept Leicester she should be accounted and allowed next heir to the crown as though she were her own born daughter;' but 'as this was certain and true on one side, so was it also certain on the other that she would not do the like with any other person.'[1]

The situation however was too serious to allow Elizabeth to persist in the Leicester foible. The narrow and irritating offer was suspended till it could be more maturely considered; and on the 1st of May the fitness or unfitness of the marriage of the Queen of Scots and Lord Darnley was discussed 'with long deliberation and argument' in the English Council. The result was a unanimous conclusion 'that the marriage with the Lord Darnley, being attended with such circumstances as did appear, was unmeet, unprofitable, directly prejudicial to the amity between the two Queens, and perilous to the concord of the realm.' But so little desirable did it seem to restrict the Queen of Scots' choice unnecessarily, so unjust it seemed to force upon her the scoundrel object of Elizabeth's own affections, that Cecil and his friends urged the necessity of meeting freely and cordially her demand for recognition; and they advised their mistress to offer the Queen of Scots 'a free election of any other of the nobility, either in the whole realm or isle or any other place.' 'For themselves,' the Council, 'thinking the like of the rest of the nobility and sage men of the realm, did for their parts humbly offer to her Majesty

[1] First draft of instructions to Sir N. Throgmorton, April 24.—*Scotch MSS. Rolls House.*

that whatever could be devised for the satisfaction of the Queen of Scots with some other meeter marriage should be allowed with their advice and furthered with their services when her Majesty should command them.'[1]

With these more generous instructions Sir N. Throgmorton started for Scotland on the 4th of May. Maitland, whom in order to prolong his absence from Edinburgh Mary Stuart had directed to go on to France, returned with the English ambassador in loyal disobedience, to add his own persuasions: he still hoped that the Queen of Scots might be tempted by the prospect of immediate recognition to accept either Arundel, Norfolk, or the Prince of Condé. If she would consent to marry either of these three, the English Government would do for her 'more than she had asked or even could expect.'[2]

But neither these offers, tempting as they would have been a few weeks before, nor the admonitory cautions of the Duke of Alva, came in time to save Mary from the rash course into which she was plunging. The presence of Lennox and Darnley had lashed the Scottish factions into fury, and Queen and court were within the influence of a whirlpool from which they could no longer extricate themselves. The lords on all sides were calling their retainers under arms. The Earl of Murray, at the expense of forfeiting the last remains of his influence over his sister, had summoned Bothwell to answer at Edinburgh a charge of high treason. Bothwell would have defied him had he dared; but Murray appeared ac-

---

[1] Determination of the Council on the Queen of Scots' marriage, signed Winchester, Norfolk, Derby, Pembroke, Clinton, W. Howard, Ed. Rogers, Fr. Knolles, W. Cecil, Ab. Cave, W. Petre, John Mason, R. Sackville.—COTTON MSS., CALIG. B. 10. Endorsed, 'This is a copy of the paper delivered to Sir N. Throgmorton.'

[2] Paul de Foix to the Queen-mother, May 2, May 10.—TEULET, vol. ii.

companied by Argyle and 7000 men on the day fixed for the trial; and the Hepburn was once more obliged to fly. On the other hand Mary was lavishing on Darnley the most extravagant demonstrations of affection. He was ill, and with confiding carelessness she installed herself as his nurse at his bedside. She accused her brother when he remonstrated of 'seeking to set the crown on his own head.' Argyle and Murray durst not appear together at the court, 'that if need were the one might relieve the other.' The miserable Chatelherault could only mutter his feeble hope that he might die in his bed; while Lennox boasted openly 'that he was sure of the greatest part of England, and that the King of Spain would be his friend.'

Lennox's men went openly to mass, and 'such pride was noted in the father and the son' that they would scarcely speak to any common nobleman. 'My young lord lying sick in his bed boasted the Duke that he would knock his pate when he was whole;' while 'the preachers looked daily to have their lives taken from them,' and 'the country was so far broken that there was daily slaughter without redress, stealing on all hands, and justice almost nowhere.'[1]

Although the report of the completion of the marriage was premature, yet the arrangements for it had been pushed forward with eager precipitancy. Mary Stuart's friends in England had informed her of the resolution of the Council; she despatched one of the Betons to delay Throgmorton at Berwick; and the leading lords were sent for one by one to Stirling, where the court was staying, and were requested to sign a paper recommending Darnley as a fitting person to be the

---

[1] Randolph to Cecil, May 3.—*Scotch MSS. Rolls House.*

Queen's husband. Murray's signature could be ill dispensed with. He was invited among the rest, and overwhelmed with courtesies—Mary, Lennox, and Darnley contending with each other in their professions of regard. Murray however was the first to refuse. 'He had no liking thereof.' The Earl of Morton had been gained over by a release from Lady Lennox of her claims on Angus; and if Murray would have complied he might have had the lands of three counties for his reward; but in vain Mary pleaded, in vain Mary threatened. She took her brother into a room apart; she placed the paper in his hand and required him to sign it on his allegiance. He asked for time: she said no time could be allowed because others were waiting for his example.

Murray's character, so much debated among historians, was in the eye of those who knew him a very simple one. He was true, faithful, honourable, earnest, stout both for the defence of God's glory and to save his sovereign's honour; and he was fearful that her doings might make a breach of amity between the two realms.'[1] For five years he had laboured to reconcile two opposing duties: he was a zealous Protestant, but he had saved his sister from persecution, and had quarrelled with his friends in her defence; he had maintained her claims on the English succession with the loyalty of a Scot; he had united his special patriotism with as noble an anxiety for the spiritual freedom of the united realms. Few men had resisted more temptations to play a selfish game than Murray; none had carried themselves with more conspicuous uprightness in a difficult and most trying service. To the last, and long after he had known the direction in which his sister's aims were tending, he had shielded

---

[1] Randolph to Cecil, May 21.—*Scotch MSS. Rolls House.*

her with his name, he had assisted her with his counsels, he had striven hard to save her from the sinister and dangerous advisers to whom she was secretly listening: but he could hesitate no longer; under the miserable influence of Ritzio and her foreign correspondents she was bringing revolution and civil war upon Scotland, and the choice was forced upon him between his country and his personal affection.

He implored the Queen to pause. She reproached him with being a slave to England. He said 'that he could not consent to her marriage with one who he could not assure himself would set forth Christ's true religion.' She told him scornfully 'it was well known from whom he had received that lesson.' 'He answered with humility, but he would not sign;' and Mary was left to act alone or with her own and Darnley's friends, and to endeavour to rid herself of Murray by such other means as might offer themselves.[1]

Her messenger meanwhile had sped fast upon his way to England, and encountered Throgmorton at Newark. Mary Stuart concealing her resentment at Maitland's disobedience, sent him by Beton's hands 'the sweetest letter that ever subject received from sovereign,' wanting neither love, eloquence, despite, anger, nor passion; she bade him go back and tell Elizabeth that she had been trifled with too long, and that she would now follow her own mind and choice; with the advice of her nobles she would take such an one as she thought good, and she would no longer be fed with yea and nay, and depend on such uncertain dealing.'

But she had far mistaken Maitland if she believed that he would travel with her on the road into which

---

[1] Randolph to Cecil, May 8.—*Scotch MSS. Rolls House.*

she had been tempted by Ritzio. So desperate it seemed to him that he would have had her dragged back from it by force.

'I never saw Lidington in such perplexity and passion,' wrote Throgmorton; 'I could not have believed he could have been so moved; he wishes I had brought with me authority to declare war if the Queen of Scots persist, as the last refuge to stay her from this unadvised act.'

Mary Stuart's orders to Maitland to return to London were so distinct that he hesitated before he again disobeyed; he remained at Newark for a few hours after Throgmorton had gone forward; but the extremity was so serious that he ran all risks and overtook the ambassador at Alnwick. At the Border they heard the alarming news that Chatelherault had been bribed into compliance with the marriage 'by a written promise to enjoy his own.' 'Let the Earl of Northumberland be stayed in London,' Throgmorton wrote back to Leicester: 'from what I hear it is very necessary. Examine Sir Richard Cholmondley, and look well and sharp to the doings of that party.' 'The Papists in these parts do rouse themselves.' 'Look to yourselves and her Majesty's safety.' 'Sir Henry Percy is dangerous.'[1]

Time pressed. On the 15th Lord Darnley was to be created Earl of Ross at Stirling; when being an English subject he would swear allegiance to the Queen of Scots without leave sought or obtained from his own sovereign. A dukedom had been first intended for him; the higher title had been suspended, and the foolish boy struck with his dagger at the justice-clerk who was sent to tell

---

[1] Throgmorton to Leicester and Cecil, from Berwick, May 11 and 12.—Scotch MSS. Rolls House.

CHAP. VIII
1565
May

him of the unwelcome change. But whether earl or duke he would alike commit treason to Elizabeth, and Throgmorton hurried forward to be in time if possible to prevent a catastrophe which would make reconciliation hopeless. A message from the Queen of Scots met him at Edinburgh that he should have his audience when the creation was over, and that he must remain where he was till she sent for him. So well he wished to Mary that he would not obey; he pushed right on to Stirling and reached the castle on the morning of the fatal day. But the gates were locked in his face; and it was not till toward evening that he received an intimation that the Queen would receive him.

Throgmorton at Stirling.

When he was at last admitted into her presence the creation was over; the oath had been sworn; and the Queen of Scots stood triumphant, her eyes flashing pride and defiance, surrounded by half the northern lords. Sir Nicholas Throgmorton and Mary Stuart had last met on the eve of her departure from France, when he had vainly entreated her to ratify the Treaty of Edinburgh. He was now witnessing another act of the same drama.

In England he had been a warm advocate of her recognition, and she received him with gracious kindness. He presented his despatches; he then said that he was sent by the Queen of England to express 'her surprise at the hasty proceedings with the Lord Darnley, seeing how he and his father had failed of their duty in enterprising such a matter without her Majesty's knowledge and consent.'

Mary Stuart affecting the utmost surprise in turn professed herself at a loss to understand Elizabeth's meaning. It was not to be supposed, she said, that she would remain always unmarried; the foreign princes who had proposed for her had been unwelcome to the Queen of

England, and she had imagined that in taking an English nobleman who was equally acceptable to both realms she would have met her sister's wishes most exactly.

The truth sprung to Throgmorton's lips; he had been a true friend to her and he would speak plainly.

He told her that she knew very well what the Queen of England had desired; and she knew also that she was doing the very thing which was not desired. The Queen of England had wished her to take some one 'who would maintain the amity between the two nations;' and by Lord Darnley that amity would not be maintained.

Argument was of course unavailing. The Queen of Scots had on her side the letter of Elizabeth's words—for Darnley was the nominee of the English Catholics; and the Catholics outnumbered the Protestants. After some discussion she promised to suspend the celebration of the marriage for three months, in the hope that in the interval Elizabeth would look more favourably on it; but Throgmorton saw that she was determined; and he doubted whether she would adhere to the small concession which she had made.

'The matter is irrevocable,' he reported to Elizabeth; 'I do find this Queen so captivate either by love or cunning—or rather to say truly by boasting or folly—that she is not able to keep promise with herself, and therefore not able to keep promise with your Majesty in these matters.'[1]

Anticipating an immediate insurrection in Northumberland and Yorkshire, he begged that Bedford, who had gone to London, might return to Berwick without an hour's delay; and that the troops there might be largely reinforced. He returned at his leisure through

---

[1] Throgmorton to Elizabeth, May 21.—*Scotch MSS. Rolls House.*

CHAP. VIII
1565
May

Measures recommended to Elizabeth by Throgmorton.

York, to inform the Council there of the names of dangerous persons which he had learnt in Scotland; and meanwhile he sketched a course of action to Leicester and Cecil which would either prevent the marriage or cripple it with conditions which would deprive it of its danger.

Elizabeth he thought should immediately make public 'the indignity' which had been offered her by the Queen of Scots, and should declare without ambiguity her intention of 'chastising the arrogancy' of subjects who had disowned their allegiance. He recommended the arrest of the Earl of Northumberland, the detention of Lady Lennox 'in close and separate confinement,' and the adoption of prompt measures to disabuse 'the Papists' of their belief 'that they were themselves in credit and estimation.' An eye should be kept on the Spanish ambassador—'there the matter imported much'—and favour should be shown to Lady Catherine Grey, who though fast sinking under hard usage still survived. The English Government should avoid differences with France and Spain; and then ' either a breach of the matter would follow or else a good composition.'[1]

Randolph after Throgmorton's departure continued at his post, and sent up accounts from week to week of the position of parties and of the progress of the crisis.

He described Darnley as a conceited arrogant intolerable fool; he spoke of Murray as true to his mistress in the highest sense, and still labouring to save her from herself—of Maitland 'as more honest than many looked for'—of Argyle and the Lords of the old Congregation as true to their principles, and working all together—of the Earl of Ruthven alone 'as to his shame stirring coals to bring the marriage to effect.' 'Of the poor Queen her-

[1] Throgmorton to Cecil and Leicester, May 21.—*Scotch MSS. Rolls House.*

self' he knew not what to say, 'so pitiful her condition seemed to him;' 'he had esteemed her before,' he said, 'so worthy, so wise, so honourable in all her doings;' and he 'found her so altered with affection towards Lord Darnley that she had brought her honour in question, her estate in hazard, her country torn to pieces.'[1]

Affection it might be, or else as Maitland thought, 'the foundation of the matter might have been anger and despite:' so far from loving the weak idiot whom she had chosen, she was more likely already shuddering at the sacrifice which her ambition and revenge had demanded; Lord Darnley had few qualities to command either love or respect from Mary Stuart.

'David Ritzio,' continued Randolph in a later letter, 'is he that now worketh all, chief secretary to the Queen and only governor to her good man. The bruits here are wonderful, men's talk very strange, the hatred towards Lord Darnley and his house marvellous great, his pride intolerable, his words not to be borne, but where no man dare speak again. He spareth not also in token of his manhood to let blows fly where he knows they will be taken. When men have said all and thought what they can, they find nothing but that God must send him a short end or themselves a miserable life. They do not now look for help from England. Whatsoever I speak is counted but wind. If her Majesty will not use force let her spend three or four thousand pounds. It is worth the expense of so much money to cut off the suspicion that men make of her Majesty that she never liked thing in her life better than to see this Queen so meanly matched. She is now so much altered from that

[1] Randolph to Leicester and Cecil, May 21.—Scotch MSS. Rolls House.

which lately she was known to be that who now beholdeth her doth not think her to be the same. Her majesty is laid aside; her wits not such as they were; her beauty other than it was; her cheer and countenance changed into I wot not what—a woman more to be pitied than any that ever I saw. The Lord Darnley has said that if there were war to-morrow between England and Scotland, this Queen should find more friends in England than the Queen's Majesty's self.'[1]

Maitland continued to write confidentially to Cecil, promising to do his best to prevent a collision between the two countries, and entreating Cecil to assist him. Randolph, distracted by the suspicions of Elizabeth's motives which he saw round him, advised that 'unless the Queen of Scots was to be allowed to take her will,' an English army should advance to the Border, and that he should be himself empowered to promise the Congregation distinct and open support. In that case all would be well. 'The Papists should be bridled at home, and all intelligence cut off between them and the Scots: and either Mary Stuart would be put to the hardest shift that ever prince was at, or such a stir in Scotland that what part soever was strongest should be the longer liver.'[2]

The agitation in England after Throgmorton's return was almost as great. A series of remarkable papers remain to illustrate the alarm with which the crisis was regarded and to reveal many unexpected features in the condition of the country.

First is a paper in Cecil's hand, dated the 2nd of June,

---

[1] Randolph to Leicester and Cecil, June 3.—*Scotch MSS. Rolls House.*
[2] Randolph to Cecil, June 12.—*Ibid.*

entitled 'The perils and troubles that may presently ensue and in time to come follow upon the marriage of the Queen of Scots with the Lord Darnley.'

CHAP VIII
1565
June

'The minds,' thus this paper runs, 'of all such as be affected to the Queen of Scots either for herself, or for the opinion of her pretences to this Crown, or for the desire to have a change in the form of religion in this realm, or for the discontentation they have of the Queen's Majesty or her successors or of the succession of any other besides the Queen of Scots, shall be by this marriage erected comforted and induced to devise and labour how to bring their desires to pass; and to make some estimate what persons these are, to the intent the quantity of the peril may be weighed, the same may be composed in these sorts either within the realm or without.

Agitation in England.

'The first are such as are especially devoted to the Queen of Scots or the Lord Darnley by bond of blood and alliance—as all the House of Lorraine and Guise for her part, and the Earl of Lennox and his wife with all such in Scotland as be of their blood there and have received displeasure by the Duke of Chatelherault and the Hamiltons.

Probable consequences of the Darnley marriage.

'The second are all manner of persons both in this realm and in other countries that are devoted to the authority of Rome and mislike of the religion here received; and in these two sorts are the substance of them comprehended that shall take comfort in this marriage.

'Next therefore is to be considered what perils and troubles these kind of men shall intend to this realm.

'The general scope and mark of all their designs is and always shall be to bring the Queen of Scots to have the royal Crown of this realm; and therefore though their devices may vary amongst themselves for the compassing hereof, according to the accidents of the times, and according to the impediments which they shall find by means of the Queen's Majesty's actions and government, yet all their purposes shall wholly and only tend to make the Queen of Scots Queen of this realm and to deprive our sovereign lady thereof. And in these their proceedings there are two manner of things to be considered, the one of which is far worse than the other. The one is intended by them that, either for malicious blindness in religion or for natural affection to the Queen of Scots or the Lord Darnley, do persuade themselves that the said Queen of Scots hath presently more right to the Crown than our sovereign the Queen, of which sort be all their kindred of both sides and all such as are devoted to the Papacy either in England Scotland Ireland or elsewhere. The other is meant of them which less maliciously are persuaded that the Queen of Scots hath only right to be the next heir to succeed the Queen's Majesty and her issue, of which sort few are without the realm but here within; and yet of them not so many as are of the contrary. And from these two sorts shall the devices and practices proceed.

'From the first are to be looked for these perils. It is to be doubted that the devil will infect some of them to imagine the hindrance of our dearest sovereign lady by such means as the devil will suggest to them; although it is to be assuredly hoped that Almighty God will—as hitherto He hath—graciously protect and preserve her from such dangers.

'There will be attempted by persuasions, by bruits and rumours and such like to alienate the minds of good subjects from the Queen's Majesty, and to conciliate them to the Queen of Scots, and in this behalf the frontier and the north will be much solicited and laboured. There will be attempted tumults and rebellions, specially in the north towards Scotland, so as thereupon may follow some open extremity by violence. There will be by the said

Queen's Council and friends a new league made with France or Spain that shall be offensive to this realm and a furtherance to their title; and it is also likely they will set on foot as many practices as they can both upon the frontier and in Ireland to occasion the Queen's Majesty to continue her charges, thereby to retain her from being wealthy or potent. From the second is not much to be feared; but they will content themselves to serve notedly the Queen's Majesty and so to impeach her not to marry; but to hope that the Queen of Scots shall have issue, which they will think to be more plausible to all men because thereby the Houses of England and Scotland shall be united in one, and thereby the occasions of war shall cease; with which persuasions many people may be seduced and abused to incline themselves to the Queen of Scots.'[1]

CHAP VIII
1565
June

The several points thus prepared by Cecil for the consideration of the Council were enlarged in the discussion which ensued on them.

'By some it was thought plainly that the peril was greater by the marriage with the Lord Darnley than with the mightiest prince abroad;' a stranger would have few friends in England; the Lord Darnley being an English subject 'whatever power he could make by the faction of the Papists or other discontented persons would be so much deducted from the power of the realm.' 'A small faction of adversaries at home was more dangerous than thrice their number abroad;' and it was remembered that 'foreign powers had never prevailed in England but with the help of some at home.'

Especial dangers anticipated from the Darnley marriage.

It 'had been observed and manifestly seen before this

[1] COTTON MSS., CALIG. B. 10.

attempt at marriage that in every corner of the realm the factions that most favoured the Scottish title had grown stout and bold;' 'they had shown themselves in the very Court itself;' and unless checked promptly 'they would grow so great and dangerous as redress would be almost desperate.' 'Scarcely a third of the population were assured to be trusted in the matter of religion, upon which only string the Queen of Scots' title did hang;' and 'comfort had been given to the adversaries of religion in the realm to hope for change,' 'by means that the bishops had dealt straightly with some persons of good religion because they had forborne to wear certain apparel and such like things—being more of form and accident than any substance.' 'The pride and arrogancy of the Catholics had been increased' by the persecution of the Protestants; while if the bishops attempted to enforce conformity on the other side 'the judges and lawyers in the realm being not the best affected in religion did threaten them with premunire, and in many cases letted not to punish and defame them,' 'so that they dared not execute the ecclesiastical laws.'

For much of all this the Queen was responsible. She it was who more than any other person had nursed 'the Scottish faction' at the Court. If the bishops had been too eager to persecute the Catholics it was she who had compelled Parker to suspend the ablest of the Protestant ministers. 'But the sum of the perils was made so apparent as no one of the Council could deny them to be both many and very dangerous.' They were agreed every one of them that the Queen must for the present relinquish her zeal for uniformity, and that the prosecutions of the clergy must cease till the question could be reconsidered by Parliament; they determined to require the oath of allegiance of the judges, 'so that they should for conscience' sake maintain the Queen's authority,' to replace the nonjuring bishops in the Tower, to declare forfeited all benefices held by ecclesiastics who were residing abroad, and to drive out a number of seditious monks and friars who had fled across the Border from Scotland and were serving as curates in the northern churches. Bedford meanwhile should go down to Berwick taking additional troops with him; the 'powers of the Border' should be held in readiness to move at an hour's notice; and a reserve be raised in London to march north in case of war. Lennox and Darnley might then be required to return to England on their allegiance. If they refused they would be declared traitors and their extradition demanded of the Queen of Scots under the treaties.

So far the Council was unanimous. As to what should be done if the Queen of Scots refused to surrender them opinions were divided. The bolder party were for declaring immediate war and sending an army to Edinburgh; others preferred to wait till events had shaped themselves more distinctly; all however agreed on the necessity of vigour speed and resolution. 'No persons deserving of mistrust were to be suffered to have any rule of her Majesty's subjects or lands in the north;' they might 'retain their fees,' 'but more trusty persons should have the rule of their people.' The Earl of Murray and his friends should be comforted and supported; and 'considering the faction and title of the Queen of Scots had for a long time received great countenance by the Queen's Majesty's favour shown to the said Queen and her ministers,' the Council found themselves compelled to desire her Majesty 'by some exterior act to show some remission of her displeasure to the Lady Catherine and the Earl of Hertford.'

Further—for it was time to speak distinctly, and her Majesty's mode of dealing in such matters being better known than appreciated—she was requested after considering these advices to choose which of them she liked, and put them in execution *in deeds and not pass them over in consultations and speeches.*[1]

Nor did the Council separate without returning once more to the vexed question of the Queen's marriage. So long as she remained single they represented gravely that 'no surety could be devised to ascertain any person of continuance of their families and posterities.' The French affair had dragged on. Elizabeth had coquetted with it as a kitten plays with a ball. The French ambassador de Foix on the 2nd of May made an effort to force an answer from her one way or the other. 'The world,' he said, 'had been made in six days and she had already spent eighty and was still undecided.' Elizabeth had endeavoured to escape by saying that the world 'had been made by a greater artist than herself; that she was constitutionally irresolute and had lost many fair opportunities by a want of promptitude in seizing them.' Four days later on the receipt of bad news from Scotland she wavered towards acceptance: she wrote to Catherine de Medici to say 'that she could not decline an offer so generously made; she would call Parliament immediately, and if her subjects approved she was willing to abide by their resolution.'[2]

A Parliamentary discussion could not be despatched in a moment. The Queen-mother on receiving Elizabeth's

---

[1] The words in italics are underlined in the original.
Summary of consultations and advices given to her Majesty, June, 1565.—COTTON *MSS.*, CALIG. B. 10. Debates in Council, June 4, 1565.—*Scotch MSS. Rolls House.*

[2] 'La response de la Reyne,' May 6.—*French MSS. Rolls House.*

letter asked how soon she might expect an answer; and when Sir T. Smith told her that perhaps four months would elapse first, she affected astonishment at the necessity of so much ceremony. If the Queen of England was herself satisfied she thought it was enough.

'Madam,' replied Smith, 'her people be not like your people; they must be trained by douleeur and persuasion not by rigour and violence. There is no realm in Christendom better governed, better policied, and in more felicity of quiet and good order than is the realm of England; and in case my sovereign should go to work as ye say, God knows what would come of it; you have an opinion that her Majesty is wise; her answer is very much in a little space and containeth more substance of matter than multitude of words.'[1]

Catherine de Medici but half accepted the excuse, regarding it only as a pretext for delay. Yet Elizabeth was probably serious, and had the English Council been in favour of the marriage, in her desperation at the attitude of Mary Stuart she might have felt herself compelled to make a sacrifice which would insure for her the alliance of France. Paul de Foix one day at the end of May found her in her room playing chess.

'Madam,' he said to her, 'you have before you the game of life. You lose a pawn; it seems a small matter; but with the pawn you lose the game.'

'I see your meaning,' she answered. 'Lord Darnley is but a pawn, but unless I look to it I shall be checkmated.'

She rose from her seat led the ambassador apart and said bitterly she would make Lennox and his son smart for their insolence.

---

[1] Smith to Elizabeth, May, 1565.—*French MSS. Rolls House.*

De Foix admitted and made the most of the danger; 'her enemies,' he allowed, 'all over the world were wishing to see Mary Stuart and Darnley married,' and unfortunately there were also clearsighted able English statesmen who desired it as well as a means of uniting the crowns. 'But your Majesty,' he added, 'has in your hands both your own safety and your rival's ruin. France has been the shield of Scotland in its English wars. Take that shield for yourself. The world is dangerous, the strongest will fare the best, and your Majesty knows that the Queen of Scots dreads no one thing so much as your marriage with the most Christian King.'

With mournful irony Elizabeth replied that she did not deserve so much happiness.[1] The English Council in pressing her to take a husband was thinking less of a foreign alliance than of an heir to the Crown; and the most Christian King was unwelcome to her advisers for the reason perhaps for which she would have preferred him to any other suitor. The full-grown able-bodied Archduke Charles was the person on whom the hearts of the truest of her statesmen had long been fixed. The Queen referred de Foix to the Council; and the Council on the 2nd of June informed him 'that on mature consideration and with a full appreciation of the greatness of the offer, the age of the King of France, the uncertainty of the English succession, and the unlikelihood of children from that marriage for several years at least obliged them to advise their mistress to decline his proposals.'[2]

The next day Elizabeth sent for the ambassador of the Duke of Wirtemberg who was acting in England in behalf of Maximilian. She told him that she had once

---

[1] Paul de Foix to the Queen-mother, June 3.—TEULET, vol. ii.
[2] MIGNET's *Mary Stuart*, vol. i. p. 146.

resolved to live and die a maiden Queen; but she deferred to the remonstrances of her subjects, and she desired him to tell the Emperor that she had at last made up her mind to marry.[1] She had inquired of the Spanish ambassador whether the King of Spain still wished to see her the wife of his cousin. The ambassador had assured her that the King could not be more anxious if the Archduke had been a child of his own. She said that she could not bind herself to accept a person whom she had never seen; but she expressed her earnest wish that the Archduke should come to England.

The minister of Wirtemberg in writing to Maximilian added his own entreaties to those of the Queen; he said that 'there was no fear for the Archduke's honour; the Queen's situation was so critical that if the Archduke would consent to come she could not dare to affront the imperial family by afterwards refusing his hand.'[2]

---

[1] 'Se constituisse nunc nubere.'
[2] Adam Schetowitz to Maximilian, June 4, 1565.—BURLEIGH Papers, vol. i.

CHAPTER IX.

THE two Queens were again standing in the same relative positions which had led to the crisis of 1560. Mary Stuart was once more stretching out her hand to grasp Elizabeth's Crown. From her recognition as heir presumptive the step to a Catholic revolution was immediate and certain; and Elizabeth's affectation of Catholic practices would avail little to save her. Again as before the stability of the English Government appeared to depend on the maintenance of the Protestants in Scotland; and again the Protestants were too weak to protect themselves without help from abroad. The House of Hamilton was in danger from the restitution of Lennox and the approaching elevation of Darnley; the Earl of Lennox claimed the second place in the Scotch succession in opposition to the Duke of Chatelherault; and the Queen of Scots had avowed her intention of entailing her Crown in the line of the Stuarts. Thus there were the same parties and the same divisions. But the Protestants were split among themselves among the counter influences of hereditary alliance and passion. The cession of her claims on the Earldom of Angus by Lady Margaret had won to Darnley's side the powerful and dangerous Earl of Morton, and had alienated from Murray the kindred houses of Ruthven and Lindsay. There was no longer an Arran marriage to cajole the patriotism of the many noblemen to whom the glory of Scotland was dearer than their creed; and all those whose hearts were set on winning for a Scotch prince or princess the English succession were now devoted to their Queen. Thus the Duke of Chatelherault with the original group who had formed the nucleus of the Congregation—Murray, Argyle, Glencairn, Boyd, and Ochiltree—found themselves alone against the whole power of their country.

Secure on the side of France, Elizabeth would have been less uneasy at the weakness of the Protestants had the loyalty of her own subjects been open to no suspicion; but the state of England was hardly more satisfactory than that of Scotland. In 1560 the recent loss of Calais and the danger of foreign invasion had united the nation in defence of its independence. Two-thirds of the peers were opposed at heart to Cecil's policy; but the menaces of France had roused the patriotism of the nation. Spain was then perplexed and neutral; and the Catholics had for a time been paralyzed by the recent memories of the Marian persecution.

Now, although the dangers were the same, Elizabeth's embarrassments were incomparably greater. The studied trifling with which she had disregarded the general anxiety for her marriage had created a party for the Queen of Scots amidst the most influential classes of the people. The settlement of the succession was a passion among them which amounted to a disease; while the union of the Crowns was an object of rational desire to every thoughtful English statesman. The Protestants were disheartened; they had gained no wisdom by suffering; the most sincere among them were as wild and intolerant as those who had made the reign of

Edward a byeword of mismanagement; the Queen was as unreasonable with them on her side as they were extravagant on theirs; while Catholicism recovering from its temporary paralysis was reasserting the superiority which the matured creed of centuries has a right to claim over the half-shaped theories of revolution. Had Mary Stuart followed the advice which Alva gave to her messenger at Bayonne, had she been prudent and forbearing and trusted her cause to time till Philip had disposed of the Turks and was at leisure to give her his avowed support, the game was in her hands. Her choice of Darnley sanctioned as it was by Spain, had united in her favour the Conservative strength of England; and either Elizabeth must have allowed the marriage and accepted the Queen of Scots as her successor, or she must have herself yielded to pressure, fulfilled her promises at last, and married the Archduke Charles.

This possibility and this alone created Mary's difficulties. She knew what Philip's engagements meant; she knew that Spain desired as little as France to see England and Scotland a united and powerful kingdom; and that if Elizabeth could be recalled out of her evil ways by a Catholic alliance, the cabinet of Madrid would think no more of Darnley or herself. She would have to exchange an immediate and splendid triumph for the doubtful prospect of the eventual succession should her rival die without a child.

Nor did Elizabeth herself misunderstand the necessity to which she would be driven unless Mary Stuart saved her by some false move. She had played so often with the Archduke's name that her words had ceased to command belief; but at last she was thinking of him seriously—the more seriously perhaps because many Englishmen who had before been most eager to provide

her with a husband were now as well or better satisfied
with the prospect of the succession of the Queen of Scots.

'The Queen,' de Silva wrote on the 8th of June to
Philip, 'has taken alarm at the divisions among her
subjects. A great many of them she is well aware are
in favour of Lord Darnley and Mary Stuart. Several
of the most powerful noblemen in England have long
withdrawn from the Court and are looking to this
marriage for the union of the two Crowns. The Queen
must now come to a resolution about the Archduke
Charles. She understands fully that a marriage with
him is the sole means left to her of preserving her
alliance with your Majesty, of resisting her enemies, and
of preventing a rebellion. She detests the thought of
it; and yet so strange is her position that she dares not
encounter Parliament for fear her excuses may be accepted.
The people have ceased to care whether she
marries or remains single; they are ready to entail the
Crown on the King and Queen of Scotland.

'Her hope at present is to throw Scotland into confusion
with the help of the Duke of Chatelherault, who
cannot endure that the House of Lennox should be preferred
to the Hamiltons. She is frightening the Huguenots
in France by telling them that if the Queen of
Scots obtains the English Crown she will avenge her
uncle's death and assist the Catholics to extirpate them.
She will temporize till she see how her tricks succeed.
If she can save herself by any other means she will not
marry.'[1]

The two players were not ill-matched, though for the
present the Queen of Scots had the advantage. 'The

---

[1] 'Por las Cartas de Londres, de viii. Junio, 1565.'—*MS. Simancas.*

matter,' said Sir Thomas Smith, 'was not so suddenly done as suddenly it did break out; the practice was of an older time. It was finely handled to make the Queen's Majesty a labourer for the restitution of the father and a sender in of the son.'[1] Elizabeth had been outmanœuvred and had placed herself in a perilous dilemma. Half the Council had advised her to demand the extradition of Darnley and Lennox and declare war if it was refused. She had rejected the bolder part of the advice; but she had allowed Throgmorton to promise Murray and his friends that if they interfered by force to prevent the marriage they should be supported by England; and if they rose in arms and failed, and if they called upon her to fulfil her engagements, she would have to comply and run all hazards, or she would justify the worst suspicions which the Scotch Protestants already entertained of her sincerity, and convert into enemies the only friends that she possessed among Mary Stuart's subjects.

In the first outburst of her anger she seemed prepared to dare everything. After the departure of Throgmorton from Scotland the Queen of Scots sent Hay of Balmerinoch with a letter in which she protested with the most innocent simplicity that in all which she had done she had been actuated only by the purest desire to meet her dear sister's wishes; that she was alike astonished and grieved to hear that she had done wrong; but that as Elizabeth was dissatisfied she would refer the question once more to a commission; and on her own side she proposed the unsuspicious names of Murray, Maitland, Morton, and Glencairn.[2]

Had Elizabeth complied with this suggestion she

Smith to Cecil, July 3.—*French MSS. Rolls House.*
[2] The Queen of Scots to the Queen of England, June 14.—KEITH.

would have committed herself to an admission that a question existed, and that the Darnley marriage was not wholly intolerable. She had no intention of admitting anything of the kind. She replied with requiring Lennox and Darnley on their allegiance to return immediately to England; and the Queen of Scots' letter she answered only with a request that they might be sent home without delay.

Neither Lennox nor Mary expected such peremptory dealing. The order of return was short of a declaration of war, and some of those who knew Elizabeth best did not believe that war was coming;[1] but Mary Stuart knew too well her own intentions to escape misgivings that the Queen of England might be as resolute as herself. When Randolph presented the letter with the message which accompanied it, she burst into tears; Lennox was silent with dismay; Darnley alone, too foolish to comprehend the danger, remained careless and defiant,[2] and said shortly 'he had no mind to return.' Mary Stuart as soon as she could collect herself said she trusted that her good sister did not mean what she had written. Randolph replied that she most certainly did mean it; and speaking plainly as his habit was, he added 'that if they refused to return and her Grace comforted them in so doing, the Queen his mistress had both

---

[1] Paul de Foix to Catherine de Medici, June 18.—TEULET, vol. ii.

[2] A sad and singular horoscope had already been cast for Darnley. 'His behaviour,' Randolph wrote to Cecil, 'is such that he is come in open contempt of all men that were his chief friends. What shall become of him I know not; but it is greatly to be feared he can have no long life amongst this people. The Queen being of better understanding, seeketh to frame and fashion him to the nature of her subjects; but no persuasion can alter that which custom hath made in him. He is counted proud, disdainful, and suspicious, which kind of men this soil of any other can least bear.'—*Randolph to Cecil, July 2.*—COTTON MSS., CALIG. B. 10. *Printed in* KEITH.

power and will to be revenged on them, being her subjects.'

From the Court Randolph went to Argyle and Murray, who had ascertained meanwhile that there was no time to lose; the Bishop of Dunblane had been sent to the Pope; Mary Stuart had obtained money from Flanders; she had again sent for Bothwell, and she meant immediate mischief. The two earls expressed their belief that 'the time was come to put to a remedy.' 'They saw their sovereign determined to overthrow religion received, and sore bent against those that desired the amity with England to be continued, which two points they were bound in conscience to maintain and defend.' They had resolved therefore 'to withstand such attempts with all their power, and to provide for their sovereign's estate better than she could at that time consider for herself.' They intended to do nothing which was not for their mistress's real advantage; Sir Nicholas Throgmorton had assured them of the Queen of England's 'godly and friendly offer to concur with and assist them;' the Queen of England's interest was as much concerned as their own; and they 'humbly desired the performance of her Majesty's promises:' they did not ask for an English army; if her Majesty would give them three thousand pounds they could hold their followers together, and would undertake the rest for themselves; Lennox and Darnley could be seized and 'delivered into Berwick,' if her Majesty would receive them.

To these communications Randolph replied with renewed assurances that Elizabeth would send them whatever assistance they required. He gave them the warmest encouragement to persevere; and as to the father and son whom they proposed to kidnap, the English

Government, he said, 'could not and would not refuse their own in what sort soever they came.'[1]

The Queen of Scots was not long in receiving intelligence of what the lords intended against her. She sent a message to her brother requesting that he would meet her at Perth. As he was mounting his horse a hint was given him that if he went he would not return alive, and that Darnley and Ritzio had formed a plan to kill him. He withdrew to his mother's castle at Lochleven and published the occasion of his disobedience. Mary Stuart replied with a countercharge that the Earl of Murray had purposed to take her prisoner and carry off Darnley to England. Both stories were probably true: Murray's offer to Randolph is sufficient evidence against himself. Lord Darnley's conspiracy against the Earl was no more than legitimate retaliation. Civil war was fast approaching; and it is impossible to acquit Elizabeth of having done her best to foster it. Afraid to take an open part lest she should have an insurrection on her own hands at home, she was ready to employ to the uttermost the assistance of the Queen of Scots' own subjects, and she trusted to diplomacy or accident to extricate herself from the consequences.

On receiving Randolph's letter, which explained with sufficient clearness the intentions of the Protestant noblemen, she not only did not find fault with the engagements to which he had committed her, but she directed him under her own hand to assure them of her perfect satisfaction with the course which they were preparing to pursue. She could have entertained no sort of doubt that they would use violence; yet she did not

---

[1] Randolph to Cecil, July 2 and July 4.—COTTON MSS., CALIG. D. 10. Printed in KEITH.

even conceal her approbation under ambiguous or uncertain phrases. She said that they should find her 'in all their just and honourable causes regard their state and continuance;' 'if by malice or practice they were forced to any inconveniency they should find no lack in her;' she desired merely that in carrying out their enterprise they would 'spend no more money than their security made necessary, nor less which might bring danger.'[1]

Measures of the General Assembly. As the collision drew near both parties prepared for it by endeavouring to put themselves right with the country. No sooner was it generally known in Scotland that the Queen intended to marry a Catholic than the General Assembly rushed together at Edinburgh. The extreme Protestants were able to appeal to the fulfilment of their predictions of evil when Mary Stuart was permitted the free exercise of her own religion. Like the children of Israel on their entrance into Canaan, they had made terms with wickedness: they had sown the wind of a carnal policy and were now reaping the whirlwind. A resolution was passed—to which Murray, though he was present, no longer raised his voice in opposition—that the sovereign was not exempt from obedience to the law of the land, that the mass should be put utterly away, and the reformed service take the place of it in the royal chapel.

Mary Stuart had been described by Randolph as so much changed that those who had known her when she was under Murray's and Maitland's tutelage were astonished at the alteration; manner, words, features, all were different; in mind and body she was said to be swollen and disfigured by the tumultuous working of her passions.

---

[1] Elizabeth to Randolph, July 10.—*Printed in* KEITH.

So perhaps she may have appeared in Randolph's eyes; and yet the change may have been more in Randolph's power of insight than in the object at which he looked. Never certainly did she show herself cooler or more adroit than in her present emergency. She replied to the Assembly with returning from Perth to Edinburgh; and as a first step towards recovering their confidence she attended a Protestant sermon. To the resolution of the General Assembly she delayed her answer, but she issued circulars protesting that neither then nor at any past time had she entertained a thought of interfering with her subjects' religion; the toleration which she had requested for herself she desired only to extend to others; her utmost wish had been that her subjects might worship God freely in the form which each most approved.[1]

A Catholic sovereign sincerely pleading to a Protestant Assembly for liberty of conscience might have been a lesson to the bigotry of mankind; but Mary Stuart was not sincere; and could the Assembly have believed her they would have thought her French teaching was bearing fruits more deadly than Popery itself. The Protestant respected the Catholic as an honest worshipper of something, though that something might be the devil. 'Liberty of conscience' was the crime of the Laodiceans, which hell and heaven alike rejected.

The attendance of Mary Stuart at sermon produced as little effect on the Congregation as Elizabeth's candles and crucifixes on the hatred of the English Papists. The elders of the Church dispersed; Argyle, Murray, and their friends withdrew to Stirling; and on the 18th of July they despatched a messenger to Elizabeth with a bond in which they pledged themselves to resist all attempts

---

[1] Circular by the Queen, July 17.

either to restore the Catholic ritual or to dissolve the English alliance. From their own sovereign they professed to hope for nothing but evil. They looked to the Queen of England 'as under God protectress most special of the professors of religion;' and they thanked her warmly for the promises of help on which it was evident that they entirely relied.[1]

They relied on those promises; and to have doubted them would have been nothing less than a studied insult. The English ambassador was ordered a second time, and more imperiously, to command Lennox and Darnley to go back to England; while avowedly by the direct instructions of his mistress he laid her thanks and wishes before the lords in a formal and written address.[2]

RANDOLPH TO THE LORDS OF SCOTLAND.[3]

July, 1565.

'Right Honourable and my very good Lords,—It is not out of your remembrance that Sir Nicholas Throgmorton being at Stirling ambassador for the Queen's Majesty my mistress to the Queen's Majesty your sovereign, it was declared at good length both to her Grace's self and also to you of her honourable Council, what misliking the Queen my mistress hath that the Lord Darnley should join marriage with the Queen your sovereign, for divers and weighty reasons;

---

[1] 'Understanding by your Highness's ambassador, Sir N. Throgmorton, and also by the information of your Majesty's servant Master Randolph, the good and gracious mind which your Majesty with continuance beareth to the maintenance of the Gospel and us that profess the same,' &c.—*The Lords in Stirling to the Queen of England, July 18.* KEITH, vol. ii. p. 329.

[2] It is necessary, at the risk of being tedious, to dwell on these particulars of Elizabeth's conduct. Each separate promise was as a nail which left a rent in her reputation when she endeavoured to free herself.

[3] LANSDOWNE *MSS.* 8.

of which some were there presently rehearsed, others for great and weighty respects left unspoken until occasion better serve to utter her Majesty's griefs for the strange manner of dealing that hath been used towards her divers ways and by divers persons contrary to that expectation she had. The Queen your sovereign having answered that she would in no wise alter her determination, the Queen my mistress commanded this resolution and answer to be propounded in Council, and to be considered according to the weight thereof, being touched thereby as well in honour as that it was against the repose and tranquillity of her Majesty's realm. And her Majesty's Council remaining in that mind that before they were of—which is that divers ways it must needs be prejudicial to the amity of the two countries, that it tendeth greatly to the subversion of Christ's true religion received and established in them both, they have not only received that with content which your lordships have subscribed with your hands, but also have become suitors to your Majesty that she will provide for her own surety and the surety of the realm against all practices and devices, from wheresoever they be intended.

'And forasmuch as nothing is more needful for both the realms than the continuance of a good and perfect amity between them and those whose hearts God hath united in one true and perfect doctrine, they have also desired that it will please her Majesty that she will have consideration of the Protestants and true professors of religion in this realm of Scotland, that Christ's holy word may be continued amongst them, and the amity remain betwixt both the countries. And because of all the apparent troubles that may ensue, as well for the subversion of Christ's word in both the countries as also for the breach of amity, the Earl of Lennox and his son the Lord Darnley are known to be the authors, and many of their practices, as well in England, Scotland and further parts, to that end discovered, it pleased the Queen my mistress to begin at the root and ground of all these mischiefs, and thereof hath presently sent her express commandment to them both, charging them to leave the realm of Scotland and repair unto her presence as they will avoid her Majesty's indignation; in refusing of which they shall give further occasion for her to proceed against them and their assisters than willingly she would.

'And to the intent it may be further known what the Queen's my mistress's purpose is if they do contrary to this charge of her Majesty, I am commanded to assure all persons here that the Queen my mistress meaneth to let the Queen your sovereign well understand by her deeds how she can measure this dishonourable kind of dealing and manner of proceeding; and according to the effect of such answers as shall be given unto me, as well from the Queen's Majesty your sovereign as from the Earl of Lennox and his son, and what thereof shall follow, her Majesty meaneth to let it manifestly appear unto the world how to use her towards such as so far forget themselves.

'To give also declaration of the tender care and good consideration the Queen my sovereign has over all those of this nation that mind to keep the realm without alteration of the religion received and will not neglect her Majesty's friendship, I am commanded to assure all such as persist therein that it is fully resolved and determined to concur with them and assist them as either need or occasion shall press them.

'This, my lords, being the effect of that which I know to be my mistress's will and express commandment given unto me to communicate unto your lordships as I saw cause, and knowing now the time most fit for that purpose, I thought good to send this same to you in writing.'

In strict conformity with these promises the Earl of Bedford returned to his charge on the Border; the Earl himself was under the impression that if the lords were in extremity he was to enter Scotland; and so satisfied and so confident was Murray that he wrote to Bedford on the 22nd of July 'as to one to whom God had granted to know the subtle devices of Satan,' telling him that the force on which the Queen of Scots most relied lay among the Maxwells, the Humes, and the Kers of the Border, and begging him, as if he was already an auxiliary in the field, 'to stay off their power.'[1]

Randolph presented his second demand for the return of the two noblemen to England. He spoke first to Mary Stuart, who half frightened, half defiant, found herself on the edge of a conflict to which her own resources were manifestly inadequate, while she could not but feel some uncertainty after all, how far she could rely on the secret promises of her English friends. She complained passionately that she had been trifled with; she spoke of Henry the Eighth's will which she dared Elizabeth to produce, in obvious ignorance that had Elizabeth consented, her hopes of a peaceable succession would be gone for ever. Randolph told her she was 'abused.' She threatened that if the English Parliament meddled with the rights either of herself or of Darnley she would 'seek friends elsewhere,' and would not fail to find them.

Randolph knew Mary well and knew her manner. He

---

[1] Murray to Bedford, July 22.—KEITH.

saw that she was hesitating and he once more attempted expostulation. 'The Queen of England,' he truly said, 'had been her kindest friend. She might have compelled her to ratify the Treaty of Edinburgh; but she had passed it over; she had defended her claims when the Scotch succession had not another supporter; unless she had taken the crown from off her own head and given it to her, she could have done no more than she had done.' Mary appeared to be moved. She asked if nothing could induce Elizabeth to allow her marriage with Lord Darnley. Randolph replied that after the attitude which she had assumed the conditions would be stringent. A declaration would have to be made by herself and the Scotch Parliament that she made no pretensions to the English crown during the life of Elizabeth or her children; she must restore to her Council the Protestant noblemen with whom she had quarrelled; and she must conform[1] to the religion established by law in Scotland.[2]

It was to ask Mary Stuart to sacrifice ambition, pride, revenge—every object for which she was mating herself with the paltry boy who was the cause of the disturbance. She said 'she would make no merchandize of her conscience.' Randolph requested in Elizabeth's name that she would do no injury to the Protestant lords who were her 'good subjects.' She replied that Elizabeth

---

[1] It is interesting to observe how the current of the Reformation had swept Elizabeth forward in spite of herself.

[2] 'Qu'elle entretienne la religion qui est aujourdhuy au Royaulme, et en ce faysant recoyve, on sa bonne grace, et en leur premier estat ceulx qu'elle a aliené d'elle; et qu'elle luy face declaration, autorisée par son Parlement qu'elle ne pretend rien au Royaulme d'elle, ne de sa posterité.'—*Analyse d'une depêche de M. de Fois au Roy, August 12.*—TEULET, vol. ii.

might call them 'good subjects;' she had found them bad subjects, and as such she meant to treat them.

The turn of Lennox and Darnley came next. The ambassador communicated Elizabeth's commands to them, and demanded a distinct answer whether they would obey or not. Lennox, to whom age had taught some lessons of moderation, replied that he was sorry to offend; but that he might not and durst not go. He with some justice might plead a right to remain; for he was a born Scot and was living under his first allegiance. Darnley, like a child who has drifted from the shore in a tiny pleasure boat, his sails puffed out with vanity, and little dreaming how soon he would be gazing back on England with passionate and despairing eyes, replied 'that he acknowledged no duty or obedience save to the Queen of Scots' whom he served and honoured; 'and seeing,' he continued, 'that the other your mistress is so envious of my good fortune, I doubt not but she may also have need of me, as you shall know within few days; wherefore to return I intend not; I find myself very well where I am, and so I purpose to keep me; and this shall be for your answer.'

'You have much forgotten your duty, sir, in such despiteful words,' Randolph answered; 'it is neither discreetly spoken of you nor otherwise to be answered by me than that I trust to see the wreck and overthrow of as many as are of the same mind.'

So saying the stout servant of Elizabeth turned on his heel 'without reverence or farewell.'[1]

Elizabeth's attitude and Randolph's language were as menacing as possible. But experience had taught Mary Stuart that between the threats and the actions of the

---

[1] Randolph to Cecil, July 21.—COTTON MSS., CALIG. B. 10.

Queen of England there was always a period of irresolution; and that with prompt celerity she might crush the disaffection of Scotland while her more dangerous enemy was making up her mind. She filled Edinburgh with the retainers of Lennox and Huntly; she summoned Murray to appear and prove his accusations against Darnley under pain of being declared a traitor; she sent a message through de Silva to Philip that her subjects had risen in insurrection against her with the support of the Queen of England to force her to change her religion;[1] and interpreting the promise of three months' delay which she had made to Throgmorton as meaning a delay into the third month, she resolved to close one element of the controversy and place the marriage itself beyond debate. On the evening of the 28th of July Edinburgh was informed by trumpet and proclamation that the Queen of Scots having determined to take to herself as her husband Henry Earl of Ross and Albany, the said Henry was thenceforth to be designated King of Scotland, and in all acts and deeds his name would be associated with her own.[2] The crowd listened in silence. A tingle voice cried 'God save his Grace!' but the speaker was Lennox.

Marriage of Mary Stuart and Darnley.

The next day July the 29th being Sunday, while the drowsy citizens of Edinburgh were still in their morning sleep, Mary Stuart became the wife of Darnley. The ceremony took place in the royal chapel just after sunrise. It was performed by a Catholic priest, and with

---

[1] De Silva to Philip, July 28.— *MS. Simancas.*
[2] The title was a mere sound. The crown matrimonial could be conferred only by Act of Parliament; nor would Mary Stuart share the reality of her power with a raw boy whose character she imperfectly knew. But Darnley was impatient for the name of king; 'He would in no case have it deferred a day,' and the Queen was contented to humour him.

the usual Catholic rites; the Queen for some strange reason appearing at the altar in a mourning dress of black velvet, 'such as she wore the doleful day of the burial of her husband.' Whether it was an accident—whether the doom of the House of Stuart haunted her at that hour with its fatal foreshadowings—or whether simply for a great political purpose she was doing an act which in itself she loathed, it is impossible to tell; but that black drapery struck the spectators with a cold uneasy awe.

But such dreamy vanities were soon forgotten. The deed was done which Elizabeth had forbidden. It remained to be seen to what extremity Elizabeth in her resentment would be provoked. The lords had been long waiting at Stirling for a sign from Berwick; but no sign came, and when the moment of extremity arrived Bedford had no definite orders. They remembered 1559, when they had been encouraged by similar promises to rebel, and when Elizabeth had trifled with her engagements so long and so dangerously. Elizabeth had given her word; but it was an imperfect security; and the uncertainty produced its inevitable effect in disheartening and dividing them. 'Though your intent be never so good to us,' Randolph wrote to Leicester on the 31st of July, 'yet we fear your delay that our ruin shall prevent your support; when council is once taken nothing is so needful as speedy execution: upon this we wholly depend; in her Majesty's hands it standeth to save our lives or suffer us to perish; greater honour her Majesty cannot have than that which lieth in her power to do for us.'[1]

While the Congregation were thus held in suspense,

---

[1] Wright's *Elizabeth*, vol. i.

Mary Stuart was all fire energy and resolution. She understood at once that Elizabeth was hesitating; she knew that she had little to fear from Argyle and Murray until they were supported in force from England; and leaving no time for faction to disintegrate her own supporters or for the Queen of England to make up her mind, she sent letters to the noblemen on whom she could rely, desiring them to meet her in arms at Edinburgh on the 9th of August.

Elizabeth as post after post came in from Scotland lost her breath at the rapidity of the Queen of Scots' movements; and resolution became more impossible as the need of it became more pressing. On receiving the news that the marriage was actually completed she despatched Tamworth, a gentleman of the bedchamber, to assure the Queen of Scots that whatever might be pretended to the contrary she had throughout been sincerely anxious to support her interests. The Queen of Scots had not given her the credit which she deserved, and was now 'imagining something else in England to content her fancy, as vain persons sometimes would.' Leaving much to Tamworth's discretion, she bade him nevertheless let the Queen of Scots see that her present intentions were thoroughly understood. 'She was following the advice of those who were labouring to extirpate out of Scotland the religion received there; 'the Protestants among her own subjects were to be destroyed ' to gain the favour of the Papists in England;' 'so as with the aid that they would hope to have of some prince abroad and from Rome also upon pretence of reformation in religion, she might when she should see time attempt the same that she did when she was married to France.' It was not for Elizabeth to say what might happen in Scotland;

'but for any other device that the Queen of Scots might be fed withal, she might be assured before God she would find all designs, consultations, intelligences, and advices, from wherever they might come to her, far or near, to be vain and deceitful.' Let her relinquish these idle imaginings, let her restore Murray to the Council and undertake to enter into no foreign alliance prejudicial to English interests, and she might yet regain the confidence of her true friends.

Had Tamworth's instructions gone no further they would have been useless without being mischievous; but a further message betrayed the fatal irresolution to which Elizabeth was yielding. A fortnight previously she had required the Queen of Scots to abandon her own creed; she now condescended to entreat that if her other requests were rejected the Scotch Protestants might at least be permitted to use their own religion without molestation.[1] She might have frightened Mary by a demonstration of force as prompt as her own. To show that she saw through her schemes, yet at the same time that she dared not venture beyond a feeble and hesitating protest, could but make the Queen of Scots desperate of further concealment, and encourage her to go forward more fearlessly than ever.

'Mary Stuart,' when Tamworth came into her presence, 'gave him words that bit to the quick.' To the Queen of England's suspicions she said she would reply with her 'own lawful demands.' 'The Queen of England spoke of imaginations and fancies;' 'she was sorry her good sister thought so disdainfully of her as she would meddle with simple devices. If things went so that she was driven to extremities and practices, she

---

[1] Instructions to Tamworth, August 1.—*MS. Rolls House.*

would make it appear to the world that her devices were not to be set at so small a price.' Playing on Elizabeth's words with a straightforward but irritating irony, she said 'that by God's grace it should appear to the world that her designs, consultations, and intelligences would prove as substantial and no more vain and deceitful than such as her neighbours themselves had at any time taken in hand;' while as to Murray's restoration she had never yet meddled between the Queen of England and her subjects; but now 'induced by her good sister's example,' 'she would request most earnestly for the release and restoration to favour' of her mother-in-law the Lady Margaret, Countess of Lennox.[1]

Had Philip of Spain been at Mary's shoulder he would have advised her to spare her sarcasms till an armada was in the Channel or till Elizabeth was a prisoner at her feet. As soon as she had made sure of Darnley he would have recommended her to omit no efforts for conciliation. She need not have relinquished one emotion of hatred or one aspiration for revenge; but she would have been taught to wait upon time to soothe down the irritation which she had roused, to cajole with promises, and to compel Elizabeth by the steady if slow pressure of circumstances to give way step by step.

But Mary Stuart was young and was a woman. Her tongue was ready and her passions strong. Philip cared sincerely for Romanism, Elizabeth cared for English liberty, the Earl of Murray cared for the doctrines of the Reformation; Mary Stuart was chiefly interested in herself, and she was without the strength of self-command which is taught only by devotion to a cause. So con-

---

[1] Answer of the Queen of Scots to Tamworth.— Printed in KEITH

fident was she that in imagination she had already
seated herself on Elizabeth's throne. To the conditions of friendship offered by Tamworth she replied
in language which could scarcely have been more
peremptory had she entered London at the head of a
victorious army. Not condescending to notice what was
demanded of herself, she required Elizabeth immediately
to declare her by Act of Parliament next in the succession; and failing herself and her children, to entail the
Crown on Lady Margaret Lennox and her children 'as
the persons by the law of God and nature next inheritable.' The Queen of England should bind herself
'neither to do nor suffer to be done either by law or
otherwise' anything prejudicial to the Scottish title; to
abstain in future from all practices with subjects of the
Scottish Crown; to enter no league and contract no
alliance which could affect the Queen of Scots' fortunes
unfavourably. On these terms, but on these alone,
she would consent to leave Elizabeth in undisturbed
possession during her own or her children's lifetime; she
would abstain from encouraging the English Catholics
to rise in rebellion in her behalf, and from inviting an
invasion from Spain or France;[1] and she condescended
to promise—to throw dust in the eyes of the Protestants
in both countries—although she was receiving the support of the Pope and seeking the support of the King of
Spain in the sole interests of Romanism—that in the
event of herself and her husband succeeding to the
throne of England, the religion established there by law
should not be interfered with.

An answer every sentence of which must have stung

---

[1] Offer of the King and Queen of Scotland, by Mr. Tamworth, August, 1565.—*Scotch MSS. Rolls House.*

Elizabeth like a whip-lash, might have for the moment satisfied Mary Stuart's passion; but her hatred of her sister of England was passing into contempt, and she believed she might trample upon her with impunity.

Tamworth having received his message desired to return with it to England. He applied for a passport, which was given him signed by Darnley as King of Scotland; and Elizabeth had forbidden him to recognize Darnley in any capacity but that of the Queen's husband. He desired that the wording might be changed: his request was refused. He requested that a guard might escort him to the Border: it could not be granted. He set out without attendance and without a safe-conduct: he was arrested and carried prisoner to Hume Castle.

The lords at Stirling had been already so perplexed by Elizabeth's timidity that they had broken up and dispersed. Argyle and Murray retired to the western Highlands, and sent an earnest message that unless they could be immediately relieved they would be overthrown.[1] The arrest of Tamworth added to their dismay. Yet in spite of past experience they could not believe Elizabeth capable of breaking promises so emphatically and so repeatedly made to them. They wrote through Randolph that they were still at the Queen of England's devotion. They would hold out as long as their strength lasted; but it was already tasked to the uttermost, and if left to themselves they would have to yield to superior force.

The catastrophe came quicker than they anticipated. The friends of the Congregation were invited by circulars to meet at Ayr on the 24th of August. On the 25th the Queen of Scots—after a tempestuous interview

---

[1] Tamworth to Cecil and Leicester, August 10.—*Scotch MSS. Rolls House.*

with Randolph, who had demanded Tamworth's release —mounted her horse and rode out of Edinburgh at the head of 5000 men to meet her enemies in the field. Darnley, in gilt armour, was at her side. She herself carried pistols in hand and pistols at her saddlebow. Her one peculiar hope was to encounter and destroy her brother, against whom, above and beyond his political opposition, she bore an especial and unexplained animosity.[1]

---

[1] 'I never heard more outrageous words than she spoke against my Lord of Murray. She said she would rather lose her crown than not be revenged upon him. She has some further cause of quarrel with him than she cares to avow.'—*Randolph to Cecil, August 27. MS. Rolls House.* Shortly after, Randolph imagined that he had discovered the 'further cause.' 'The hatred conceived against my Lord of Murray is neither for his religion nor yet for that she now speaketh—that he would take the crown from her, as she said lately to myself—but that she knoweth that he knoweth some such secret fact, not to be named for reverence sake, that standeth not with her honour, which he so much detesteth, being her brother, that neither can he show himself as he hath done, nor she think of him but as of one whom she mortally hateth. Here is the mischief, this is the grief; and how this may be solved and repaired it passeth man's wit to consider. This reverence, for all that he hath to his sovereign, that I am sure there are very few that know this grief; and to have this obloquy and reproach of her removed, I believe he would quit his country for all the days of his life.'—*Randolph to Cecil, October 13. MS. Ibid.*

The mystery alluded to was apparently the intimacy of Mary Stuart with Ritzio, which was already so close and confidential as to provoke calumny. In the face of Randolph's language it is difficult to say for certain that Mary Stuart had never transgressed the permitted limits of propriety; yet it is more likely that a person so careless of the opinions of others, and so warm and true in her friendships, should have laid herself open to remark through some indiscretion, than that she should have seriously compromised her character. It seems certain that Murray intended to have hanged Ritzio. Paul de Foix asked Elizabeth for an explanation of the Queen of Scots' animosity against her brother:—

'Elle s'estant ung peu teue, et secoué sa teste, me respondit que c'estoit pour ce que la Royne d'Escosse avoit esté informée que le Comte de Murray avoit voullu pendre ung Italien nommé David qu'elle aymoit et favorisoit, luy donnant plus de credit que ses affaires et honneur ne devoient.'—*Paul de Foix au Roy.* TEULET, vol. ii.

With the money sent her from abroad she had contrived to raise six hundred 'harquebussmen,' whom the half-armed retainers of the lords could not hope to engage successfully. Passing Linlithgow and Stirling she swept swiftly round to Glasgow, and cut off the retreat of the Protestants into the western hills. A fight was looked for at Hamilton, where 'a hundred gentlemen of her party determined to set on Murray in the battle, and either slay him or tarry behind lifeless.'[1]

Outnumbered—for they had in all but 1300 horse—and outmanœuvred by the rapid movements of the Queen, the Protestants fell back on Edinburgh, where they expected the citizens to declare for them. On the last of August, six days after Mary Stuart had left Holyrood, Chatelherault, Murray, Glencairn, Rothes, Boyd, Kirkaldy, and a few more gentlemen, rode with their servants into the West Port, and sending a courier to Berwick with a pressing entreaty for help, they prepared to defend themselves. But the Calvinist shopkeepers who could be so brave against a miserable priest had no stomach for a fight with armed men. The Queen was coming fast behind them like an avenging fury; and Erskine, who was inclining to the royal side, began to fire on the lords from the castle. 'In the town they could find neither help nor support from any one,' and the terrified inhabitants could only entreat and even insist that they should depart. A fortnight before, a little money and a few distinct words from England would have sufficed to save them. Mary Stuart's courage and Elizabeth's remissness had by this time so strengthened the party of the Queen that 'little

---

[1] Randolph to Cecil, September 4.—*MS. Rolls House.*

good could now be done without greater support than
could be in readiness in any short time.' The lords
could only retire towards the Border and wait Elizabeth's
pleasure. 'What was promised,' Randolph passionately
wrote to Cecil, 'your honour knoweth. Oh that her
Majesty's mind was known! If the Earl of Bedford
have only commission to act in this matter both Queens
may be in one country before long. In the whole world
if there be a more malicious heart towards the Queen
my sovereign than hers that here now reigneth, let me
be hanged at my home-coming or counted a villain for
ever.'[1]

Mary meanwhile had re-entered Edinburgh, breathing
nothing but anger and defiance. Argyle was in his own
Highlands wasting the adjoining lands of Athol and
Lennox; but she scarcely noticed or cared for Argyle.
The affection of a sister for a brother was curdled into a
hatred the more malignant because it was unnatural.
Her whole passion was concentrated on Murray, and after
Murray on Elizabeth.

The day before she had left Holyrood for the west an
Englishman named Yaxlee had arrived there from Flanders. This person, who has been already mentioned as
in the service of Lady Lennox, had been employed by
her as the special agent of her correspondence with
the continental courts. Lady Lennox being now in
the Tower, Yaxlee followed the fortunes of her son,
and came to Scotland to place himself at the disposal of
Mary Stuart. He was a conspirator of the kind most
dangerous to his employers, vain, loud, and confident,
fond of boasting of his acquaintance with kings and
princes, and 'promising to bring to a good end whatso-

---

[1] Randolph to Cecil, September 4.—*MS. Rolls House.*

ever should be committed to him.' 'The wiser sort' soon understood and avoided him. The Queen of Scots however allowed herself to be persuaded by her husband, and placed herself in Yaxlee's power. She told him all her schemes at home and all the promises which had been made to her abroad. The Bishop of Dunblane at Rome had requested the Pope to lend her twelve thousand men, and the Pope was waiting only for Philip's sanction and co-operation to send them.[1] She selected Yaxlee to go on a mission to Spain to explain her position and to 'remit her claims, prospects, and the manner of the prosecution thereof' to Philip's judgment and direction.

Vain of the trust reposed in him the foolish creature was unable to keep his counsel. His babbling tongue revealed all that he knew and all that he was commissioned to do; and the report of it was soon in Cecil's hands.[2]

Philip would no doubt be unwilling to move. Philip like Elizabeth was fond of encouraging others to run into difficulties by promises which he repudiated if they were inconvenient; and in this particular instance Mary Stuart had gone beyond his advice and had placed herself in a position against which the Duke of Alva had pointedly warned her. But the fears of the Spaniards for the safety of the Low Countries were every day increasing; they regarded England as the fountain from which the heresies of the continent were fed; and they looked

---

[1] Capitulo de Cartas del Cardinal Pacheco á su Mag^d., 2 September, 1565.—*MS. Simancas.*

[2] 'Memoir of the proceedings of Francis Yaxlee,' in Cecil's handwriting.—COTTON *MSS.*, CALIG. B. 10. The name of the person is left blank in Cecil's manuscript, but a French translation of the memoir was found in Paris by M. Teulet, and on the margin is written, 'Celluy qui est laissé en blanc c'est Yaxlee.'

to the recovery of it to the Church as the only means of restoring order in their own provinces.[1]

Elizabeth was perfectly aware of the dangers which were thickening round her, and the effect was to end her uncertainty and to determine her to shake herself clear from the failing fortunes of the noblemen whom she had invited to rebel. They had halted at Dumfries, close to the Border, where Murray thinking that 'nothing worse could happen than an agreement while the Queen of Scots had the upper hand and they without a force in the field,' was with difficulty keeping together the remnant of his party.[2] The Earl of Bedford, weary of waiting for instructions which never came, wrote at last half in earnest and half in irony to Elizabeth to propose that she should play over again the part which she had played with Winter; he would himself enter Scotland with the Berwick garrison, and 'her Majesty could afterwards seem to blame him for attempting such things as with the help of others he could bring about.'[3] But Elizabeth was too much frightened to consent even to a vicarious fulfilment of her promises. She replied that if the lords were in danger of being taken the Earl might cover their retreat into England; she sent him three thousand pounds which if he pleased he might place in their hands; but he must give them to understand precisely that both the one and the other were his own acts, for which she would accept neither thanks nor responsibility.

---

[1] 'Esta materia de Faccoia y de aqui es de tanta importancia como se puede considerar: porque si este Reyno se reduxiese, parece que se quitara la fuente de los hereges de Flandes y de Francia, y aun las intelligencias de Alemania, que, como aqui, hay necessidad destas malas ayudas para sostenerse.'—De Silva to Philip, August 20. MS. Simancas.

[2] Murray to Randolph, September 8.—MS. Rolls House.

[3] Bedford to Elizabeth.—MS. Ibid.

'You shall make them perceive your case to be such,' she said, 'as if it should appear otherwise your danger should be so great as all the friends you have could not be able to save you towards us.'[1]

At times she seemed to struggle with her ignominy, but it was only to flounder deeper into distraction and dishonour. Once she sent for the French ambassador: she told him that the Earl of Murray and his friends were in danger for her sake and through her means; the Queen of Scots was threatening their lives; and she swore she would aid them with all the means which God had given, and she would have all men know her determination. But the next moment, as if afraid of what she had said, she stooped to a deliberate lie. De Foix had heard of the 3000*l*., and had ascertained beyond doubt that it had been sent from the Treasury; yet when he questioned Elizabeth about it she took refuge behind Bedford, and swore she had sent no money to the lords at all.[2]

'It fears me not a little,' wrote Murray on the 21st, 'that these secret and covered pretendings of the Queen's Majesty there, as matters now stand, shall never put this cause to such end as we both wish, but open declaration would apparently bring with it no doubt.'[3] 'If her Majesty will openly declare herself,' said Bedford, 'uncertain hearts will be determined again and all will go well.'[4]

Paul de Foix himself, notwithstanding his knowledge of Elizabeth, was unable to believe that she would persevere in a course so discreditable and so dangerous. So easy it would be for her to strike Mary Stuart down, if she had half the promptitude of Mary herself, that it

---

[1] Elizabeth to Bedford, September 12.—*Scotch MSS. Rolls House.*
[2] De Foix to the Queen-mother, September 18.—TEULET, vol. ii.
[3] Murray to Bedford, September 21.—*Scotch MSS. Rolls House.*
[4] Bedford to Cecil.—*MS. Ibid.*

seemed impossible to him that she would neglect the opportunity. As yet the party of the Queen of Scots had no solid elements of strength: Ritzio was the chief councillor; the Earl of Athol was the general—'a youth without judgment or experience, whose only merit was a frenzied Catholicism.'[1] Catherine de Medici, who thought like de Foix, and desired to prevent Elizabeth from becoming absolute mistress of Scotland, sent over Castelnau de Mauvissière to mediate between the Queen of Scots and her subjects. But Mary Stuart understood better the temperament with which she had to deal; she knew that Elizabeth was thoroughly cowed and frightened, and that she had nothing to fear. She sent a message to Castelnau that she would allow neither France nor England to interfere between her and her revolted subjects; while her rival could only betake herself to her single resource in difficulty, and propose again to marry the Archduke.

There was something piteous as well as laughable in the perpetual recurrence of this forlorn subject. She was not wholly insincere. When pushed to extremity she believed that marriage might become her duty, and she imagined that she was willing to encounter it. The game was a dangerous one, for she had almost exhausted the patience of her subjects, who might compel her at last to fulfil in earnest the hopes which she had excited. It would have come to an end long before had it not been that Philip, who was irresolute as herself, allowed his wishes for the marriage to delude him into believing Elizabeth serious whenever it was mentioned; while the desirableness of the Austrian alliance in itself, and the extreme anxiety for it among English statesmen, kept

---

[1] De Foix to the Queen-mother, September 18.—TEULET, vol. ii.

CHAP IX
1565
September

alive the jealous fears of the French. To de Silva the Queen appeared a vain capricious woman, whose pleasure it was to see the princes of Europe successively at her feet; yet he too had expected that if her Scotch policy failed she would take the Archduke in earnest at last, and thus the value of the move was not yet wholly played away, and she could use his name once more to hold her friends and her party together.

As a matter of course when the Archduke was talked of on one side the French had their candidate on the other; and Charles the Ninth being no longer in question Paul de Foix threw his interest on the side of Leicester. While the Queen of Scots was displaying the spirit of a sovereign and accomplishing with uncommon skill the first steps of the Catholic revolution, Elizabeth was amusing herself once more with balancing the attractions of her lover and the Austrian prince: not indeed that she any longer wished to marry even the favoured Lord Robert; 'If she ever took a husband,' she said to de Foix, 'she would give him neither a share of her power nor the keys of her treasury; her subjects wanted a successor, and she would use the husband's services to obtain such a thing; but under any aspect the thought of marriage was odious to her, and when she tried to make up her mind it was as if her heart was being torn out of her body.'[1]

Elizabeth's private feelings on her marriage.

Yet Leicester was fooled by the French into a brief hope of success. He tried to interest Cecil in his cause

---

[1] She said she was resolved—'Ne departir jamais à celuy qui scroit son mary ni de ses biens ni forces ni moyens, ne voulant s'ayder de luy que pour laisser successeur d'elle à ses subjectz; mais quand elle pensoit de ce faire, il luy sembloit que l'on luy arrachast le cœur du ventre; tant elle en estoit de son naturel esloongnée.'—*Paul de Foix to the Queen-mother, August 22.*—TEULET, vol. ii.

by assuring him that the Queen would marry no one but himself; and Cecil mocked him with a courteous answer, and left on record in a second table of contrasts with the Archduke his own intense conviction of Leicester's worthlessness.[1]

A ludicrous court calamity increased the troubles of the Queen and with them her unwillingness to declare war against the Queen of Scots. The three daughters of the Duke of Suffolk had been placed one after the other in the line of succession by Henry the Eighth. Lady Jane was dead; Lady Catherine was dying from the effects of her long and cruel imprisonment; the third, Lady Mary, had remained at the Court, and one evening in August when the Scotch plot was thickening got herself married in the palace itself 'by an old fat priest in a short gown' to Thomas Keys the sergeant porter.[2] Lady Mary was 'the smallest woman in the Court,' Keys was the largest man, and that seemed to have been the chief bond of connexion between them. The lady was perhaps anxious for a husband and knew that Elizabeth would keep her single till she died. Discovery followed before worse had happened than the ceremony. The burly sergeant porter was sent to the Fleet to grow thin on discipline and low diet; the Lady Mary went into private confinement; and both were only too eager to release each other and escape from punishment. The bishops were set to work by the Council to undo the knot and found it no easy matter.[3] Elizabeth had a fresh excuse for her detestation of the Greys and a fresh

---

[1] 'De Matrimonio Reginæ Angliæ.' Reasons against the Earl of Leicester. —BURLEIGH *Papers*, vol. i.

[2] This marriage was before mentioned by me as having taken place at the same time with that of Lady Jane Grey and Guildford Dudley. I was misled by Dugdale.

[3] Privy Council Register, August, 1565. Proceedings of Council on the

topic on which to descant in illustration of the iniquities of matrimony.

De Mauvissière meanwhile undeterred by the Queen of Scots' message had made his way to Edinburgh, but only to find that he had come upon a useless errand. The Earl of Bothwell had rejoined Mary Stuart in the middle of her triumph, 'a man,' said Randolph, ' fit to be made a minister of any shameful act against God or man ;'[1] and Bothwell's hatred for Murray drew him closer than ever to Mary's side. In the full confidence of success and surrounded by persons whose whole aim was to feed the fire of her passion she would listen to nothing which de Mauvissière could urge. In vain he warned her of the experience of France; in vain he reminded her of the siege of Leith and of the madness of risking a quarrel with her powerful and dangerous neighbour. 'Scotland,' she said, 'should not be turned into a republic; she would sooner lose her crown than wear it at the pleasure of her revolted subjects and the Queen of England; instead of advising her to make peace, Catherine de Medici should have stepped forward to her side and assisted her to avenge the joint wrongs of France and Scotland; if France failed her in her extremity, grieved as she might be to leave her old allies, she would take the hand which was offered her by Spain ; she would submit to England—never.'[2]

From the moment when she had first taken the field, she had given her enemies no rest; she had swept Fife, the hotbed of the Protestants as far as St. Andrew's. The old Laird of Lundy—he who had called the mass

---

marriage of the Lady Mary Grey. —*MS. Domestic, Eliz., Rolls House.* Bishop of London to Cecil.—*MS. Ibid.*

[1] Randolph to Cecil, September 20.—*Scotch MSS. Rolls House.*
[2] Castelnau de Mauvissière to Paul de Foix, September.—TEULET, vol. II.

the mickle deil—was flung into prison and his friends and his family had to fly for their lives. At the end of September she was pausing to recover breath at Holyrood before she made her last swoop upon the party at Dumfries. The Edinburgh merchants found her money, her soldiers with lighted matchlocks assisting them to unloose their purse strings. With October she would march to the Border, and in her unguarded moments she boasted that she would take her next rest at the gates of London.[1]

It was now necessary for Elizabeth to come to some resolution which she could avow—either to interfere at once or distinctly to declare that she did not mean to interfere. Cecil according to his usual habit reviewed the situation and drew out in form its leading features. The two interests at stake were religion and the succession to the Crown. For religion 'it was doubtful how to meddle in another prince's controversy;' 'so far as politic laws were devised for the maintenance of the Gospel Christian men might defend it,' 'yet the best service which men could render to the truth was to serve God faithfully and procure by good living the defence thereof at His Almighty hand.' The succession was at once more critical and more impossible to leave untouched. The Queen of Scots appeared to intend to exact her recognition as 'second person' at the point of the sword. The unwillingness of the Queen of England to marry had unsettled the minds of her subjects, who 'beholding the state of the crown to depend only on the breath of one person' were becoming restless and uneasy; and there were symptoms on all sides which pointed 'towards a civil quarrel in the realm.' The best remedy would be the fulfilment of the hopes which had been so

---

[1] Paul de Foix to the King of France, September 29.—TRULET, vol. ii.

long held out to the nation. If the Queen would marry all danger would at once be at an end. If she could not bring herself to accept that alternative, she might make the intrigues of the Scottish Queen with her Catholic subjects, the practising with Rome, the language of Darnley to Randolph, and the continued refusal to ratify the Treaty of Edinburgh, a ground for declaring war.[1]

Every member of the Council was summoned to London. The suspected Earls of Cumberland, Westmoreland, and Northumberland were invited to the Court, to remove them from the Border where they would perhaps be dangerous; and day after day the advisers of the Crown sat in earnest and inconclusive deliberation. A lucid statement was drawn up of Mary Stuart's proceedings from the day of Elizabeth's accession; every aggressive act on her part, every conciliatory movement of the Queen of England were laid out in careful detail to assist the Council in forming a judgment; the history was brought down to the latest moment, and one only important matter seems to have been withheld—the unfortunate promises which Elizabeth had made to the Earl of Murray and his friends at a time when she believed that a demonstration in Scotland would be sufficient to frighten Mary Stuart and that she would never be called on to fulfil them.

In favour of sending assistance to the Protestant noblemen it was urged that the Queen of Scots notoriously intended to overthrow the reformed religion and to make her way to the English throne; the title of the Queen of England depended on the Reformation; if the Pope's authority was restored she would no longer be regarded as legitimate. To sit still in the face of the

---

[1] Note in Cecil's hand, September, 1565.—*MS. Rolls House.*

attitude which the Queen of Scots had assumed was to encourage her to continue her practices; and it was more prudent to encounter an enemy when it could be done at small cost and in her own country than to wait to be overtaken at home by war and rebellion which would be a thousand times more dangerous and costly.

On the other hand to defend the insurgent subjects of a neighbouring sovereign was a dangerous precedent. If Elizabeth was justified in maintaining the Scotch Protestants the King of Spain might claim as fair a right to interfere in behalf of the English Catholics. The form which a war would assume and the contingencies which might arise from it could not be foreseen, while the peril and expense were immediate and certain.

The arguments on both sides were so evenly balanced that it was difficult to choose between them. The Council however, could it be proved that the Queen of Scots was in communication with the Pope to further her designs on England, were ready to consider that 'a great matter.' The name of the Pope was detested in England by men who believed themselves to hold every shred of Catholic doctrine; the creed was an opinion; the Pope was a political and most troublesome fact with which under no circumstances were moderate English gentlemen inclined to have any more dealings. The Pope turned the scale; and the Council after some ineffectual attempts to find a middle course resolved on immediately confiscating the estates of the Earl of Lennox; while they recommended the Queen to demand the ratification of the Treaty of Edinburgh, to send a fleet into the Forth, and to despatch a few thousand men to Berwick to be at the disposal of the Earl of Bedford.[1]

[1] Notes of the Proceedings in Council at Westminster, September 24. In Cecil's hand.—COTTON MSS. CALIG. D. 10. Scotch MSS. Rolls House.

Had these steps been taken either Mary Stuart must have yielded, or there would have been an immediate war. But the Council though consenting and advising a decided course were still divided: Norfolk, Arundel, Winchester, Mason, and Pembroke were in favour in the main of the Queen of Scots' succession, and they regarded Calvinists and Calvinism with a most heartfelt and genuine detestation. Elizabeth in her heart resented the necessity of identifying herself with the party of John Knox, and her mood varied from day to day. After the resolution of the Council on the 24th she spoke at length to the French ambassador in praise of Murray, who if his sister could but have known it, she said, was her truest friend—a noble, generous and good man; she was fully aware of the Queen of Scots' designs against her; and when de Foix entreated her not to break the peace she refused to give him any assurances, and she told him that if France assisted Mary Stuart she should receive it as an act of hostility against herself.[1]

But her energy spent itself in words, or rather both the Queen and those advisers whom she most trusted, even Sir William Cecil himself, oscillated backwards into a decision that the risk of war was too great to be encountered. The example might be fatal: the Catholic powers might interfere in England; the Romanists at home might mutiny; while to move an army was 'three times more chargeable than it was wont to be, whereof the experience at Havre might serve for example.'[2] Two days after their first resolution therefore the Council assembled again, when Cecil informed them 'that he found a lack of disposition in the Queen's Majesty to

---

[1] Paul de Foix to the King of France, September 29.—TEULET, vol. ii.
[2] 'Causes that move me not to consent presently to war,' September 26. Note in Cecil's hand.—COTTON MSS., CALIG. B. 10.

allow of war or of the charges thereof;' she would break
her word to the lords whom she had encouraged into
insurrection; but it was better than to run the risk of
a conflagration which might wrap all England in its
flames. The idea of forcible interference was finally
abandoned. De Mauvissière remained at Edinburgh sincerely endeavouring to keep Mary within bounds; and
Cecil himself wrote a private letter of advice to her which
he sent by the hands of a Captain Cockburn. There were
reasons for supposing that her violence might have begun
to cool. Darnley had desired that the command of the
army might be given to his father; the Queen of Scots
had insisted on bestowing it upon Bothwell,[1] who had
won her favour by promising to bring in Murray dead
or alive;[2] and Lennox was holding off from the Court in
jealous discontent.

Cockburn on his arrival at Holyrood placed himself
in communication with de Mauvissière. They waited
on Mary together; and expatiating on the ruinous effect
of the religious wars of the Guises which had filled
France with rage and hatred, they entreated her for her
own sake to beware of the miserable example. The
French ambassador told her that if she looked for aid
from abroad she was deceiving herself; France would
not help her and would not permit the interference of
Spain; so that she would bring herself 'to a hard end.'
Cockburn 'spoke his mind freely to her to the same
effect' and 'told her she was in great danger.'[3]

Mary Stuart 'wept wondrous sore;' but construing

---

[1] Randolph speaking of Mary Stuart's relation with Bothwell at this time says:—'I have heard a thing most strange, whereof I will not make mention till I have better assurance than now I have.'—*Randolph to Cecil, October* 13. *MS. Rolls House.*

[2] Cockburn to Cecil, October 2.—*MS. Ibid.*

[3] Ibid.

Elizabeth's unwillingness to declare war into an admission of her own strength, she was deaf to advice as she had been to menace. She disbelieved de Mauvissière and trusted soon to hear from Yaxlee that the Spanish fleet was on its way to the English Channel; at least she would not lose the chance of revenge upon her brother: 'she said she could have no peace till she had Murray's or Chatelherault's head.'[1]

A few hundred men from Berwick would probably have ended her power of so gratifying herself; yet on the other hand it might have been a spark to explode an insurrection in England; and Elizabeth preferred to hold aloof with her arm half raised—wishing yet fearing to strike—and waiting for some act of direct hostility against herself. As far as the peace of her own country was concerned her policy was no doubt a prudent one; but it was pursued at the expense of her honour; it ruined for the time her party in Scotland; and it was an occasion of fresh injury to the fugitives at Dumfries.

As soon as Murray with his few dispirited friends had reached the Border he despatched Sir Robert Melville to London to explain his situation and to request in form the assistance which had been promised him. Elizabeth assured Melville that she was sorry for their condition. She bade him return and tell Murray that she would do her very best for himself and his cause; but she could not support him by arms without declaring war against the Queen of Scots, and she could not declare war 'without just cause.' If the Queen of Scots therefore were to offer him 'any tolerable conditions' she would not have him refuse; 'if on the other hand the indignation of the Queen was so cruelly intended as he and his com-

---

[1] Randolph to Cecil, October 5.—*Scotch MSS. Rolls House.*

panions could obtain no end with preservation of their
lives, her Majesty both for her private love towards
those that were noblemen and of her princely honour and
clemency towards such as were tyrannically persecuted
would receive them into her protection, save their persons and their lives from ruin, and so far would give
them aid and succour;' she would send a commissioner
to Scotland to intercede with the Queen, 'and with him
also an army to be used as her Majesty should see just
occasion given to her.'[1]

The Lords had become 'desperate of hope and as men
dismayed;' they had repented bitterly of 'having
trusted so much to England:'[2] Chatelherault, Glencairn,
Kirkaldy—all in fact save Murray—desired to make
terms with Mary, and were feeling their way towards
recovering her favour at the expense of the Queen of
England, whom they accused of betraying them. When
Melville returned with Elizabeth's answer it was interpreted into a fresh promise of interference in their behalf,
not only by the lords, whom anxiety might have made
sanguine, but by the bearer of the message to whom
Elizabeth had herself spoken. They immediately recovered their courage, broke off their communications
with the Queen of Scots, and prepared to continue their
resistance.

Elizabeth would have done better if she had spoken
less ambiguously. Mary Stuart who had paused to ascertain what they would do set out at once for the Border
with Athol, Bothwell, and a motley force of 18,000 men.
She rode in person at their head in steel bonnet and
corselet, 'with a dagg at her saddlebow,'[3] declaring that

---

[1] Answer to Robert Melville, October 1.—Scotch MSS. Rolls House.
[2] Bedford to Cecil, October 5.—MS. Ibid.
[3] Randolph to Cecil, October 13.—MS. Ibid.

'all who held intercourse with England should be treated as enemies to the realm;' while Darnley boasted that he was about 'to be made the greatest that ever reigned in the isle of Britain.'[1] Ritzio was still the presiding spirit in Mary's council chamber. 'You may think,' wrote Randolph, 'what the matter meaneth that a stranger and a varlet should have the whole guiding of the Queen and country.'[2] The army was but a confused crowd: of loyal friends the Queen could really count on none but Bothwell, young Athol, and perhaps Huntly; 'the rest were as like to turn against her as stand by her.' She perhaps trusted to some demonstration from Berwick to kindle them into enthusiasm through their patriotism; but Elizabeth disappointed equally both her enemies and her friends; she would give no excuse to the Queen of Scots to complain that England had broken the peace. The 'few hundreds' with whose assistance the lords undertook to drive their sovereign back to Edinburgh were not forthcoming; the army more than half promised to Melville was a mere illusion; and Bedford was confined by his orders to Carlisle, where he was allowed only to receive Murray and his party as fugitives: they had now therefore no resource except to retreat into England; the Queen of Scots following in hot pursuit glared across the frontier at her escaping prey, half tempted to follow them and annihilate the petty guard of the English commander:[3] but prudence for once prevailed; she halted and drew back.

So ended the insurrection which had been undertaken

---

[1] Randolph to Leicester, October 18.—*Scotch MSS. Rolls House.*

[2] *MS. Ibid.*

[3] 'A few hundred men would have kept all right. I fear they will break with us from words which she has used, and we are all unprovided.' —*Bedford to Cecil, October 13. MS. Ibid.*

at Elizabeth's instigation and mainly in Elizabeth's interests. Having failed to prevent the catastrophe she would gladly now have heard no more of it; but she was not to escape so easily. Even among her own subjects there were some who dared to speak unpalatable truths to her. Bedford who had been sent to the north with an army which he believed that he was to lead to Edinburgh, wrote in plain stern terms to the Queen herself 'that the lords, in reliance upon her Majesty's promise, had stood out against their sovereign, and now knew not what to do;'[1] while to Cecil, not knowing how deeply Cecil was responsible for the Queen's conduct, he wrote in serious sorrow. In a previous letter he had spoken of 'the Lords of the Congregation,' and Elizabeth had taken offence at a term which savoured of too advanced a Protestantism.

'The poor noblemen,' he now said, 'rest so amazed and in so great perplexity they know not what to say, do, or imagine. My terming them Lords of the Congregation was but used by me because I saw it received by others; for that it is not plausible I shall omit it henceforth, wishing from my heart the cause was plausibly received, and then for terms and names it should be no matter. The Earl of Murray I find constant and honourable, though otherwise sore perplexed, poor gentleman, the more the pity. As her Majesty means peace we must use the necessary means to maintain peace; albeit I know that the Queen useth against the Queen's Majesty our sovereign all such reproachful and despiteful words as she can; besides her practices with foreign realms, which her Majesty's father I am sure would have thought much of. Yet as her Majesty winketh at the

---

[1] Bedford to the Queen, October 13.—*Scotch MSS. Rolls House.*

same, I must know what I am to do, whether in dealing with the wardens on the Border I am to recognize commissions signed by the Lord Darnley as King of Scotland.'[1]

Randolph ashamed and indignant at the deception of which he and Throgmorton had been the instruments, insisted 'that the Queen of Scots meant evil and nothing but evil,' and that however long she was borne with she would have to be brought to reason by force at last. 'You, my lord,' he wrote anxiously to Leicester, 'do all you can to move her Majesty; it is looked for at your hand, and all worthy and godly men of this nation shall love and honour you for ever; let it be handled so that this Queen may know how she has been misguided and ill-advised to take so much upon her—not only against these noblemen, but far above that if she had power to her will.'[2]

But it was from Murray himself that Elizabeth had to encounter the most inconvenient remonstrances. To save England from a Catholic revolution and to save England's Queen from the machinations of a dangerous rival, the Earl of Murray had taken arms against his sovereign, and he found himself a fugitive and an outlaw, while the sacred cause of the Reformation in his own country had been compromised by his fall. His life was safe, but Mary Stuart having failed to take or kill him was avenging herself on his wife, and the first news which he heard after reaching England was that Lady Murray had been driven from her home, and within a few weeks of her confinement was wandering shelterless in the woods. Submis-

---
[1] Bedford to Cecil, October 13 and October 26.—*Scotch MSS. Rolls House.*
[2] Randolph to Leicester, October 18.—*MS. Ibid.*

sion and soft speeches would have been his more prudent part, but Murray, a noble gentleman of stainless honour, was not a person to sit down patiently as the dupe of timidity or fraud.

He wrote shortly to the English Council to say that in reliance on the message brought him by Sir Robert Melville he had encouraged his friends to persevere in resistance at a time when they could have made their peace; and through 'their Queen's cold dealing' both he and they were now forced to enter England. If there was an intention of helping them he begged that it might be done at once, and that Scotland might be saved from ruin.[1]

By the same messenger he wrote more particularly to Cecil: 'He did not doubt,' he said, 'that Cecil understood fully the motives both of himself and his friends; they had enterprised their action with full foresight of their sovereign's indignation, being moved thereto by the Queen of England and her Council's hand writ directed to them thereupon;' the 'extremities' had followed as they expected; the Queen of Scots would now agree to no condition, relying on the Queen of England's 'coldness:' he was told that the Queen's Majesty's conscience was not resolved to make open war without further motive and occasion; the Queen's Majesty was perfectly aware 'that he had undertaken nothing for any particularity of his own, but for good affection to follow her own counsel; her Majesty had been the furtherer and the doer, and he with the other noblemen had assisted therein to their power.'[2]

Nor were the lords contented with written protests:

---

[1] Murray to the Council, October 14.—*Scotch MSS. Rolls House.*
[2] Murray to Cecil, October 14.—*MS. Ibid.*

they were determined to hear from Elizabeth's own lips an explanation of their desertion. Murray himself and the Abbot of Kilwinning were chosen as the representatives of the rest; and Bedford after an affectation of opposition which he did not carry beyond a form, sent to the Queen on the 17th of October to prepare for their appearance in London. Pressed by the consequences of her own faults Elizabeth would have concealed her conduct if possible from her own eyes; least of all did she desire to have it thrown in her teeth before all the world. She had assured Paul de Foix at last that she would give the lords no help, and would wait to be attacked. She wished to keep clear of every overt act which would justify the Queen of Scots in appealing to France and Spain. She had persuaded herself that Mary Stuart's army would disperse in a few days for want of supplies, that the lords would return over the Border as easily as they had crossed it;[1] and that she could assist them with money behind the scenes without openly committing herself. These plans and hopes would be fatally disconcerted by Murray's appearance at the court, and she sent Bedford's courier flying back to him with an instant and angry command to prevent so untoward a casualty. She had said again and again that 'she would give no aid that should break the peace.' The coming up of the Earl of Murray 'would give manifest cause of just complaint to the Queen of Scots;' and she added with curious self exposure, 'neither are these kind of matters in this open sort to be used.' If Murray had not yet set out she required Bedford 'to stay him by his authority;' if he had started he must be sent after and recalled.[2]

---

[1] Paul de Foix to the King of France, October 16.—TEULET, vol. ii.
[2] Elizabeth to Bedford, October 20.—*Scotch MSS. Rolls House.*

The harshness of Elizabeth's language was softened by the Council, who expressed their regret 'that the common cause had not hitherto had better success;' they promised their own support 'so far as their power and credit might extend;' but they entreated Murray 'patiently to accommodate himself to her Majesty's resolution.'[1]

Unluckily for Elizabeth, Murray had anticipated the prohibition, and had followed so closely behind the announcement of his approach that the couriers charged with the letters of the Queen and Council met him at Ware. He opened the despatch which was addressed to himself, and immediately sent on a note to Cecil regretting that he had not been sooner made aware of the Queen's wishes, but saying that as he had come so far he should now remain where he was till he was informed of her further pleasure.

Embarrassed, irritated, and intending at all hazards to disavow her connexion with the lords, Elizabeth, since Murray had chosen to come to her, resolved to turn his presence to her advantage. When she had once made up her mind to a particular course she never hesitated on the details whatever they might cost. The Earl of Murray was told that he would be received; he went on to London, and 'on the night of his arrival the Queen sent for him and arranged in a private interview the comedy which she was about to enact.'[2]

---

[1] The Council to Murray, October 20.—*Scotch MSS. Rolls House.* The letter is signed by Norfolk, Pembroke, Lord William Howard, and Cecil.

[2] 'Yo fué avisado que la noche antes desta platica el de Murray estuvó con ella y con el secretario Cecil buen rato, donde se debió consultar lo que pasó el dia siguiente.'— De Silva to Philip, November 5. And again, 'La Reyna oyó al de Murray la noche que llegó en secreto, y otro dia hizó aquella demostracion delante del Embajador de Francia.' —*Same to the same,* November 10. *MS. Simancas.* A report of the proceedings in the Rolls House, which was drawn up for the inspection of

Chap IX
1565 October

The following morning, the 22nd of October, he was admitted to an audience in public, at which de Foix and de Mauvissière who had by this time returned from Scotland, were especially invited to be present. De Silva describes what ensued, not as an eye-witness, but from an account which was given to him by the Queen herself.[1]

Elizabeth receives Murray in form.

Elizabeth having taken her place with the Council and the ambassadors at her side, the Earl of Murray entered modestly dressed in black. Falling on one knee he began to speak in Scotch, when the Queen interrupted him with a request that he would speak in French, which she said she could better understand. Murray objected that he had been so long out of practice that he could not properly express himself in French; and Elizabeth whose object was to produce an effect on de Foix and his companion, accepted his excuse for himself; but she said that although he might not be sufficient master of the idiom to speak it, she knew that he understood it when he heard it spoken; she would therefore in her own part of the conversation make use of that language.

She then went on 'to express her astonishment that being declared an outlaw as he was by the Queen of Scots, the Earl of Murray should have dared to come unlicensed into her presence. The Queen of Scots had been her good sister, and such she always hoped to find her. There had been differences between them which had

---

Mary Stuart herself, and the Courts of France and Spain, states that 'the Queen received Murray openly and none otherwise.' The consciousness that she had received him otherwise explains words which else might have seemed superfluous.

[1] The account in Sir James Melville's *Memoirs* is evidently taken from the official narrative, with which in most points it verbally agrees. De Silva's is but little different. The one variation of importance will be noticed.

made her fear for their friendship; but the King of France had kindly interposed his good offices between herself, her sister, and her sister's subjects; and the two ministers who had been his instruments in that good service being at the moment at her court, she had requested both them and others to attend on the present occasion to hear what she was about to say. She wished it to be generally understood that she would do nothing which would give just offence to the Queen of Scots or which would impair her own honour. The world she was aware was in the habit of saying that her realm was the sanctuary for the seditious subjects of her neighbours; and it was even rumoured that she had instigated or encouraged the insurrection in Scotland. She would not have done such a thing to be sovereign of the universe. God, who was a just God, she well knew would punish her with the like troubles in her own country; and if she encouraged the subjects of another prince in disobedience He would stir her own people into insurrection against herself. So far as she knew there were two causes for the present disturbances in Scotland; the Queen of Scots had married without the consent of her Estates and had failed to apprize the princes her neighbours of her intentions; the Earl of Murray had attempted to oppose her and had fallen into disgrace. This was the first cause. The second was that the Earl of Lennox and his house were opposed to the reformed religion; the Earl of Murray feared that he would attempt to destroy it, and with his friends preferred to lose his life rather than allow what he believed to be the truth to be overthrown. The Earl had come to the English court to request her to intercede with his sovereign that he might be heard in his defence. There were faults which proceeded of malice which deserved the rigour of justice—one of these was treason against the person of the sovereign; and were she to understand that the Earl of Murray had meditated treason she would arrest and chastise him according to his demerits; but she had known him in times past to be well-affectioned to his mistress; he had loved her she was confident with the love which a subject owes to his prince. There were other faults—faults committed through imprudence, through ignorance, or in self-defence, which might be treated mercifully. The Earl of Murray's fault might be one of these; she bade him therefore say for which cause he had instigated the late disturbances.'

Elizabeth had exercised a wise caution in preparing Murray for this preposterous harangue. He commanded himself, and replied by calling God to witness of the loyalty with which he had ever served his sovereign: she had bestowed lands, honour, and rewards upon him far beyond his desert; he had desired nothing less than to offend her, and he would have stood by her with life and goods to the utmost of his ability.

Elizabeth then began again: 'She held a balance in her hand,' she said; 'in the one scale was the sentence of outlawry pronounced against him by the Queen of Scots, in the other were the words which he had just spoken. But the word of a Queen must outweigh the word of a subject in the mind of a sister sovereign, who was bound to show most favour to her own like and equal. The Earl had committed actions deserving grave reprehension: he had refused to appear when lawfully summoned; he had taken up arms and had made a league with others like himself to levy war against his sovereign. She had been told that he was afraid of being murdered, but if there had been a conspiracy against him he should have produced the proofs of it in his sovereign's presence.'

Murray replied in Scotch, the Queen interpreting as he went on. He said that it was true that there had been a conspiracy; the condition of his country was such that he could not have saved his life except by the means which he had adopted. Elizabeth had doubtless made it a condition of her further friendship that he should say nothing by which she could herself be incriminated; and he contented himself with entreating her to intercede for him to obtain the Queen of Scots' forgiveness.

*Chap IX
1565
October*

Elizabeth affected to hesitate. The Queen of Scots, she said, had so often refused her mediation that she knew not how she could offer it again, but she would communicate with her Council, and when she had ascertained their opinions he should hear from her. Meanwhile she would have him understand that he was in great danger, and that he must consider himself a prisoner.

The Earl was then permitted to withdraw. The Queen went aside with the Frenchmen, and assuring them that they might accept what they had witnessed as the exact truth, she begged that they would communicate it to the King of France. To de Silva, when he was next admitted to an audience, she repeated the story word by word, and to him as well as to the others she protested that rebels against their princes should receive from her neither aid nor countenance.[1]

Elizabeth declares that she had spoken nothing but the truth.

So ended this extraordinary scene. Sir James Melville's narrative carries the extravagance one point further. He describes Elizabeth as extorting from Murray an acknowledgment that she had not encouraged the rebellion, and as then bidding him depart from her presence as an unworthy traitor. Sir James Melville

---

[1] De Silva to Philip, November 5.—*MS. Simancas.*

does but follow an official report which was drawn up under Elizabeth's eye and sanction, to be sent to Scotland and circulated through Europe. It was thus therefore that she herself desired the world to believe that she had spoken; and one falsehood more or less in a web of artifice could scarcely add to her discredit. For Murray's sake however it may be hoped that he was spared this further ignominy, and that de Silva's is the truer story.

If the Earl did not declare in words however that Elizabeth was unconnected with the rebellion, he allowed her to disavow it in silence, and by his forbearance created for himself and Scotland a claim upon her gratitude. He was evidently no consenting party to the deception; and after leaving her presence he wrote to her in a letter what he had restrained himself from publicly declaring.

Private protest of Murray.

'Her treatment of him would have been more easy to bear,' he said, 'had he known in what he had offended;' 'he had done his uttermost with all his power to serve and gratify her;' and 'the more he considered the matter it was ever the longer the more grievous to him:' noblemen who had suffered in former times for maintaining English interests in Scotland, 'when their cause was not to be compared to the present, had been well received and liberally gratified;' while he who had 'endeavoured to show a thankful heart in her service when any occasion was presented, could in no wise perceive by her Highness's answer any affection towards his present state;' 'her declaration had been more grievous to him than all his other troubles;' he trusted that 'he might in time receive from her some more comfortable answer.'[1]

---

[1] The Earl of Murray to Queen Elizabeth, from Westminster, October 31.—*Scotch MSS. Rolls House.*

It does not appear that Elizabeth saw Murray any more. She was only anxious to be rid of his presence, which was an intolerable reproach to her; and with these words—the least which the occasion required, yet not without a sad dignity—he returned to his friends who had been sent on to Newcastle, where they were ordered for the present to remain. Elizabeth was left to play out in character the rest of her ignoble game. To the ambassadors, whom she intended to deceive, it was a transparent farce; and there was probably not a house in London, Catholic or Protestant, where her conduct, which she regarded as a political masterpiece, was not ridiculed as it deserved. But it must be allowed at least the merit of completeness. An elaborate account of the interview with Murray was sent to Randolph to be laid before the Queen of Scots; Elizabeth accompanied it with an autograph letter in which she attempted to impose on the keenest-witted woman living by telling her she wished 'she could have been present to have heard the terms in which she addressed her rebellious subject.' 'So far was she from espousing the cause of rebels and traitors,' she said, 'that she should hold herself disgraced if she had so much as tacitly borne with them;' 'she wished her name might be blotted out from the list of princes as unworthy to hold a place among them,' if she had done any such thing.[1]

---

[1] 'Answy je luy (Randolph) ay declaré tout au long le discours entre moy et ung de vos subjects lequel j'espere vous contentera; souhaitant que vos oreilles en eussent été juges pour y entendre et l'honneur et l'affection que je monstrois en vostre endroit; tout au rebours de ce qu'on dict que je defendois vos mauvaises subjects contre vous; laquelle chose se tiendra tousjours tres eloignée de mon cœur, estant trop grande ignominie pour une princesse à souffrir, non que à faire; souhaitant alors qu'on me ablouisme du rang des princes comme estant indignede tenir lieu.'—*Elizabeth to the Queen of Scots*, October 29. Scotch MSS. Rolls House.

At the same time she wrote to Randolph himself saying frankly that her first impulse on Murray's arrival had been to accept partially if not entirely the conditions of peace which the Queen of Scots had offered to Tamworth. If the Queen of Scots would promise not to molest either herself or her children in the possession of the English throne, she had been ready to pledge her word that nothing should be done in England in prejudice of the Queen of Scots' title to 'the second place.' On reflection however it had seemed imprudent to show excessive eagerness. She had therefore written a letter which Randolph would deliver; and he might take the opportunity of saying that although the Darnley marriage had interrupted the friendship which had subsisted between the Queen of Scots and herself, yet that she desired only to act honourably and kindly towards her; and if the Queen of Scots would undertake to keep the peace and would give the promise which she desired, she would send commissioners to Edinburgh to make a final arrangement.[1]

In a momentary recovery of dignity she added at the close of her letter that if the Queen of Scots refused, 'she would defend her country and subjects from such annoyance as might be intended, and would finally use all such lawful means as God should give her to redress all offences and injuries already done or hereafter to be done to her or her subjects.'[2] But an evil spirit of trickery and imbecility had taken possession of Elizabeth's intellect. The Queen of Scots naturally expressed the utmost readiness to receive commissioners sent from England to concede so much of what she had asked. By

---

[1] Elizabeth to Randolph, October 29.—*Scotch MSS. Rolls House.*
[2] Ibid.

the time Mary's answer came, her Majesty being no
longer in a panic, had become sensible of the indignity of
her proposal. She therefore bade Randolph 'so compass
the matter that the Queen of Scots should rather send
commissioners to England, as more honourable to herself;' and 'if the Queen of Scots said, as it was like she
would, that the Queen of England had offered to send a
commission thither, *he should answer that he indeed said
so and thought so,* but that he did perceive he had mistaken her message.'[1]

Elizabeth's strength, could she only have known it,
lay in the goodness of the cause which she represented.
The essential interests both of England and Scotland
were concerned in her success. She was the champion
of liberty, and through her the two nations were eman-
cipating themselves from spiritual tyranny. By the
side of the Jesuits she was but a shallow driveller in
the arts to which she condescended; and she was about
to find that after all the paths of honour were the paths
of safety, and that she could have chosen no weapon
more dangerous to herself than the chicanery of which
she considered herself so accomplished a mistress. She
had mistaken the nature of English and Scottish gentlemen in supposing that they would be the instruments
of a disgraceful policy, and she had done her rival
cruel wrong in believing that she could be duped with
artifices so poor.

'Send as many ambassadors as you please to our
Queen,' said Sir William Kirkaldy to Bedford; 'they
shall receive a proud answer. She thinks to have a force
as soon ready as you do, besides the hope she has to
have friendship in England. If force of men and ships

---

[1] Elizabeth to Randolph, November 26.—*Scotch MSS. Rolls House.*

come not with the ambassadors, their coming and travail shall be spent in vain.'[1]

Even Cecil perhaps now deplored the effects of his own timidity. 'I have received,' wrote Bedford to him, 'your gentle and sorrowful letter. It grieveth me that things will frame no better. The evil news will be the overthrow of three hundred gentlemen of Scotland that are zealous and serviceable.' Too justly Bedford feared that the Scotch Protestants in their resentment would 'become the worst enemies that England ever had;' too clearly he saw that Elizabeth by her miserable trifling had ruined her truest friends; that however anxious she might be for peace 'the war would come upon her when least she looked for it;' and that Mary Stuart now regarded her with as much contempt as hatred. 'Alas! my lord,' he wrote to Leicester, 'is this the end? God help us all and comfort these poor lords. There is by these dealings overthrown a good duke, some earls, many other barons, lords, and gentlemen, wise, honest, religious. Above all am I driven to bemoan the hard case of the Earl of Murray and the Laird of Grange, whose affection to this whole realm your lordship knows right well. I surely think there came not a greater overthrow to Scotland these many years; for the wisest, honestest, and godliest are discomfited and undone. There is now no help for them, unless God take the matter in hand, but to commit themselves to their prince's will and pleasure. And what hath England gotten by helping them in this sort? even as many mortal enemies of them as before it had dear friends; for otherwise will not that Queen receive them to mercy, if she deal no worse with them; nor

---

[1] Kirkaldy to Bedford, October 31.—*Scotch MSS. Rolls House.*

without open and evident demonstration of the same cannot they assure themselves of her favour; and the sooner they thus do the sooner they shall have her to conceive a good opinion of them, and the sooner they shall be restored to their livelihoods.'[1]

'Greater account might have been made of the lords' good-will,' wrote Randolph. 'If there be living a more mortal enemy to the Queen my mistress than this woman is, I desire never to be reputed but the vilest villain alive.'[2] 'The lords,' concluded Bedford scornfully, 'abandoned by man and *turned over to God*, must now do the best they can for themselves.'

And what that was, what fruit would have grown from those strokes of diplomatic genius, had Mary Stuart been equal to the occasion, Elizabeth would ere long have tasted in deposition and exile or death. Randolph, faithful to the end, might say and unsay, might promise and withdraw his word, and take on himself the blame of his mistress's changing humour; Bedford, with ruin full in view before him, might promise at all risks 'to obey her bidding.' But the lords of Scotland were no subjects of England, to be betrayed into rebellion in the interests of a country which they loved with but half their hearts, and when danger came to be coolly 'turned over to God.' Murray might forgive, for Murray's noble nature had no taint of self in it; but others could resent for him what he himself could pardon. Argyle, his brother-in-law, when he heard of that scene in London, bade Randolph tell his mistress 'he found it very strange; the Queen of Scots had made him many offers, and till that time he had refused them all; if

---

[1] Bedford to Leicester, November 5.—*Scotch MSS. Rolls House.*
[2] Randolph to Leicester, November 8.—*Ibid.*

CHAP IX
1565
November

Revoltment of the Earl of Argyle.

the Queen of England would reconsider herself he would stick to the English cause and fight for it with lands and life; but he demanded an answer within ten days. If she persisted he would make terms with his own sovereign.'[1] The ten days passed and no answer came. Argyle withdrew the check which through the Scots of the Isles he had held over Shan O'Neil, and Ireland blazed into fury and madness; while Argyle himself from that day forward till Mary Stuart's last hopes were scattered at Langside, became the enemy of all which till that hour he had most loved and fought for.

Nor was Argyle alone in his anger. Sir James Melville saw the opportunity and urged on his mistress a politic generosity. From the day of her return from France he showed her that she had 'laboured without effect to sever her nobility from England.' The Queen of England had now done for her what for herself she could not do; and if she would withdraw her prosecutions, pardon Murray, pardon Chatelherault, pardon Kirkaldy and Glencairn, she might command their devotion for ever.'[2] Melville found an ally where he could have least looked for it to repeat the same advice. Sir Nicholas Throgmorton had for the last six years been at the heart of every Protestant conspiracy in Europe. He it was of whose experienced skill Elizabeth had availed herself to light the Scotch insurrection. His whole nature revolted against the paltry deception of which he had been made the instrument; and now throwing himself passionately into the interests of the Queen of Scots he advised the lords 'to sue for pardon at their own Queen's hands, and engage never to offend her again for the satisfaction of any prince alive;' while

[1] Randolph to Cecil, November 19.
[2] MELVILLE's *Memoirs*.

more daringly and dangerously he addressed Mary Stuart herself.

Sir Nicholas Throgmorton writes to Mary Stuart.

1565 November

'Your Majesty,' he said, 'has in England many friends who favour your title for divers respects; some for conscience thinking you have the right; some from personal regard; some for religion; some for faction; some for the ill-will they bear to Lady Catherine your competitor. Your friends and enemies alike desire to see the succession settled. Parliament must meet next year at latest; and it must be your business meanwhile to assure yourself of the votes of the majority, which if you will you can obtain. You have done wisely in marrying an Englishman; we do not love strangers. Make no foreign alliance till you have seen what we can do for you. Keep on good terms with France and Spain, but do not draw too close to them. Go on moderately in religion as you have hitherto done, and you will find Catholics as well as Protestants on your side. Show clemency to the banished lords. You will thus win many hearts in England. Be careful, be generous, and you will command us all. I do not write as "a fetch" to induce you to take the lords back; it is thought expedient for your service by many who have no favour to them and are different from them in religion.

'The Earl of Murray has offended you it is true; but the Protestants persuade themselves that his chief fault in your eyes is his religion, and on that ground they take his side. Pardon him, restore him to favour, and win by doing so all Protestant hearts. The lords will in no wise if they can eschew it be again in the Queen of England's debt, neither by obtaining of any favour at your hand by her intervention, nor yet for any support in time of their banishment. Allow them their charges out of their own lands, and the greater part even of the English bishops will declare for you.'¹

Never had Elizabeth been in greater danger; and the worst features of the peril were the creations of her own untruths. Without a fuller knowledge of the strength and temper of the English Catholics than the surviving evidence reveals, her conduct cannot be judged with entire fairness. Undoubtedly the utmost caution was necessary to avoid giving the Spaniards a pretext for interference; and it is due to her to admit that her own unwillingness to act openly on the side of the northern lords had been endorsed by that of Cecil. Yet she had been driven into a position from which, had Mary Stuart understood how to use her advantage, she would scarcely have been able to extricate herself. If the Queen of Scots had relied on her own judgment she would probably have accepted the advice of Melville and Throgmorton and her other English friends; she would have declared an amnesty, and would have rallied all parties except the extreme Calvinistic fanatics to her side. But such a policy would have involved an indefinite prolongation of the yoke which she had already found intolerable; she must have concealed or suspended her intention of making a religious revolution, and she must have continued to act with a forbearance towards the Protestants which her passionate temper found more and more difficulty in maintaining. The counsels of David Ritzio were worth an army to English liberty: she had surrendered herself entirely and exclusively to Ritzio's guidance; and when Melville attempted to move the dark and dangerous Italian 'he evidenced a disdain of danger and despised counsel.'

---

¹ Letter from Sir N. Throgmorton to the Queen of Scots.—*Printed by Sir James Melville: abridged.*

Ritzio, 'the minion of the Pope,' preferred the more direct and open road of violence and conquest, which he believed, in his ignorance of the people amongst whom he was working, to be equally safe for his mistress, while it promised better for other objects which he had in view for himself. Already every petition addressed to the crown was passing through his hands, and he was growing rich upon the presents which were heaped upon him to buy his favour. He desired rank as well as wealth; and to be made a peer of Scotland, the reward which Mary Stuart intended for him, he required a share of the lands of the banished earls, the estates of Murray most especially, as food at once for his ambition and revenge.

It is time to return to his friend and emissary Francis Yaxlee, who went at the end of August on a mission to Philip.

The conditions under which the King of Spain had promised his assistance seemed to have arrived. Mary Stuart had married Lord Darnley as he advised; her subjects had risen in insurrection with the secret support of the Queen of England, who was threatening to send an army into Scotland for their support. She had run into danger in the interests of the Church of Rome, and she looked with confidence to the most Catholic King to declare for her cause. Yaxlee found Philip at the beginning of October at Segovia. Elizabeth's diplomacy had been so far successful that the Emperor Maximilian was again dreaming that she would marry the Archduke Charles. He was anxious to provide his brother with a throne: he had been wounded by Mary Stuart's refusal to accept the Archduke, when his marriage with her had been arranged between himself and the Cardinal of Lorraine, with the sanction of the Council of Trent. Elizabeth had played upon his humour, and he had reverted to the scheme which had at one time been so anxiously entertained by his father and Philip.¹ The King of Spain's own hopes of any such solution of the English difficulty were waning; yet he was unwilling to offend the Emperor, and he would not throw away a card which might after all be the successful one. It was perhaps the suspicion that Philip was not acting towards her with entire sincerity which urged Mary Stuart into precipitancy; or she might have wished to force Elizabeth into a position in which it would be impossible for any Catholic sovereign to countenance her. But Elizabeth on the one hand had been too cautious, and Philip on the other, though wishing well to the Queen of Scots and evidently believing that she was the only hope of the Catholic cause in England, yet could not overcome his constitutional slowness. He was willing to help her, yet only as Elizabeth had helped the Scotch insurgents, with a secrecy which would enable him to disavow what he had done. He was afraid of the Huguenot tendencies of the French Government; he was afraid that if he took an open part he might set a match to the mine which was about to explode in the Low Countries: he therefore repeated the cautions which Alva had given Beton at Bayonne; he gave Yaxlee a bond for twenty thousand crowns which would be paid him by Granvelle at Brussels; he promised if Elizabeth declared war to contribute such further sums as should be necessary, but he

---

¹ À noche recibí una carta de Chantonnay del 27 del pasado en que me escribe que habiendo dicho al Emperador de parte de V. M⁴. que si era necesario que, para que se hiciese el negocio del matrimonio del Archiduque con la de Inglaterra, V. M⁴. escribiese á la Reyna de su mano sobrello, y que el Emperador le habia respondido que no estaba deshuciado deste negocio, y le diria lo que sobrello habia de escribir á V. M⁴. El deseo es grande que [el Emperador] tiene á este negocio.'— *De Silva to Philip*, November 10. *MS. Simancas.*

would do it only under shelter of the name of the Pope
and through the Pope's hands; in his own person he
would take no part in the quarrel; the time, he said,
was not ripe. He insisted especially that Mary Stuart
should betray no intention of claiming the English throne
during Elizabeth's lifetime. It would exasperate the
Queen of England into decisive action, and justify her to
some extent in an immediate appeal to arms.[1] As little
would he encourage the Queen of Scots to seek assistance
from her uncles in France. She might accept money
wherever she could get it, but to admit a French army
into Scotland would create a greater danger than it
would remove.[2]

With this answer Yaxlee was dismissed; and so
anxious was Philip that Mary Stuart should know his
opinion that he enclosed a duplicate of his reply to de
Silva, with directions that it should be forwarded immediately to Scotland, and with a further credit for money
should the Queen of Scots require it.

Yet Philip was more anxious for her success and more
sincere in his desire to support her than might be
gathered from his cautious language to her ambassador;
and his real feelings may be gathered from a letter
which he wrote after Yaxlee had left Segovia to Cardinal
Pacheco his minister at Rome.

PHILIP II. TO CARDINAL PACHECO.[3]

October 16.

'I have received your letter of the 2nd of September,
containing the message from his Holiness on the assist-

---

[1] 'Porque esto la escandalizaria mucho y daria gran ocasion para ejecutar contra ellos lo que pudiese, y en alguna manera seria justificar su causa.'—*Answer to Yaxlee.* MUNKE vol. ii. p. 200.
[2] Ibid.
[3] *MS. Simancas.*

ance to be given to the Queen of Scots. As his Holiness desires to know my opinion you must tell him first that his anxiety to befriend and support that most excellent and most Christian princess in her present straits is worthy of the zeal which he has ever shown for the good cause, and is what his disposition would have led me to expect. The Queen of Scots has applied to myself as well as to his Holiness; and possessing as I do special knowledge of the condition of that country, and having carefully considered the situation of affairs there, I have arrived at the following conclusions:—

'There are three possibilities—

'1. Either the Queen of Scots may find herself at war only with her own subjects, and may require assistance merely to reduce her own country to obedience and to maintain religion there; or,

'2. The Queen of England afraid for her own safety may openly support the rebels and heretics in their insurrection, and herself undisguisedly declare war; or,

'3. The Queen of Scots may attempt to extort by arms the recognition of her claims on the English succession.

'In either or all of these contingencies his Holiness will act in a manner becoming his position and his character if he take part avowedly in her behalf. I myself am unwilling to come prominently forward, but I am ready to give advice and assistance, and that in the following manner:—

'Suppose the first case that the Scotch rebels find no support from any foreign prince, their strength cannot then be great, and the Queen of Scots with very little aid from us will be able to put them down. It will be sufficient if we send her money, which can be managed secretly; and if his Holiness approves he will do well to send whatever sum he is disposed to give without delay. I shall myself do the same, and indeed I have already sent a credit to my ambassador in England for the Queen of Scots' use.

'If the Queen of England takes an open part, more will be required of us, and secrecy will hardly be possible even if we still confine ourselves to sending money. Whatever be done however, it is my desire that it be done entirely in his Holiness's name. I will contribute in my full proportion; his Holiness shall have the fame and the honour.

'The last alternative is far more difficult. I foresee so many inconveniences as likely to arise from it that the most careful consideration is required before any step is taken. Nothing must be done prematurely; and his Holiness I think should write to the Queen of Scots and caution her how she proceeds. A false move may ruin all, while if she abide her time she cannot fail to succeed. Her present care should be to attach her English friends to herself more firmly, and wherever possible to increase their number; but above all she should avoid creating a suspicion that she aims at anything while the Queen of England is alive. The question of her right to the succession must be continually agitated, but no resolution should be pressed for until success is certain. If she grasp at the crown too soon she will lose it altogether. Let her bide her time before she disclose herself: and meanwhile I will see in what form we can best interfere. The cause is the cause of God, of whom the Queen of Scots is the champion. We now know assuredly that she is the sole gate through which religion can be restored in England; all the rest are closed.'

The unfortunate Yaxlee having received his money in Flanders was hurrying back to his mistress when he was caught in the Channel by a November gale, and was flung up on the coast of Northumberland a mangled body, recognizable only by the despatches found upon his person. They told Elizabeth little which she did not know already. She was perhaps relieved from the fear of an immediate interposition from Spain, the expectation of which as much as any other cause had led to the strangeness of her conduct. But she knew herself to be surrounded with pitfalls into which a false step might at any moment precipitate her; and she could resolve on nothing. One day she thought of trying to persuade the Queen of Scots to establish 'religion' on the English model; 'or if that could not be obtained that there might be liberty of conscience, that the Protestants might serve God their own way without molestation.'[1] Then again in a feeble effort to preserve her dignity she would once more attempt to entrap the Queen of Scots into sending commissioners to England to sue for a settlement of the succession, which naturally did but increase Mary Stuart's exasperation.[2] Bothwell made a raid on the Borders and carried off five or six English prisoners. The Earl of Bedford made reprisals, in the faint hope that it might force Elizabeth into a more courageous attitude. She first blamed Bedford; then stung by an insolent letter from the Queen of Scots she flashed up with momentary pride and became conscious of her injustice to Murray.

---

[1] Instructions to Commissioners going to Scotland, November 1565.—COTTON MSS., CALIG. B. 10.

[2] Randolph to Cecil, December 15.—Scotch MSS. Rolls House.

The Scotch Parliament was summoned for the ensuing February, when Murray and his friends would be required to appear, and if they failed to present themselves would be proceeded against for high treason. The Queen of Scots at Ritzio's instigation was determined to carry an act of attainder and forfeiture against them, which Elizabeth felt herself bound in honour to make an effort to prevent. So anxious she had been for the first two months after they had come to England to disclaim connexion with them that she had almost allowed them to starve; and Randolph on Christmas-day wrote to Cecil that Murray 'had not at that time two crowns in the world.'[1] But this neglect was less the result of deliberate carelessness than of temporary panic; and as the alarm cooled down she recovered some perception of the obligations under which she lay.

At length therefore she consented for herself to name two commissioners if the Queen of Scots would name two others; and in writing on the subject to Randolph, under her first and more generous impulse, she said that 'her chief intention in their meeting was, if it might be, that some good might be done for the Earl of Murray.' Her timidity came back upon her before she had finished her letter; she scored out the words and wrote instead 'the chief intention of this meeting on our part is, *covertly though not manifestly*, to procure that some good might be done for the Earl.'[2] More painful evidence she could scarcely have given of her perplexity and alarm.

Bedford and Sir John Foster were named to represent England. The Queen of Scots, as if in deliberate

---

[1] Randolph to Cecil, December 25.—*Scotch MSS. Rolls House.*
[2] Elizabeth to Randolph, January 10.—*Ibid.*

insult, named Bothwell as a fit person to meet with them; and even this, though wounded to the quick, Elizabeth endured, lest a refusal might 'increase her malice.'[1]

So the winter months passed away; and the time was fast approaching for the meeting of the Scottish Parliament. The Queen of Scots was by this time pregnant. Her popularity in England was instantly tenfold increased; while from every part of Europe warnings came thicker and thicker that mischief was in the wind. 'The young King and Queen of Scots,' wrote Sir Thomas Smith from Paris, 'do look for a further and a bigger crown and have more intelligence and practice in England and in other realms than you think for. Both the Pope's and the King of Spain's hands be in that dish further and deeper than I think you know. The ambassadors of Spain, Scotland, and the Cardinal of Lorraine be too great in their devices for me to like. The Bishop of Glasgow looks to be a cardinal, and to bring in Popery ere it be long, not only into Scotland but into England. I have cause to say to you *vigilate*!'[2]

'It is written,' Randolph reported to Leicester, 'that this Queen's faction increaseth greatly among you. I commend you for that; for so shall you have religion overthrown, your country torn in pieces, and never an honest man left alive that is good or godly. Woe is me for you when David's (Ritzio's) son shall be a king of England.'[3]

At length a darker secret stole abroad that Pius the

---

[1] Elizabeth to Randolph, February 2.—LANSDOWNE MSS. 8.
[2] Sir T. Smith to Cecil, March 1565-6.—*French* MSS. Rolls House.
[3] Randolph to Leicester, January 29.—*Scotch* MSS. Rolls House.

Fifth, who had just succeeded to the Papal chair, had drawn away Catherine de Medici from the freer and nobler part of the French people; that she had entered on the dark course which found its outcome on the day of St. Bartholomew; and that a secret league had been formed between the Pope and the King of France and the Guises for the uprooting of the reformed faith out of France by fair means or foul. Nor was the conspiracy confined to the Continent; a copy of the bond had been sent across to Scotland which Randolph ascertained that Mary Stuart had signed.[1] At the moment when it arrived she had been moved in some slight degree by Melville's persuasions, and perhaps finding that Philip also advised moderation, she was hesitating whether she should not pardon the lords after all. But the Queen-mother's messenger, M. de Villemont, entreated that she would under no circumstance whatever permit men to return to Scotland who had so long thwarted and obstructed her. The unexpected support from France blew her passion into flame again;[2] and she looked only to the meeting of the Parliament, from which the strength of the Protestants would now be absent, not only to gratify her own and Ritzio's revenge but to commence her larger and long-cherished projects. She determined to make an effort to induce the Estates to re-establish Catholicism as the religion of Scotland, leaving the Protestants for the present with liberty of conscience, but with small prospect of retaining long a privilege which when in power they had refused to their opponents.

The defeat of the lords and the humiliating exhibition

---

[1] Randolph to Cecil, February 7.—*Scotch MSS. Rolls House.*
[2] MELVILLE's *Memoirs.*

of Elizabeth's fears had left Mary Stuart to outward appearance mistress of the situation. There was no power in Scotland which seemed capable of resisting her. She wrote to Pius to congratulate him on her triumph over the enemies of the faith, and to assure him that 'with the help of God and his Holiness she would leap over the wall.'[1] Bedford and Randolph ceased to hope; and Murray, in a letter modestly and mournfully beautiful, told Cecil that unless Elizabeth interfered, of which he had now small expectation, 'for anything that he could judge' he and his friends were wrecked for ever.[2]

Suddenly, and from a quarter least expected, a little cloud rose over the halcyon prospects of the Queen of Scots, wrapped the heavens in blackness, and burst over her head in a tornado. On the political stage Mary Stuart was but a great actress. The 'woman' had a drama of her own going on behind the scenes; the theatre caught fire; the mock heroics of the Catholic crusade burnt into ashes; and a tremendous domestic tragedy was revealed before the astonished eyes of Europe.

Differences between the Queen of Scots and her husband.

Towards the close of 1565 rumours went abroad in Edinburgh, coupled with the news that the Queen was enceinte, that she was less happy in her marriage than she had anticipated. She had expected Darnley to be passive in her hands, and she was finding that he was too foolish to be controlled: a proud ignorant self-willed boy was at the best an indifferent companion to an accomplished woman of the world; and when he took upon himself the airs of a king, when he affected to rule the country and still more to rule the Queen, he very soon

---

[1] Mary Stuart to the Pope, January 21, 1566.—MIGNET.
[2] Murray to Cecil, January 9.—*Scotch MSS. Rolls House.*

became intolerable. The first open difference between them arose from the appointment of Bothwell as lieutenant-general in preference to Lennox. The Lennox clan and kindred, the Douglases, the Ruthvens, the Lindsays, who were linked together in feudal affinity, took the affront to themselves; and Darnley supported by his friends showed his resentment by absenting himself from the Court.

'The Lord Darnley,' wrote Randolph on the 20th of December,[1] 'followeth his pastimes more than the Queen is content withal; what it will breed hereafter I cannot say, but in the mean time there is some misliking between them.'

It was seen how Darnley at the time of his marriage grasped at the title of King. As he found his wishes thwarted he became anxious, and his kinsmen with him, that the name should become a reality, and 'the crown matrimonial' be legally secured to him at the approaching Parliament. But there were signs abroad that his wish would not be acceded to; Mary Stuart was unwilling to part with her power for the same reason that Darnley required it.

On Christmas-day Randolph wrote again of 'strange alterations.' 'A while ago,' he said,[2] 'there was nothing but King and Queen; now the Queen's husband is the common word. He was wont in all writings to be first named; now he is placed in the second. Lately there were certain pieces of money coined with their faces Henricus et Maria; these are called in and others framed. Some private disorders there are among themselves; but because they may be but *amantium iræ* or "household

---

[1] *Scotch MSS. Rolls House.*
[2] *Ibid.*

words " as poor men speak, it makes no matter if it grow no further.'

In January a marked affront was passed on Darnley. M. Rambouillet brought from Paris 'the Order of the Cockle' for him. A question rose about his shield. Had 'the crown matrimonial' been intended for him he would have been allowed to bear the royal arms. The Queen coldly 'bade give him his due,' and he was enrolled as Duke of Rothsay and Earl of Ross.[1] Darnley retaliated with vulgar brutality. He gave roistering parties to the young French noblemen in Rambouillet's train and made them drunk.[2]

Loose living of Darnley.

One day he was dining with the Queen at the house of a merchant in Edinburgh. He was drinking hard as usual, and when she tried to check him 'he not only paid no attention to her remonstrance, but also gave her such words as she left the place with tears.' Something else happened also, described as 'vicious,' the nature of which may be guessed at, at some festivity or other on 'Inch Island;'[3] and as a natural consequence the Queen 'withdrew her company' from the Lord Darnley; a staircase connected their rooms, but they slept apart.[4]

Intimacy between Mary Stuart and Ritzio.

Side by side with the estrangement from her husband Mary Stuart admitted Ritzio to closer and closer intimacy. Signor David, as he was called, became the Queen's inseparable companion in the council-room and the cabinet. At all hours of the day he was to be found with her in her apartments. She kept late hours, and he was often alone with her till midnight. He had the control of all the business of the State; as Darnley grew troublesome

---

[1] KNOX; *History of the Reformation.*

[2] 'Sick with draughts of aqua composita.'

[3] Sir William Drury to Cecil, February 16. — COTTON *MSS.*, CALIG. B. 10.—*Printed in* KEITH.

[4] RUTHVEN's *Narrative.*—KEITH.

his presence was dispensed with at the Council, and a signet, the duplicate of the King's, was intrusted to the favoured secretary. Finding himself so deeply detested by the adherents of Lennox, Ritzio induced the Queen to show favour to those among the banished lords who were most hostile to the King and were least determined in their Protestantism. Chatelherault was pardoned and allowed to return as a support against the Lennox faction in case of difficulty;[1] while among the Congregation—as was seen in one of Randolph's letters —the worst construction was placed on the relations between the Queen and the favourite.

Thus a King's party and a Queen's party had shaped themselves within six months of the marriage: Scotland was the natural home of conspiracies, for law was powerless there, and social duty was overridden by the more sacred obligation of affinity or private bond. On the 13th of February (the date is important) Randolph thus wrote to Leicester:—

'I know now for certain that this Queen repenteth her marriage, that she hateth the King and all his kin; I know that he knoweth himself that he hath a partaker in play and game with him; I know that there are practices in hand contrived between the father and the son to come by the crown against her will; I know that if that take effect which is intended, David, with the con-

---

[1] 'The Duke of Chatelherault, finding so favourable address, hath much displeased both the King and his father, who is in great misliking of the Queen. She is very weary of him. Thus it is that those that depend wholly on him are not liked of her, nor they that follow her in like manner are not liked of him, as David and others. If there should between her and the Lord Darnley arise such controversy as she could not well appease, the Duke's aid she would use.'—*Drury to Cecil, February* 16. COTTON *MSS.*, CALIG. B. 10.

sent of the King, shall have his throat cut within these ten days. Many things and grievouser and worse are brought to my ears, yea of things intended against the Queen's own person.'[1]

It was observed on the first return of Lennox that the enmities and friendships of his family intersected and perplexed the leading division between Catholics and Protestants. Lord Darnley had been brought to Scotland as the representative of the English Catholics and as a support to the Catholic faction; but it was singular that the great Scottish families most nearly connected with him were Protestants; while the Gordons, the Hamiltons, the Betons, the relations generally of Chatelherault, who was Lennox's principal rival, were chiefly on the opposite side. The confusion hitherto had worked ill for the interests of the Reformers. The House of Douglas had preferred the claims of blood to those of religion: the Earl of Ruthven though Murray's friend was Darnley's uncle,[2] and had stood by the Queen through the struggle of the summer; Lindsay a Protestant to the backbone had married a Douglas and went with the Earl of Morton; the desire to secure the crown to a prince of their own blood and race had overweighed all higher and nobler claims.

The desertion of so large a section of his friends had been the real cause of Murray's failure; Protestantism was not dead in Scotland, but other interests had paralyzed its vitality, just as four years before Murray's eagerness to secure the English succession for his sister

---

Printed in TYTLER's *History of Scotland*.
[2] Ruthven had married a half-sister of Lady Margaret Lennox.

had led him into his first and fatal mistake of supporting her in refusing to ratify the Treaty of Edinburgh. The quarrel between the Queen and her husband flung all parties back into their natural places; Lennox who twenty years before had been brought in from France in the interest of Henry the Eighth as a check on Cardinal Beton, drifted again into his old position in the front of the Protestant league; and Darnley's demand for the matrimonial crown, though in himself the mere clamour of disappointed vanity, was maintained by powerful noblemen, who though they neither possessed nor deserved the confidence of the Reformers yet were recognizing too late that they had mistaken their interest in leaving them.

But the matrimonial crown it became every day more clear that Darnley was not to have; Ritzio above all others was held responsible for the Queen's resolution to refuse it, and for this, as for a thousand other reasons, he was gathering hatred on his devoted head. A foreigner who had come to Scotland two years before as a wandering musician was thrusting himself into the administration of the country, and pushing from their places the fierce lords who had been accustomed to dictate to their sovereign. As a last stroke of insolence he was now aiming at the Chancellorship, of which the Queen was about to deprive in his favour the great chief of the House of Douglas.

While their blood was set on fire with these real and fancied indignities Lord Darnley, if his word was to be believed, went one night between twelve and one to the Queen's room. Finding the door locked he knocked but could get no answer. At length after he had called many times and had threatened to break the lock the Queen drew back the bolt. He entered and she appeared

CHAP IX
1566
February

Darnley
accuses the
Queen of
unfaithfulness.

to be alone, but on searching he found Ritzio half-dressed in a closet.[1]

Darnley's word was not a good one: he was capable of inventing such a story to compass his other purposes, or if it was true it might have been innocently explained. The Queen of Scots frequently played cards with Ritzio late into the night, and being a person entirely careless of appearances she might easily have been alone with him with no guilty intention under the conditions which Darnley described. However it was, he believed or pretended that he had found evidence of his dishonour, and communicated his discovery to Sir George Douglas another of his mother's brothers, who at Darnley's desire on the 10th of February informed the Earl of Ruthven.

Once before, it appeared, 'the nobility had given Darnley counsel suitable to his honour'—that is to say they had intimated to him their own views of Ritzio's proceedings and character. Darnley had betrayed them to the Queen, who had of course been exasperated. Ruthven had been three months ill; he was then scarcely able to leave his bed and was inclined at first to run into no further trouble; but pressed at length by Darnley's oaths and entreaties he saw in what had occurred an opportunity for undoing his work of the summer and

---

[1] 'L'une cause de la mort de David est que le Roy quelques jours auparavant, environ une heure après minuict, seroit allé heurter à la chambre de ladicte dame, qui estoit au dessus de la sienne; et d'autant que après avoir plusieurs fois heurté l'on ne luy respondoit point il auroit apellé souvent la Royne, la priant de ouvrir, et enfin la menaçant de rompre la porte; à cause de quoy elle lui auroit ouvert. Laquelle ledict Roy trouva seule dedans ladicte chambre; mais ayant cherché partout il auroit trouvé dedans son cabinet ledict David en chemise, couvert seullement d'une robbe fourrée.'—Analyse d'une dépêche de M. de Foix à la Royne mère. TEULET, vol. ii. p. 267.

for bringing back the banished lords. Parliament was to meet in the first week in March to proceed with the forfeitures, so that no time was to be lost. Ruthven consulted Argyle who was ready to agree to anything which would save Murray from attainder. Maitland who since his conduct about the marriage had been under an eclipse gave his warm adhesion; and swiftly and silently the links of the scheme were welded. The plan was to punish the miserable minion who, whatever his other offences, was notoriously the chief instigator of the Queen's bitterness against her brother, and to give the coveted crown matrimonial to Darnley, provided he on his part 'would take the part of the lords, bring them back to their old rooms, and establish religion as it was at the Queen's home-coming.'[1]

The conspirators for their mutual security drew a 'bond,' to which they required Darnley's signature, that he might not afterwards evade his responsibility. On their side they 'undertook to be liege subjects to the said Prince Henry, to take part with him in all his lawful actions causes and quarrels, to be friends to his friends and enemies to his enemies.' At the Parliament they would obtain for him 'the crown matrimonial for his life;' and 'failing the succession of their sovereign they would maintain his right to the crown of Scotland after her death.' Religion should be 'maintained and established as it was on the arrival of their sovereign lady in the realm.' 'They would spare neither life, lands, goods, nor possessions in setting forward all things to the advancement of the said noble prince, and would intercede with the Queen of England for favour to be shown both to himself and to his mother.'

---

[1] Randolph to Cecil, February 20.—*Scotch MSS. Rolls House.*

Chap IX
1466 February

Darnley promised in return that the banished noblemen 'should have free remission of all their faults' as soon as the possession of the crown matrimonial enabled him to pardon them, and till he obtained it he undertook to prevent their impeachment. The lords might return at once to Scotland in full possession of 'their lands, titles and goods.' If they 'were meddled with' he would stand by them to the uttermost, and religion should be established as they desired.[1]

Copies of these articles were carried by swift messengers to Newcastle. Ritzio's name was not mentioned; there was nothing in them to show that more was intended than a forcible revolution on the meeting of Parliament; and such as they were, they were promptly signed by Murray and his friends. Argyle subscribed, Maitland subscribed, Ruthven subscribed; Morton hesitated, but at the crisis of his uncertainty Mary Stuart innocently carried out her threat of depriving him of the Chancellorship, and he added his name in a paroxysm of anger. It need not be supposed that the further secret was unknown to any of them, but it was undesirable to commit the darker features of the plot to formal writing.

Randolph is expelled from Scotland.

Meanwhile the Queen of Scots all unconscious of the deadly coil which was gathering round her had chosen the moment to order Randolph to leave Scotland. She entertained not the faintest suspicion of the conspiracy, but she knew that the English ambassador had shared Murray's secrets, that he had been Elizabeth's instrument in keeping alive in Scotland the Protestant faction, and that so long as he remained the party whom she most detested would have a nucleus to gather round.

---
[1] Bond subscribed March 6, 1566.—*Scotch MSS. Rolls House.*

Believing that she could do nothing which Elizabeth would dare to resent, she called him before the Council, charged him with holding intercourse with her rebels, and bade him begone.[1] The opportunity was ill selected, for Elizabeth had been for some time recovering her firmness; she had sent Murray money for his private necessities; in the middle of February she had so far overcome both her economy and her timidity that she supplied him with a thousand pounds 'to be employed in the common cause and maintenance of religion;'[2] and before she heard of the treatment of Randolph she had taken courage to write with something of her old manner to the Queen of Scots herself.

'She had not intended,' she said, 'to have written on the subject again to her, but hearing that her intercession hitherto in favour of the lords had been not only fruitless but that at the approaching Parliament the Queen of Scots meant to proceed to the worst extremities she would no longer forbear to speak her mind.' The Earl of Murray had risen in arms against her only to prevent her marriage and for the defence of his own life from the malice which was borne him; he was the truest and best of her subjects; and therefore, she said, 'in the interest of both the realms we are moved to require you to have that regard that the Earl and others with him may be received to your grace, or if not that you will forbear proceeding against him and the others until some better opportunity move you to show them favour.'[3]

In this mood Elizabeth was not inclined to bear with

---

[1] The Queen of Scots to Elizabeth, February 20.—*Scotch MSS. Rolls House.*

Acknowledgment by the Earl of Murray of the receipt of moneys from the Queen's Majesty, February, 1566.—*MS. Ibid.*

[3] Elizabeth to the Queen of Scots, February 24.—*Scotch MSS. Rolls House.*

patience the dismissal of her ambassador. Proudly and coldly she replied to Mary Stuart's announcement of what she had done, 'that inasmuch as the Queen of Scots had been pleased to break the usages of nations and pass this affront upon her, as this was the fruit of the long forbearance which she had herself shown, she would be better advised before she entered into any further correspondence; she would take such measures as might be necessary for her own defence; and for the Earl of Murray to deal plainly she could not for her honour and for the opinion she had of his sincerity and loyalty towards his country but see him relieved in England, whereof she thought it convenient to advertise the Queen of Scots; if harm came of it she trusted God would convert the evil to those that were the cause of it.'[1]

The first and probably the second of these letters never reached their destination: the events which were going forward in Scotland rendered entreaties and threats in behalf of Murray alike unnecessary.[2] Randolph though ordered off was unwilling to go till he saw the execution of the plot: he made excuses for remaining till an escort came to his door with orders to see him over the frontiers, and he was compelled to obey. Bothwell met him on the road to Berwick with apologies and protests; but Randolph said he knew that Bothwell and one other— no doubt Ritzio—were those who had advised his expulsion. They desired to force Elizabeth to declare war, when Bothwell hoped 'to win his spurs.'[2]

---

[1] Elizabeth to the Queen of Scots, March 3.—LANSDOWNE *MSS.* 8.

[2] 'A great business is in hand in Scotland, which will bring about the recall of the Earl of Murray, so that we have forborne to forward your Majesty's letters in his behalf.' —*Randolph and Bedford to Elizabeth, March 6. Scotch MSS. Rolls House.*

[3] Randolph to Cecil, March 6.— *MS. Ibid.*

Far enough was the Queen of Scots from the triumphant war which she was imagining; far enough was Bothwell from his spurs and Ritzio from his Chancellorship and the investiture of the lands of Murray. The mine was dug, the train was laid, the match was lighted to scatter them and their projects all to the winds.

The Parliament was summoned for Monday the 11th of February; on the 12th the Bill of Attainder against the lords was to be brought forward and pressed to immediate completion. On Friday the 8th the conspirators sent a safe-conduct signed by Darnley to bring Murray back to Scotland. Lord Hume had been gained over and had undertaken to escort his party through the marches, and before the Earl and his companions could reach Edinburgh all would be over.[1]

The outline of the intended proceedings was sketched by Randolph for Cecil's information on his arrival at Berwick.

BEDFORD AND RANDOLPH TO CECIL.[2]

Berwick, March 6.

'The Lord Darnley weary of bearing the name of a king and not having the honour pertaining to such a dignity is in league with certain of the lords for a great attempt, whereby the noblemen now out of their country may without great difficulty be restored and in the end tranquillity ensue in that country. Somewhat we are sure you have heard of diverse discords and jars between the Queen and her husband; partly for that she hath refused him the crown matrimonial, partly for that he hath assured knowledge of such usage of himself as

[1] Bedford and Randolph to Cecil and Leicester, March 8.—*Scotch MSS. Rolls House.*
[2] *MS. Ibid.*

altogether is intolerable to be borne, which if it were not over-well known we would both be very loth that it could be true. To take away this occasion of slander he is himself determined to be at the apprehension and execution of him whom he is able manifestly to charge with the crime, and to have done him the most dishonour that can be to any man, much more being as he is. We need not more plainly describe the person—you have heard of the man whom we mean.

'The time of execution and performance of these matters is before the Parliament, as near as it is. To this determination there are privy in Scotland these—Argyle, Morton, Ruthven, Boyd, and Lidington; in England these—Murray, Grange, Rothes, myself (Bedford), and the writer hereof (Randolph).

'If the Queen will not yield to persuasion, we know not how they propose to proceed. If she make a power at home she will be fought with; if she seek aid from abroad the country will be placed at the Queen's Majesty's disposal to deal as she think fit.'

In the blindness of confidence, and to prevent the chance of failure in Parliament, Mary Stuart had collected the surviving peers of the old 'spiritual estate,' the Catholic bishops and abbots, and placed them 'in the antient manner,' intending as she herself declared,[1] 'to have done some good anent the restoring the auld religion, and to have proceeded against the rebels according to their demerits.' On Thursday the 7th she presided in person at the choice of the Lords of the Articles, naming with her own mouth 'such as would say what she thought expedient to the forfeiture of the

---

[1] The Queen of Scots to the Archbishop of Glasgow, April 2.—KEITH.

banished lords;[1] and on Friday there was a preliminary meeting at the Tolbooth to prepare the Bill of Attainder. The Lords of the Articles,[2] carefully as they had been selected, at first reported 'that they could find no cause sufficient for so severe a measure.'[3] The next day—Saturday—the Queen appeared at the Tolbooth in person, and after 'great reasoning and opposition' carried her point. 'There was no other way but the lords should be attainted.'[4] The Act was drawn, the forfeiture was decreed, and required only the sanction of the Estates.[5]

The same day, perhaps at the same hour, when Mary Stuart was exulting in the consciousness of triumph, the conspirators were completing their preparations. Sunday the 10th had been the day on which they had first fixed to strike their blow. But Darnley was impatient. He swore that 'if the slaughter was not hasted' he would stab David in the Queen's presence with his own hand. Each hour of delay was an additional risk of discovery, and it was agreed that the deed should be done the same evening. Ruthven proposed to seize Ritzio in his own room, to try him before an extemporized tribunal, and to hang him at the market cross. So commonplace a proceeding however would not satisfy the imagination of Darnley, who desired a more dramatic revenge; he would have his enemy seized in the Queen's own room, in the very sanctuary of his intimacy; 'where she

---

[1] RUTHVEN's narrative.—'Who chose the Lords of the Articles?' Ruthven said to the Queen. 'Not I,' said the Queen. 'Saving your presence,' said he, 'you chose them all, and nominated them.'

[2] The Lords of the Articles were a committee chosen from the Three Estates, and according to law, chosen by the Estates, to prepare the measures which were to be submitted to Parliament.

[3] RUTHVEN's narrative.

[4] Knox.

[5] The Queen of Scots to the Archbishop of Glasgow, April 2.—KEITH.

might be taunted in his presence because she had not entertained her husband as she ought of duty.' The ill-spirited boy, in retaliation for treatment which went it is likely no further than coldness and contempt, had betrayed or invented his own disgrace, to lash his kindred into fury and to break the spirit of the proud woman who had humbled him with her scorn.

The Queen's friends — Huntly, Athol, Sutherland, Bothwell, Livingston, Fleming, Sir James Balfour, and others — were in Edinburgh for the Parliament, and had rooms in Holyrood; but as none of them dreamt of danger there were no troops there but the ordinary guard, which was scanty and could be easily overpowered. It was arranged that as soon as darkness had closed in the Earl of Moreton with a party of the Douglases and their kindred should silently surround the palace: at eight o'clock the doors should be seized and no person permitted to go out or in; while Morton himself with a sufficient number of trusted friends should take possession of the staircase leading to the Queen's rooms, and cut off communication with the rest of the building. Meanwhile the rest———. But a plan of the rooms is necessary to make the story intelligible. The suite of apartments occupied by Mary Stuart were on the first floor in the north-west angle of Holyrood Palace. They communicated in the usual way by a staircase with the large inner quadrangle. A door from the landing led directly into the presence chamber; inside the presence chamber was the bedroom; and beyond the bedroom a small cabinet or boudoir not more than twelve feet square, containing a sofa, a table, and two or three chairs. Here after the labours of the day the Queen gave her little supper parties. Darnley's rooms were immediately below, connected with the bedroom by a narrow spiral staircase, which opened close to the little door leading into the cabinet.

'Knowing the King's character, and that he would have a lusty princess afterwards in his arms,' the conspirators required his subscription to another bond, by which he declared that all that was done 'was his own device and intention;' and then after an early supper together, Ruthven, though so ill that he could hardly stand, with his brother George Douglas, Ker of Faldonside, and one other, followed Darnley to his room, and thence with hushed breath and stealthy steps they ascended the winding stairs. A tapestry curtain hung before the cabinet. Leaving his companions in the bedroom, Darnley raised it and entered. Supper was on the table; the Queen was sitting on the sofa, Ritzio in a chair opposite to her, and Murray's loose sister the Countess of Argyle on one side. Arthur Erskine the equerry, Lord Robert Stuart, and the Queen's French physician were in attendance standing.

Darnley placed himself on the sofa at his wife's side. She asked him if he had supped. He muttered something, threw his arm round her waist, and kissed her. As she shrank from him half surprised, the curtain was again lifted, and against the dark background, alone, his corslet glimmering through the folds of a crimson sash, a steel cap on his head, and his face pale as if he had risen from the grave, stood the figure of Ruthven.

Glaring for a moment on Darnley, and answering his kiss with the one word 'Judas,' Mary Stuart confronted the awful apparition, and demanded the meaning of the intrusion.

Pointing to Ritzio, and with a voice sepulchral as his features, Ruthven answered:

'Let yon man come forth; he has been here over long.'

'What has he done?' the Queen answered; 'he is here by my will.' 'What means this?' she said, turning again on Darnley.

The caitiff heart was already flinching. 'Ce n'est rien!' he muttered. 'It is nothing!'[1] But those whom he had led into the business would not let it end in nothing.

'Madame,' said Ruthven, 'he has offended your honour; he has offended your husband's honour; he has caused your Majesty to banish a great part of the nobility that he might be made a lord; he has been the destroyer of the commonwealth, and must learn his duty better.'

'Take the Queen your wife to you,' he said to Darnley, as he strode forward into the cabinet.

The Queen started from her seat 'all amazed,' and threw herself in his way, while Ritzio cowered trembling behind her and clung to her dress.

Stuart, Erskine, and the Frenchman recovering from their astonishment and seeing Ruthven apparently alone, 'made at him to thrust him out.'

'Lay no hands on me,' Ruthven cried, and drew his dagger; 'I will not be handled.' In another moment Faldonside and George Douglas were at his side. Faldonside held a pistol at Mary Stuart's breast; the bedroom door behind was burst open, and the dark throng of Morton's followers poured in. Then all was confusion; the table was upset, Lady Argyle catching a candle as it

---

[1] Bedford and Randolph in their report from Berwick, said the King answered 'It was against her honour.' But these words were used by Ruthven. An original report, printed by TEULET, vol. ii. p. 262, compared with that given by Mary herself in the letter to the Archbishop of Glasgow, printed in KEITH, creates a belief that the words in the text were those which Darnley really used. They are more in keeping with his character.

fell. Ruthven thrust the Queen into Darnley's arms and bade him hold her; while Faldonside bent Ritzio's little finger back till he shrieked with pain and loosed the convulsive grasp with which he clung to his mistress.

'Do not hurt him,' Mary said faintly. 'If he has done wrong he shall answer to justice.'

'This shall justify him,' said the savage Faldonside, drawing a cord out of his pocket. He flung a noose round Ritzio's body, and while George Douglas snatched the King's dagger from its sheath, the poor wretch was dragged into the midst of the scowling crowd and borne away into the darkness. He caught Mary's bed as he passed; Faldonside struck him sharply on the wrist; he let go with a shriek, and as he was hurried through the anteroom the cries of his agony came back upon Mary's ear; 'Madame, madame, save me! save me!—justice—I am a dead man! spare my life!'

Unhappy one! his life would not be spared. They had intended to keep him prisoner through the night and hang him after some form of trial; but vengeance would not wait for its victim. He was borne alive as far as the stairhead, when George Douglas, with the words 'This is from the King,' drove Darnley's dagger into his side: a moment more and the whole fierce crew were on him like hounds upon a mangled wolf; he was stabbed through and through with a hate which death was not enough to satisfy, and was then dragged head foremost down the staircase, and lay at its foot with sixty wounds in him.

So ended Ritzio, unmourned by living soul save her whose favour had been his ruin, unheeded now that he was dead as common carrion, and with no epitaph on his remains except a few brief words from an old servant of the palace, so pathetic because so commonplace. The

CHAP IX
1566
March 9

body was carried into the lodge and flung upon a chest to be stripped for burial. 'Here is his destiny,' the porter moralized as he stood by; 'for on this chest was his first bed when he came to this place, and there now he lieth a very niggard and misknown knave.'[1]

The Queen meanwhile fearing the worst but not knowing that Ritzio actually was dead, had struggled into her bedroom, and was there left with Ruthven and her husband. Ruthven had followed the crowd for a moment, but not caring to leave Darnley alone with her had returned. She had thrown herself sobbing upon a seat; the Earl bade her not be afraid, no harm was meant to her; what was done was by the King's order.

'Yours!' she said, turning on Darnley as on a snake; 'was this foul act yours? Coward! wretch! did I raise you out of the dust for this?'

Driven to bay he answered sullenly that he had good cause; and then his foul nature rushing to his lips he flung brutal taunts at her for her intimacy with Ritzio, and complaints as nauseous of her treatment of himself.[2]

'Well,' she said, 'you have taken your last of me and your farewell; I shall never rest till I give you as sorrowful a heart as I have at this present.'

---

[1] RUTHVEN's narrative.

[2] The expressions themselves are better unproduced. The conversation rests on the evidence of Ruthven, which is considerably better than Darnley's, and if it was faithfully related might justify Randolph's view of the possible parentage of James the Sixth. But the recollection of a person who had been just concerned in so tremendous a scene was not likely to be very exact. Bedford and Randolph believed the worst:

'It is our part,' they said in a despatch to the English Council, 'rather to pass the matter over in silence than to make any rehearsal of things committed to us in secret; but we know to whom we write;' and they went on to describe the supposed conversation word for word as Ruthven related it. Those who are curious in Court scandals may refer to this letter, which has been printed by Mr. Wright in the first volume of *Elizabeth and her Times*.

Ruthven tried to soothe her, but to no purpose. Could she have trampled Darnley into dust upon the spot she would have done it. Catching sight of the empty scabbard at his side, she asked him where his dagger was.

He said he did not know.

'It will be known hereafter,' she said; 'it shall be dear blood to some of you if David's be spilt. Poor David!' she cried, 'good and faithful servant! may God have mercy on your soul.'

Fainting between illness and excitement, Ruthven with a half apology sank into a chair and called for wine.

'Is this your sickness?' she said bitterly. 'If I die of my child and the commonwealth come to ruin, there are those who will revenge me on the Lord Ruthven. Running over the proud list of friends with which she had fooled her fancy, she threatened him with Philip and Charles and Maximilian and her uncles and the Pope.

'Those are over great persons,' Ruthven answered, 'to meddle with so poor a man as me. No harm is meant you. If aught has been done to-night which you mislike, your husband and none of us is the cause.'

The courage and strength with which the Queen had hitherto borne up began to give way.

'What—what have I done to be thus handled?' she sobbed.

'Ask your husband,' said the Earl.

'No,' she said, 'I will ask you. I will set my crown before the Lords of the Articles, and if they find I have offended, let them give it where they please.'

'Who chose the Lords of the Articles?' Ruthven answered with a smile, 'you chose them all.'

At this moment the boom was heard of the alarm bell in Edinburgh. A page rushed in to say that there was fighting in the quadrangle; and the Earl, leaning heavily on a servant's arm, rose and went down. Huntly, Sutherland, and Bothwell hearing the noise and confusion had come out of their rooms to know what it meant. Morton's followers required them to surrender: they had called a few servants about them and were defending themselves against heavy odds when Ruthven appeared. Ill as he was he thrust himself into the mêlée, commanded both sides to drop their arms, and by the glare of a torch read to them Darnley's bond. 'The banished earls,' he said, 'would be at Holyrood in the morning, and he prayed that all feuds and passions might be buried in the dead man's grave.'

The Queen's friends, surprised and outnumbered, affected to be satisfied; the leaders on both sides shook hands; and Bothwell and Huntly withdrew to their own apartments, forced open the windows, dropped to the ground and fled.

This disturbance was scarcely over when the Provost of Edinburgh came out of the Canongate with four hundred of the town guard and demanded the meaning of the uproar. The Provost was a supporter of the Queen; Mary dashed from her seat, wrenched back the casement and cried out for help.

'Sit down,' some ruffian cried. 'If you stir you shall be cut in collops and flung over the walls.'[1] She was dragged away, and Darnley whose voice was well known called out that the Queen was well, that what had been

---

[1] The speaker is not known. Mary says in her letter to the Archbishop of Glasgow, 'The Lords in our face declared that we should be cut down.' It was not Ruthven, who was still absent.

done was done by orders from himself, and that they might go home. The citizens bore no good will to Ritzio: too familiar with wild scenes to pay much heed to them they inquired no further, and went back to their homes, leaving eighty of their number to assist Morton in the guard of the palace.

Ruthven returned for a moment, but only to call Darnley away and leave the Queen to her rest. The King withdrew, and with him all the other actors in the late tragedy who had remained in the scene of it. The ladies of the court were forbidden to enter, and Mary Stuart was locked alone into her room amidst the traces of the fray, to seek such repose as she could find.

So closed Saturday the 9th of March at Holyrood. The same night another dark deed was done in Edinburgh, which passed scarce noticed in the agitation of the murder of Ritzio. Mary of Lorraine the year before her death had a chaplain named Adam Black; he was a lax kind of man, and after being detected in sundry moral improprieties had been banished to England, where he held a cure in the English Church near Newcastle. His old habits remained with him; he acknowledged to Lord Bedford one bad instance of seduction; but it is to be supposed that he had merit of some kind, for Mary Stuart as soon as she was emancipated from the first thraldom of the Puritans recalled him, took him into favour, and appointed him one of the court preachers. He had better have remained in Northumberland. A citizen encountered him a little before Christmas in some room or passage where he should not have been. He received 'two or three blows with a cudgel and one with a dagger,' and had been since unable to leave his bed. While Edinburgh was shuddering over the scene in the palace, a brother or husband who had matter against the chaplain—the same perhaps who had stabbed him—finished his work, and murdered the wounded wretch where he lay.[1]

In the morning at daybreak a proclamation went out in the King's name that the Parliament was postponed and that 'all bishops, abbots, and Papists should depart the town.' Murray was expected in a few hours; no one knew how deep or how far the conspiracy had gone, and the Catholics, uncertain what to do, offered no resistance. What was to be done with the Queen was the next difficulty. They had caged their bird, but it might be less easy to hold her; and if they believed the Queen was crushed or broken the conspirators knew little of the temper which they had undertaken to control: sleeping behind that grace of form and charm of manner there lay a spirit which no misfortune could tame—a nature like a panther's, merciless and beautiful—and along with it every dexterous art by which women can outwit the coarser intellects of men.

In the silence and solitude of that awful night she nerved herself for the work before her. With the grey of the twilight she saw Sir James Melville passing under her window and called to him to bring the city guard and rescue her; but Melville bowed and passed on; at that moment rescue was impossible; she had nothing to depend upon but her own courage and her husband's folly. Could she escape her friends would rally round her, and her first thought was to fly in the disguise of one of her gentlewomen. But to escape alone, even if possible, would be to leave Darnley with the lords; she resolved to play a bolder game, to divide him from them, and carry him off, and to leave them without the name of a king to shield their deed.

---

[1] Randolph to Cecil, March 13.—*Scotch MSS. Rolls House.*

In the first agony of passion she had been swept away from her self-control, and she had poured on her husband the full stream of her hate and scorn. He returned to her room on the Sunday morning to find her in appearance subdued, composed, and affectionate. To Mary Stuart it was an easy matter to play upon the selfish cowardly and sensual nature of Darnley. As Ruthven had foreseen, she worked upon him by her caresses; she persuaded him that he had been fatally deceived in his supposed injuries; but she affected to imagine that he had been imposed on by the arts of others, and when he lied she pretended to believe him. She uttered no word of reproach, but she appealed to him through the child—his child—whose safety was endangered; and she prayed that at least, situated as she was, she might not be left entirely among men, and that her ladies might be allowed to attend her.

Soft as the clay of which he was made, Darnley obtained the reluctant consent of Morton and Ruthven. The ladies of the palace were admitted to assist at the Queen's morning toilet, and the instant use she made of them was to communicate with Huntly and Bothwell. The next point was to obtain larger liberty for herself. Towards the afternoon 'she made as though she would part with her child;' a midwife was sent for, who with the French physician insisted that she must be removed to a less confined air. To Darnley she maintained an attitude of dependent tenderness; and fooled in his idle pride by the prayers of the woman whom he believed that he had brought to his feet, he was led on to require that the guard should be removed from the gate, and that the exclusive charge of her should be committed to himself.

The conspirators 'seeing that he was growing effeminate, liked his proposals in no way;' they warned him that if he yielded so easily 'both he and they would have cause to repent;' and satisfied that the threat of miscarriage was but 'trick and policy,' they refused to dismiss a man from his post and watched the palace with unremitting vigilance.

So passed Sunday. As the dusk closed in a troop of horse appeared on the road from Dunbar. In a few moments more the Earl of Murray was at the gate.

It was not thus that Mary Stuart had hoped to meet her brother. His head sent home by Bothwell from the Border, or himself brought back a living prisoner, with the dungeon, the scaffold, and the bloody axe—these were the images which a few weeks or days before she had associated with the next appearance in Edinburgh of her father's son. Her feelings had undergone no change. He knew some secrets about her which she could not pardon the possessor, and she hated him with the hate of hell; but the more deep-set passion paled for the moment before a thirst for revenge on Ritzio's murderers.

On alighting the Earl was conducted immediately to the Queen's presence. The accomplished actress threw herself sobbing into his arms.

'Oh my brother,' she said as she kissed him, 'if you had been here I should not have been so uncourteously handled.'

Murray had 'a free and generous nature.' But a few hours had passed since she had forced the unwilling Lords of the Articles to prepare a Bill of Attainder against him; but her shame, her seeming helplessness, and the depth of her fall touched him, and he shed tears.

The following morning Murray, Ruthven, Morton, and the rest of the party, met to consider the next step which they should take. Little is known of their deliberations except from the suspected source of a letter from Mary Stuart to the Archbishop of Glasgow. .Some, she said, proposed to keep her a perpetual prisoner, some to put her to death, some 'that she should be warded in Stirling Castle till she had approved in Parliament what they had done, established their religion, and given to the King the whole government of the realm.'

Some measure of this sort they were without doubt prepared to venture; it had been implied in the very nature of their enterprise: yet to carry it out they required Darnley's countenance, and fool and coward as they knew him to be they had not fathomed the depth of his imbecility and baseness. While the lords were in consultation the Queen had wormed the whole secret from him; he told her of the plot for the return of Murray and his friends, with the promises which had been made to himself; he revealed every name that he knew, concealing nothing save that the murder had been his own act and design and provoked by his accusations against herself; he had forgotten that his own handwriting could be produced in deadly witness against him. From that moment she played upon him like an instrument; she showed him that if he remained with the lords he would be a tool in their hands; she assured him of the return of her own affection for him, and flattered his fancy with visions of greatness which might be in store for him if he would take his place again at her side; she talked of 'his allies the confederate princes,' who would be displeased if he changed his religion; she appealed again to the unborn heir of their united greatness, and she bound him soul and body to do her bidding.

After possessing him with the plans which she had formed to escape, she sent him to the lords to promise in her name that she was ready to forget the past and to bury all unkindness in a general reconciliation. They felt instinctively that what they had done could never really be pardoned; but Ruthven, Morton, and Murray returned with Darnley to her presence, when again with the seeming simplicity of which she was so finished a mistress, she repeated the same assurances. She was ready, she said, to bind herself in writing if they would not trust her word; and while the two other noblemen were drawing a form for her to sign she took Murray by the hand and walked with him for an hour. She then retired to her room. Darnley as soon as the bond was ready, took charge of it, promising to return it signed on the following day; and meanwhile he pressed again that after so much concession on her part they were bound to meet her with corresponding courtesy and to spare her the ignominy of being longer held a prisoner in her own palace.

Had they refused to consent, an attempt would have been made that night by Bothwell to carry her off by force. But to reject the request of Darnley, whose elevation to a share of the throne was the professed object of the conspiracy, was embarrassing and perhaps dangerous; they gave way after another warning; the guard was withdrawn, Ruthven protesting as he yielded that 'whatever bloodshed followed should be on the King's head.'

The important point gained, Darnley would not awake suspicion by returning to the Queen; he sent her word privately that 'all was well;' and at eight in the evening Stewart of Traquair Captain of the Royal Guard, Arthur Erskine, 'whom she would trust with a thousand lives,' and Standen, a young and gallant gentleman, assembled in the Queen's room to arrange a plan for the escape from Holyrood. The first question was where she was to go. Though the gates were no longer occupied the palace would doubtless be watched; and to attempt flight and to fail would be certain ruin. In the Castle of Edinburgh she would be safe with Lord Erskine, but she could reach the castle only through the streets which would be beset with enemies; and unfit as she was for the exertion she determined to make for Dunbar.

She stirred the blood of the three youths with the most touching appeal which could be made to the generosity of man. Pointing to the child that was in her womb she adjured them by their loyalty to save the unborn hope of Scotland. So addressed they would have flung themselves naked on the pikes of Morton's troopers. They swore they would do her bidding be it what it would; and then 'after her sweet manner and wise directions, she dismissed them till midnight to put all in order as she herself excellently directed.'

'The rendezvous appointed with the horses was near the broken tombs and demolished sepultures in the ruined Abbey of Holyrood.'[1] A secret passage led underground from the palace to the vaults of the abbey; and at midnight Mary Stuart, accompanied by one servant and her husband—who had left the lords under pretence of going to bed—'crawled through the charnel-house, among the bones and skulls of the antient kings,' and 'came out of the earth' where the horses were shivering in the March midnight air.

The moon was clear and full. 'The Queen with incredible animosity was mounted *en croup* behind Sir Arthur Erskine upon a beautiful English double gelding,' 'the King on a courser of Naples;' and then away

---

[1] Then standing at the south-eastern angle of the Royal Chapel.

—away—past Restalrig, past Arthur's Seat, across the bridge and across the field of Musselburgh, past Seton, past Prestonpans, fast as their horses could speed; 'six in all—their Majesties, Erskine, Traquair, and a chamberer of the Queen.' In two hours the heavy gates of Dunbar had closed behind them, and Mary Stuart was safe.[1]

Whatever credit is due to iron fortitude and intellectual address must be given without stint to this extraordinary woman. Her energy grew with exertion; the terrible agitation of the three preceding days, the wild escape, and a midnight gallop of more than twenty miles within three months of her confinement, would have shaken the strength of the least fragile of human frames: but Mary Stuart seemed not to know the meaning of the word exhaustion; she had scarce alighted from her horse than couriers were flying east, west, north, and south, to call the Catholic nobles to her side; she wrote her own story to her minister at Paris, bidding the Archbishop in a postscript anticipate the false rumours which would be spread against her honour, and tell the truth —her version of the truth—to the Queen-mother and the Spanish ambassador.

To Elizabeth she wrote with her own hand, fierce, dauntless, and haughty, as in her highest prosperity.[2] 'Ill at ease with her escape from Holyrood, and suffer-

---

[1] The account of the escape is taken from a letter of Antony Standen, preserved among the CECIL MSS. at Hatfield; the remaining details of the murder and the circumstances connected with it, are collected from RUTHVEN's narrative, printed in KEITH; the letters of Bedford and Randolph, printed by WRIGHT; the two Italian accounts in the seventh volume of LABANOFF; CALDERWOOD's History; Mary Stuart's letter to the Archbishop of Glasgow, and a letter of Paul de Foix, printed by TEULET.

[2] This letter may be seen in the Rolls House; the strokes thick and slightly uneven from excitement, but strong, firm, and without sign of tremulousness.

ing from the sickness of pregnancy, she demanded to know whether the Queen of England intended to support the traitors who had slain her most faithful servant in her presence. If she listened to their calumnies and upheld them in their accursed deeds, she was not so unprovided of friends as her sister might dream; there were princes enough to take up her quarrel in such a cause.'

The loyalty of Scotland answered well its sovereign's summons. The faithwell Bothwell, ever foremost in good or evil in Mary Stuart's service, brought in the night-riders of Liddesdale, the fiercest of the Border marauders; Huntly came, forgetting his father and brother's death and his own long imprisonment; the Archbishop of St. Andrew's—an evil omen to Darnley—was followed by a thousand Hamiltons; Erskine from the Castle sent word of his fidelity; and the Earl Marshal, Athol, Caithness, and a hundred more hurried to Dunbar with every trooper that they could raise. In four days the Queen found herself at the head of a small army of eight thousand men.

On the other hand the conspirators' plans were disconcerted hopelessly by the flight of the King. Perplexed, divided, uncertain what to do when the slightest hesitation was ruin—they lost confidence in one another and in their cause. Had they held together they could still have collected force enough to fight. The Western Highlands were at the devotion of Argyle, and he at any time could command his own terms; but Elizabeth's behaviour in the preceding autumn had for ever shaken Argyle's policy. The Queen 'not venturing,' as she said herself, 'to have so many at once on her hands,' sent to say she would pardon the rebellion of the summer and would receive into favour all who had not been present at or been concerned in the murder of Ritzio. 'They seeing now their liberty and restitution offered them were content to leave those who were the occasion of their return, and took several appointments as they could.'[1] Glencairn joined Mary at Dunbar; Rothes followed; and then Argyle, the central pillar of the Protestant party. Three only of those who had been in England refused to desert their friends—the stainless noble Murray, Kirkaldy of Grange, and the Laird of Paturrow. 'These standing so much upon their honour and promise would not leave the other without likelihood to do them good.'[2]

Mary Stuart returns to Edinburgh.

Thus within a week from her flight Mary Stuart was able to return in triumph to Edinburgh. She had succeeded so entirely that she was already able to throw off the mask towards Darnley. Sir James Melville met her on the road: she 'lamented to him the King's folly and ingratitude;' and it was to no purpose that the old far-sighted diplomatist warned her against indulging this new resentment; the grudge never left her heart,[3] and she had made the object of it already feel the value of the promises with which she had wrought upon his weakness. 'The King spoke to me of the lords,' said Melville, 'and it appeared that he was troubled that he had deserted them, finding the Queen's favour but cold.'[4]

Flight of the conspirators.

The conspirators, or 'the Lords of the new attemptate' as they were called, made no effort to resist. Erskine threatened to fire on them from the Castle, and before the Queen reached Holyrood, Ruthven, Morton, Maitland, Lindsay, Faldonside, even Knox, were gone their several ways, most of them making for the Border

---

[1] Randolph to Cecil, March 21.
[2] Ibid.
[3] MELVILLE's *Memoirs*.
[4] Ibid.

to take shelter with Bedford at Berwick. Murray too left Edinburgh with them, and intended to share their fortunes; but Ruthven and Morton, generous as himself, wrote to beg him 'as the rest had fallen off, not to endanger himself on their account, but to make his peace if he was able;'[1] and Murray feeling that he would do more good for them and for his country by remaining at home than by going with them into a second exile, returned to his sister and was received with seeming cordiality.

Bothwell whose estates had been forfeited for his share in the Arran conspiracy was rewarded for his services by 'all that had belonged to Lidington.' The unfortunate King, 'contemned and disesteemed of all,' was compelled to drain the cup of dishonour. He declared before the Council 'that he had never counselled, commanded, consented to, assisted, or approved' the murder of Ritzio. His words were taken down in writing and published at the market-cross of every town in Scotland. The conspirators retorted with sending the Queen the bond which they had exacted from him, in which he claimed the deed as exclusively his own; while the fugitives at Berwick addressed a clear brief statement of the truth to the Government in England:

MORTON AND RUTHVEN TO CECIL.[2]

Berwick, March 27.

'The very truth is this:—the King having conceived a deadly hatred against David Ritzio an Italian, and some others his accomplices, did a long time ago move unto his ally the Lord Ruthven that he might in no way

---

[1] Randolph to Cecil, March 21.—*Scotch MSS. Rolls House.*
[2] *Scotch MSS. Rolls House.*

endure the misbehaviour and offence of the foresaid David, and that he might be fortified by him and some others of the nobility to see the said David executed according to his demerits; and after due deliberation the said Lord Ruthven communicated this the King's mind to the Earl of Morton, with whom having deeply considered the justice of the King's desires in respect of the manifold misbehaviours and misdeeds of the said David Ritzio, tending so manifestly to the great danger of the King's and Queen's Majesties and the whole estate of that realm and commonweal—he not ceasing to abuse daily his great estate and credit to the subversion of religion and the justice of the realm, as is notoriously known to all Scotland and more particularly to us—we upon the considerations aforesaid found good to follow the King's determination anent the foresaid execution; and for divers considerations we were moved to haste the same considering the approaching Parliament, wherein determination was taken to have ruined the whole nobility that then was banished; whereupon we perceived to follow a subversion of religion within the realm, and consequently of the intelligence betwixt the two realms grounded upon the religion; and to the execution of the said enterprise the most honest and the most worthy were easily induced to approve and fortify the King's deliberation.

'How be it in action and manner of execution, more was followed of the King's advice kindled by an extreme choler than we minded to have done.

'This is the truth whatever the King say now, and we are ready to stand by it and prove it.'

CHAPTER X.

THE murder of Ritzio had deranged Mary Stuart's projects in Scotland, and had obliged her to postpone her intended restoration of Catholicism; but her hold on parties in England was rather increased than injured by the interruption of a policy which would have alarmed the moderate Protestants. The extreme Puritans still desired to see the succession decided in favour of the children of Lady Catherine Grey; but their influence in the state had been steadily diminishing as the Marian horrors receded further into the distance. The majority of the peers, the country gentlemen, the lawyers and the judges, were in favour of the pretensions which were recommended at once by justice and by the solid interests of the realm. The union of the crowns of Scotland and England was the most serious desire of the wisest of Elizabeth's statesmen, and the marriage of Mary Stuart with Darnley had removed the prejudice which had attached before to her alien birth.

The difficulty which had hitherto prevented her recognition had been the persistency with which she identified herself with the party of revolution and ultramontane fanaticism. The English people had no desire for a Puritan sovereign, but as little did they wish to see again the evil days of Bonner and Gardiner. They were jealous of their national independence; they had done once for all with the Pope, and they would have no priesthoods Catholic or Calvinist to pry into their opinions or meddle with their personal liberty. For a creed they would be best contented with a something which would leave them in communion with Christendom and preserve to them the form of superstition without the power of it.

Had Elizabeth allowed herself to be swayed by the ultra-Protestants, Mary Stuart would have appealed to arms and would have found the weightiest portion of the nation on her side. Had the Queen of Scots' pretensions been admitted so long as her attitude to the Reformation was that of notorious and thorough-going hostility, she would have supplied a focus for disaffection. A prudent and reasonable settlement would have been then made impossible; and England sooner or later would have become the scene of a savage civil war like that which had lacerated France.

Elizabeth with the best of her advisers expected that as she grew older Mary Stuart would consent to guarantee the liberties which England essentially valued, and that bound by conditions which need not have infringed her own liberty of creed, she could be accepted as the future Queen of the united island. It was with this view that the reversion of the crown had been held before Mary Stuart's eyes coupled with the terms on which it might be hers, while the Puritans had been forbidden to do anything which might have driven her to the ultimatum of force.

The intrigues with Spain, the Darnley marriage, and the attitude which the Queen of Scots had assumed in connexion with it, had almost precipitated a crisis. Elizabeth had been driven in despair to throw herself on the fanaticism of the Congregation, to endorse the de-

mands of Knox that the Queen of Scots should abjure
her own religion, and afterwards to retreat from her
position with ignominious and dishonourable evasions.
Yet the perplexity of a sovereign whose chief duty at
such a time was to prevent a civil war, deserves or demands a lenient consideration. Had Elizabeth declared
war in the interest of Murray and the Protestants, she
would have saved her honour, but she would have provoked a bloody insurrection; while it would have become
more difficult than ever to recognise the Queen of Scots,
more hopeless than ever to persuade her into moderation
and good sense. If Elizabeth's conduct in its details had
been alike unprincipled and unwise, the broader bearings
of her policy were intelligible and commendable; her
caprice and vacillation arose from her consciousness of
the difficulties by which she was on every side surrounded. The Queen of Scots herself had so far shown
in favourable contrast with her sister of England: she had
deceived her enemies, but she had never betrayed a friend.
The greater simplicity of conduct however was not wholly
a virtue: it had been produced by the absence of all
high and generous consideration. Ambition for herself
and zeal for a creed which suited her habits were motives
of action which involved and required no inconsistencies.
From the day on which she set foot in Scotland she had
kept her eye on Elizabeth's throne, and she had determined to restore Catholicism; but her public schemes
were but mirrors in which she could see the reflection of her own greatness, and her creed was but the
form of conviction which least interfered with her self-
indulgence: the passions which were blended with her
policy made her incapable of the restraint which was
necessary for her success; while her French training had
taught her lessons of the pleasantness of pleasure, for

CHAP X
1566

Prospects of
the Queen
of Scots.

which she was at any time capable of forgetting every other consideration. Elizabeth forgot the woman in the Queen, and after her first mortification about Leicester preserved little of her sex but its caprices. Mary Stuart when under the spell of an absorbing inclination could fling her crown into the dust and be woman all.

Could she have submitted to the advice so consistently pressed upon her by Philip, Alva, Melville, Throgmorton, by every wise friend that she possessed, the impatience of the English for a settlement of the succession would have rendered her victory certain. She had only to avoid giving occasion for just complaint or suspicion, and the choice of the country notwithstanding her creed—or secretly perhaps in consequence of it—would have inevitably at no distant time have been determined in her favour. Elizabeth she knew to be more for her than against her. The Conservative weight of the country party would have far outbalanced the Puritanism of the large towns.

But a recognition of her right to an eventual inheritance was not at all the object of Mary Stuart's ambition; nor in succeeding to the English throne did she intend to submit to trammels like those under which she had chafed in Scotland. She had spoken of herself not as the prospective but as the actual Queen of England;[1] she had told the lords who had followed her to Dumfries that she would lead them to the gates of London; she would not wait; she would make no compromise; she would wrench the sceptre out of Elizabeth's hands

---

[1] 'That Queen the other day was in a merchant's house in Edinburgh where was a picture of the Queen's Majesty; when some had said their opinions how like or unlike it was to the Queen's Majesty of England, "No," said she, "it is not like, for I am Queen of England." These high words, together with the rest of her doings and meanings towards this realm, I refer to others to consider.'— *Bedford to Leicester, February 14, 1566.* PEPYSIAN MSS. *Cambridge.*

with a Catholic army at her back as the first step of a Catholic revolution. Even here—so far had fortune favoured her—she might have succeeded could she but have kept Scotland united, could she but have availed herself skilfully of the exasperation of the Lords of the Congregation when they found themselves betrayed and deserted, could she have remained on good terms with her husband and his father, and kept the friends of the House of Lennox in both countries true to her cause. That opportunity she had allowed to escape. It remained to be seen whether she had learnt prudence from the catastrophe from which she had so narrowly escaped; whether she would now abandon her more dangerous courses, and fall back on moderation; or whether if she persisted in trying the more venturous game she could bring herself to forego the indulgence of those personal inclinations and antipathies which had caused the tragedy at Holyrood. If she could forget her injuries, if she could renounce with Ritzio's life her desire to revenge his murder, if she avoided giving open scandal to the Catholic friends of Darnley and his mother, her prospects of an heir would more than re-establish her in the vantage-ground from which she had been momentarily shaken.

Elizabeth either through fear or policy seemed as anxious as ever to disconnect herself from the Congregation. The English Government had been informed a month beforehand of the formation of the plot; they had allowed it to be carried into execution without remonstrance; but when the thing was done and Murray was restored the Queen made haste to clear herself of the suspicion of having favoured it. Sir Robert Melville was residing in London, and was occupied notoriously in gaining friends for the Scotch succession. Elizabeth sent for him, and when it was too late to save Ritzio she revealed to him the secret information which had been supplied by Randolph; nay, in one of the many moods into which she drifted in her perplexities, she even spoke of Argyle and Murray as 'rebels pretending reformation of religion.' There were too many persons in England and Scotland who were interested in dividing the Protestant noblemen from the English court. The Queen's words were carried round to rend still further what remained of the old alliance; and Randolph, discredited on all sides, could but protest to Cecil against the enormous mischief which Elizabeth's want of caution was producing.[1]

Elizabeth takes Mary Stuart's side.

It appeared as if the Queen had veered round once more and was again throwing herself wholly into Mary Stuart's interests. She replied to the letter which the Queen of Scots addressed to her from Dunbar by sending Melville to Scotland with assurances of sympathy and help; she wrote to Darnley advising him 'to please the Queen of Scots in all things,' and telling him that she would take it as an injury to herself if he offended her again; she advised Murray 'to be faithful to the Queen his sovereign' under pain of her own displeasure.[2] As to the second set of fugitives who had taken shelter in England—Morton, Ruthven, and the rest—she told Bedford that she would neither acquit nor condemn them till she was more fully informed of their conduct, and that for the present they might remain under his protection;[3] but she insisted that they must move to a distance from the frontier, and Melville was allowed to

---

[1] Randolph to Cecil, June 17. The letter is addressed significantly 'To Mr. Secretary's self, and only for himself.'—BURLEIGH *Papers*, vol. i.

[2] Sir R. Melville to Elizabeth, April 1.—*Scotch MSS. Rolls House.*
[3] Elizabeth to Bedford, April 2.—*MS. Ibid.*

promise Mary Stuart 'that they should meet with nothing but rigour.'

De Silva informed Philip that the terror of the scene through which she had passed had destroyed the hope which the Queen of Scots had entertained of combining her subjects against the Queen of England. 'She had found them a people fierce, strange, and changeable; she could trust none of them;[1] and she had therefore responded graciously to the tone which Elizabeth assumed towards her.' In an autograph letter of passionate gratitude Mary Stuart placed herself as it were under her sister's protection; she told her that in tracing the history of the late conspiracy she had found that the lords had intended to imprison her for life, and if England or France came to her assistance they had meant to kill her; she implored Elizabeth to shut her ears to the calumnies which they would spread against her, and with engaging frankness she begged that the past might be forgotten; she had experienced too deeply the ingratitude of those by whom she was surrounded to allow herself to be tempted any more into dangerous enterprises; for her own part she was resolved never to give offence to her good sister again; nothing should be wanting to restore the happy relations which had once existed between them; and should she recover safely from her confinement she hoped that in the summer Elizabeth would make a progress to the north, and that at last she might have an opportunity of thanking her in person for her kindness and forbearance.'[2]

This letter was sent by the hands of a certain

---

[1] De Silva to Philip.—*MS. Simancas.*
[2] The Queen of Scots to Elizabeth, April 4.—*Scotch MSS. Printed by* LABANOFF, vol. vii. p. 300.

Thornton, a confidential agent of Mary Stuart, who had been employed on messages to Rome. 'A very evil and naughty person, whom I pray you not to believe,' was Bedford's credential for him in a letter of the 1st of April to Cecil. He was on his way to Rome again on this present occasion. The public in Scotland supposed that he was sent to consult the Pope on the possibility of divorcing Darnley; and it is remarkable that the Queen of Scots at the close of her own letter desired Elizabeth to give credit to him on some secret matter which he would communicate to her. She perhaps hoped that Elizabeth would now assist her in the dissolution of a marriage which she had been so anxious to prevent.

It was not till her return to Edinburgh that the whole circumstances became known to her which preceded the murder; and—whether she had lost in Ritzio a favoured lover, or whether the charge against her had been invented by Darnley to heat the blood of his kindred—in either case his offence against the Queen was irreparable and deadly, and every fresh act of baseness into which he plunged increased the loathing with which she regarded him. The poor creature laboured to earn his pardon by denouncing accomplice after accomplice. Maitland's complicity was unsuspected till it was revealed by Darnley. He gave up the names of three other gentlemen 'whom only he and no man else knew to be privy.'[1] Maitland's lands were seized, and he had himself to fly into the Highlands. One of the three gentlemen was executed; but the Queen while she used his information repaid his baseness with deserved scorn. The bond which he had signed was under her eyes; and the stories which he had told against her were brought

---

[1] Randolph to Cecil, April 2.—*Scotch MSS. Rolls House.*

forward by the lords in their own justification. While distrust and fear and suspicion divided home from home and friend from friend, the contempt and hate of all alike was centred on the unhappy caitiff who had betrayed both parties in turn; and Darnley, who was so lately dreaming of himself as sovereign of England and Scotland, was left to wander alone about the country as if the curse of Cain was clinging to him.[1]

Meanwhile Elizabeth was reaping a harvest of inconveniences from exaggerated demonstrations of friendliness. The Queen of Scots taking her at her word demanded that Morton and Ruthven should be either surrendered into her hands or at least should not be permitted to remain in England. Elizabeth would have consented if she had dared, but Argyle and Murray identified their cause with that of their friends. Murray was so anxious that they should do well that 'he wished himself banished for them to have them as they were.' Though they had generously begged him to run no risks in their interest he had told his sister 'that they had incurred their present danger only on his account;' while Argyle sent word to Elizabeth that if she listened to the Queen of Scots' demands he would join Shan O'Neil.[2] Vainly Elizabeth struggled to extricate herself from her dilemma; resentment was still pursuing her for her treachery in the past autumn. She dared not shelter the conspirators, for the Queen of Scots would no longer believe her fair speeches, and de Silva was watching her with keen and jealous

---

[1] 'He is neither accompanied nor looked upon by any nobleman; attended by certain of his own servants and six or eight of his guard, he is at liberty to do or go what or where he will.'—*Randolph to Cecil, April 25. Scotch MSS. Rolls House.*

[2] Randolph to Cecil, May 13 and May 23.—*MS. Ibid.*

eyes;[1] she dared not surrender or expel them lest the last Englishman in Ireland should be flung into the sea. She could but shuffle and equivocate in a manner which had become too characteristic. Ruthven was beyond the reach of human vengeance: he had risen from his sick bed to enact his part in Holyrood, he had sunk back upon it to die. To Morton she sent an order, a copy of which could be shown to the Queen of Scots, to leave the country; but she sent with it a private hint that England was wide, and that those who cared to conceal themselves could not always be found.[2] Argyle she tried to soothe and work upon, and she directed Randolph to 'deal with him.' She understood, she said, 'that there was a diminution of his good will towards her service, and specially in the matter of Ireland,' and that 'he alleged a lack of her favour in time of his need.' 'She had been right sorry for the trouble both of him and his friends; she had done all that in honour she could do, omitting nothing for the Earl of Murray's preservation but open hostility; she trusted therefore that he would alter his mind and withdraw him from the favouring of that principal rebel being sworn cruel adversary to the state of all true religion.' If possible Randolph was to move Argyle by reasoning and remonstrance; if he failed, 'sooner than O'Neil should receive any aid from thence she would be content to have some portion of money bestowed secretly by way of reward to the hindrance of it.' And yet, she said—her thrifty

---

[1] 'Con todas las promesas y demostraciones que esta Reyna ha hecho á la de Escocia al presente de la prometer ayuda y serle amiga y no consentir estos ultimos conspiradores en su Reyno, como oygo estan en Newcastle.'—*De Silva to Philip, May 18. MS. Simancas.*

[2] Morton to Cecil, May 16. Leicester to Cecil, July 11.—*Scotch MSS. Rolls House.*

nature coming up again—the money was not to be promised if the Earl could be prevailed on otherwise; 'of the matter of money she rather made mention as of a thing for Randolph to think upon until he heard farther from her than that he should deal with any person therein.'[1]

But Elizabeth was not to escape so easily, and Argyle's resentment had reached a heat which a more open hand than Elizabeth's would have failed to cool. Murray was ready to forget his own wrongs, but Argyle would not forget them for him, and would not forget his other friends. 'If the Queen of England,' the proud M'Cullum-More replied, 'would interfere in behalf of the banished lords, and would undertake that in Scotland there should be no change of religion,' he on his part 'would become O'Neil's enemy and hinder what he could the practices between the Queen his sovereign and the Papists of England.'[2] But Elizabeth must accept his terms; it was a matter with which money in whatever quantity had nothing to do. The practices with the English Catholics had begun again, or rather, in spite of Mary Stuart's promises to abstain from such transactions for the future, they had never ceased; and a curious discovery was about to be made in connexion with them. A report had been sent by Murray to Cecil that there was an Englishman about the court at Holyrood who was supposed to have come there on no good errand; he was one of the Rokebies of Yorkshire, and was closely connected with the great Catholic families there. But Cecil it seems knew more of Rokeby's doings than Murray knew. He had gone across the Border to be out of the way of the bailiffs; and Cecil,

---

[1] Elizabeth to Randolph, May 23.—*Scotch MSS. Rolls House, and Lansdowne MSS.* 9.

Randolph to Cecil, June 13.—*Scotch MSS. Ibid.*

who suspected that Mary Stuart was still playing her old game, and had before been well acquainted with Rokeby, sent him word 'that he might purchase pardon and help if he would use his acquaintance in Scotland to the contentation of the Queen's Majesty,' in other words if he would do service as a spy. Rokeby, who wanted money and had probably no honour to lose, made little objection. His brother-in-law, Lascelles, who was one of Mary Stuart's stanchest friends and correspondents, gave him letters of introduction, and with these he hastened to Edinburgh and was introduced by Sir James Melville to the Queen.

In a letter to Cecil he thus describes his reception:—

'In the evening, after ten o'clock, I was sent for in secret manner, and being carried into a little closet in Edinburgh Castle the Queen came to me; and so doing the duty belonging to a prince I did offer my service, and with great courtesy she did receive me, and said I should be very welcome to her, and so began to ask me many questions of news from the court of England and of the Queen and of the Lord Robert. I could say but little; so being very late she said she would next day confer with me in other causes, and willed me take my ease for the night.

'The next night after I was sent for again, and was brought to the same place where the Queen came to me, she sitting down on a little coffer without a cushion and I kneeling beside. She began to talk of her father, Lascelles, and how much she was beholden to him, and how she trusted to find many friends in England whensoever time did serve; and did name Mr. Stanley, Herbert, and Dacres, from whom she had received letters, and by means she did make account to win friendship of many of the nobility—as the Duke of Norfolk, the Earls of Derby, Shrewsbury, Northumberland, Westmoreland and Cumberland. She had better hopes of them for that she thought them all to be of the old religion, which she meant to restore again with all expedition, and thereby win the hearts of the common people. Besides this she practised to have two of the worshipful of every shire of England, and such as were of her religion to be made her friends, and sought of me to know the names of such as were meet for that purpose. I answered and said I had little acquaintance in any shire of England but only Yorkshire, and there were great plenty of Papists. She told me she had written a number of letters to Christopher Lascelles with blank superscriptions; and he to direct them to such as he thought meet for that purpose. She told me she had received friendly letters from diverse, naming Sir Thomas Stanley and one Herbert, and Dacres with the crooked back—thus meaning that after she had friended herself in every shire in England with some of the worshipful or of the best countenance of the country, she meant to cause wars to be stirred in Ireland, whereby England might be kept occupied; then she would have an army in readiness, and herself with her army to enter England—and the day that she should enter her title to be read and she proclaimed Queen. And for the better furniture of this purpose she had before travailed with Spain, with France, and with the Pope for aid; and had received fair promises with some money from the Pope and more looked for.'[1]

Such a revelation as this might have satisfied Eliza-

---

[1] Christopher Rokeby to Cecil, June 1566.—*Hatfield MSS. Printed in the BURLEIGH Papers*, vol. i.

both that it was but waste of labour to attempt any more to return to cordiality and confidence with the Queen of Scots; yet either from timidity, or because she would not part with the hope that Mary Stuart might eventually shake off her dreams and qualify herself for the succession by prudence and good sense, she would not submit to the conditions on which Argyle offered to remain her friend. She could not conceal that she was aware of Mary Stuart's intrigues with her subjects; but she chose to content herself with reading her a lecture as excellent as it was useless on the evil of her ways. Messengers were passing and repassing continually between the court at Holyrood and Shan O'Neil. Other and more sincere English Catholics than Rokeby were coming day after day to Holyrood to offer their swords and to be admitted to confidence. Elizabeth in the middle of June sent Sir Henry Killigrew to remonstrate, and 'to demand such present answer as should seem satisfactory,'[1] while to his public instructions she added a private letter of her own.

'Madam,' she wrote to the Queen of Scots, 'I am informed that open rebels against my authority are receiving countenance and favour from yourself and your councillors. The news madam I must tell you with your pardon do much displease us. Remove these briars I pray you lest some thorn prick the hand of those who are to blame in this. Such matters hurt to the quick. It is not by such ways as these that you will attain the object of your wishes. These be the bypaths which those follow who fear the open road. I say not this for any dread I feel of harm that you may do me. My trust

---

[1] Instructions to Sir H. Killigrew, sent to the Queen of Scots, June 15. Cecil's hand.—*Scotch MSS. Rolls House.*

is in Him who governs all things by His justice, and with this faith I know no alarm. The stone recoils often on the head of the thrower, and you will hurt yourself —you have already hurt yourself—more than you can hurt me. Your actions towards me are as full of venom as your words of honey. I have but to tell my subjects what you are, and I well know the opinion which they will form of you. Judge you of your own prudence— you can better understand these things than I can write them. Assure me under your own hand of your good meaning, that I may satisfy those who are more inclined than I am to doubt you. If you are amusing yourself at my expense, do not think so poorly of me that I will suffer such wrong without avenging it. Remember my dear sister, that if you desire my affection you must learn to deserve it.'[1]

Essentially Elizabeth was acting with the truest regard for the Queen of Scots' interests, and was in fact behaving with extraordinary forbearance. It was unfortunate that petty accidents should have so perpetually given her rival a temporary advantage and an excuse for believing herself the injured party. Among the Catholics of whose presence at her court Sir H. Killigrew was instructed to complain, the spy of Cecil had been especially named. Already the Queen of Scots had been warned to beware how she trusted Rokeby; and at once, with an affected anxiety to meet Elizabeth's wishes, she ordered his arrest and the seizure of his papers. Cecil's letters to him were discovered in his correspondence, and the evidence of the underplot was too plain to permit Elizabeth to return upon so doubtful a ground.[2]

---

[1] Elizabeth to the Queen of Scots, June 13.— *Scotch MSS. Rolls House.*
[2] Killigrew to Cecil, July 4.—*MS. Ibid.*

These however and all subsidiary questions were soon merged in the great event of the summer. On the 19th of June, in Edinburgh Castle, between nine and ten in the morning was born James Stuart heir presumptive to the united crowns of England and Scotland. Better worth to Mary Stuart's ambition was this child than all the legions of Spain and all the money of the Vatican; the cradle in which he lay, to the fevered and anxious glance of English politicians, was as a Pharos behind which lay the calm waters of an undisturbed succession and the perpetual union of the too long divided realms. Here if the occasion was rightly used lay the cure for a thousand evils; where all differences might be forgotten, all feuds be laid at rest, and the political fortunes of Great Britain be started afresh on a newer and brighter career.

Scarcely even in her better mind could the birth of the Prince of Scotland be less than a mortification to Elizabeth—knowing as she could not fail to know, the effect which it would produce upon her subjects. Parliament was to have met in the spring, and she had attempted to force herself into a resolution upon her own marriage, which would enable her to encounter the House of Commons. In the middle of February she believed that she had made up her mind to the Archduke. Sir Richard Sackville had been selected as a commissioner to arrange preliminaries at Vienna; and she had gone so far as to arrange in detail the conditions on which her intended husband was to reside in England.

'I do understand this to be the state of his [Sackville's] despatch,' wrote Sir N. Throgmorton to Leicester.[1]

---

[1] February, 1566, endorsed in Leicester's hand —'A very considerable letter.'—PEPYSIAN MSS. Magdalen College, Cambridge.

'Her Majesty will tolerate the public contract for the exercise of the Archduke's Roman religion, so as he will promise secretly to her Majesty to alter the said religion hereafter. She doth further say that if the Archduke will come to England she promiseth to marry him unless there be some apparent impediment. She maketh the greatest difficulty to accord unto him some large provision to entertain him at her and the realm's cost as he demandeth.'

So far had her purpose advanced—even to a haggling over the terms of maintenance; yet at the last moment the thought of losing Leicester for ever became unbearable. He was absent from the court, and Elizabeth determined to see him once more before the fatal step was taken.

'After this was written,' Throgmorton concluded, 'I did understand her Majesty had deferred the signing of Sackville's despatch until your Lordship's coming.'

Cecil at the same time wrote to inform Leicester of the Queen's resolution; and either the Earl believed that it was his policy to appear to consent, or else if he may be credited with any interval of patriotism, he was ready for the moment to forget his own ambition in the interest of England.[1]

---

[1] 'I heartily thank you, Mr. Secretary, for your gentle and friendly letter, wherein I perceive how far her Majesty hath resolved touching the matter she dealt in on my coming away. I pray God her Highness may so proceed therein as may bring but contentation to herself and comfort to all that be hers. Surely there can be nothing that shall so well settle her in good estate as that way— I mean her marriage—whensoever it shall please God to put her in mind to like and to conclude. I know her Majesty hath heard enough thereof, and I wish to God she did bear that more that here abroad is wished and prayed for. Good will it doth move in many, and truly it may easily appear necessity doth require of all. We bear ourselves much also when we be there, but methinks it is good sometimes that some that be there should be abroad, for that is

CHAP X.
1566
June

As however it had been Mary Stuart's first success after her marriage with Darnley which had driven Elizabeth towards a sacrifice which she abhorred; so Ritzio's murder, the return of Murray and his friends, and the recovered vitality of the Protestants in Scotland gave her again a respite. As Mary Stuart's power to hurt her grew fainter, the Archduke once more ceased to appear indispensable; and when Leicester came back to the court Sackville's mission was again put off. Again the Queen began to nourish convulsive hopes that she could marry her favourite after all. Again Cecil had to interfere with a table of damning contrasts between the respective merits of the Austrian Prince and the English Earl;[1]

sooner believed that is seen than heard; and in hope, Mr. Secretary, that her Majesty will now earnestly intend that which she hath of long time not yet minded, and delay no longer her time, which cannot be won again for any gift, I will leave that with trust of happiest success, for that God hath left it the only means to redeem us in this world.'—*Leicester to Cecil, February 20, 1566. Domestic MSS., Eliz., vol. xxxix., Rolls House.*

[1] DE MATRIMONIO REGINÆ ANGLIÆ CUM EXTERO PRINCIPE.
April, 1566.

Reasons to move the Queen to accept Charles.

'Besides his person { his birth. his alliance.

1. 'She shall not diminish the honour of a prince to match with a prince.
2. 'When she shall receive messages from kings, her husband shall have of himself by birth and countenance to receive them.
3. 'Whatsoever he shall bring to the realm he shall spend it here in the realm.

Reasons against the Earl of Leicester.

1. 'Nothing is increased by marriage of him, either in riches, estimation, or power.
2. 'It will be thought that the slanderous speeches of the Queen with the Earl have been true.
3. 'He shall study nothing but to enhance his own particular friends to wealth, to office, to lands, and to offend others—

Sir H. Sidney.　Leighton.
Earl Warwick.　Christmas.
Sir James Crofts.　Middleton.
Henry Dudley.　Middlemore.

[4. 'He　　　　　　　　　　　[John

and again when remonstrance seemed to fail, the pale
shadow of Amy Robsart was called up out of the tomb
and waved the lovers once more asunder.[1]

Thus the season passed on; summer came, and James's
birth found Elizabeth as far from marriage as ever;
Parliament had been once more postponed, but the public
service could be conducted no longer without a subsidy,
and a meeting at Michaelmas was inevitable.

Scarcely was Mary Stuart delivered and the child's
sex made known, than Sir James Melville was in the

John Dudley.	Colshill.
Foster.	Wiseman.
Sir F. Johnson.	Killigrew.
Appleyard.	Molyneux.
Horsey.	
4. 'He shall have no regard to any person but to please the Queen.	4. 'He is inflamed by the death of his wife.
5. 'He shall have no opportunity nor occasion to tempt him to seek the crown after the Queen, because he is a stranger, and hath no friends in the realm to assist him.	5. 'He is far in debt.
6. 'By marriage with him the Queen shall have the friendship of King Philip, which is necessary, considering the likelihood of falling out with France.	6 'He is like to prove unkind, or jealous of the Queen's Majesty.

7. 'No Prince of England ever remained without good amity of the House
of Burgundy, and no prince ever had less alliance than the Queen of England
hath, nor any prince ever had more cause to have friendship and power to
assist her estate.

8. 'The French King will keep Calais against his pact.

9. 'The Queen of Scots pretendeth title to the crown of England, and so
did never foreign prince since the Conquest.

10. 'The Pope also, and all his parties, are watching adversaries to this
crown.'—BURLEIGH *Papers*, vol. I. p. 444.

[1] It was probably at this time Appleyard made his confession that 'he had covered his sister's murder,' and that Sir Thomas Blount was secretly examined by the Council. There is little room for doubt that the menace of exposure was the instrument made use of to prevent Elizabeth from ruining herself.—See cap. 4.

Chap X
1566
June

Sir James Melville announces the birth of James.

saddle. The night of the 19th he slept at Berwick; on the evening of the 22nd he rode into London. A grand party was going forward at Greenwich: the Queen was in full force and spirit, and the court in its summer splendour. A messenger glided through the crowd and spoke to Cecil; Cecil whispered to his mistress, and Elizabeth flung herself into a seat, dropped her head upon her hand, and exclaimed 'The Queen of Scots is the mother of a fair son, and I am but a barren stock.' Bitter words!—how bitter those only knew who had watched her in the seven years' struggle between passion and duty.

She could have borne it better perhaps had her own scheme been carried out for a more complete self-sacrifice, and had Leicester been the father of the future king. Then at least she would have seen her darling honoured and great; then she would have felt secure of her rival's loyalty and of the triumph of those great principles of English freedom for which she had fought her long, and as it now seemed, her losing battle. The Queen of Scots had challenged her crown, intrigued with her subjects, slighted her councils, and defied her menaces, and this was the result.

But Elizabeth had been apprenticed in self-control. By morning she had overcome her agitation and was able to give Melville an audience.

The ambassador entered her presence radiant with triumph. The Queen affected, perhaps she forced herself to feel, an interest in his news, and she allowed him to jest upon the difficulty with which the prince had been brought into the world. 'I told her,' he reported afterwards,[1] 'that the Queen of Scots had dearly bought her

---

[1] MELVILLE's *Memoirs*.

child, being so sore handled that she wished she had never been married. This I said by the way to give her a scare from marriage and from Charles of Austria.' Elizabeth smiled painfully and spoke as graciously as she could, though Melville believed that at heart she was burning with envy and disappointment. The trial was doubtless frightful, and the struggle to brave it may have been but half successful; yet when he pressed her to delay the recognition no longer she seemed to feel that she could not refuse, and she promised to take the opinion of the lawyers without further hesitation. So great indeed had been the disappointment of English statesmen at the last trifling with the Archduke that they had abandoned hope. The Scottish Prince was the sole object of their interest, and all the motives which before had recommended Mary Stuart were working with irresistible force. Whatever might be the Queen's personal reluctance, Melville was able to feel that it would avail little; the cause of his mistress, if her game was now played with tolerable skill, was virtually won. Norfolk declared for her, Pembroke declared for her, no longer caring to conceal their feelings; even Leicester, now that his own chances were over, became 'the Queen of Scots' avowed friend,' and pressed her claims upon Elizabeth, 'alleging that to acknowledge them would be her greatest security, and that Cecil would undo all.'[1] All that Melville found necessary was to give his mistress a few slight warnings and cautions.

Her recognition as second person he knew that she regarded as but a step to the dethronement of Elizabeth; nor did he advise her to abandon her ambition. He did not wish her to slacken her correspondence with the

---

[1] MELVILLE's *Memoirs*.

Catholics; she need not cease 'to entertain O'Neil;' but he required her only to be prudent and secret. 'Seeing the great mark her Majesty shot at, she should be careful and circumspect, that her desires being so near to be obtained should not be overthrown for lack of management.'[1]

Schooled for once by advice Mary Stuart wrote from her sick bed to Melville's brother Robert. The letter appeared to be meant only for himself, but it was designed to be shown among the Protestant nobility of England. She declared in it that she meant nothing but toleration in religion, nothing but good in all ways; she protested that she had no concealed designs, no unavowed wishes; her highest ambition went no further than to be recognized by Parliament, with the consent of her dear sister.

With these words in their hands the Melvilles made swift progress in England. Elizabeth's uncertainties and changes had shaken her truest friends; and even before Parliament some popular demonstrations were looked for.

Prospect of disturbances in England.

'There are threats of disturbance,' de Silva wrote in August, 'and trouble is looked for before the meeting of Parliament. For the present we are reassured, but it is likely enough that something will happen. The Queen is out of favour with all sides: the Catholics hate her because she is not a Papist, the Protestants because she is less furious and violent in heresy than they would like to see her; while the courtiers complain of her parsimony.'[2] James Melville was soon able to send the gratifying assurance to the Queen of Scots that should

---

[1] MELVILLE's *Memoirs*.
[2] De Silva to Philip, August 23, 1566.—*MS. Simancas.*

Elizabeth continue the old excuses and delays 'her friends were so increased that many whole shires were ready to rebel, and their captains already named by election of the nobility.'[1]

CHAP X
1566
August

In such a world and with such humours abroad the approaching session could not fail to be a stormy one; and Elizabeth knew, though others might affect to be ignorant, that if she was forced into a recognition of Mary Stuart a Catholic revolution would not be many months distant.

At the beginning of August, to gather strength and spirit for the struggle, she went on progress, not to the northern counties where the Queen of Scots had hoped to meet her, but first to Stamford on a visit to Cecil, thence round to Woodstock, her old prison in the perilous days of her sister, and finally, on the evening of the 31st, she paid Oxford the honour which two years before she had conferred on the sister University. The preparations for her visit were less gorgeous, the reception itself far less imposing, yet the fairest of her cities in its autumnal robe of sad and mellow loveliness, suited the Queen's humour, and her stay there had a peculiar interest.

She travelled in a carriage. At Wolvercot, three miles out on the Woodstock road, she was met by the heads of houses in their gowns and hoods. The approach was by the long north avenue leading to the north gate; and as she drove along it she saw in front of her the black tower of Bocardo, where Cranmer had been long a prisoner, and the ditch where with his brother martyrs he had given his life for the sins of the people. The scene was changed from that chill sleety morning, and the soft glow

Elizabeth at Oxford.

[1] MELVILLE's Memoirs.

of the August sunset was no unfitting symbol of the change of times; yet how soon such another season might tread upon the heels of the departing summer none knew better than Elizabeth. She went on under the archway and up the corn-market between rows of shouting students. The students cried in Latin 'Vivat Regina.' Elizabeth amidst bows and smiles answered in Latin also, 'Gratius ago, gratias ago.'

At Carfax, where Bishop Longlands forty years before had burnt Tyndal's Testaments, a professor greeted her with a Greek speech, to which with unlooked for readiness she replied again in the same language. A few more steps brought her down to the great gate of Christ Church, the splendid monument of Wolsey and of the glory of the age that was gone. She left the carriage, and with de Silva at her side she walked under a canopy across the magnificent quadrangle to the Cathedral. The dean after evening service entertained her at his house.

Disputations in the schools. The days of her stay were spent as at Cambridge—in hearing plays or in attending the exercises of the University. The subjects chosen for disputation in the schools mark the balance of the two streams of ancient and modern thought, and show the matter with which the rising mind of England was beginning to occupy itself. There were discussions on the tides—whether or how far they were caused by the attraction of the moon. There were arguments on the currency—whether a debt contracted when the coin was pure could be liquidated by the payment of debased money of the same nominal value. The keener intellects were climbing the stairs of the temple of Modern Science, though as yet they were few and feeble and they were looked upon askance with orthodox suspicion. At their side the descendants of the schoolmen were working on the old safe methods, proving paradoxes by laws of logic amidst universal applause. The Professor of Medicine maintained in the Queen's presence that it was not the province of the physician to cure disease, because diseases were infinite, and the infinite was beyond the reach of art; or again because medicine could not retard age, and age ended in death, and therefore medicine could not preserve life. With trifles such as these the second childhood of the authorities was content to drowse away the hours. More interesting than either science or logic were perilous questions of politics, which Elizabeth permitted to be agitated before her.

The Puritan formula that it was lawful to take arms against a bad sovereign was argued by examples from the Bible and from the stories of the patriot tyrannicides of Greece and Rome. Doctor Humfrey deserted his friends to gain favour with the Queen, and protested his horror of rebellion; but the defenders of the rights of the people held their ground and remained in possession of it. Pursuing the question into the subtleties of theology they even ventured to say that God himself might instigate a regicide, when Bishop Jewel who was present, stepped down into the dangerous arena and closed the discussion with a vindication of the divine right of kings.

More critically—even in that quiet haven of peaceful thought—the great subject of the day, which Elizabeth called her death-knell, still pursued her. An eloquent student discoursed on the perils to which a nation was exposed when the sovereign died with no successor declared. The comparative advantages were argued of elective and hereditary monarchy. Each side had its hot defenders; and though the votes of the University were in favour of the natural laws of succession, the champion of election had the best of the argument, and apparently best pleased the Queen. When in the peroration of his speech he said he would maintain his opinion 'with his life, and if need were with his death,'[1] she exclaimed 'Excellent—oh, excellent!'

At the close of the exercises she made a speech in Latin as at Cambridge. She spoke very simply, deprecating the praises which had been heaped upon her. She had been educated well, she said, though the seed had fallen on a barren soil; but she loved study if she had not profited by it, and for the Universities she would do her best that they should flourish while she lived, and after her death continue long to prosper.

So five bright days passed swiftly, and on the sixth she rode away over Magdalen Bridge to Windsor. As she crested Headington Hill she reined in her horse and once more looked back. There at her feet lay the city in its beauty, the towers and spires springing from amidst the clustering masses of the college elms; there wound beneath their shade the silvery lines of the Cherwell and the Isis.

'Farewell, Oxford!' she cried, 'farewell, my good subjects there!—farewell, my dear scholars, and may God prosper your studies!—farewell, farewell!'[2]

The Queen of Scots meanwhile had recovered rapidly from her confinement, and it seemed as if she had now but to sit still and wait for the fortune which time had so soon to bestow; yet Melville on his return to Scotland found her less contented than he expected. The

---

[1] 'Hoc vitâ et si opus est et morte comprobabo.'
[2] NICHOLLS's *Progress of Elizabeth*.

Pope, if it was true that she had desired a divorce from her husband, had not smiled upon her wishes; and Melville's well-meant efforts to console her for her domestic troubles with her prospects in England failed wholly of their effect. Five days after James's birth Killigrew reported that although Darnley was in the castle and his father in Edinburgh 'small account was made of them;' Murray, though he continued at the court, 'found his credit small and his state scarce better than when he looked daily for banishment;' Maitland was still a fugitive, and his estates with the splendid royalties of Dunbar were in possession of Bothwell; 'Bothwell's credit with the Queen was more than all the rest together.'[1]

It seemed as if Mary Stuart, brave as she might be, in that stormy sea of faction and conspiracy required a man's arm to support her: she wanted some one on whose devotion she could depend to shield her from a second night of terror, and such a man she had found in Bothwell—the boldest, the most reckless, the most unprincipled of all the nobles in Scotland. Her choice though imprudent was not unnatural. Bothwell from his earliest manhood had been her mother's stanchest friend; Bothwell, when the English army was before Leith—though untroubled with faith in Pope or Church or God, had been more loyal than the Catholic lords; and though at that time but a boy of twenty-two he had fought the cause of France and of Mary of Lorraine when Huntly and Seton were standing timidly aloof. Afterwards when Mary Stuart returned, and Murray and Maitland ruled Scotland, Bothwell continued true to his old colours, and true to the cause which the Queen of

---

[1] Killigrew to Cecil, June 24.

Scots in her heart was cherishing. Hating England, hating the Reformers, hating Murray above all living men, he had early conceived projects of carrying off his mistress by force from their control—nor was she herself supposed to have been ignorant of his design. The times were then unripe, and Bothwell had retired from Scotland to spend his exile at the French court, in the home of Mary Stuart's affection; and when he came back to her out of that polished and evil atmosphere, she found his fierce northern nature varnished with a thin coating of Parisian culture, saturated with Parisian villany, and the Earl himself with the single virtue of devotion to his mistress, as before he had been devoted to her mother. Her own nature was altogether higher than Bothwell's; yet courage, strength, and a readiness to face danger and dare crime for their sakes, attract some women more than intellect however keen, or grace however refined. The affection of the Queen of Scots for Bothwell is the best evidence of her innocence with Ritzio.

As soon as she had become strong enough to move she left the close hot atmosphere of the Castle, and at the end of July, attended by her cavalier, she spent her days upon the sea or at the Castle of Alloa on the Forth. She had condescended to acquaint Darnley with her intention of going, but with no desire that he should accompany her; and when he appeared uninvited at Alloa he was ordered back to the place from which he came. 'The Queen and her husband,' wrote the Earl of Bedford on the 3rd of August, 'agree after the old manner. It cannot for modesty nor for the honour of a Queen be reported what she said of him.'[1] Sir James Melville who dreaded the effect in England of the aliena-

---

[1] Bedford to Cecil, August 3.—COTTON MSS., CALIG. B. 10.

tion of the friends of Lady Lennox, again remonstrated and attempted to cure the slight with some kind of attention. But Melville was made to feel that he was going beyond his office; in her violent moods Mary Stuart would not be trifled with, and at length he received a distinct order 'to be no more familiar with the Lord Darnley.'[1] Water parties and hunting parties in the Highlands consumed the next few weeks. Though inexorable towards her husband the Queen as the summer went on found it necessary to take her brother into favour again, and to gain the confidence of the English Protestants by affecting a readiness to be guided by his advice. Maitland's peace had been made also though with more difficulty. Bothwell who was in possession of his estates refused to part with them; and in a stormy scene in the Queen's presence Murray told him 'that twenty as honest men as he should lose their lives ere he reft Liddington.'[2] The Queen felt however that her demand for recognition in England would be effective in proportion to the unanimity with which she was supported by her own nobility; she felt the want of Maitland's help; and visiting her resentment for the death of Ritzio on her miserable husband alone, she was ready to forget the share which Maitland had borne in it and exerted herself to smooth down and reconcile the factions at the court. She contrived to bring Maitland, Murray, Argyle and Bothwell secretly together; 'the matter in dispute' was talked over and at last amicably settled.[3]

From Maitland to Morton was a short step. The lords now all combined to entreat his pardon from the Queen, and in the restoration to favour of the nobles

---
[1] MELVILLE's *Memoirs*.
[2] Advertisements out of Scotland, August. 1566.—*MS. Rolls House*.
[3] Maitland to Cecil, September 20.—*MS. Ibid.*

whom he had invited to revenge his own imagined wrongs and had thus deserted and betrayed, the miserable King read his own ruin. One after another he had injured them all; and his best hope was in their contempt. Even Murray's face he had good cause to dread. He with Ritzio had before planned Murray's murder, and now seeing Murray at the Queen's side he let fall some wild passionate words as if he would again try to kill him. So at least the Queen reported, for it was she who carried the story to Murray, 'and willed the Earl to speer it at the King;' it was believed afterwards that she desired to create a quarrel which would rid her of one or both of the two men whom she hated worst in Scotland. But if this was her object she had mistaken her brother's character; Murray was not a person to trample on the wretched or stoop to ignoble game; he spoke to Darnley 'very modestly' in the Queen's presence; and the poor boy might have yet been saved could he have thrown himself on the confidence of the one noble-hearted person within his reach. He muttered only some feeble apology however and fled from the court 'very grieved.' He could not bear, so some one wrote, 'that the Queen should use familiarity with man or woman, especially the Lords of Argyle and Murray which kept most company with her.'[1]

Lennox, as much neglected as his son, was living privately at Glasgow, and between Glasgow and Stirling the forlorn Darnley wandered to and fro 'misliked of all,' helpless and complaining and nursing vague impossible schemes of revenge. He had signed the articles by which he bound himself to maintain the Reformation; he now dreamt of taking from Mary the defence of the

---

[1] Advertisements out of Scotland, August, 1566.—*MS. Rolls House.*

Church. He wrote to the Pope and to Philip complaining that the Queen of Scots had ceased to care for religion and that they must look to him only for the restoration of Catholicism. His letters instead of falling harmless by going where they were directed were carried to Mary, and might have aggravated her animosity against him had it admitted of aggravation. Still more terrified he then thought of flying from the kingdom. The Scotch Council was about to meet in Edinburgh in the middle of September; the Queen desired that he would attend the session with her; he refused, and as soon as she was gone he made arrangements to escape in an English vessel which was lying in the Forth. 'In a sort of desperation' he communicated his project to the French ambassador du Croq, who had remained after the Queen's departure at Stirling. He told him it seems that he should go to the Scilly Isles; perhaps like Sir Thomas Seymour with a notion of becoming a pirate chief there. When du Croq questioned him on his reasons for such a step he complained 'that the Queen would give him no authority;' 'all the lords had abandoned him he said; he had no hope in Scotland and he feared for his life.'

Better far it would have been had they allowed him to go, better for himself, better for Mary Stuart, better for human history which would have escaped the inky stain which blots its page; yet his departure at such a time and in such a manner would attract inconvenient notice in England—it would be used in Parliament in the debate on the succession. Du Croq carried word to Mary Stuart. Lennox after endeavouring in vain to dissuade him wrote to her also in the hope that he might appease her by giving proofs of his own loyalty;

and Darnley finding his purpose betrayed followed the French ambassador to Edinburgh, and on the evening of the 29th of September presented himself at the gates of Holyrood. He sent in word of his arrival—but he said he would not enter as long as Murray, Argyle, and Maitland were in the palace. The Queen went out to him, carried him to her private apartments and kept him there for the night. The next morning the council met and he was brought or led into their presence. There they sat—a hard ring of stony faces: on one side the Lords of the Congregation who had risen in insurrection to prevent his marriage with the Queen, whom afterwards he had pledged his honour to support and whom he had again betrayed—now by some inexplicable turn of fortune restored to honour while he was himself an outcast; on the other side Huntly, Caithness, Bothwell, Athol, the Archbishop of St. Andrew's, all Catholics, all Ritzio's friends, yet hand in hand now with their most bitter enemies, united heart and soul to secure the English succession for a Scotch Princess, and pressing with the weight of unanimity on the English Parliament; yet he who had been brought among them in the interest of that very cause was excluded from share or concern in the prize; every noble present had some cause of mortal enmity against him; and as he stood before them desolate and friendless he must have felt how short a shrift was allowed in Scotland for a foe whose life was inconvenient.

The letter of the Earl of Lennox was read aloud. Mary Stuart said that she had tried in vain to draw from her husband the occasion of his dissatisfaction; she trusted that he would tell the lords what he had concealed from herself; and then turning to him with clasped hands like a skilled actress on the stage, 'Speak,' she said, 'speak; say what you complain of; if the blame is with me do not spare me.'

The lords followed, assuring him with icy politeness that if he had any fault to find they would see it remedied.

Du Croq implored him to take no step which would touch his own honour or the Queen's.

What could he say? Could he tell the truth that he believed his Royal Mistress and those honourable lords were seeking how to rid the world of him? That was his fear; and she and they and he alike knew it—but such thoughts could not be spoken. And yet he had spirit enough to refuse to cringe or to stand at the bar to be questioned as a prisoner. He said a few unmeaning words and turned to go, and they did not dare detain him. 'Adieu Madam,' he said as he left the room, 'you will not see my face for a long space; gentlemen adieu.'[1]

Four days later they heard that the ship was ready in which he was about to sail; and it appears as if they had resolved to let him go. But in an evil hour for himself he had another interview with the French ambassador; du Croq after a long conversation persuaded him that the clouds would clear away and that fortune would again look beneficently upon him. The English ship sailed away and Darnley remained behind to drift upon destruction, 'hated,' as du Croq admitted, 'by all men and by all parties—because being what he was he desired to be as he had been and to rule as a king.'[2] In him

---

[1] Du Croq to the Archbishop of Glasgow, October 15. The Lords of Scotland to the Queen-mother of France, October 8.—*Printed in* KEITH.
[2] Du Croq to the Queen-mother of France, October 17.—TEULET, vol. II.

the murderers of Ritzio found a scapegoat, and the Queen accepted with seeming willingness the vicarious sacrifice. The political relations between England and Scotland relapsed into their old bearings. Maitland was found again corresponding with the English ministers on the old subject of the union of the realms, while the Queen of Scots herself wrote to Cecil with affected confidence and cordiality, just touching—enough to show that she understood it—on the treachery of Rokeby, but professing to believe that Cecil wished well to her and would assist her to gain her cause.[1]

So stood the several parties in the two kingdoms when Elizabeth returned from her progress and prepared to meet her Parliament.[2] Four years had passed since the last troubled session: spring after spring, autumn after autumn, notice of a Parliament had gone out; but ever at the last moment Elizabeth had flinched, knowing

---

[1] Maitland to Cecil, October 4. The Queen of Scots to Cecil, October 5.—*MS. Rolls House.*

[2] An entry in the Privy Council Register shows how anxiously the English Government were still watching the Queen of Scots, and how little they trusted her assurances.

October 8, 1566.

'A letter to Sir John Foster, Warden of the Middle Marches, touching the intelligence received out of Scotland of the sending of the Earl of Argyle towards Shan O'Neil with a hundred soldiers of those that were about the Scottish Queen's own person with commission also to levy all his own people and the people of the Isles to assist Shan against the Queen's Majesty. And because the understanding of the truth of this matter is of great importance, and necessary to be boulted out with speed, he is required that under pretence of some other message he take occasion to send with convenient speed some discreet person to the Scottish Court, to procure by all the best means he may to boult out the very certainty hereof. And in case he shall find indeed that the said advertisements are true, then to demand audience of the Scottish Queen and to deliver unto her the Queen's Majesty's letter,[1] sent herewith, requiring answer with speed; and in case he shall find the said enterprise is intended only, and not executed, then he shall procure to stay the same by the best means he may.'

---

[1] Not found.

well what lay before her. Further delay was at last impossible: the Treasury was empty, the humour of the people was growing dangerous. Thus at last on the 30th of September the Houses reassembled. The first fortnight was spent in silent preparations; on the 14th the campaign opened with a petition from the bishops, which was brought forward in the form of a statute in the House of Commons. It will be remembered that after the Bill was passed in the last session empowering the Anglican prelates to tender the vote of allegiance to their predecessors in the Tower, they had been checked in their first attempt to put the law in execution by a denial of the sacredness of their consecration, and the judges had confirmed the objection. To obviate this difficulty and to enable the bench at last to begin their work of retaliation, a Bill was brought in declaring that 'inasmuch as the bishops of the Church of England had been nominated according to the provisions of the Act of Henry the Eighth,[1] and had been consecrated according to the form provided in the Prayer-book, they should be held to have been duly and lawfully appointed, any statute law or canon to the contrary notwithstanding.' In this form, untrammelled by further condition, the Act went from the Commons to the Lords, and had it passed in its first form there would have been an immediate renewal of the attempt to persecute. The Lords however were better guardians than the Commons of English liberties. Out of 81 peers 22 were the bishops themselves, who as the promoters of the Bill unquestionably voted for it in its fullness; yet it was sent back, perhaps as an intimation that there had been enough of spiritual tyranny, and that the Church of England was not to disgrace itself with

---

[1] 25 Hen. VIII. cap. 20.

imitating the iniquities of Rome. A proviso was added that the Act should be retrospective only as it affected the general functions of the episcopal office,[1] but was not to be construed as giving validity to the requisition of the oath of allegiance in the episcopal courts, or as giving the bishops power over the lives or lands of the prisoners who had refused to swear.[2] The Bill although thus modified left the bench with powers which for the future they might abuse; and although there was an understanding that those powers were not to be put in force eleven lay peers still spoke and voted absolutely against admitting the episcopal position of men who had

---

[1] 'Provided always that no person or persons shall at any time hereafter be impeached or molested in body, lands, livings, or goods, by occasion or means of any certificate by any Archbishop or Bishop heretofore made, or before the last day of this present Session of Parliament to be made by authority of any Act passed in the first session of this present Parliament, touching or concerning the refusal of the oath declared and set forth by Act of Parliament in the first year of the reign of our Sovereign Lady the Queen: and that all tenders of the said oath made by any Archbishop or Bishop aforesaid, or before the last day of the present Session to be made by authority of any Act established in the first Session of this present Parliament, and all refusals of the same oath so tendered, or before the last day of this present Session to be tendered by any Archbishop or Bishop by authority of any law established in the first session of this present Parliament, shall be void, and of none effect or validity in the law.'—*Statutes of the Realm*, 8 ELIZ. cap. 1.

[2] 'La peticion que se dió en el Parlamento por parte de los obispos Protestantes acerca de su confirmacion se pasó por la Camara baja sin contradicion. En la alta tuvó once contradiciones, pero pasóse; no confirmandolo ellos sino á lo que hasta aqui se habia hecho en el ejercicio de su officio; con tanto que no se entendiese la confirmacion contra lo que hubiessen hecho ni podrian hacer en materia de sangre ni de bienes temporales. Lo de la sangre se entiende por el juramento que pedian á Bonner el buen Obispo de Londres, y á otros, acerca de lo de la religion, que es por lo que principalmente dicen que pedian la confirmacion; aunquedaban á entenderque por otros fines lo de bienes temporales han sentido; pero no fué segun entiendo este el intento; sino que obviar á que no les pierdan los, que no querian hacer el juramento.'—*De Silva to the King, November* 11, 1566. *MS. Simancas.*

been thrust into already occupied sees.[1] To have thrown the measure out altogether however would have been equivalent to denying the Church of England a right to exist: it passed with this limitation, and the bishops with a tacit intimation that they were on their good behaviour were recognized as legitimate.

The Consecration Bill was however but a preliminary skirmish, preparatory to the great question which both Houses, with opposite purposes, were determined to bring forward. The House of Commons was the same which had been elected at the beginning of the reign in the strength of the Protestant reaction. The oscillation of public feeling had left the majority of the members unaffected; they were still anxious to secure the reversion of the crown to the dying Lady Catherine and her children; and the tendencies of the country generally in favour of the Scotch succession made them more desirous than ever not to let the occasion pass through their hands. The House of Lords was in the interest of Mary Stuart, but some divisions had been already created by her quarrel with Darnley. The Commons perhaps thought that although the peers might prefer the Queen of Scots, they would acquiesce in the wife of Lord Hertford sooner than endure any more uncertainty; the Peers may have hoped the same in favour of their own candidate: they may have felt assured that when the question came once to be discussed, the superior right of the Queen of Scots, the known opinions of the lawyers in her favour, the scarcely concealed preference of the great body of English gentlemen, with the political ad-

---

[1] Non-contents—Earls Northumberland, Westmoreland, Worcester, and Sussex; Lords Montague, Morley, Dudley, Darcy, Mounteagle, Cromwell, and Mordaunt.

vantages which would follow on the union of the crowns, must inevitably turn the scale for Mary Stuart, whatever the Commons might will. Both Houses at all events were determined to bear Elizabeth's vacillation no longer, to believe no more in promises which were made only to be broken, and either to decide once for all the future fortunes of England, or lay such a pressure on the Queen that she should be forbidden to trifle any more with her subjects' anxiety for her marriage.

On the 17th of October Cecil brought forward in the Lower House a statement of the expenses of the French and Irish wars. On the 18th Mr. Molyneux a barrister proposed at once amidst universal approbation 'to revive the suit for the succession,' and to consider the demands of the exchequer only in connexion with the determination of an heir to the throne.[1]

Elizabeth's first desire was to stifle the discussion at its commencement. Sir Ralph Sadler rose when Molyneux sat down, and 'after divers propositions' 'declared that he had heard the Queen say in the presence of the nobility that her highness minded to marry.' Sadler possessed the confidence of the Protestants, and from him, if from any one, they would have accepted a declaration with which so steady an opponent of the Queen of Scots was satisfied; but the disappointment of the two previous sessions had taught them the meaning of words of this kind; a report of something said elsewhere to 'the nobility' would not meet the present irritation; 'their mind was to continue their suit, and to know her Highness's answer.'

Elizabeth found it necessary to be more specific. The

---

[1] 'October 18.—Motion made by Mr. Molyneux for the reviving of the suit for the succession, and to proceed with the subsidy, was very well allowed by the House.'—Commons' Journals, 8 Eliz.

next day, first Cecil, then Sir Francis Knowles, then Sir
Ambrose Cave declared formally that 'the Queen by
God's special providence was moved to marry, that she
minded for the wealth of the commons to prosecute the
same, and persuaded to see the sequel of that before further
suit touching the succession.'¹ Cecil and Cave were
good Protestants, Knowles was an advanced Puritan, yet
they were no more successful than Sadler; 'the lawyers' still insisted; the House went with them in declining to endure any longer a future which depended on
the possible 'movements' of the Queen's mind; and a vote
was carried to press the question to an issue and to invite
the Lords to a conference. The Lords as eager as the
Commons instantly acquiesced. Public business was
suspended, and committees of the two Houses sat daily
for a fortnight, preparing an address to the crown.²

---

¹ *Commons' Journals*, 8 ELIZ.

² Cecil, who was a member of the Commons' Committee, has left a paper of notes touching the main points of the situation:—

'*October*, 1566.

'To require both marriage and the stablishing of the succession is the uttermost that can be desired.

'To deny both the uttermost that can be denied.

'To require marriage is most natural, most easy, most plausible to the Queen's Majesty.

'To require certainty of succession is most plausible to all people.

'To require the succession is hardest to be obtained, both for the difficulty to discuss the right and the loathsomeness of the Queen's Majesty to consent thereto.

'The difficulty to discuss it is by reason of—

1. 'The uncertainty of indifferency in the parties that shall discuss it.

2. 'The uncertainty of the right pretended.

'The loathsomeness to grant it is by reason of natural suspicion against a successor that hath right by law to succeed.

'Corollarium.

'The mean betwixt them is to determine effectually to marry, and if it succeed not, then proceed to discussion of the right of succession.'— *Domestic MSS.*, ELIZ., vol. xl.

Another paper, also in Cecil's hand, contains apparently a rough sketch for the address to the Crown:—

'That the marriage may proceed effectually.

'That it may be declared how necessary it is to have the succession stablished for sundry causes.

'Surety and quietness of the

In spite of her struggles the Queen saw the net closing round her. Fair speeches were to serve her turn no longer, and either she would have to endure some husband whom she detested the very thought of, or submit to a settlement the result of which it was easy to foresee. Into her feelings, or into such aspect of them as she chose to exhibit, we once more gain curious insight through a letter of de Silva. So distinctly was Elizabeth's marriage the object of the present move of the House of Commons that the Queen of Scots, in dread of it, was contented to withdraw the pressure for a determination in her own favour, and consented to bide her time.

GUZMAN DE SILVA TO PHILIP II.[1]

October 26.

'The Parliament is in full debate on the succession. The Queen is furious about it; she is advised that if the question come to a vote in the Lower House the greatest number of voices will be for the Lady Catherine. This Queen's Majesty that no person may attempt anything to the furtherance of any supposed title when it shall be manifest how the right is settled. Whereunto may also be added sundry devices to stay every person in his duty, so as her Majesty may reign assuredly.

'The comfort of all good subjects that may remain assured, how and whom to obey lawfully, and how to avoid all errors in disobedience, whereby civil wars may be avoided.

'And because presently it seemeth very uncomfortable to the Queen's Majesty to hear of this at this time, and that it is hoped that God will direct her heart to think more comfortably hereof, it may be required that her marriage may proceed with all convenient speed; and that if her Majesty cannot condescend to enter into the disquisition and establishing of the succession in this Session, that yet for the satisfaction of her people she will prorogue this Parliament until another short time, within which it may be seen what God will dispose of her marriage, and then to begin her Parliament again, and to proceed in such sort as shall seem meetest then for the matter of succession, which may with more satisfaction be done to her Majesty if she shall then be married.'—*Domestic MSS. Rolls House.*

---

[1] *MS. Simancas.*

lady and her husband Lord Hertford are Protestants; and a large number, probably an actual majority of the Commons, being heretics also, will declare for her in self-defence.

'I have never ceased to urge upon the Queen the inconvenience and danger to which she will be exposed if a successor is declared, and on the other hand her perfect security as soon as she has children of her own. She understands all this fully, and she told me three days ago that she would never consent. The Parliament she said had offered her two hundred and fifty thousand pounds as the price of her acquiescence; but she had refused to accept anything on conditions. She had requested a subsidy for the public service in Ireland and elsewhere, and it should be given freely and graciously or not at all. She says she will not yield one jot to them let them do what they will; she means to dissemble with them and hear what they have to say, so that she may know their views, and the lady which each declares for[1]—meaning the Queen of Scots and Lady Catherine. I told her that if she would but marry, all this worry would be at an end. She assured me she would send this very week to the Emperor and settle everything; and yet I learn from Sir Thomas Heneage, who is the person hitherto most concerned in the Archduke affair, that she has grown much cooler about it.

'The members of the Lower House are almost all Protestants, and seeing the Queen in such a rage at them, I took occasion to point out to her the true character of this new religion, which will endure no rule and will have everything at its own pleasure without regard to the sovereign authority; it was time for her

---

[1] 'Por conocer las voluntades y saber la dama de cada uno.'

to see to these things, and I bade her observe the contrast between these turbulent heretics and the quiet and obedience of her Catholic subjects. She said she could not tell what those devils were after.[1] They want liberty, madam, I replied, and if princes do not look to themselves and work in concert to put them down, they will find before long what all this is coming to.[2]

'She could not but agree with me: she attempted a defence of her own subjects, as if there was some justice in their complaints of the uncertainty of the succession; but she knows at heart what it really means, and by and by when she finds them obstinate she will understand it better. I told her before that I knew they would press her, and she would not believe me.

'Melville the agent of the Queen of Scots was with me yesterday. Her disagreement with her husband is doing her much mischief here; yet that Queen has so much credit with the good all over the realm that the blame is chiefly laid on the Lord Darnley. I have told Melville to urge upon them the necessity of reconciliation; and I have written to the Commendador Major of Castile at Rome to speak to the Pope about it, and to desire his Holiness to send them his advice to the same effect. Melville tells me the lords there are working

---

[1] 'Respondióme que no sabia que querian estos demonios.'

[2] Elizabeth had before affected to be alarmed at the revolutionary tendencies of Protestantism. On the 15th of the preceding July, de Silva wrote—

'The Queen must be growing anxious. She often says to me that she wonders at the tendency of subjects now-a-days to anarchy and revolution. I invariably reply that this is the beginning, middle, and end of the inventors of new religions. They have an eye only to their own interests; they care neither for God nor law, as they show by their works; and princes ought to take order among themselves and unite to chastise their excesses.'—MS. Simancas.

together wonderfully well. He has given this Queen to understand that since she is reluctant to have the succession discussed, his mistress is so anxious to please her that she will not press for it; she will only ask that if the question is forced forward after all, she may have notice in time that she may send some one to plead in her behalf.

'This Queen is full of gratitude for her forbearance; she has told her that her present resolution is to keep the matter quiet; should her endeavours be unsuccessful however, the Queen of Scots shall have all the information and all the help which she herself can give.

'Molville learns from a private source that this Queen will fail in her object. The question will be forced in the Queen of Scots' interest, and with the best intentions. Her friends are very numerous; we shall soon see how things go.'

Melville's information was right. Having failed in full Parliament, Elizabeth tried next to work on the committee. The Marquis of Winchester was put forward to prevent the intended address. He brought to bear the weight of an experience which was older than the field of Bosworth; but he was listened to with impatience; not a single voice either from Peers or Commons was found to second him. Unable to do anything through others, the Queen sent for the principal noblemen concerned to remonstrate with them herself in private.

The Duke of Norfolk was the first called, and rumour said, though she herself afterwards denied the words, that she called him traitor and conspirator. Leicester, Pembroke, Northampton, and Lord William Howard came next. Norfolk had complained of his treatment to Pembroke: Pembroke told her that the Duke was a good friend both to the realm and to herself; if she would not listen to advice and do what the service of the commonwealth required, they must do it themselves.

She was too angry to argue; she told Pembroke he spoke like a foolish soldier, and knew not what he was saying. Then seeing Leicester at his side, 'You, my lord,' she said, 'you! If all the world forsook me I thought that you would be true!'

'Madam,' Leicester said, 'I am ready to die at your feet!'

'What has that to do with it?' she answered.

'And you, my Lord Northampton,' she went on—turning from one to the other; 'you who when you had a wife of your own already could quote Scripture texts to help you to another;[1] you forsooth must meddle with marriages for me! You might employ yourself better I think.'

She could make nothing of them nor they of her. Both Queen and lords carried their complaints to de Silva; the lords urging him to use his influence to force her into taking the Archduke; Elizabeth complaining of their insolence and especially of the ingratitude of Leicester. Her very honour she said had suffered for the favour which she had shown to Leicester; and now she would send him to his house in the country, and the Archduke should have nothing to be jealous of.[2]

The committee went on with the work. On the 2nd of November the form of the address was still undetermined; they were undecided whether to insist most on the marriage, or on the nomination, or on both. In some shape or other however a petition of a serious kind

---

[1] Northampton's divorce and second marriage had been one of the great scandals of the days of Edward.
[2] De Silva to Philip, November 4.—*MS. Simancas.*

would unquestionably be presented, and Elizabeth prepared to receive it with as much self-restraint as she could command. Three days later she understood that the deliberations were concluded. To have the interview over as soon as possible Elizabeth sent for the committee at once; and on the afternoon of the 5th of November, 'by her highness's special commandment,' twenty-five lay Peers, the Bishops of Durham and London, and thirty members of the Lower House presented themselves at the palace at Westminster.

The address was read by Bacon.

After grateful acknowledgments of the general government of the Queen the two Houses desired, first, to express their wish that her Highness would be pleased to marry 'where it should please her, with whom it should please her, and as soon as it should please her.'

Further, as it was possible that her Highness might die without children, her faithful subjects were anxious to know more particularly the future prospects of the realm. Much as they wished to see her married, the settlement of the succession was even more important, 'carrying with it such necessity that without it they could not see how the safety of her royal person or the preservation of her imperial crown and realm could be or should be sufficiently and certainly provided for.' 'Her late illness (the Queen had been unwell again), the amazedness that most men of understanding were by fruit of that sickness brought unto,' and the opportunity of making a definite arrangement while Parliament was sitting, were the motives which induced them to be more urgent than they would otherwise have cared to be. History and precedent alike recommended a speedy decision. They hoped that she might live to have a child of her own; but she was mortal, and should she die before her subjects knew to whom their allegiance was due, a civil war stared them in the face. The decease of a prince leaving the realm without a government was the most frightful disaster which could befall the commonwealth; with the vacancy of the throne all writs were suspended, all commissions were void, law itself was dead. Her Majesty was not ignorant of these things. If she refused to provide a remedy 'it would be a dangerous burden before God upon her Majesty!' They had therefore felt it to be their duty to present this address; and on their knees they implored her to consider it and to give them an answer before the session closed.[1]

Elizabeth had prepared her answer; as soon as Bacon ceased, she drew herself up and spoke as follows:—

'If the order of your cause had matched the weight of your matter, the one might well have craved reward, and the other much the sooner be satisfied. But when I call to mind how far from dutiful care, yea rather how nigh a traitorous trick this tumbling cast did spring, I muse how men of wit can so hardly use that gift they hold. I marvel not much that bridleless colts do not know their rider's hand whom bit of kingly rein did never snaffle yet. Whether it was fit that so great a cause as this should have had this beginning in such a public place as that, let it be well weighed. Must all evil bodings that might be recited be found little enough to hap to my share? Was it well meant, think you, that those that knew not how fit this matter was to be granted by the prince, would prejudicate their prince in aggravating the matter? so all their arguments tended to my careless care of this my dear realm.'

[1] Dewes' Journals, 8 Eliz.

So far she spoke from a form which remains in her own handwriting.[1] She continued perhaps in the same style; but her words remain only in the Spanish of de Silva.

'She was not surprised at the Commons,' she said; 'they had small experience and had acted like boys; but that the Lords should have gone along with them she confessed had filled her with wonder. There were some among them who had placed their swords at her disposal when her sister was on the throne, and had invited her to seize the crown;[2] she knew but too well that if she allowed a successor to be named, there would be found men who would approach him or her with the same encouragement to disturb the peace of the realm. If she pleased she could name the persons to whom she alluded. When time and circumstances would allow she would see to the matter of their petition before they asked her; she would be sorry to be forced into doing anything which in reason and justice she was bound to do; and she concluded with a request that her words should not be misinterpreted.'

So long as she was speaking to the lay Peers she controlled her temper; but her passion required a safety-valve, and she rarely lost an opportunity of affronting and insulting her bishops.

Turning sharp round where Grindal and Pilkington were standing—

---

[1] Answer to the Parliament by the Queen; Autograph.—*Domestic MSS.*, Eliz., vol. xli. *Rolls House.*

[2] 'Entre los cuales habia habido algunos que reynando su hermana le ofrecian á ella ayuda y la querian mover á que quisiese procurar en su vida la corona.'—*De Silva al Rey*, 11 *November*, 1566. *MS. Simancas.* It is tolerably certain that the Queen used these words. De Silva heard them first from the Queen herself, and afterwards from the Lords who were present.

'And you *doctors*,' she said—it was her pleasure to ignore their right to a higher title;[1] 'you I understand make long prayers about this business. One of you dared to say in times past that I and my sister were bastards; and you must needs be interfering in what does not concern you. Go home and amend your own lives and set an honest example in your families. The Lords in Parliament should have taught you to know your places; but if they have forgotten their duty I will not forget mine. Did I so choose I might make the impertinence of the whole set of you an excuse to withdraw my promise to marry; but for the realm's sake I am resolved that I will marry; and I will take a husband that will not be to the taste of some of you. I have not married hitherto out of consideration for you, but it shall be done now, and you who have been so urgent with me will find the effects of it to your cost. Think you the prince who will be my consort will feel himself safe with such as you, who thus dare to thwart and cross your natural Queen?'

She turned on her heel and sailed out of the hall of audience, vouchsafing no other word. At once she sent for de Silva, and after profuse thanks to himself and Philip for their long and steady kindness, swelling with anger as she was, she gave him to understand that her course was chosen at last and for ever; she would accept the Archduke and would be all which Spain could desire.

Many of the peers came to her in the evening to make their excuses: they said that they had been misled by

---

[1] 'Volviendose á los obispos que se halláron presentes á la platica, dijó, Vosotros doctores, no les llamando obispos, que haceis muchas oraciones,' &c.

the Council, who had been the most in favour of the address; and they had believed themselves to be acting as she had herself desired. The Upper House she might have succeeded in controlling; but the Commons were in a more dangerous humour. They were prepared for a storm when they commenced the debate; and they were not disposed to be lectured into submission. The next day Cecil rose in his place: the Queen he said had desired him to tell them that she was displeased, first, that the succession question should have been raised in that House without her consent having been first asked; and secondly, because 'by the publication abroad of the necessity of the matter,' and the danger to the realm if it was left longer undecided, the responsibility of the refusal was thrown entirely upon her Majesty. The 'error' she was ready to believe had risen chiefly from want of thought, and she was ready to overlook it. For the matter itself her Highness thought that by her promises to marry she had rather deserved thanks than to be troubled with any new petition. 'The word of a prince spoken in a public place' should have been taken as seriously meant; and if her Majesty had before told them that she was unwilling, they should have been more ready to believe her when she said that she had made up her mind. Time and opportunity would prove her Majesty's sincerity, and it was unkind to suppose that she would fail in producing children. Loyal subjects should hope the best. Her Majesty had confidence in God's goodness; and except for the assurance that she would have an heir, she would not marry at all. On this point she required the Houses to accept her word. For the succession she was not surprised at their uneasiness; she was as conscious as they could be of the desirableness of a settlement. At the present moment however, and in the existing state of parties in the realm the thing was impossible, and she would hear no more of it.[1]

The Queen expected that after so positive a declaration she would escape further annoyance; but times were changing, and the relations with them between sovereigns and subjects. The House listened in silence, not caring to conceal its dissatisfaction. The Friday following, being the 8th of November, 'Mr. Lambert began a learned oration for iteration of the suit to the Queen on the succession.'[2]

Whether they were terrified by the spectre of a second York and Lancaster war, or whether they were bent on making an effort for Lady Hertford before they were dissolved and another House was elected in the Scottish interest, or whether they disbelieved Elizabeth's promises to marry, notwithstanding the vehemence of her asseverations, the Commons seemed resolute at all hazards to persevere. Other speeches followed on the same side, expressing all of them the same fixed determination; and matters were now growing serious. The Spanish ambassador never lost a chance of irritating the Queen against the Protestant party; and on Saturday, stimulated by do Silva's invectives, and convinced, perhaps with justice, that she was herself essentially right, Elizabeth sent down an order that the subject should be approached no further on pain of her displeasure. The same night a note was flung into the presence-chamber saying that the debate on the succession had been undertaken because the commonwealth required it, and that if the Queen interfered it might be the worse for her.[3]

In the most critical period of the reign of Henry the

---

[1] Report made to the Commons' House by Mr. Secretary.—*Domestic MSS. Rolls House.*

[2] *Commons' Journals.*

[3] 'A noche embáron en la camera de presencia un escrito que contenia en sustancia que se habia tratado en el Parlamento de la sucesion porque

Eighth, speech in Parliament had been ostentatiously free; the Act of Appeals had been under discussion for two years and more, Catholic and Protestant had spoken their minds without restraint; yet among the many strained applications of the treason law no peer or commoner had been called to answer for words spoken by him in his place in the legislature. The Queen's injunction of silence had poured oil into the fire, and raised a fresh and more dangerous question of privilege. As soon as the House met again on Monday morning Mr. Paul Wentworth rose to know whether such an order 'was not against the liberties' of Parliament.[1] He and other members inquired whether a message sent by a public officer was authority sufficient to bind the House, or if neither the message itself nor the manner in which it was delivered was a breach of privilege, 'what offence it was for any of the House to declare his opinion to be otherwise.'[2] The debate lasted five hours, and (a rare if not unprecedented occurrence) was adjourned.

Elizabeth more angry than ever sent for the Speaker; she insisted 'that there should be no further argument:' if any member of either House was dissatisfied he must give his opinion before the Council.

The Commons having gone so far had no intention of yielding; and de Silva watched the crisis with a malicious hope of a collision between the two Houses and of both with the Queen. The Lower House he said was determined to name a successor, and was all but unanimous for Lady Catherine; the Peers were as decided for the Queen

---

convenia al bien del Reyno, y que si la Reyna no consentia que se tratase dello que veria algunas cosas que no le placerian.'—*De Silva to Philip, November* 11. *MS. Simancas.*

[1] *Commons' Journals,* 8 ELIZ.
[2] Note of Proceedings in Parliament, *November* 11.—*Domestic MSS.,* ELIZ. vol. xli.

of Scots.[1] A dissolution would leave the Treasury without a subsidy, and could not be thought of save at the last extremity. On the return of the Speaker the Commons named a committee to draw up an answer which though in form studiously courteous was in substance as deliberately firm.[2] The finishing touch was given to it by Cecil, and the sentences added in his hand were those which insisted most on the liberty of Parliament, and most justified the attitude which the Commons had assumed.

After thanking the Queen for her promise to marry, and assuring her that whatever she might think to the contrary they meant nothing but what became them as loyal subjects, they said that they submitted reluctantly to her resolution to postpone the settlement of the succession, *being most sorry that any manner of impediment had appeared to her Majesty so great as to stay her from proceeding in the same.*'[3] They had however received a message implying 'that they had deserved to be deprived, or at least sequestrated, *much to their discomfort and infamy,*[4] from their ancient and laudable custom, always from the beginning necessarily annexed to their assembly, and by her Majesty *always*[5] confirmed—that is, a lawful sufferance and dutiful liberty to treat and devise matters honourable

---

[1] 'Ellos pretenden libertad de proceder á lo del nombramiento de la sucesion en la qual en la camara superior tendra mucha parti la de Escocia; su tiene por cierto y assi lo creo que Caterina tendra casi todos los de la Camara baja, y assi parece que inclina todo á emocion.'—*De Silva to Philip, November 13. MS. Simancas.*

[2] Draft of an Address to the Queen, submitted to the Committee of the Commons' House.—*Domestic MSS., Eliz.*, vol. xli.

[3] The words in Italics were added by Cecil.

[4] Added in Cecil's hand.

[5] The word first written was 'graciously.' Cecil scratched through 'graciously,' as if it implied that the liberties of the House of Commons depended on the pleasure of the Sovereign, and substituted 'always.'

to her Majesty and profitable to the realm.' Before this message reached them 'they had made no determination to deal in any way to her discontentation; they therefore besought her of her motherly love that they might continue in their course of duty, honouring and serving her like children, without any unnecessary, *unaccustomed*[1] or undeserved yoke of commandment; so[2] should her Majesty continue the singular favour of her honour, wherein she did excel all monarchs, for ruling her subjects without misliking; and they also would enjoy the like praise above all other people for obeying without constraint—than the which no prince could desire more earthly honour, nor no people more earthly praise.'

No one knew better than Elizabeth how to withdraw from an indefensible position, and words so full of firmness and dignity might perhaps have produced an effect; but before the address could be presented a fresh apple of discord was thrown into the arena.

A book had appeared in Paris, written by a refugee Scot named Patrick Adamson. The subject of it was the birth of James; and the Queen of Scots' child was described as the heir of the English throne. Copies had been scattered about London, and Elizabeth had already directed Mary Stuart's attention to the thing 'as a matter strange and not to be justified.'[3]

On the 21st of November, on occasion of a measure laid before the House against the introduction of seditious books from abroad, a Mr. Dalton brought forward this production of Adamson in the fiercest Protestant spirit.

'How say you,' he exclaimed, 'to a libel set forth in

---
[1] Cecil's hand. [2] The conclusion is entirely Cecil's.
[3] Elizabeth to Bedford, November 13.—*Scotch MSS. Rolls House.*

print calling the Infant of Scotland Prince of England, Scotland and Ireland? Prince of England, Scotland, and Ireland! What enemy to the peace and quietness of the realm of England—what traitor to the crown of this realm hath devised, set forth, and published this dishonour against the Queen's most excellent Majesty and the crown of England? Prince of England, and Queen Elizabeth as yet having no child!—Prince of England, and the Scottish Queen's child!—Prince of Scotland and England, and Scotland before England! who ever heard or read that before this time? What true English heart may sustain to hear of this villany and reproach against the Queen's highness and this her realm? It is so that it hath pleased her highness at this time to bar our speech; but if our mouths shall be stopped, and in the mean time such despite shall happen and pass without revenge, it will make the heart of a true Englishman break within his breast.'

'With the indignity of the matter being,' as he afterwards said, 'set on fire,' Dalton went on to touch on dangerous matters, and entered on the forbidden subject of the Scottish title. The Speaker gently checked him, but not before he had uttered words which called out the whole sympathy of the Commons, and gave them an opportunity of showing how few friends in that House Mary Stuart as yet could count upon.[1]

The story was carried to the Queen: she chose to believe that the House of Commons intended to defy her; she ordered Dalton into arrest and had him examined before the Star Chamber; she construed her own orders into

---

[1] Mr. Dalton's Speech, according to the Report.—*Domestic MSS.*, ELIZ. vol. xli.

a law, and seemed determined to govern the House of Commons as if it was a debating society of riotous boys.

The Commons behaved with great forbearance: they replied to the seizure of the offending member by requesting 'to have leave to confer upon the liberties of the House.' The original question of the succession was lost in the larger one of privilege, and the address which they had previously drawn seemed no longer distinct enough for the occasion. The Council implored Elizabeth to consider what she was doing. As soon as her anger cooled she felt herself that she had gone too far, and not caring to face a conference, 'foreseeing that thereof must needs have ensued more inconvenience than were meet,' she drew back with temper not too ruffled to save her dignity in giving way. Her intention had been to extort or demand the sanction of the House for the prosecution of Dalton. Discovering in time that if they refused she had no means of compelling them, she would not risk an open rupture. The prisoner was released 'without further question or trial,' and on the 25th she sent orders to the Speaker 'to relieve the House of the burden of her commandment.' She had been assured, she said, that they had no intention of molesting her, and that they had been 'much perplexed' by the receipt of her order; 'she did not mean to prejudice any part of the laudable liberties heretofore granted to them;' she would therefore content herself with their obedient behaviour, and she trusted only that if any person should begin again to discuss any particular title, the Speaker would compel him to be silent.[1]

The Commons were prudent enough to make the

---

[1] Note of the words of the Queen to the Speaker of the House of Commons.—*Domestic MSS.*, ELIZ., vol. xli. Leicester to Cecil, November 27.— *MS. Ibid.*

Queen's retreat an easy one. Having succeeded in resisting a dangerous encroachment of the crown they did not press their victory. The message sent through the Speaker was received by the House 'most joyfully, with most hearty prayers and thanks for the same,'[1] and with the consent of all parties the question of Parliamentary privilege was allowed to drop.

Yet while ready to waive their right of discussing further the particular pretensions of the claimants of the crown, the Commons would not let the Queen believe that they acquiesced in being left in uncertainty. Two months had passed since the beginning of the session, and the subsidy had not been so much as discussed. The succession quarrel had commenced with the first motion for a grant of money, and had lasted with scarcely an interval ever since.

It was evident that although Elizabeth's objection to name a successor was rested on general grounds, it applied as strongly to Lady Catherine as to the Queen of Scots, and had arisen professedly from the Queen's own experience in the lifetime of her sister; yet the Commons either suspected that she was secretly working in the Scottish interest, or they thought at all events that her procrastination served only to strengthen that interest, and that Mary Stuart's friends every day grew more numerous.

The Money Bill was reintroduced on the 27th. The House was anxious to compensate by its liberality for the trouble which it had given on other subjects, and the Queen was privately informed that the grant would be made unusually large. Elizabeth, determined not to be outdone, replied that although for the public service she might require all which they were ready to offer,

---

[1] *Commons' Journals*, 8 Eliz.

'she counted her subjects in respect of their hearty good will her best treasurers;' and 'she therefore would move them to forbear at that time extending their gift as they proposed.' The manner as well as the matter of the message was pointedly gracious, yet the Commons would have preferred her taking the money and listening to their opinions; and the bribe was as unsuccessful as the menace, in keeping them silent. They voted freely the sum which she would consent to take. It amounted in a rough estimate to an income tax of seven per cent. for two years; but an attempt was made to attach a preamble to the Bill which would commit the Queen in accepting it to what she was straining every nerve to avoid. Referring to the promise which she had made to the Committee, 'the Commons humbly and earnestly besought her with the assistance of God's grace, having resolved to marry, to accelerate without more loss of time all her honourable actions tending thereto;' while 'submitting themselves to the will of Almighty God, in whose hands all power and counsel did consist, they would at the same time beseech Him to give her Majesty wisdom well to foresee, opportunity speedily to consult, and power with assent of the realm sufficiently to fulfil without unnecessary delay, all that should be needful to her subjects and their posterity in the stablishing the succession of the crown, first in her own person and progeny, and next in such persons as law and justice should peaceably direct—according to the answer of Moses: "The Lord God of the spirit of all flesh set one over this great multitude which may go out and in before them, and lead them out and in, that the Lord's people may not be as sheep without a shepherd."'[1]

---

[1] Preamble for the Subsidy Bill. *Domestic MSS.*, vol. xli. *Rolls House.*

The meaning of language such as this could not be mistaken. All the political advantages of the Scottish succession would not compensate to 'the Lord's people' for such a shepherd as the person into whose hands they seemed to be visibly drifting. It was a grave misfortune for the Protestants that they could produce no better candidate than Lady Catherine Grey, who had professed herself a Catholic when Catholicism seemed likely to serve her turn; and to whom, notwithstanding her legal claim through the provisions of the will of Henry the Eighth, there were so many and so serious objections. The friends of the Queen of Scots had set in circulation a list of difficulties in the way of her acknowledgment, the weight of which fanaticism itself could not refuse to admit.[1]

It is uncertain whether the preamble was ever forced

---

[1] 'Whatever be said, it is notorious that when Sir Charles Brandon married the French Queen he had a wife already living.

'The Lady Katherine is therefore illegitimate.

'Even if this were not so, yet such hath been her life and behaviour, and so much hath she stained herself and her issue, as she is to be thought unworthy of the crown. For she was married, as you know, to the Lord Herbert; the marriage was performed and perfected by all necessary circumstances; there was consent of parties, consent of parents, open solemnizing, continuance till lawful years of consent, and in the meantime, carnal copulation; all which, save the last, are commonly known, and the last, which might be most doubtful, is known by confession of them both. She herself hath earnestly acknowledged the same.

'A divorce was procured by the Earl of Pembroke, in Queen Mary's reign, against their wills, so that it cannot be legal.

'Afterwards, she by dalliance fell to carnal company with the Earl of Hertford, which was not descried till the bigness of her belly bewrayed her ill hap. The marriage between them was declared unlawful by the bishop who examined it.

'The mother wicked and lascivious; the issue bastardled.

'If she were next in the blood royal, her fault is so much the more to have so foully spotted the same. She can have no lawful children. Deut. xiii. 23:—It is written, "a bastard and unlawful-born person may not bear rule in the church and commonweal;" a law devised to punish

on Elizabeth's attention. The draft of it alone remains to show what the Commons intended; and either they despaired of prevailing on the Queen to accept the grant while such a prelude was linked to it, and were unwilling to embarrass the public service; or they preferred another expedient to which they trusted less objection might be raised: the preamble at all events was abandoned; they substituted for it a general expression of gratitude for the promise to marry, and sent the Bill to the Lords on the 17th of December.

Meanwhile on the 5th a measure was introduced which, if less effective in the long run for the protection of the Reformation than the declaration of a Protestant

---

the parents for their sins, so that such a mother ought in no case to be allowed to succeed.

'Next as to King Henry's will:—

'He had no power to bequeath the crown, except so far as Parliament gave him leave; and Parliament could only give him leave so far as the power of Parliament extended. The words of the statute give him no absolute or unlimited power to appoint an unfit person to the crown, not capable of the same—as unto a Turk, an Infidel, an infamous or opprobrious person, a fool or a madman.

'But again, he had power to order the succession, either by Letters Patent, or by his will, signed with his own hand.

'He has not done it by Letters Patent; of that there is no doubt.

'His will, there are witnesses sufficient, and some of them that subscribed the same testament can truly and plainly testify, that he did not subscribe.

'The stamp might be appended when the King was void of memory, or else when he was deceased, as indeed it happened, as more manifestly appeared by open declaration made in Parliament by the late Lord Paget and others, that the King did not sign it with his own hand, and as it is plain and probable enough by the pardon obtained for one William Clerke for putting the stamp to the said will after the King was departed.

'As to the enrolment in Chancery, and the evidence on the Rolls that the will was accepted and acted on, this is nothing. It was his will whether signed or not, and so far as legacies, etc., were concerned, such as he had power to make by the common law, so far it might be acted on. But in so far as the succession was concerned, it was invalid, because the form prescribed by the empowering statute, 35 Hen. VIII., had not been observed.'—*Answer to Mr. Hales' Book of the Succession, December*, 1566. *Domestic MSS., Eliz.*, vol. xli.

successor, would have ended at once the ambiguity of the religious position of Elizabeth. The Thirty-nine Articles, strained and cracked by three centuries of evasive ingenuity, scarcely embarrass now the feeblest of consciences. The clergyman of the nineteenth century subscribes them with such a smile as might have been worn by Samson when his Philistine mistress bound his arms with the cords and withes. In the first years of Elizabeth they were the symbols by which the orthodox Protestant was distinguished from the concealed Catholic. The liturgy with purposed ambiguity could be used by those who were Papists save in the name; the Articles affirmed the falsehood of doctrines declared by the Church to be divine, and the Catholic who signed them either passed over to the new opinions or imperilled his soul with perjury. In their anxiety for conciliation, and for the semblance of unanimity, Elizabeth's Government had as yet held these formulas at arm's length: the Convocation of 1562 had reimposed them so far as their powers extended; but the decrees of Convocation were but shadows until vitalized by the legislature; and both Queen and Parliament had refused to give the authority of law to a code of doctrines which might convulse the kingdom.

On the failure of the suit for the succession, a Bill was brought into the Lower House to make subscription to the Articles a condition for the tenure of benefices in the Church of England. The move was so sudden and the Commons were so swift that there was no time for resistance. It was hurried through its three readings and given to the bishops to carry through the Lords. A letter from de Silva to Philip shows the importance which both Catholic and Protestant attached to it:—

DE SILVA TO PHILIP II.

December, 1566.

'Religion is again under discussion here; these heretic bishops are urging forward their malicious pretences; they say that it is desirable for the realm to profess an uniform belief, and they desire to have their doctrine enforced by temporal penalties as soon as it has been sanctioned by Parliament.

'The Catholics are in great alarm and entreat the Queen to withhold her sanction. I spent some time with her yesterday, and to bring on the subject I said that the Subsidy Bill having been passed it would be well if she let the Parliament end. The longer it lasted the more annoyance it would cause to her; and she might assure herself that these popular assemblies could not fail to produce disquiet, more particularly where the Commons had liberty of speech and were so much inclined to novelties.

'She agreed with me in this. She said the Commons had now entered upon a subject which was wholly alien to their duties; they were acting in contradiction to their late professions, and she would endeavour to send them about their business before Christmas.

'I pointed out to her the mischievous intention of the men who had brought these religious questions forward. They had no care for her or for the commonwealth and they simply meant sedition. She was at peace so far and had lived and reigned in safety all these years on the principles on which Cecil had carried on the government. If there was now to be a change, the insolence of the upholders of novelties would disturb everything. Hitherto the Pope and the Catholic powers had abstained from declaring against her, in the belief that her subjects were equitably and wisely governed, and that she would allow no one to be injured or offended. Should they now see her preparing to change her course they would perhaps reconsider the situation and troubles might ensue, of which I as the minister of your Majesty who so ardently desired her well-being could not but give her honest warning.

'She went into the subject at some length. She said that those who were engaged upon it had given her to understand that it was for her own good and had promised every one of them to stand by her and defend her against all her enemies.

'I told her she could not but see that these new religionists were only frightening her—in order that they might bring her to declare more decisively for them and against the Catholics. They pretended that if she separated herself from them—if she did not yield in all points to what they wished—she would be in danger on account of the sentence which had been given at Rome in favour of Queen Catherine. I could assure her that she had but to express a desire to that effect and the Pope would immediately remove the difficulty; I knew in fact that he was extremely anxious to remove it. Being her father's daughter, born in his house, having been named by him with consent of Parliament to succeed after her sister, and being Queen in possession, she had nothing really to fear—she would find powerful friends everywhere.

'It was true, she admitted, that the Pope had offered to reverse the sentence, but he had made it a condition that she should submit to him absolutely and unreservedly.

'If his Holiness had done this, I said, he was not actuated by any covetous ambition but by the sincerest interest in herself and the realm. In the present Pope she might feel the fullest confidence; and at all events

there was no more reason for making innovations now
than there had been at the beginning of her reign. She
would do better to wait till time should enable her to
see her way.

'She said that she thought as I did: she believed
however that her people were afraid if she married the
Archduke that the old religion would be brought in
again; they were pressing forward these changes as a
precaution.

'A little while ago, I said, her Council were most
afraid that she would not marry at all.

'True, she answered; that was their fear or their pretended fear—and their present conduct showed how dishonest they had been. Marry however she would if it was only to vex them. She would have been glad, she said, had there been any one in Parliament who could have checked the Bill in its progress; if it passed the Lords she feared she would be unable to resist the pressure which would be brought to bear upon her.'

Either Elizabeth feared another quarrel and distrusted her own strength, or she wished to deceive de Silva into believing her opposition to the Bill to be more sincere than it really was. The remonstrances of the Catholics however and her own better judgment prevailed at last. She collected her courage and sent a message to the Peers desiring that the Bill of Religion should go no further. The bishops were the persons in the Upper House for whom alone the question had much interest; and Elizabeth understood how to manage them. The Commons had resisted one order—the bishops thought they could resist another. Their first impulse was to entreat the Queen to reconsider her command—to let the debate go forward, and 'if the Bill was found good by the Lords that she would be pleased for the glory of

God to give her gracious assent to the same.'[1] A petition to this effect was presented carrying the signatures of the two archbishops and thirteen bishops. The Queen sent immediately for Parker and three or four more, and inquired which of them had been the first promoters of the Bill. Though it first appeared in the Lower House, she said, it must have originated with some one on the Bench; and though she had no objection to the doctrine of the Articles—'for it was that which she did openly profess'—she objected seriously to sudden irregular action 'without her knowledge and consent' on a question of such magnitude.

Had Elizabeth scolded in the tone usual with her towards the Church authorities she might have found them obstinate; but she spoke reasonably and they were frightened. The archbishops, though their names headed the signatures to the petition, disclaimed eagerly the responsibility of the initiation. She bade them find out by whom it had been done. The Archbishop of Canterbury reported to Cecil 'that most of his brethren answered, as he had done, that they knew nothing of it.' Having extracted a disavowal from the majority of the Bench, Elizabeth was able to shield her objections behind their indifference; she had checkmated them and the obnoxious measure disappeared.

Thus gradually the storms of the session were blowing over. The Queen seemed at last to have really resolved on marriage, and her determination gave her courage to encounter her other difficulties with an increase of firmness. She promised the advocates of the Scotch title that the will of Henry the Eighth should be examined immediately on the close of the session, and that

---

[1] Petition of the Bishops to the Queen, December, 1566.—*Domestic MSS.*, ELIZ., vol. xli.

a fair legal opinion should be taken on the Queen of
Scots' claims;[1] and she gave Mary Stuart a significant
evidence of her good will in closing promptly and peremptorily a discussion which had commenced at Lincoln's
Inn in the interests of the rival candidate. The lawyers
disappointed of their debate in the House of Commons
began it again in the Inns of Court—where there was no
privilege to protect incautious speakers. Mr. Thornton,
an eloquent advocate of Lady Catherine, was sent to the
Tower; and even Cecil earned the thanks of the Queen
of Scots by the energy with which he seconded his mistress in silencing opposition.[2]

---

[1] De Silva to Philip, December 16.—MS. Simancas.

[2] On the 5th of January, Murray thanked Cecil in his own and the Queen's name for 'his cordial dealing.' 'Her Majesty,' wrote Maitland to him, 'is very well satisfied with your behaviour. I pray you so continue, not doubting but you shall find her a thankful princess.' 'Melville,' he added, 'reports nothing but good of you, touching the repairing the injury done against my mistress at Lincoln's Inn.'—Scotch MSS. Rolls House.

Cecil's conduct in the succession struggle is not easy to make out. Neither memorandum nor letter of his own remains to show his real feelings; but though he might naturally have been looked for among the supporters of Lady Catherine Grey, he seems to have given thorough satisfaction to the friends of the Queen of Scots. He must have written to Maitland immediately after Elizabeth's first answer to the address of the Houses, regretting her resolution to leave the question unsettled; and he must have led Maitland to suppose that he had wished Mary Stuart to have been the person nominated; for Maitland, answering his letter on the 11th of November, gave him 'hearty thanks for the pains which he had taken in the busy matter which he had had in hand,' and then went on more pointedly—

'I look not in my time to see the matter in any perfection, for I think it is not the pleasure of God to have the subjects of this isle thoroughly settled in their judgment; for which cause he doth keep things most necessary undetermined, so as they shall always have somewhat wherewith to be exercised. The experience I have had of late in my own person makes me the less to marvel when I hear your doings are misconstrued by backbiters. Whomsoever will meddle with public affairs and princes must be content to bear that burden. I never doubted the sincerity of your intentions, and I doubt not time shall convince those that think the contrary even in their own conscience, whenas themselves shall be content

Elizabeth herself wrote to the Queen of Scots, no longer insisting on the Treaty of Leith—no longer stipulating for embarrassing conditions. Substantially conceding all the points which were in dispute between them, she proposed that they should mutually bind themselves by a contract in which Mary Stuart should undertake to do nothing against Elizabeth during the lifetime of herself or her children; while Elizabeth would 'engage never to do or suffer anything to be done to the prejudice of the Queen of Scots' title and interest as her next cousin.'[1]

The Queen of Scots declared herself, in reply, assured of Elizabeth's 'good mind and entire affection' towards her; 'she did not doubt that in time her sister would proceed to the perfecting and consideration of that which she had begun to utter, as well to her own people as to other nations—the opinion which her sister had of the equity of her cause;' and she promised to send a commission to London to settle the terms in which the

---

to justify your councils, which now are ignorant to what scope they are directed.'

On the 17th of November, Mary Stuart herself wrote to Cecil, saying 'that the bruits were passed which reported him to be a hinderer to her advancement, and that she knew him to be a wise man.'

On the 18th Murray wrote that 'he had always found Cecil most earnest to produce good feeling and a sound understanding between England and Scotland, and between the two Queens; and so,' he said, 'my trust is that ye will continue favourable to the end in all her Highness's affairs, which for my own part I will

most earnestly crave of you, being most assured there is no daughter in the isle doth more reverence her natural mother nor my Sovereign the Queen your mistress. Nor sure I am can she be induced by any means to seek or procure that which may in any sort offend her Majesty.'—*Scotch MSS. Rolls House.*

It is possible that even Cecil's vigilance had been laid asleep by the submissive attitude which the Queen of Scots had assumed towards Elizabeth, and by the seeming restoration of Murray to her confidence.

[1] Elizabeth to the Queen of Scots, December, 1566.—*MS. Rolls House.*

contract 'might pass orderly to both their contentments.'[1]

Thus the struggle was over; though unrecognized by a formal Act of Parliament Mary Stuart had won the day and was virtually regarded as the heir presumptive to the English throne. Elizabeth's own wishes had pointed throughout to this conclusion, if the Queen of Scots would consent to seek her object in any other capacity than as the representative of a revolution. The reconciliation of the two factions in Scotland and the restoration of Murray and Maitland to confidence and authority were accepted as an indication of a changed purpose; and harassed by her subjects, goaded into a marriage which she detested, and exhausted by a struggle which threatened a dangerous breach between herself and the nation, Elizabeth closed the long chapter of distrust, and yielded or prepared to yield all that was demanded of her.

Having thus made up her mind she resolved to break up the Parliament and to punish the refractory House of Commons by a dissolution. After another election the Puritans would be in a minority. The succession could be legally established without division or quarrel, guarded by such moderate guarantees as might secure the mutual toleration of the two creeds.

For the first time in parliamentary history a session had been wasted in barren disputes. On the 2nd of January between two and three in the afternoon the Queen appeared in the House of Lords to bring it to an end. The Commons were called to the bar; the Speaker Mr. Onslow read a complimentary address, in which he described the English nation as happy in a sovereign

---

[1] The Queen of Scots to Elizabeth, Jan. 3, 1567.—*Scotch MSS. Rolls House.*

who understood her duties, who prevented her subjects from injuring one another and knew 'how to make quiet among the ministers of religion.' He touched on the many excellences of the constitution and finally with some imprudence ventured an allusion to the restrictions on the royal authority.

'There be,' he said, 'for the prince provided princely prerogatives and royalties, yet not such as the prince can take money or other things or do as she will at her own pleasure without order; but quietly to suffer her subjects to enjoy their own without wrongful oppression; whereas other princes by their liberty do take as pleaseth them.'

'Your Majesty,' he went on turning to Elizabeth, 'has not attempted to make laws contrary to order but orderly has called this Parliament, which perceived certain wants and thereunto have put their helping hands, and for help of evil manners good laws are brought forth.'

Then going to the sorest of all sore and wounding subjects he concluded, 'we give hearty thanks to God for that your highness has signified your pleasure of your inclination to marriage, which afore you were not given unto; which is done for our safeguard that when God shall call you you may leave of your own body to succeed you. Therefore God grant us that you will shortly embrace the holy state of matrimony when and with whom God shall appoint and shall best like your Majesty.'

Elizabeth's humour, none the happiest at the commencement, was not improved by this fresh chafing of her galled side. She had come prepared to lecture others not to listen to a homily. She beckoned Bacon to her and spoke a few words to him. He then rose and said that the general parts of the Speaker's address her

Majesty liked well, and therefore he need not touch on them; on the latter and more particular expressions used in it a few words were necessary.

'Politic orders,' he said, 'be the rules of all good acts, and touching them that you have made to the overthrowing of good laws' (your Bill of Religion, with which you meant to tyrannize over conscience), 'these deserve reproof as well as the others deserve praise. In which like cause you err in bringing her Majesty's prerogative into question, and for that thing wherein she meant not to hurt any of your liberties. Her Majesty's nature however is mild; she will not be austere; and therefore though at this time she suffer you all to depart quietly into your counties for your amendment, yet as it is needful she hopeth the offenders will hereafter use themselves well.'

The Acts of the session were then read out and received the royal assent; all seemed over, and it was by this time dusk; when Elizabeth herself in the uncertain light rose from the throne, stood forward in her robes and spoke.

'My Lords and other Commons of this assembly: although the Lord Keeper hath according to order very well answered in my name, yet as a periphrasis I have a few words further to speak unto you, notwithstanding I have not been used nor love to do it in such open assemblies. Yet now, not to the end to amend his talk, but remembering that commonly princes' own words are better printed in the hearers' memory than those spoken by her command, I mean to say thus much unto you.

'I have in this assembly found such dissimulation where I always professed plainness, that I marvel thereat; yea two faces under one hood, and the body rotten, being covered with the two vizors succession and liberty —which they determined must be either presently granted, denied, or deferred; in granting whereof they had their desire; and denying or deferring thereof, those things being so plausible as indeed to all men they are, they thought to work me that mischief which never foreign enemy could bring to pass—which is the hatred of my Commons.

'But alas! they began to pierce the vessel before the wine was fined, and begun a thing not foreseeing the end, how by this means I have seen my well-willers from my enemies, and can as meseemeth very well divide the House into four:—

'1. The broachers and workers thereof, who are in the greatest fault.

'2. The speakers who by eloquent tales persuaded the rest are next in degree.

'3. The agreers who being so light of credit that the eloquence of those tales so overcame them that they gave more credit thereunto than unto their own wits.

'4. Those that sat still and mute and meddled not therewith, but rather wondered disallowing the matter; who in my opinion are most to be excused.

'But do you think that either I am so unmindful of your surety by succession wherein is all my care, considering I know myself to be but mortal? No, I warrant you. Or that I went about to break your liberties? No, it never was in my meaning; but to stay you before you fell into the ditch. For all things have their time; and although perhaps you may have after me a better-learned or wiser, yet I assure you, none more careful over you; and therefore henceforth, whether I live to see the like assembly or no, or whoever it be, yet beware how you prove your prince's patience as you have now done mine.

'And now to conclude all this; notwithstanding, not meaning to make a Lent of Christmas, the most part of you may assure yourselves that you depart in your prince's grace.

'My Lord Keeper you will do as I bid you.'

Again Bacon rose and in a loud voice said, 'The Queen's Majesty doth dissolve this Parliament. Let every man depart at his pleasure.'

Elizabeth swept away in the gloom, passed to her barge, and returned to the palace. The Lords and Commons scattered through the English counties, and five years went by before another Parliament met again at Westminster in a changed world.

On that evening the immediate prospect before England was the Queen's marriage with an Austrian Catholic prince, the recognition more or less distant of the Catholic Mary Stuart as heir presumptive, the establishment with the support and sanction of the Catholic powers of some moderate form of government, under which the Catholic worship would be first tolerated and then creep on towards ascendancy. It might have ended, had Elizabeth been strong enough, in broad intellectual freedom; more likely it would have ended in the reappearance of the Marian fanaticism, to be encountered by passions as fierce and irrational as itself; and to the probable issue of that conflict conjecture fails to penetrate.

But the era of toleration was yet centuries distant; and the day of the Roman persecutors was gone never more to reappear. Six weeks later a powder barrel exploded in a house in Edinburgh, and when the smoke cleared away the prospects of the Catholics in England were scattered to all the winds.

CHAP X.
1567
January

The murder of Henry Stuart Lord Darnley is one of those incidents which will remain till the end of time conspicuous on the page of history. In itself the death of a single boy, prince or king though he might be, had little in it to startle the hard world of the sixteenth century. Even before the folly and falsehood by which Mary Stuart's husband had earned the hatred of the Scotch nobility, it had been foreseen that such a frail and giddy summer pleasure-boat would be soon wrecked in those stormy waters. Had Darnley been stabbed in a scuffle or helped to death by a dose of arsenic in his bed, the fair fame of the Queen of Scots would have suffered little, and the tongues that dared to mutter would have been easily silenced. But conspiracies in Scotland were never managed with the skilful villany of the Continent; and when some conspicuous person was to be removed out of the way, the instruments of the deed were either fanatic religionists who looked on themselves as the servants of God, or else they had been wrought up to the murder point by some personal passion which was not contented with the death of its victim, and required a fuller satisfaction in the picturesqueness of dramatic revenge. The circumstances under which the obstacle to Mary Stuart's peace was disposed of challenged the attention of the whole civilized world, and no after efforts availed in court, creed or nation, to hide the memory of the scenes which were revealed in that sudden lightning flash.

The Queen of Scots goes to Jedburgh.

The disorders of the Scots upon the Border had long been a subject of remonstrance from the English Government. The Queen of Scots, while the Parliament was sitting at Westminster, desired to give some public proof of her wish to conciliate; and after the strange appearance of Darnley in September at the Council at Edinburgh, she proposed to go in person to Jedburgh and hear the complaints of Elizabeth's wardens. The Earl of Bothwell had taken command of the North Marches: he had gone down to prepare the way for the Queen's appearance, and on her arrival she was greeted with the news that he had been shot through the thigh in a scuffle and was lying wounded in Hermitage Castle. The Earl had been her companion throughout the summer; her relations with him at this time—whether innocent or not—were of the closest intimacy; and she had taken into her household a certain Lady Reres, who had once been his mistress.

She heard of his wound with the most alarmed anxiety: on every ground she could ill afford to lose him;[1] and careless at all times of bodily fatigue or danger, she rode on the 15th of October twenty-five miles over the moors to see him. The Earl's state proved to be more painful than dangerous, and after remaining two hours at his bed-side she returned the same day to Jedburgh. She had not been well: 'thought and displeasure,' which as she herself told Maitland,[2] 'had their root in the King,' had already affected both her health and spirits. The long ride, the night air, and 'the great distress of her mind for the Earl,' proved too much for her; and though she sat her horse till her journey's end she fainted when she was lifted from the saddle, and remained two hours unconscious. Delirium followed with violent fever, and in this condition she continued for a week. She was frequently insensible: food refused to remain upon her stomach; yet for the first few days there seemed to be 'no tokens of death;' she slept tolerably, and on Tuesday

---

[1] 'Ce ne lay eust pas esté peu de perte de le perdre!' were the unsuspicious words of du Croq on the 17th of October.—TEULET, vol. ii. p. 289.
[2] Maitland to the Archbishop of Glasgow.—Printed in KEITH.

and Wednesday the 22nd and 23rd she was thought to be improving. An express had been sent to Glasgow for Darnley, but he did not appear. On Friday the 25th there was a relapse; shiverings came on, the body grew rigid, the eyes were closed, the mouth set and motionless; she lost consciousness so entirely that she was supposed to be dying or dead; and in expectation of an immediate end a menacing order to keep the peace was sent out by Murray, Maitland, Huntly, and the other Lords who were in attendance on her.

The physician, 'Master Nuw,' however, 'a perfyt man of his craft,' 'would not give the matter over.' He restored the circulation by chafing the limbs; the Queen came to herself at last, broke into a profuse perspiration, and fell into a natural sleep. When she awoke, the fever was gone, but her strength was prostrated. For the few next days she still believed herself in danger, and with the outward signs, and so far as could be seen with the inward spirit of Catholic piety, she prepared to meet what might be coming upon her. The Bishop of Ross was ever on his knees at her bed-side; and courageous always, she professed herself ready to die if so it was to be. She recommended the Prince to the lords; through Murray she bequeathed the care of him to Elizabeth—through du Croq to the King of France and Catherine de Medici—and for Scotland she implored them all as her last request 'to trouble no man in his conscience that professed the Catholic faith,' in which she herself had been brought up and was ready to die.

How much of all this was real, how much theatrical, it is needless to inquire; the most ardent admirer of Mary Stuart will not claim for her a character of piety, in any sense of the word which connects it with the moral law; those who regard her with most suspicion will not refuse her the credit of devotion to the Catholic cause.

In a week all alarm was at an end. At length, but so late that his appearance was an affront, Darnley arrived: he was received with coldness; but for the interposition of Murray he would not have been allowed to remain a single night, and the next morning he was dismissed to return to his father. In unhappy contrast the Earl of Bothwell was brought as soon as he could be moved to Jedburgh; and on the 10th of November the court broke up, and proceeded by slow journeys towards Edinburgh for the Prince's baptism. At Kelso the Queen found a letter from her husband. It seems that he had been again writing in complaint of her to the Pope and the Catholic powers.[1] He was probably no less unwise in the words which he used to herself; and she exclaimed passionately in Murray's and Maitland's presence 'that unless she was freed of him in some way she had no pleasure to live, and if she could find no other remedy she would put hand to it herself.'[2]

Leaving Kelso and skirting the Border, she looked from Halydon Hill over Berwick and the English lines, and that fair vision of the future where Darnley was the single darkening image. A train of knights and gentlemen came out to do her homage and attend her to Ayemouth; the Berwick batteries as she went by saluted the heiress of the English crown; all through Northumberland, through Yorkshire, to the very gates of London, had she cared to visit Elizabeth, Mary Stuart

---

[1] De Silva in a letter, late in the winter, to Philip, spoke of writing to the Queen of Scots—' Á carca del mal oficio que su marido habia hecho contra ella con V. M⁴ y con el Papa y Principes en lo de su religion.'— MS. Simancas.

[2] CALDERWOOD.

would have been then received with all but regal honours. The Earl of Bedford—of all English nobles the most determined of her opponents—was preparing to be present at the approaching baptism to make his peace as Elizabeth's representative. From Dunbar she wrote to Cecil and the rest of the Council as to 'her good friends,' to whom she committed the care of 'her cause.' From thence she passed on to Craigmillar[1] to recruit her strength in the keen breezy air.

Some heavy weight still hung upon her spirits: her brilliant prospects failed to cheer her. 'The Queen is at Craigmillar,' wrote du Croq at the end of November; 'she is still sick, and I believe the principal part of her disease to consist of a deep grief and sorrow: nor can she, it seems, forget the same; again and again she says she wishes she were dead.'[2]

To the lords who had attended her to Dalkeith the cause of her trouble was but too notorious. Instead of listening to her entreaties to relieve her of her husband, the Pope had probably followed the advice of de Silva, and had urged her to be reconciled to him: at any rate she must have known the anxiety of her English friends, and must have felt more wearily than ever the burden of the chain with which she had bound herself. Bothwell, Murray, Maitland, and Huntly continued at her side, and at Craigmillar they were joined by Argyle.

The lords and gentlemen who had been concerned in Ritzio's murder had by this time most of them received their pardon; but the Queen had still found herself unable to forgive Morton who, with Lindsay, young Ruthven and Ker, was still in exile in England. Their

---

[1] Three miles south of Edinburgh, on the road to Dalkeith.
[2] Du Croq to the Archbishop of Glasgow.—KEITH.

friends had never ceased to intercede for them. One morning while Argyle was still in bed, Murray and Maitland came to his room; and Maitland beginning upon the subject, said that the 'best way to obtain Morton's pardon was to promise the Queen to find means to divorce her from her husband.'

Argyle said he did not know how it could be done.

'My Lord,' said Maitland, 'care you not for that, we shall find the means to make her quit of him well enough, if you and Lord Huntly will look on and not take offence.'

Scotland was still entangled in the Canon Law, and some trick could be made available if the nobles agreed to allow it. Huntly entered as the others were talking. They offered him the restoration of the Gordon estates if he would consent to Morton's return: he took the price and agreed with the rest to forward the divorce.

The four noblemen then went together to Bothwell, who professed equal readiness; he accompanied them to the Queen; and Maitland in the name of the rest undertook to deliver her from Darnley on condition that she pardoned Morton and his companions.

Mary Stuart was craving for release: she said generally that she would do what they required; but embarrassed as she was by her connexion with Rome she was unable to understand how a divorce could be managed, or how if they succeeded they could save the legitimacy of her child. So obvious a difficulty could not have been unforeseen. Under the old law of the Church the dissolution of marriage was so frequent and facile, that by a kind of tacit agreement children born from connexions assumed at the time to be lawful, were like Mary and Elizabeth of England, allowed to pass as legitimate, and to succeed to their fathers' estates. The Earl of Angus and Queen Margaret were divorced, yet the English Council had tried in vain to fix a stigma on the birth of Lady Lennox. Archbishop Parker more recently had divorced Hertford and Lady Catherine Grey, yet their son was still the favourite, for the succession of the English Protestants. Bothwell was ready with an instance from his own experience. The marriage between his own father and mother had been declared invalid, yet he had inherited the earldom without challenge.

The interests which depended on the young Prince of Scotland however were too vast to be lightly put in hazard; there was another and a shorter road out of the difficulty.

'Madam,' said Maitland, 'we are here the chief of your Grace's council and nobility; we shall find the means that your Majesty shall be quit of your husband without prejudice of your son, and albeit that my Lord of Murray here present be little less scrupulous for a Protestant than your Grace is for a Papist, I am assured he will look through his fingers thereto, and will behold our doings, saying nothing to the same.'

The words were scarcely ambiguous, yet Murray said nothing. Such subjects are not usually discussed in too loud a tone, and he may not have heard them distinctly. He himself swore afterwards 'that if any man said he was present when purposes were held in his audience tending to any unlawful or dishonourable end he spoke wickedly and untruly.'[1]

But Mary herself—how did she receive the dark suggestion? This part of the story rests on the evidence of her own friends, and was drawn up in her excuse and

---

[1] Reply of Murray to the declarations of the Earls of Huntly and Argyle.—KEITH.

defence. According to Argyle and Huntly she said she 'would do nothing to touch her honour and conscience;' 'they had better leave it alone;' 'meaning to do her good it might turn to her hurt and displeasure.'[1]

She may be credited with having refused her consent to the proposals then made to her; and yet that such a conversation should have passed in her presence (of the truth of the main features of it there is no room for doubt) was serious and significant. The secret was ill kept: it reached the ears of the Spanish ambassador who though he could not believe it true wrote an account of it to Philip.[2] The Queen was perhaps serious in her reluctance; perhaps she desired not to know what was intended till the deed was done.

> 'This they should have done,
> And not have spoken of it. In her 'twas villany;
> In them it had been good service.'

Those among the lords at all events who were most in Mary Stuart's confidence concluded that if they went their own way they had nothing to fear from her resentment. Four of the party present—Argyle, Huntly, Maitland, and Bothwell, with a cousin of Bothwell, Sir James Balfour—signed a bond immediately afterwards, while the court was still at Craigmillar, to the following purpose:—

'That for sae meikle as it was thought expedient and profitable for the commonweal, by the nobility and lords

---

[1] Declarations of Huntly and Argyle.—KEITH.

[2] 'Había entendido que viendo algunos el desgusto que había entre estos Reyes, habian ofrecido á la Reyna de hacer algo contra su marido, y que ella no había venido en ello. Aunque tuve este aviso de buena parte, parecióme cosa que no se debía creer que se hubiese tratado con la Reyna semejante plática.'— *De Silva to Philip, January* 18. *MS. Simancas.*

underwritten, that sic an young fool and proud tyran (as the King) should not bear rule of them—for divers causes therefore they all had concluded that he should be put forth by one way or other—and whosoever should take the deed in hand or do it, they should defend and fortify it, for it should be by every one of them reckoned and holden done by themselves.'[1]

The curtain which was thus for a moment drawn aside again closes. The Queen went in the first week of December to Stirling, where Darnley was allowed to join her; and the English Catholics, who had been alarmed at the rumours which had gone abroad, flattered themselves into a hope that all would again go well. The King would make amends for the past by affection and submission; Mary Stuart would in time obliterate the painful feelings which her neglect of him had aroused.[2]

A few days after, the Earl of Bedford arrived from England; the Parliament was then approaching its conclusion; the storm had subsided, and Elizabeth, free to act for herself, had commissioned Bedford to tell the Queen of Scots that her claims should be investigated as soon as possible, and 'should receive as much favour as she could desire to her contentation.'[3] The ambassador had brought with him a magnificent font of gold weighing 330 ozs. as a splendid present to the heir of the English throne. The Prince, who was to have been dipped in it at his baptism, had grown too large by the delay of the

---

[1] Ormston's confession. — PITCAIRN's *Criminal Trials of Scotland.*

[2] 'El Rey de Escocia ha ya viente dias que esta con la Reyna, y comen juntos; y aunque parece que no perderá tan presto del todo el desgusto del Rey por las cosas pasadas, todavia piensa que el tiempo, y estar juntos, y el Rey determinado de complacerle, hará mucho en la buena reconciliacion.'—*De Silva to Philip*, December 18. MS. Simancas.

[3] Instructions to the Earl of Bedford going to Scotland.—KEITH.

ceremony; but Elizabeth suggested that it might be used for 'the next child.'¹

The time had been when these things would have satisfied Mary Stuart's utmost hopes, and have filled her with exultation. Her thoughts, interests, and anxieties were now otherwise occupied. On the 15th, at five in the evening the Prince was baptized by torch-light in Stirling Chapel; the service was that of the Catholic Church; the Archbishop of St. Andrew's, the most abandoned of all Episcopal scoundrels, officiated, supported by three of his brethren. The French ambassador carried the child into the aisle; the Countess of Argyle, the same who had been present at Ritzio's murder, held him at the font as Elizabeth's representative; and three of the Scottish noblemen—Eglinton, Athol, and Ross—were present at the ceremony. The rest, with the English ambassador, stood outside the door. It boded ill for the supposed reconciliation that the Prince's father, though in the castle at the time, remained in his own room, either still brooding over his wrongs and afraid that some insult should be passed upon him, or else forbidden by the Queen to appear.

As soon as the baptism was over the suit for the restoration of Morton was continued: Bedford added his intercession to that of Murray; Bothwell, Athol, and all the other noblemen joined in the entreaty; and on the 24th the Queen with some affectation of reluctance gave way. George Douglas, who had been the first to strike Ritzio, and Faldonside, who had held a pistol to her breast, were alone excepted from a general and final pardon.²

Under any circumstances it could only have been with

---

¹ Instructions to the Earl of Bedford going to Scotland.—KEITH.
² Bedford to Cecil, December 30.—*Scotch MS. Rolls House.*

terror that Darnley could have encountered Morton and young Ruthven; but the conversation at Craigmillar which had stolen into England, had been carried equally to his own ear. He knew that the pardon of Ritzio's murderers had been connected with his own destruction; and a whisper had reached him also of the bond which, though unsigned by the Queen, had been 'drawn by her own device.'[1] So long as Morton remained in exile he could hope that the conspiracy against him was incomplete. The proclamation of the pardon was his deathknell, and the same night, swiftly, 'without word spoken or leave taken, he stole away from Stirling and fled to his father.'

Darnley flies from Stirling and is taken ill.

That at such a crisis he should have been attacked by a sudden and dangerous illness was to say the least of it a singular coincidence. A few miles from the castle blue spots broke out over his body, and he was carried into Glasgow languid and drooping, with a disease which the court and the friends of the court were pleased to call small-pox.

There for a time he lay, his father absent, himself hanging between life and death, attended only by a few faithful servants, while the Queen with recovered health and spirits spent her Christmas with Bothwell at Drummond Castle and Tullibardine, waiting the issue of the disease.

Unfortunately for all parties concerned, the King after a few days was reported to be slowly recovering. Either the natural disorder was too weak to kill him, or the poison had failed of its work. The Queen returned to Stirling: the favourite rode south to receive the exiles on their way back from England. 'In the yard of the

---

[1] Deposition of Thomas Crawford.—*Scotch MSS. Rolls House.*

hostelry of Whittingham,' Bothwell and Morton met; and Morton, long after—on the eve of his own execution, when to speak the truth might do him service where he was going, and could do him no hurt in this world—thus described what passed between them :—

'The Earl of Bothwell,' said Morton, 'proposed to me the purpose of the King's murder, seeing that it was the Queen's mind that he should be taken away, because she blamed the King of Davie's slaughter more than me.'

Morton 'but newly come from one trouble, said that he was in no haste to enter into a new,' and required to be assured that the Queen indeed desired it.

Bothwell said 'he knew what was in the Queen's mind, and she would have it done.'

'Bring me the Queen's hand for a warrant,' Morton said that he replied, 'and then I will answer you.'[1]

Rash and careless as Mary Stuart's passion made her, she was not so blind to prudence as to commit her signature as her husband had done. Bothwell promised that he would produce an order from her, but it never came, and Morton was saved from further share in the conspiracy.

On the 14th of January the Queen brought the Prince to Edinburgh; on the 20th she wrote a letter to the Archbishop of Glasgow at Paris complaining of her husband's behaviour to her, while the poor wretch was still lying on his sick bed;[2] and about the same time she was rejoined by Bothwell on his return from the Border. So far the story can be traced with confidence. At this point her conduct passes into the debateable land, where her friends meet those who condemn with charges of

---

[1] The Earl of Morton's confession.—*Illustrations of Scottish History*, p. 494.
[2] The Queen of Scots to the Archbishop of Glasgow, January 20.—KEITH.

falsehood and forgery. The evidence is neither conflicting nor insufficient: the dying depositions of the instruments of the crime taken on the steps of the scaffold, the 'undesigned coincidences' between the stories of many separate witnesses, with letters which after the keenest inquiry were declared to be in her own handwriting, shed a light upon her proceedings as full as it is startling; but the later sufferings of Mary Stuart have surrounded her name with an atmosphere of tenderness, and half the world has preferred to believe that she was the innocent victim of a hideous conspiracy.

The so-called certainties of history are but probabilities in varying degrees; and when witnesses no longer survive to be cross-questioned, those readers and writers who judge of truth by their emotions can believe what they please. To assert that documents were forged, or that witnesses were tampered with, costs them no effort; they are spared the trouble of reflection by the ready-made assurance of their feelings.

The historian who is without confidence in these easy criteria of certainty can but try his evidence by such means as remain. He examines what is doubtful by the light of what is established, and offers at last the conclusions at which his own mind has arrived, not as the demonstrated facts either of logic or passion, but as something which after a survey of the whole case appears to him to be nearest to the truth.[1]

---

[1] The story in the text is taken from the depositions in ANDERSON and PITCAIRN; from the deposition of Crawford, in the Rolls House; and from the celebrated casket letters of Mary Stuart to Bothwell. The authenticity of these letters will be discussed in a future volume in connexion with their discovery, and with the examination of them which then took place. Meantime I shall assume the genuineness of documents, which, without turning history into a mere creation of imaginative sympathies, I do not

The Queen then, after writing the letter of complaint against her husband to the Archbishop of Glasgow, suddenly determined to visit his sick bed. On Thursday the 23rd of January she set out for Glasgow attended by her lover. They spent the night at Callendar together.[1] In the morning they parted; the Earl returned to Edinburgh; Mary Stuart pursued her journey attended by Bothwell's French servant Paris, through whom they had arranged to communicate.

The news that she was on her way to Glasgow anticipated her appearance there. Darnley was confined to his bed; Lennox who suspected mischief, when he heard that she was coming, sent a gentleman, named Crawford, a noble, fearless kind of person, to apologize for his inability to meet her. It seems that after hearing of the bond at Craigmillar Darnley had written some letter to her, the inconvenient truths of which had been irritating; and she had used certain bitter expressions about him which had been carried to his ears. Both father and son believed that she intended to be revenged;

feel at liberty to doubt. They come to us after having passed the keenest scrutiny both in England and Scotland. The handwriting was found to resemble so exactly that of the Queen that the most accomplished expert could detect no difference. One of the letters could have been invented only by a genius equal to that of Shakspeare; and that one once accomplished, would have been so overpoweringly sufficient for its purpose that no forger would have multiplied the chances of detection by adding the rest. The inquiry at the time appears to me to supersede authoritatively all later conjectures. The English Council, among whom were many friends of Mary Stuart, had the French originals before them, while we have only translations, or translations of translations.

[1] 'When Bothwell was conducting the Queen to Glasgow, where she was going to the King, at Callendar after supper, late, Lady Reres came to Bothwell's room, and seeing me there, said, "What does M. Paris here?" "It is all the same," said he, "Paris will say nothing." And thereupon she took him to the Queen's room.' — *Examination of French Paris*, ANDERSON's *Collection*. Paris was Bothwell's servant.

and Crawford when he gave his message did not hide from her that his master was afraid of her.

'There is no remedy against fear,' the Queen said shortly.

'Madam,' Crawford answered, 'I know so far of my master that he desires nothing more than that the secrets of every creature's heart were writ in their faces.'[1]

Crawford's suspicions were too evident to be concealed. The Queen did not like them; she asked sharply if he had more to say; and when he said he had discharged his commission, she bade him 'hold his peace.'

Lord Darnley had made some use of his illness; as he lay between life and death he had come to understand that he had been a fool, and for the first time in his life had been thinking seriously. When the Queen entered his room she found him lying on his couch, weak and unable to move. Her first question was about his letter; it was not her cue to irritate him, and she seemed to expostulate on the credulity with which he had listened to calumnies against her. He excused himself faintly. She allowed her manner to relax, and she inquired about the cause of his illness.

A soft word unlocked at once the sluices of Darnley's heart; his passion gushed out uncontrolled, and with a wild appeal he threw himself on his wife's forgiveness.

'You are the cause of it,' he said; 'it comes only from you who will not pardon my faults when I am sorry for them. I have done wrong, I confess it; but others besides me have done wrong, and you have forgiven them, and I am but young. You have forgiven me often you may say; but may not a man of my age for want of counsel, of which I am very destitute, fall

---

[1] Crawford's deposition.—*MS. Rolls House.*

twice or thrice and yet repent and learn from experience? Whatever I have done wrong forgive me; I will do so no more. Take me back to you; let me be your husband again or may I never rise from this bed. Say that it shall be so,' he went on with wild eagerness; ' God knows I am punished for making my God of you—for having no thought but of you.'[1]

He was flinging himself into her arms as readily as she could hope or desire; but she was afraid of exciting his suspicions by being too complaisant. She answered kindly that she was sorry to see him so unwell; and she asked him again why he had thought of leaving the country.

He said that ' he had never really meant to leave it; yet had it been so there was reason enough; she knew how he had been used.'

She went back to the bond of Craigmillar. It was necessary for her to learn who had betrayed the secret and how much of it was known.

Weak and facile as usual Darnley gave up the name of his informant; it was the Laird of Minto; and then he said that ' he could not believe that she who was his own proper flesh would do him harm;' 'if any other would do it,' he added with something of his old bravado, ' they should buy him dear unless they took him sleeping.'

Her part was difficult to act. As she seemed so kind he begged that she would give him his food; he even wished to kiss her, and his breath after his illness was not pleasant. ' It almost killed me,' she wrote to Bothwell, ' though I sate as far from him as the bed would allow: he is more gay than ever you saw him; in fact

---

[1] Crawford's deposition. The conversation, as related by Darnley to Crawford, tallies exactly with that given by Mary herself to Bothwell in the casket letters.

A A 2

he makes love to me, of the which I take so great pleasure that I enter never where he is but incontinent I take the sickness of my sore side which I am so troubled with.'[1]

When she attempted to leave the room he implored her to stay with him. He had been told, he said, that she had brought a litter with her; did she mean to take him away?

She said she thought the air of Craigmillar would do him good; and as he could not sit on horseback she had contrived a means by which he could be carried.

The name of Craigmillar had an ominous sound. The words were kind, but there was perhaps some odd glitter of the eyes not wholly satisfactory.

He answered that if she would promise him on her honour to live with him as his wife and not to leave him any more he would go with her to the world's end, and care for nothing; if not he would stay where he was.

It was for that purpose, she said tenderly, that she had come to Glasgow; the separation had injured both of them, and it was time that it should end; 'and so she granted his desire and promised it should be as he had spoken, and thereupon gave him her hand and faith of her body that she would love him and use him as her husband;' she would wait only till his health was restored; he should use cold baths at Craigmillar, and then all should be well.

Again she returned to his letter; she was still uneasy about his knowledge of the bond, and she asked whether he had any particular fear of either of the noblemen. He had injured Maitland most, and he shivered when she named him. He felt but too surely with what indifference Maitland would set his heel on such a worm as he was.

---

[1] Mary Stuart to Bothwell.—ANDERSON's *Collection.*

She spoke of Lady Reres, Bothwell's evil friend. Darnley knew what that woman had been and suspected what she might be. He said he liked her not, and wished to God she might serve the Queen to her honour; but he would believe her promise, he would do all that she would have him do, and would love all that she loved.

She had gained her point; he would go with her, and that was all she wanted. A slight cloud rose between them before she left the room. He was impatient at her going, and complained that she would not stay with him: she on her part said that he must keep her promise secret; the lords would be suspicious of their agreement, and must not know of it.

He did not like the mention of the lords; the lords, he said, had no right to interfere; he would never excite the lords against her, and she he trusted would not again make a party against him.

She said that their past disagreements had been no fault of hers. He and he alone was to blame for all that had gone wrong.

With these words she left him. Mary Stuart was an admirable actress; rarely perhaps on the world's stage has there been a more skilful player. But the game was a difficult one; she had still some natural compunction, and the performance was not quite perfect.

Darnley, perplexed between hope and fear, affection and misgiving, sent for Crawford. He related the conversation which had passed, so far as he could recollect it, word for word, and asked him what he thought.

Crawford, unblinded by passion, answered at once 'that he liked it not;' if the Queen wished to have him living with her, why did she not take him to Holyrood? Craigmillar—a remote and lonely country house—was no proper place for him; if he went with her he would go rather as her prisoner than her husband.

Darnley answered that he thought little less himself; he had but her promise to trust to, and he feared what she might mean; he had resolved to go however; 'he would trust himself in her hands though she should cut his throat.'[1]

And Mary, what was her occupation after parting thus from her husband? Late into the night she sat writing an account of that day's business to her lover, 'with whom,' as she said, 'she had left her heart.' She told him of her meeting with Crawford, and of her coming to the King; she related with but slight verbal variations Darnley's passionate appeal to her, as Darnley himself had told it to his friend.

'I pretend,' she wrote, 'that I believe what he says; you never saw him better or heard him speak more humbly. If I did not know his heart was wax, and mine a diamond whereinto no shot can enter but that which comes from your hand, I could almost have had pity on him; but fear not, the plan shall hold to the death.'

If Mary Stuart was troubled with a husband, Bothwell was inconvenienced equally with a wife.

'Remember in return,' she continued, 'that you suffer not yourself to be won by that false mistress of yours, who will travel no less with you for the same; I believe they learnt their lesson together. He has ever a tear in his eye. He desires I should feed him with my own

---

[1] Crawford's deposition.—Scotch MSS. Rolls House.

hands. I am doing what I hate. Would you not laugh
to see me lie so well and dissemble so well, and tell
truth botwixt my hands? We are coupled with two bad
companions. The devil sunder us and God knit us
together to be the most faithful couple that ever he
united. This is my faith—I will die in it. I am writing
to you while the rest are sleeping, since I cannot sleep
as they do, and as I would desire—that is in your arms,
my dear love; whom I pray God preserve from all evil
and send you repose.'

Without much moral scrupulousness about her, Mary
Stuart had still feelings which answer to a loose man's
'senso of honour.'

'I must go forward,' she said, 'with my odious
purpose. You make me dissemble so far that I abhor it,
and you cause me to do the office of a traitress. If
it were not to obey you I had rather die than do it; my
heart bleeds at it. He will not come with me except I
promise him that I shall be with him as before, and
doing this he will do all I please and come with me.
To make him trust me I had to fence in some things
with him; so when he asked that when he was well we
should both have but one bed, I said that if he changed
not purpose between now and then it should be so; but
in the mean time I bade him take care that he let
nobody know of it, because the lords would fear if we
agreed together, he would make them feel the small account they made of him. In fine, he will go anywhere
that I ask him. Alas! I never deceived anybody; but
I remit me altogether to your pleasure. Send me word
what to do and I will do it. Consider whether you can
contrive anything more secret by medicine. He is to

take medicine and baths at Craigmillar. He suspects greatly, and yet he trusts me. I am sorry to hurt any one that depends on me; yet you may command me in all things. About Lady Reres he said, I pray God she may serve you to your honour. He suspects the thing you know, and of his life; but as to the last when I speak two or three kind words he is happy and out of doubt. Burn this letter, for it is dangerous and nothing well said in it.'

Then following the ebb and flow of her emotions to that strange point where the criminal passion of a woman becomes almost virtue in its utter self-abandonment, she appealed to Bothwell not to despise her for the treachery to which for his sake she was condescending.

'Have no evil opinion of me for this,' she concluded; 'you yourself are the cause of it; for my own private revenge I would not do it to him. Seeing then that to obey you, my dear love, I spare neither honour, conscience, hazard, nor greatness, take it I pray you in good part. Look not at that woman whose false tears should not be so much regarded as the true and faithful labour which I am bearing to deserve her place; to obtain which—against my nature—I betray those that may hinder me. God forgive me, and God give you, my only love, the happiness and prosperity which your humble and faithful friend desires for you. She hopes soon to be another thing to you. It is late. I could write to you for ever; yet now I will kiss your hand and end.'[1]

With these thoughts in her mind Mary Stuart Queen of Scotland lay down upon her bed—to sleep, doubtless

---

[1] Mary Stuart to Bothwell.—ANDERSON's *Collection*.

—sleep with the soft tranquillity of an innocent child. Remorse may disturb the slumbers of the man who is dabbling with his first experiences of wrong. When the pleasure has been tasted and is gone, and nothing is left of the crime but the ruin which it has wrought, then too the Furies take their seats upon the midnight pillow. But the meridian of evil is for the most part left unvexed; and when a man has chosen his road he is let alone to follow it to the end.

The next morning the Queen added a few closing words:

'If in the meantime I hear nothing to the contrary, according to my commission I will bring the man to Craigmillar on Monday—where he will be all Wednesday—and I will go to Edinburgh to draw blood of me. Provide for all things and discourse upon it first with yourself.'

This letter and another to Maitland she gave in charge to Paris to take to Edinburgh. In delivering them she bade him tell Bothwell that she had prevented the King from kissing her, as Lady Reres could witness; and she told him to ask Maitland whether Craigmillar was to be the place, or whether they had changed their plan. They would give him answers with which he would come back to her immediately. She would herself wait at Glasgow with the King till his return.

Paris after being a day upon the road, reached Edinburgh with his despatches on the night of Saturday the 25th. On going to Bothwell's room the next morning he found the Earl absent, and a servant directed him to a house belonging to Sir Robert Balfour, brother of James Balfour who signed the Craigmillar bond.

St. Mary's-in-the-Fields called commonly Kirk-a-Field was a roofless and ruined church, standing just inside the old town walls of Edinburgh, at the north-western corner of the present College. Adjoining it there stood a quadrangular building which had at one time belonged to the Dominican monks. The north front was built along the edge of the slope which descends to the Cowgate; the south side contained a low range of unoccupied rooms which had been 'priests' chambers;' the east consisted of offices and servants' rooms; the principal apartments in the dwelling into which the place had been converted were in the western wing, which completed the square. Under the windows there was a narrow strip of grass-plat dividing the house from the town wall; and outside the wall were gardens into which there was an opening through the cellars by an underground passage. The principal gateway faced north and led direct into the quadrangle.

Here it was that Paris found Bothwell with Sir James Balfour. He delivered his letter and gave his message. The Earl wrote a few words in reply. 'Commend me to the Queen,' he said as he gave the note, 'and tell her that all will go well. Say that Balfour and I have not slept all night, that everything is arranged, and that the King's lodgings are ready for him. I have sent her a diamond. You may say I would send my heart too were it in my power—but she has it already.'

A few more words passed, and from Bothwell Paris went to Maitland, who also wrote a brief answer. To the verbal question he answered, 'Tell her Majesty to take the King to Kirk-a-Field;' and with these replies the messenger rode back through the night to his mistress.

She was not up when he arrived; her impatience could not rest till she was dressed, and she received him in bed. He gave his letters and his message. She asked if there was anything further. He answered that

Bothwell bade him say 'he would have no rest till he
had accomplished their enterprise, and that for love of her
he would train a pike all his life.' The Queen laughed.
'Please God,' she said, 'it shall not come to that.'[1]

A few hours later she was on the road with her
victim. He could be moved but slowly. She was
obliged to rest with him two days at Linlithgow; and it
was not till the 30th that she was able to bring him to
Edinburgh. As yet he knew nothing of the change of
his destination, and supposed that he was going on to
Craigmillar. Bothwell however met the cavalcade outside the gates and took charge of it. No attention was
paid either to the exclamations of the attendants or the
remonstrances of Darnley himself; he was informed that
the Kirk-a-Field house was most convenient for him, and
to Kirk-a-Field he was conducted.

'The lodgings' prepared for him were in the west
wing, which was divided from the rest of the house by a
large door at the foot of the staircase. A passage ran
along the ground floor from which a room opened which
had been fitted up for the Queen. At the head of the
stairs a similar passage led first to the King's room—
which was immediately over that of the Queen—and
further on to closets and rooms for the servants.

Here it was that Darnley was established during the last
hours which he was to know on earth. The keys of the
doors were given ostentatiously to his groom of the
chamber, Thomas Nelson; the Earl of Bothwell being
already in possession of duplicates. The door from the
cellar into the garden had no lock, but the servants were
told that it could be secured with bolts from within.
The rooms themselves had been comfortably furnished,

---

[1] Examination of Paris.—PITCAIRN's *Criminal Trials*, vol. i.

and a handsome bed had been set up for the King with new hangings of black velvet. The Queen however seemed to think that they would be injured by the splashing from Darnley's bath, and desired that they might be taken down and changed. Being a person of ready expedients too she suggested that the door at the bottom of the staircase was not required for protection. She had it taken down and turned into a cover for the bath-vat; 'so that there was nothing left to stop the passage into the said chamber but only the portal door.'[1]

After this little attention she left her husband in possession; she intended herself to sleep from time to time there, but her own room was not yet ready.

The further plan was still unsettled. Bothwell's first notion was to tempt Darnley out into the country some sunny day for exercise and then to kill him. But 'this purpose was changed because it would be known;'[2] and was perhaps abandoned with the alteration of the place from Craigmillar.

The Queen meanwhile spent her days at her husband's side, watching over his convalescence with seemingly anxious affection, and returning only to sleep at Holyrood. In the starry evenings, though it was mid-winter, she would go out into the garden with Lady Reres, and 'there sing and use pastime.'[3] After a few days her apartment at Kirk-a-Field was made habitable; a bed was set up there in which she could sleep, and particular directions were given as to the part of the room where it was to stand. Paris through some mistake misplaced it. 'Fool that you are,' the Queen

---

[1] Examination of Thomas Nelson.—PITCAIRN.
[2] Hepburn's confession.—ANDERSON.
[3] Depositions of Thomas Nelson.—PITCAIRN.

said to him when he saw it, 'the bed is not to stand there; move it yonder to the other side.'[1] She perhaps meant nothing, but the words afterwards seemed ominously significant. A powder barrel was to be lighted in that room to blow the house and every one in it into the air. They had placed the bed on the spot where the powder was to stand, immediately below the bed of the King.

Whatever she meant, she contrived when it was moved to pass two nights there. The object was to make it appear as if in what was to follow her own life had been aimed at as well as her husband's. Wednesday the 5th she slept there, and Friday the 7th, and then her penance was almost over, for on Saturday the thing was to have been done.

Among the wild youths who followed Bothwell's fortunes three were found who consented to be the instruments—young Hay the Laird of Tallo, Hepburn of Bolton, and the Laird of Ormeston—gentlemen retainers of Bothwell's house, and ready for any desperate adventure.[2] Delay only created a risk of discovery, and the Earl on Friday arranged his plans for the night ensuing.[3]

It seems however that at the last moment there was an impression either that the powder might fail or that Darnley could be more conveniently killed in a scuffle

---

[1] 'Sot que tu es, je ne veulx pas que mon lit soyt en cest endroyt la, et du fait le feint oster.'—*Examination of Paris.* PITCAIRN.

[2] Hepburn on his trial said that when Bothwell first proposed the murder to him, 'he answered it was an evil purpose, but because he was servant to his Lordship he would do as the rest.' So also said Hay and Ormeston. Paris according to his own story was alike afraid to refuse and to consent. Bothwell told him the lords were all agreed. He asked what Murray said. 'Murray, Murray!' said the Earl, 'il ne se veult n'ayder ni nuyre, mais c'est tout ung.' 'Monsieur,' Paris replied, 'il est sage.'—*Examination of Paris.* PITCAIRN.

[3] Examination of Hay of Tallo.—ANDERSON.

with an appearance of accident. Lord Robert Stuart, Abbot of St. Cross, one of James the Fifth's wild brood of children whom the church had provided with land and title, had shared in past times in the King's riots, and retaining some regard for him had warned the poor creature to be on his guard. Darnley making love to destruction, told the Queen; and Stuart, knowing that his own life might pay the forfeit of his interference, either received a hint that he might buy his pardon by doing the work himself, or else denied his words and offered to make the King maintain them at the sword's point. A duel, could it be managed, would remove all difficulty; and Bothwell would take care how it should end.

Something of this kind was in contemplation on the Saturday night, and the explosion was deferred in consequence. The Queen that evening at Holyrood bade Paris tell Bothwell 'that the Abbot of St. Cross should go to the King's room and do what the Earl knew of.' Paris carried the message, and Bothwell answered, 'Tell the Queen that I will speak to St. Cross and then I will see her.'[1]

But this too came to nothing. Lord Robert went, and angry words according to some accounts were exchanged between him and Darnley; but a sick man unable to leave his couch was in no condition to cross swords; and for one more night he was permitted to survive.

So at last came Sunday, eleven months exactly from the day of Ritzio's murder; and Mary Stuart's words that she would never rest till that dark business was revenged were about to be fulfilled. The Earl of Murray knowing perhaps what was coming, yet unable to inter-

---

[1] Examination of Paris.—ANDERSON.

fore, had been long waiting for an opportunity to leave Edinburgh. Early that morning he wrote to his sister to say that Lady Murray was ill at St. Andrew's, and that she wished him to join her; the Queen with some reluctance gave him leave to go.

It was a high day at the Court: Sebastian one of the musicians was married in the afternoon to Margaret Cawood, Mary Stuart's favourite waiting-woman. When the service was over the Queen took an early supper with the Bishop of Argyle, and afterwards accompanied by Cassilis, Huntly, and the Earl of Argyle, she went as usual to spend the evening with her husband, and professed to intend to stay the night with him. The hours passed on. She was more than commonly tender; and Darnley absorbed in her caresses paid no attention to sounds in the room below him, which had he heard them might have disturbed his enjoyment.

At ten o'clock that night two servants of Bothwell, Powrie and Patrick Wilson, came by order to the Earl's apartments in Holyrood. Hepburn, who was waiting there, pointed to a heap of leather bags and trunks upon the floor, which he bade them carry to the gate of the gardens at the back of Kirk-a-Field. They threw the load on a pair of pack-horses and led the way in the dark as they were told; Hepburn himself went with them, and at the gate they found Bothwell, with Hay, Ormeston, and another person, muffled in their cloaks. The horses were left standing in the lane. The six men silently took the bags on their shoulders and carried them to the postern door which led through the town wall. Bothwell then went in to join the Queen, and told the rest to make haste with their work and finish it before the Queen should go. Powrie and Wilson were dismissed; Hepburn and the three others dragged the bags through the cellar into Mary Stuart's room. They had intended to put the powder into a cask, but the door was too narrow, so they carried it as it was and poured it out in a heap upon the floor.

They blundered in the darkness. Bothwell who was listening in the room above heard them stumbling at their work, and stole down to warn them to be silent; but by that time all was in its place. The dark mass in which the fire-spirit lay imprisoned rose dimly from the ground; the match was in its place, and the Earl glided back to the Queen's side.

It was now past midnight. Hay and Hepburn were to remain with the powder alone. 'You know what you have to do,' Ormeston whispered; 'when all is quiet above, you fire the end of the lint and come away.'

With these words Ormeston passed stealthily into the garden. Paris who had been assisting in the arrangement went upstairs to the King's room, and his appearance was the signal concerted beforehand for the party to break up. Bothwell whispered a few words in Argyle's ear; Argyle touched Paris on the back significantly: there was a pause—the length of a Paternoster[1]—when the Queen suddenly recollected that there was a masque and a dance at the Palace on the occasion of the marriage, and that she had promised to be present. She rose, and with many regrets that she could not stay as she intended, kissed her husband, put a ring on his finger, wished him good night, and went. The lords followed her. As she left the room, she said as if by accident, 'It was just this time last year that Ritzio was slain.'[2]

In a few moments the gay train was gone. The Queen walked back to the glittering halls in Holyrood;

---

[1] Examination of Paris.—PITCAIRN.
[2] (BUCHANAN.—History of Scotland.)

Darnley was left alone with his page, Taylor, who slept in his room, and his two servants, Nelson and Edward Seymour. Below in the darkness, Bothwell's two followers shivered beside the powder heap, and listened with hushed breath till all was still.

The King, though it was late, was in no mood for sleep, and Mary's last words sounded awfully in his ears. As soon as she was gone he went over 'her many speeches,' he spoke of her soft words and her caresses which had seemed sincere, 'but the mention of Davie's slaughter marred all his pleasure.'[1]

'What will she do?' said he, 'it is very lonely.' The shadow of death was creeping over him; he was no longer the random boy who two years before had come to Scotland filled with idle dreams of vain ambition. Sorrow, suffering, disease, and fear had done their work. That night before or after the Queen's visit he was said to have opened the Prayer-book, and to have read over the 55th Psalm,[2] which by a strange coincidence was in the English service for the day that was dawning.

True or false such was the tale at the time; and the words have a terrible appropriateness.

'Hear my prayer, O Lord, and hide not thyself from my petition.

'My heart is disquieted within me, and the fear of death is fallen upon me.

'Fearfulness and trembling are come upon me, and an horrible dread hath overwhelmed me.

'It is not an open enemy that hath done me this dishonour, for then I could have borne it.

---

[1] [CALDERWOOD, vol. ii. p. 344.]
[2] [Sir William Drury, the authority for this statement, says that he went over the 55th Psalm a few hours before his death.'—*Drury to Cecil, March,* 1567. *Border MSS. Rolls House.*]

'It was even thou my companion, my guide, and my own familiar friend.'

Forlorn victim of a cruel age! Twenty-one years old —no more. At the end of an hour he went to bed, with his page at his side. An hour later they two were lying dead in the garden under the stars.

The exact facts of the murder were never known— only at two o'clock that Monday morning, a 'crack' was heard which made the drowsy citizens of Edinburgh turn in their sleep, and brought down all that side of Balfour's house of Kirk-a-Field in a confused heap of dust and ruin. Nelson, the sole survivor, went to bed and slept when he left his master, and 'knew nothing till he found the house falling about him;' Edward Seymour was blown in pieces; but Darnley and his page were found forty yards away, beyond the town wall, under a tree, with 'no sign of fire on them,' and with their clothes scattered at their side.

Some said that they were smothered in their sleep; some that they were taken down into a stable and 'wirried;' some that 'hearing the keys grate in the doors below them, they started from their beds and were flying down the stairs, when they were caught and strangled.' Hay and Hepburn told one consistent story to the foot of the scaffold:—When the voices were silent overhead they lit the match and fled, locking the doors behind them. In the garden they found Bothwell watching with his friends, and they waited there till the house blew up, when they made off and saw no more. It was thought however that in dread of torture they left the whole dark truth untold; and over the events of that night a horrible mist still hangs unpenetrated and unpenetrable for ever.

This only was certain, that with her husband Mary

Stuart's chances of the English throne perished also, and with them all serious prospect of a Catholic revolution. With a deadly instinct the world divined the author of the murder; and more than one nobleman on the night on which the news reached London, hastened to transfer his allegiance to Lady Catherine Grey.[1] The faithful Melville hurried up to defend his mistress —but to the anxious questions of de Silva, though he called her innocent, he gave confused answers.[2] 'Lady Lennox demands vengeance upon the Queen of Scots,' de Silva said; 'nor is Lady Lennox alone in the belief of her guilt; they say it is revenge for the Italian secretary. The heretics denounce her with one voice; the Catholics are divided; her own friends acquit her; the connexions of the King cry out upon her without exception.'[3]

On the 1st of March, Moret, the Duke of Savoy's ambassador at the Scotch court, passed through London on his way to the Continent. He had been in Edinburgh at the time of the murder; and de Silva turned to him for comfort. But Moret had no comfort to give. 'I pressed him,' said de Silva, 'to tell me whether he thought the Queen was innocent; he did not condemn her in words, but he said nothing in her favour;'[4] 'the spirits of the Catholics are broken;' should it turn out that she is guilty, her party in England is gone, and by her means there is no more chance of a restoration of religion.'[5]

---

[1] De Silva to Philip, February 17. —*MS. Simancas.*

[2] 'Aunque este salvó á la Reyna, veo lo algo confuso.'— *De Silva to Philip, February 22. MS. Ibid.*

[3] Ibid.

[4] 'Apretandole que me dixese lo que le parecia conforme á lo que el habia visto y colegido al la Reyna tenia culpa dello, annque no la le condeño de palabra, no le salbó nada.'— *De Silva to Philip, March 1. MS. Ibid.*

[5] 'Mucho ha este caso enflaquecido los animos de los Catolicos.'—*Ibid.*

[6] Ibid.

CHAPTER XI.

THE Earl of Sussex having failed alike to beat Shan O'Neil in the field or to get him satisfactorily murdered, had at last been recalled, leaving the government of Ireland in the hands of Sir Nicholas Arnold. An unsuccessful public servant never failed to find a friend in Elizabeth, whose disposition to quarrel with her ministers was usually in proportion to their ability. She had shared the confidence of the late Deputy in what to modern eyes appears unpardonable treachery; she received him on his return to England with undiminished confidence, and she allowed him to confirm her in her resolution to spend no more money in the hopeless enterprise of bringing the Irish into order; while she left Arnold to set the bears and bandogs to tear each other, and watched contentedly the struggle in Ulster between O'Neil and the Scots of the Isles.

The breathing-time would have been used to better advantage had the reform been carried to completeness which had been commenced with the mutinous miscreants miscalled the English army. But the bands could not be discharged with decency till they had received their wages; without money they could only continue to maintain themselves on the plunder of the farmers of the Pale; and the Queen, provoked with the past expenses to which she had so reluctantly assented, knotted her purse-strings, and seemed determined that Ireland should in future bear the cost of its own government. The worst peculations of the principal officers were inquired into and punished: Sir Henry Ratcliff, Sussex's brother, was deprived of his command and sent to the castle; but Arnold's vigour was limited by his powers. The paymasters continued to cheat the Government in the returns of the number of their troops; the Government defended themselves by letting the pay run into arrear; the soldiers revenged their ill-usage on the people; and so it came to pass that in O'Neil's country alone in Ireland—defended as it was from attacks from without, and enriched with the plunder of the Pale—were the peasantry prosperous, or life or property secure.

Munster was distracted by the feuds between Ormond and Desmond; while the deep bays and creeks of Cork and Kerry were the nests and hiding-places of English pirates, whose numbers had just received a distinguished addition in the person of Sir Thomas Stukely, with a barque of four hundred tons and 'a hundred tall soldiers, besides mariners.'

Stukely had been on his way to Florida with a license from the Crown to make discoveries and to settle there; but he had found a convenient halting-place in an Irish harbour, from which he could issue out and plunder the Spanish galleons.[1] He had taken up his quarters at Kinsale, 'to make the sea his Florida;'[2] and in antici-

---

[1] 'Stukely's piracies are much ralled at here in all parts. I hang down my head with shame. Alas! though it cost the Queen roundly, let him for honour's sake be fetched in. These pardons to such as be *hostes humani generis* I like not.'—*Chaloner to Cecil, Madrid, December* 14, 1564. *Spanish MSS. Rolls House.*

[2] Sir Thomas Wroth to Cecil, November 17.—*Irish MSS. Ibid.*

pation of the terms on which he was likely to find himself with Elizabeth, he contrived to renew an acquaintance which he had commenced in England with Shan O'Neil. The friendship of a buccaneer who was growing rich on Spanish plunder might have seemed inconvenient to a chief who had offered Ireland as a fief to Philip; but Shan was not particular: Philip had as yet shown but a cold interest in Irish rebellion, and Stukely filled his cellars with sherry from Cadiz, amused him with his magniloquence, and was useful to him by his real dexterity and courage. So fond Shan became of him that he had the impertinence to write to Elizabeth in favour 'of that his so dearly loved friend and her Majesty's worthy subject,' with whom he was grieved to hear that her Majesty was displeased. He could not but believe that she had been misinformed; but if indeed so good and gallant a gentleman had given her cause of offence, Shan entreated that her Majesty, for his sake and in the name of the services which he had himself rendered to England, would graciously pardon him; and he, with Stukely for a friend and confidant, would make Ireland such as Ireland never was since the world began.[1]

The Irish bishops.

Among so many mischiefs 'religion' was naturally in a bad way. 'The lords and gentlemen of the Pale went habitually to mass.'[2] The Protestant bishops were chiefly agitated by the vestment controversy. Adam Loftus, the titular Primate, to whom sacked villages, ravished women, and famine-stricken skeletons crawling about the fields were matters of every-day indifference, shook with terror at the mention of a surplice.[3] Robert Daly

---

[1] Shan O'Neil to Elizabeth, June 18, 1565.—*Irish MSS. Rolls House.*
[2] Adam Loftus to Elizabeth, May 17.—*MS. Ibid.*
[3] Adam Loftus to Cecil, July 16.—*MS. Ibid.*

wrote in anguish to Cecil, in dismay at the countenance to 'Papistry' and at his own inability to prolong a persecution which he had happily commenced.[1]

Some kind of shame was felt by statesmen in England at the condition in which Ireland continued. Unable to do anything real towards amending it, they sketched out among them about this time a scheme for a more effective government. The idea of the division of the country into separate presidencies lay at the bottom of whatever hopes they felt for an improved order of things. So long as the authority of the sovereign was represented only by a Deputy residing at Dublin, with a few hundred ragged marauders called by courtesy 'the army,' the Irish chiefs would continue, like O'Neil, to be virtually independent; while by recognizing the reality of a power which could not be taken from them, the English Government could deprive them of their principal motive for repudiating their allegiance.

The aim of the Tudor sovereigns had been from the first to introduce into Ireland the feudal administration

---

[1] 'The bruit of the alteration in religion is so talked of here among the Papists, and they so triumph upon the same, it would grieve any good Christian heart to hear of their rejoicing; yea, is so much that my Lord Primate, my Lord of Meath, and I, being the Queen's commissioners in ecclesiastical causes, dare not be so bold now in executing our commissions in ecclesiastical causes as we have been to this time. To what end this talk will grow I am not able to say. I fear it will grow to the great contempt of the Gospel and of the ministers of the same, except that spark be extinguished before it grow to flame. The occasion is that certain learned men of our religion are put from their livings in England; upon what occasion is not known here as yet. The poor Protestants amazed at the talk do often resort to me to learn what the matter means; whom I comfort with the most faithful texts of Scripture that I can find. . . . But I beseech you send me some comfortable words concerning the stablishing of our religion, wherewith I may both confirm the wavering hearts of the doubtful, and suppress the stout brags of the sturdy and proud Papists.'— Robert Daly to Cecil, July 2. Irish MSS. Rolls House.

of the English counties; they had laboured to persuade the chiefs to hold their lands under the Crown, with the obligations which landed tenures in England were supposed always to carry with them. The large owner of the soil, to the extent that his lordship extended, was in the English theory the ruler of its inhabitants, magistrate from the nature of his position, and representative of the majesty of the Crown. Again and again they had endeavoured to convince the Irish that order was better than anarchy; that their faction fights, their murders, their petty wars and robberies, were a scandal to them; that till they could amend their ways they were no better than savages. Fair measures and foul had alike failed so far. Once more a project was imagined of some possible reformation, which might succeed at least on paper.

In the system which was at last to bring a golden age to Ireland, the four provinces were to be governed each by a separate president and council. Every county was to have its sheriff; and the Irish noblemen and gentlemen were to become the guardians of the law which they had so long defied. The poor should no longer be oppressed by the great; and the wrongs which they had groaned under so long should be put an end to for ever by their own Parliament. 'No poor persons should be compelled any more to work or labour by the day or otherwise without meat, drink, wages, or some other allowance during the time of their labour;' no 'earth-tillers, nor any others inhabiting a dwelling under any lord should be distrained or punished in body or goods for the faults of their landlord;' nor any honest man lose life or lands without fair trial, by Parliamentary attainder, 'according to the antient laws of England and Ireland.' Noble provisions were pictured out for the rebuilding of the ruined churches at the Queen's expense, with 'twelve free grammar schools,' where the Irish youth should grow into civility, and 'twelve hospitals for aged and impotent folk.' A University should be founded in Elizabeth's name, and endowed with lands at Elizabeth's cost; and the devisers of all these things, warming with their project, conceived the Irish nation accepting willingly a reformed religion, in which there should be no more pluralities, no more abuse of patronage, no more neglect, or idleness, or profligacy. The bishops of the Church of Ireland were to be chosen among those who had risen from the Irish schools through the Irish University. The masters of the grammar schools should teach the boys 'the New Testament, Paul's Epistles, and David's Psalms, in Latin, that they being infants might savour of the same in age, as an old cask doth of its first liquor.' In every parish from Cape Clear to the Giant's Causeway, there should be a true servant of God for a pastor, who would bring up the children born in the same in the knowledge of the Creeds, the Lord's Prayer, the Ten Commandments, and the Catechism; 'the children to be brought to the Bishop for confirmation at seven years of age, if they could repeat them, or else to be rejected by the Bishop for the time with reproach to their parents.'[1]

Here was an ideal Ireland, painted on the retina of some worthy English minister; but the real Ireland was still the old place: as it was in the days of Brian Boroihme and the Danes, so it was in the days of Shan O'Neil and Sir Nicholas Arnold; and the Queen who was to found all these fine institutions cared chiefly to burden her exchequer no further in the vain effort to

---

[1] Device for the better government of Ireland.—*Irish MSS. Rolls House.*

drain the black Irish morass—fed as it was from the perennial fountains of Irish nature.

The Pope might have been better contented with the condition of his children: yet he too had his grounds of disquiet, and was not wholly satisfied with Shan, or with Shan's rough-riding Primate. A nuncio had resided secretly for four years at Limerick, who from time to time sent information of the state of the people to Rome; and at last an aged priest named Creagh, who in past days had known Charles the Fifth, and had been employed by him in relieving English Catholic exiles, went over with letters from the nuncio recommending the Pope to refuse to recognize the appointment of Terence Daniel to the Primacy, and to substitute Creagh in his place. The old man, according to his own story, was unambitious of dignity, and would have preferred 'to enter religion' and end his days in a monastery. The Pope however decided otherwise. Creagh was consecrated Archbishop of Armagh in the Sistine Chapel, and was sent back 'to serve among those barbarous wild uncivil folk,' taking with him a letter from Pius to Shan O'Neil, 'whom he did not know whether to repute for his foe or his friend.'

Thus Ireland had three competing Primates: Adam Loftus, the nominee of Elizabeth; Shan's Archbishop, Terence Daniel; and Creagh, sent by the Pope. The latter however had the misfortune to pass through London on his way home, where Cecil heard of him. He was seized and sent to the Tower, where 'he lay in great misery, cold, and hunger,' 'without a penny,' 'without the means of getting his single shirt washed, and without gown or hose.'

The poor old man petitioned 'to be let go to teach youth.' 'He would do it for nothing,' he said, 'as he had done all the days of his life, never asking a penny of the Church or any benefice of any man;[1] and so modest a wish might have been granted with no great difficulty, considering that half the preferments in England were held by men who scarcely affected to conceal that they were still Catholics. Either Creagh however was less simple than he pretended, or Cecil had reason to believe that his presence in Ireland would lead to mischief; he was kept fast in his cage, and would have remained there till he died, had he not contrived one night to glide over the walls into the Thames.

His imprisonment was perhaps intended as a gratification to Shan O'Neil. No sooner had he escaped than Elizabeth considered that of the two Catholic Archbishops Terence Daniel might be the least dangerous, and that to set Shan against the Pope might be worth a sacrifice of dignity. It was intimated that if Shan would be a good subject he should have his own Primate, and Adam Loftus should be removed to Dublin.[2] Shan on his part gave the Queen to understand that when Terence was installed at Armagh, and he himself was created Earl of Tyrone, she should have no more trouble; and the events of the spring of 1565 made the English Government more than ever anxious to come to terms with a chieftain whom they were powerless to crush.

Since the defeat of the Earl of Sussex, Shan's influence and strength had been steadily growing. His return unscathed from London, and the fierce attitude which he assumed on the instant of his reappearance in Ulster,

---

[1] Questions for Creagh, with Creagh's answers, February 22, 1565. Further answers of Creagh, March 17.—*Irish MSS. Rolls House.*
[2] Private Instructions to Sir Henry Sidney. Cecil's hand, 1565.—*MS. Ibid.*

CHAP XI
1565

Shan O'Neil defeats the Scots.

convinced the petty leaders that to resist him longer would only ensure their ruin. O'Donnell was an exile in England, and there remained unsubdued in the north only the Scottish colonies of Antrim, which were soon to follow with the rest. O'Neil lay quiet through the winter. With the spring and the fine weather, when the rivers fell and the ground dried, he roused himself out of his lair, and with his galloglasse and kern, and a few hundred 'harquebussmen,' he dashed suddenly down upon the 'Redshanks,' and broke them utterly to pieces. Six or seven hundred were killed in the field; James M'Connell and his brother Sorleboy[1] were taken prisoners; and for the moment the whole colony was swept away. James M'Connell himself, badly wounded in the action, died a few months later, and Shan was left undisputed sovereign of Ulster.

The facile pen of Terence Daniel was employed to communicate to the Queen this 'glorious victory,' for which 'Shan thanked God first, and next the Queen's Majesty; affirming the same to come of her good fortune.'[2] The English Government, weary of the ill success which had attended their own dealings with the Scots, were disposed to regard them as a 'malicious and dangerous people, who were gradually fastening on the country;'[3] and with some misgivings, they were inclined to accept Shan's account of himself; while Shan finding Elizabeth disinclined to quarrel with him, sent Terence over to her to explain more fully the excellence of his intentions. Sir Thomas Cusack added his own commendations both of Terence and his master, and urged that now was the time to make O'Neil a friend for ever. Sir

---

[1] Spelt variously Sorleboy, Sarleboa, Surlebois, and Surlyboy.
[2] Terence Daniel to Cecil, June 24.—*Irish MSS. Rolls House.*
[3] Opinion of Sir H. Sidney, May 20.—*MS. Ibid.*

Nicholas Arnold, with more discrimination, insisted that it was necessary to do one thing or the other, but he too seemed to recommend the Queen, as the least of two evils, to be contented with Shan's nominal allegiance, and to leave him undisturbed.

'If,' he said, 'you use the opportunity to make O'Neil a good subject, he will hardly swerve hereafter. The Pale is poor and unable to defend itself. If he do fall out before the beginning of next summer there is neither outlaw, rebel, murderer, thief, nor any lewd or evil-disposed person—of whom God knoweth there is plenty swarming in every corner amongst the wild Irish, yea, and in our own border too—which would not join to do what mischief they might.'[1]

Alas! while Arnold wrote there came news that Shan's ambition was still unsatisfied. He had followed up his successes against the Scotch by seizing the Queen's castles of Newry and Dundrum. Turning west he had marched into Connaught 'to require the tribute due of owld time to them that were kings in that realm.' He had exacted pledges of obedience from the western chiefs, frightened Clanrickard into submission, 'spoiled O'Rourke's country,' and returned to Tyrone driving before him four thousand head of cattle. Instead of the intended four presidencies in Ireland, there would soon be only one; and Shan O'Neil did not mean to rest till he had revived the throne of his ancestors, and reigned once more in 'Tara's halls.'

'Excuse me for writing plainly what I think,' said Lord Clanrickard to Sir William Fitzwilliam. 'I assure you it is an ill likelihood toward—that the realm if it be

---

[1] Sir T. Cusack to Cecil, August 23. O'Neil to Elizabeth, August 25. Sir N. Arnold to the English Council, August 31.—*Irish MSS. Rolls House.*

not speedily looked unto will be at a hazard to come as far out of her Majesty's hands as ever it was out of the hands of any of her predecessors. Look betimes to these things, or they will grow to a worse end.'[1]

The evil news reached England at the crisis of the convulsion which had followed the Darnley marriage. The Protestants in Scotland had risen in rebellion, relying on Elizabeth's promises; and Argyle, exasperated at her desertion of Murray, was swearing that he would leave his kinsmen unrevenged, and would become Shan's ally and friend. Mary Stuart was shaking her sword upon the Border at the head of 20,000 men; and Elizabeth, distracted between the shame of leaving her engagements unredeemed or bringing the Irish and Spaniards upon her head, was in no humour to encounter fresh troubles. Shan's words were as smooth as ever; his expedition to Connaught was represented as having been undertaken in the English interest. On his return he sent 'a petition' to have 'his title and rule' determined without further delay; while 'in consideration of his good services' he begged 'to have some augmentation of living granted him in the Pale,' and 'her Majesty to be pleased not to credit any stories which his evil-willers might spread abroad against him.'[2]

Elizabeth allowed herself to believe what it was most pleasant to her to hope. 'We must allow something,' she wrote to Sir Henry Sidney, 'for his wild bringing up, and not expect from him what we should expect from a perfect subject; if he mean well he shall have all his reasonable requests granted.'[3]

But it was impossible to leave Ireland any longer

---

[1] Clanrickard to Fitzwilliam, Oct. 11.—*Irish MSS. Rolls House.*
[2] Shan O'Neil to Elizabeth, October 27.—*MS. Ibid.*
[3] Elizabeth to Sir H. Sidney, November 11.—*MS. Ibid.*

without the presence of a deputy. Sir Nicholas Arnold had gone over with singular and temporary powers; the administration was out of joint, and the person most fitted for the government by administrative and military capacity was Leicester's brother-in-law Sir Henry Sidney, President of Wales.

Sidney knew Ireland well from past experience. He had held command there under Sussex himself; he had seen deputy after deputy depart for Dublin with the belief that he at last was the favoured knight who would break the spell of the enchantment; and one after another he had seen them return with draggled plumes and broken armour. Gladly would he have declined the offered honour. 'If the Queen would but grant him leave to serve her in England, or in any place in the world else saving Ireland, or to live private, it should be more joyous to him than to enjoy all the rest and to go thither.' It was idle to think that O'Neil could be really 'reformed' except by force; and 'the Irishry had taken courage through the feeble dealing with him.' If he was to go, Sidney said, he would not go without money. Ten or twelve thousand pounds must be sent immediately to pay the outstanding debts. He must have more and better troops; two hundred horse and five hundred foot at least, in addition to those which were already at Dublin. He would keep his patent as President of Wales; he would have leave to return to England at his discretion if he saw occasion; and for his personal expenses, as he could expect nothing from the Queen, he demanded—strange resource to modern eyes—permission to export six thousand kerseys and clothes free of duty.[1]

---

[1] Petition of Sir H. Sidney going to Ireland.—*Irish MSS. Rolls House.*

CHAP XI
1565
October

His requests were made excessive perhaps to ensure their refusal; but the condition of Ireland could not be trifled with any longer, and if he hoped to escape he was disappointed.

Expenses of the Irish government.

'In the matter of Ireland was found such an example as was not to be found again in any place; that a sovereign prince should be owner of such a kingdom, having no cause to fear the invasion of any foreign prince, neither having ever found the same invaded by any foreign power, neither having any power born or resident within that realm that denied or ever had directly or indirectly denied the sovereignty of the Crown to belong to her Majesty; and yet, contrary to all other realms, the realm of Ireland had been and yet continued so chargeable to the Crown of England, and the revenues thereof so mean, and those which were, so decayed and so diminished, that great yearly treasures were carried out of the realm of England to satisfy the stipends of the officers and soldiers required for the governance of the same.'[1]

Sir H. Sidney is chosen Deputy.

Sir Henry Sidney paid the penalty of his ability in being selected to terminate in some form or other a state of things which could no longer be endured. Again before he would consent he repeated and even exaggerated his conditions. He would not go as others had gone, 'fed on the chameleon's dish,' to twine ropes of sand and sea-slime to bind the Irish rebels with. He would go with a force to back him, or he would not go at all. He must have power, he said, to raise as many men as the Queen's service required; and she must trust

---

[1] Instructions to Sir H. Sidney, October 5.—*Irish MSS. Rolls House.*

his honour to keep them no longer than they were absolutely wanted. No remedial measures could be attempted till anarchy had been trampled down; and then the country would prosper of itself.

'To go work by force,' he said, 'will be chargeable it is true; but if you will give the people justice and minister law among them, and exercise the sword of the sovereign, and put away the sword of the subject—omnia hæc adjicientur vobis—you shall drive the now man of war to be an husbandman, and he that now liveth like a lord to live like a servant; and the money now spent in buying armour and horses and waging of war should be bestowed in building of towns and houses. By ending these incessant wars ere they be aware, you shall bereave them both of force and beggary, and make them weak and wealthy. Then you can convert the military service due from the lords into money; then you can take up the fisheries now left to the French and the Spaniards; then you can open and work your mines, and the people will be able to grant you subsidies.'[1]

The first step towards the change was to introduce a better order of government: and relapsing upon the scheme for the division into presidencies, Sidney urged Elizabeth to commence with appointing a President of Munster, where Ormond and Desmond were tearing at each other's throats. The expense—the first consideration with her—would be moderate. The President would be satisfied with a mark (13s. 4d.) a day; fifty men—horse and foot—would suffice for his retinue, with 9d. and 8d. a day respectively; and he would require two

[1] Opinions of Sir H. Sidney.—*Irish MSS. Rolls House.*

clerks of the signet, with salaries of a hundred pounds a year. The great Munster noblemen—Ormond, Desmond, Thomond, Clancarty, with the Archbishop of Cashel and the Bishops of Cork, Waterford, and Limerick, would form a standing council; and a tribunal would be established where disputes could be heard and justice administered without the perpetual appeal to the sword.[1]

A clause was added to the first sketch in Cecil's hand: 'The Lord President to be careful to observe Divine service and to exhort others to observe it; and also to keep a preacher who shall be allowed his diet in the household, to whom the said President shall cause due reverence to be given in respect of his office which he shall have for the service of God.'

---

[1] It is noticeable that we find in an arrangement which was introduced as a reform and as a means of justice the following clause:—

'Also it shall be lawful for the President and Council or any three of them, the President being one, in cases necessary, upon vehement suspicion and presumption of any great offence in any party committed against the Queen's Majesty, to put the same party to torture as they shall think convenient.'—*Presidency of Munster*, February 1, 1566. *Irish MSS. Rolls House.*

Even in England torture continued to be freely used. On December 28, 1566, a letter was addressed by the Privy Council to the Attorney-General and others, that:—

'Where they were heretofore appointed to put Clement Fisher, now prisoner in the Tower, in some fear of torture whereby his lewdness and such as he might detect might the better come to light, they are requested, for that the said Fisher is not minded to be plain, as thereby the faults of others might be known, to cause the said Fisher according to their discretion to feel some touch of the rack, for the better hoalting out and opening of that which is requisite to be known.'—*Council Register.* ELIZ. *MSS.*

And again, Jan. 18, 1567. A letter to the Lieutenant of the Tower:—

'One Rice, a buckler-maker, committed there, is discovered to have been concerned in a robbery of plate four years before; the lieutenant to examine the said Rice about this robbery, and if they shall perceive him not willing to confess the same then to put him in fear of the torture, and to let him feel some smart of the same whereby he may be the better brought to confess the truth.'—*Irish MSS. Rolls House.*

With an understanding that this arrangement for Munster should be immediately carried out, that the precedent, if successful in the south, should be followed out in the other provinces, and that his other requests should be complied with, Sidney left London for Ireland in the beginning of December. Every hour's delay had increased the necessity for his presence. Alarmed at the approach of another deputy, and excited on the other hand by the Queen of Scots' successes, Shan O'Neil had attached himself eagerly to her fortunes. In October he offered to assist her against Argyle, who was then holding out against her in the Western Highlands.[1] His pleasure was as great as his surprise when he found Argyle ready to allow the Western Islanders to join with him to drive the English out of Ireland, and punish Elizabeth for her treachery to Murray. So far Argyle carried his resentment, that he met Shan somewhere in the middle of the winter, and to atone for the disgrace of his half sister, he arranged marriages between a son and daughter which she had borne to Shan, and two children of James M'Connell, whom Shan had killed; O'Neil undertook to settle on them the disputed lands of Antrim, and Argyle consented at last to the close friendship in the interest of the Queen of Scots for which the Irish chief had so long been vainly suing.

No combination could be more ominous to England. Foul weather detained Sidney for six weeks at Holyhead. In the middle of January, but not without 'the loss of all his stuff and horses,' which were wrecked on the coast of Down, he contrived to reach Dublin. The state of things which he discovered on his arrival was worse than the worst which he had looked for. The

---

[1] Adam Loftus to Leicester, November 20.—*Irish MSS. Rolls House.*

English Pale he found 'as it were overwhelmed with vagabonds; stealth and spoils daily carried out of it; the people miserable; not two gentlemen in the whole of it able to lend twenty pounds; without horse, armour, apparel, or victual.' 'The soldiers were worse than the people: so beggarlike as it would abhor a general to look on them.' 'Never a married wife among them,' and therefore 'so allied with Irish women,' that they betrayed secrets, and could not be trusted on dangerous service; 'so insolent as to be intolerable; so rooted in idleness as there was no hope by correction to amend them.'

So much for the four shires. 'In Munster,' as the fruit of the Ormond and Desmond wars, 'a man might ride twenty or thirty miles and find no houses standing,' in a county which Sidney had known 'as well inhabited as many counties in England.' Connaught was quiet so far, and Clanrickard was probably loyal; but he was weak and was in constant expectation of being overrun.

'In Ulster,' Sidney wrote, 'there tyrannizeth the prince of pride; Lucifer was never more puffed up with pride and ambition than that O'Neil is; he is at present the only strong and rich man in Ireland, and he is the dangerousest man and most like to bring the whole estate of this land to subversion and subjugation either to him or to some foreign prince, that ever was in Ireland.'[1]

The Deputy's first step after landing was to ascertain the immediate terms on which the dreaded chief of the North intended to stand towards him. He wrote to desire Shan to come into the Pale to see him, and Shan at first answered with an offer to meet him at Dundalk;

---

[1] Sidney to Leicester, March 5.—*Irish MSS. Rolls House.*

but a letter followed in which he subscribed himself as
Sidney's 'loving gossip to command,' the contents of
which were less promising. For himself, Shan said, he
had so much affection and respect for Sir Henry, that he
would gladly go to him anywhere; but certain things
had happened in past years which had not been wholly
forgotten. The Earl of Sussex had twice attempted to
assassinate him. Had not the Earl of Kildare interfered
the Earl of Sussex when he went to Dublin to embark
for England, 'would have put a lock upon his hands, and
have carried him over as a prisoner.' His 'timorous and
mistrustful people' after these experiences would not
trust him any more in English hands.[1]

All this was unpleasantly true, and did not diminish
Sidney's difficulties. It was none the less necessary for
him however to learn what he was to expect from Shan.
Straining a point at the risk of offending Elizabeth, he
accepted the services of Stukely, which gave the latter an
opportunity of covering part of his misdoings by an act
of good service, and sent him with another gentleman to
Shan's castle, 'to discover if possible what he was, and
what he was like to attempt.'[2] A better messenger, supposing him honest, could not have been chosen. Shan
was at his ease with a person whose life was as lawless
as his own. He had ceased to care for concealment, and
spoke out freely. At first 'he was very flexible but very
timorous to come to the Deputy, apprehending traitorous
practices.' One afternoon 'when the wine was in him,'
he put his meaning in plainer language. Stukely had
perhaps hinted that there would be no earldom for him
unless his doings were more satisfactory. The Irish
heart and the Irish tongue ran over.

[1] Shan O'Neil to Sidney, February 18.—*Irish MSS. Rolls House.*
[2] Sidney to Leicester, March 5.—*MS. Ibid.*

'I care not,' he said, 'to be made an earl unless I may be better and higher than an earl, for I am in blood and power better than the best of them; and I will give place to none but my cousin of Kildare, for that he is of my house. You have made a wise earl of M'Carty More. I keep as good a man as he. For the Queen I confess she is my Sovereign, but I never made peace with her but by her own seeking. Whom am I to trust? When I came to the Earl of Sussex on safe conduct he offered me the courtesy of a handlock. When I was with the Queen, she said to me herself that I had, it was true, safe conduct to come and go, but it was not said when I might go; and they kept me there till I had agreed to things so far against my honour and profit, that I would never perform them while I live. That made me make war, and if it were to do again I would do it. My ancestors were kings of Ulster; and Ulster is mine, and shall be mine. O'Donnell shall never come into his country, nor Bagenal into Newry, nor Kildare into Dundrum or Lecale. They are now mine. With this sword I won them; with this sword I will keep them.'

'My Lord,' Sidney wrote to Leicester, ' no Attila nor Totila, no Vandal or Goth that ever was, was more to be doubted for overrunning any part of Christendom than this man is for overrunning and spoiling of Ireland. If it be an angel of heaven that will say that ever O'Neil will be a good subject till he be thoroughly chastised, believe him not, but think him a spirit of error. Surely if the Queen do not chastise him in Ulster, he will chase all hers out of Ireland. Her Majesty must make up her mind to the expense, and chastise this cannibal. She must send money in such sort as I may pay the garrison throughout. The present soldiers who are idle, treache-

rous, and incorrigible, must be changed. Better have no
soldiers than those that are here now—and the wages
must be paid. It must be done at last, and to do it at
once will be a saving in the end. My dear Lord, press
these things on the Queen. If I have not money, and
O'Neil make war, I will not promise to encounter with
him till he come to Dublin. Give me money, and
though I have but five hundred to his four thousand, I
will chase him out of the Pale in forty-eight hours. If I
may not have it, for the love you bear me have me home
again. I have great confidence in Lord Kildare. As to
Sussex and Arnold, it is true that all things are in disorder
and decay; but the fault was not with them—
impute it to the iniquity of the times. These malicious
people so hated Sussex as to ruin him they would have
ruined all. Arnold has done well and faithfully; and
Kildare very well. Remember this, and if possible let
him have the next garter that is vacant.'[1]

To the long letter to his brother-in-law, Sidney added
a few words equally anxious and earnest to Cecil. 'Ireland,'
he said, 'would be no small loss to the English
Crown, and it was never so like to be lost as now. O'Neil
has already all Ulster, and if the French were so eager
about Calais, think what the Irish are to recover their
whole island. I love no wars; but I had rather die
than Ireland should be lost in my government.'[2]

Evidently, notwithstanding all his urgency before he
left England, notwithstanding the promises which he extracted
from Elizabeth, the treasury doors were still locked.
Months had passed; arrears had continued to grow; the

---

[1] Sidney to Leicester, March 5. (condensed).—*Irish MSS. Rolls House.*
[2] Sidney to Cecil, March, 1566.—*MS. Ibid.*

troops had become more disorganized than ever, and the summer was coming, which would bring O'Neil and his galloglasse into the Pale, while the one indispensable step was still untaken which must precede all preparations to meet him. Nor did these most pressing letters work any speedy change. March went by and April came; and the smacks from Holyhead sailed up the Liffey, but they brought no money for Sidney and no despatches. At length unable to bear his suspense and disappointment longer, he wrote again to Leicester:—

'My Lord, if I be not speedier advertised of her Highness's pleasure than hitherto I have been, all will come to naught here, and before God and the world I will lay the fault on England, for there is none here. By force or by fair means the Queen may have anything that she will in this country if she will minister means accordingly, and with no great charge. If she will resolve of nothing, for her Majesty's advantage and for the benefit of this miserable country, persuade her Highness to withdraw me, and pay and discharge this garrison. As I am, and as this garrison is paid, I undo myself; the country is spoiled by the soldiers, and in no point defended. Help it my Lord for the honour of God one way or the other.'[1]

Two days later a London post came in, and with it letters from the Council. The help would have come long since had it rested with them. On the receipt of his first letter, they had agreed unanimously that every wish should be complied with. Money, troops, discretionary power—all should have been his—'so much was

---

[1] Sidney to Leicester, April 13.—*Irish MSS. Rolls House.*

every man's mind inclined to the extirpation of that proud rebel, Shan.' The Munster Council, which had hung fire also, should have been set on foot without a day's delay; and Sir Warham St. Leger, according to Sidney's recommendation, would have been appointed the first President. Elizabeth only had fallen into one of her periodic fits of ill-humour and irresolution, and would neither consent nor refuse. She had not questioned the justice of Sidney's report; she was 'heated and provoked with the monster' who was the cause of so much difficulty. Yet to ask her for money was to ask her for her heart's blood. 'Your lordship's experience of negotiation here in such affairs with her Majesty,' wrote Cecil, 'can move you to bear patiently some storms in the expedition;' 'the charge was the hindrance;' and while she could not deny that it was necessary, she could not forgive the plainness with which the necessity had been forced upon her.

She quarrelled in detail with everything which Sidney did; she disapproved of the Munster Council because Ireland could not pay for it; and it was useless to tell her that Ireland must be first brought into obedience. She was irritated because Sidney, unable to see with sufficient plainness the faults of Desmond and the exclusive virtues of Ormond, had refused to adjudicate without the help of English lawyers, in a quarrel which he did not understand. She disapproved of Sir Warham St. Leger because his father Sir Antony had been on bad terms with the father of Ormond; she insisted that Sidney should show favour to Ormond, 'in memory of his education with that holy young Solomon King Edward;'[1] and she complained bitterly of the employment of Stukely.

---

[1] Cecil to Sidney, March 27.—*Irish MSS. Rolls House.*

It was not till April was far advanced that the Council forced her by repeated importunities to consent that 'Shan should be extirpated;' and even then she would send only half of what was wanted to pay the arrears of the troops. 'Considering the great sums of money demanded and required of her in Ireland and elsewhere, she would be most glad that for reformation of the rebel any other way might be devised,' and she affronted the Deputy by sending Sir Francis Knolles to control his expenditure. If force could not be dispensed with, Sir Francis might devise an economical campaign. 'The cost of levying troops in England was four times as great as it used to be;' and it would be enough, she thought, if five or six hundred men were employed for a few weeks in the summer. O'Donnell, O'Reilly, and M'Guyre might be restored to their castles, and they could then be disbanded.[1] Such at least was her own opinion; should those, however, who had better means of knowing the truth, conclude that the war so conducted would be barren of result, she agreed with a sigh that they must have their way. She desired only that the cost might be as small as possible; 'the fortification of Berwick and the payment of our foreign debts falling very heavily on her.'[2]

Such was ever Elizabeth's character. She had received the Crown encumbered with a debt which with self-denying thrift she was laboriously reducing, and she had her own reasons for disliking over frequent sessions of Parliament. At the last extremity she would yield usually to what the public service demanded, but she gave with

---

[1] Instructions to Sir F. Knolles. By the Queen, April 18.—*Irish MSS. Rolls House.*

[2] Ibid.

grudging hand and irritated temper; and while she admitted the truth, she quarrelled with those who brought it home to her.

Shan meanwhile was preparing for war. He doubted his ability to overreach Elizabeth any more by words and promises, while the growth of the party of the Queen of Scots, his own connexion with her, and the Catholic reaction in England and Scotland, encouraged him to drop even the faint disguise behind which he had affected to shield himself. He mounted brass 'artillery' in Dundrum Castle, and in Lifford at the head of Lough Foyle. The friendship with Argyle grew closer, and another wonderful marriage scheme was in progress for the alliance between the Houses of M'Callum-More and O'Neil. 'The Countess' was to be sent away, and Shan was to marry the widow of James M'Connell whom he had killed—who was another half-sister of Argyle, and whose daughter he had married already and divorced. This business 'was said to be the Earl's practice.'[1] The Irish chiefs it seemed, three thousand years behind the world, retained the habits and the moralities of the Greek princes in the tale of Troy, when the bride of the slaughtered husband was the willing prize of the conqueror; and when only a rare Andromache was found to envy the fate of a sister

'Who had escaped the bed of some victorious lord.'

Aware that Sidney's first effort would be the restoration of O'Donnell, O'Neil commenced the campaign with a fresh invasion of Tyrconnoll, where O'Donnell's brother still held out for England; he swept round by Lough Erne, swooped on the remaining cattle of M'Guyre, and

---

[1] Sidney to the English Council, April 15.—*Irish MSS. Rolls House.*

'struck terror and admiration into the Irishry.'[1] Then stretching out his hands for foreign help, he wrote in the style of a king to Charles the Ninth of France.

'Your Majesty's father King Henry in times past required the Lords of Ireland to join with him against the heretic Saxon, the enemies of Almighty God, the enemies of the Holy Church of Rome, your Majesty's enemies and mine.[2] God would not permit that alliance to be completed, notwithstanding the hatred borne to England by all of Irish blood, until your Majesty had become King in France, and I was Lord of Ireland. The time is come however when we all are confederates in a common bond to drive the invader from our shores; and we now beseech your Majesty to send us six thousand well armed men. If you will grant our request there will soon be no Englishman left alive among us, and we will be your Majesty's subjects evermore. Help us, we implore you, to expel the heretics and schismatics, and to bring back our country to the holy Roman see.'[3]

The letter never reached its destination; it fell into English hands. Yet in the 'ticklo' state of Europe and with the progress made by Mary Stuart, French interference was an alarming possibility. More anxious and more disturbed than ever, Elizabeth made Sidney her scapegoat. Lord Sussex, ill repaying Sir Henry's generous palliation of his own shortcomings, envious of the ability of Leicester's brother-in-law, and wishing to escape the charge which he had so well deserved of being

---

[1] The Bishop of Meath to Sussex, April 27, 1566.—WRIGHT, vol. I.
[2] 'Vestræ Majestatis et nostræ simul inimicos.'
[3] O'Neil to Charles IX. 1566.—Irish MSS. Rolls House.

the cause of Shan's 'greatness,' whispered in her ear that in times past Sidney had been thought to favour 'that great rebel;' that he had addressed him long before in a letter by the disputed title of 'O'Neil,' and was perhaps his secret ally.

Elizabeth did not seriously believe this preposterous story; but it suited her humour to listen to a suspicion which she could catch at as an excuse for economy. The preparations for war were suspended, and instead of receiving supplies, Sidney learnt only that the Queen had spoken unworthy words of him.

Sidney's blood was hot; he was made of bad materials for a courtier. He wrote at once to Elizabeth herself, 'declaring his special grief at hearing that he was fallen from her favour,' and 'that she had given credit to that improbable slander raised upon him by the Earl of Sussex.' He wrote to the Council, entreating them not to allow these idle stories to relax their energies in suppressing the rebellion; but he begged them at the same time to consider his own 'unaptness to reside any longer in Ireland, or to be an actor in the war.' The words which the Queen had used of him were gone abroad in the world. 'He could find no obedience.' 'His credit being gone, his power to be of service was gone also.' He therefore demanded his immediate recall 'that he might preserve the small remnant of his patrimony already much diminished by his coming to Ireland.' As for the charge brought against him by the Earl of Sussex, he would reply with his sword and body 'against an accusation concealed hitherto he knew not with what duty, and uttered at last with impudency and unshamefastness.'[1]

---

[1] Sidney to the English Council, May 18.—*Irish MSS. Rolls House.*

CHAP XI
1566
May

But Elizabeth meant nothing less than to recall Sidney. She neither distrusted his loyalty nor questioned his talents; she chose merely to find fault with him while she made use of his services. It was her habit towards those among her subjects whom she particularly valued. Sir Francis Knolles when he arrived at Dublin could report only that Sidney had gained the love and the admiration of every one; and that his plan for proceeding against O'Neil was the first which had ever promised real success. Campaigns in Ireland had hitherto been no more than summer forays—mere inroads of devastation during the few dry weeks of August and September. Sidney proposed to commence at the end of the harvest, when the corn was gathered in, and could either be seized or destroyed; and to keep the field through the winter and spring. It would be expensive; but money well laid out was the best economy in the end, and Sidney undertook, if he was allowed as many men as he thought requisite, and was not interfered with, 'to subdue, kill, or expel Shan, and reduce Ulster to as good order as any part of Ireland.'[1]

At first Elizabeth would not hear of it; she would not ruin herself for any such hairbrained madness. The Deputy must defend the Pale through the summer, and the attack on O'Neil, if attempted at all, should be delayed till the spring ensuing. But Sir Francis, who was sent to prevent expense, was the foremost to insist on the necessity of it. He explained that in the cold Irish springs the fields were bare, the cattle were lean, and the weather was so uncertain, that neither man nor horse could bear it; whereas in August food everywhere was abundant, and the soldiers would have time to become hardened to

Plan for the campaign.

---

[1] Sidney to Cecil, April 17.—*Irish MSS. Rolls House.*

their work. They could winter somewhere on the Bann, harry Tyrone night and day without remission, and so break Shan to the ground and ruin him. Two brigantines would accompany the army with supplies, and control the passage between Antrim and the Western Isles; and beyond all, Knolles re-echoed what Sidney had said before him on the necessity of paying wages to the troops instead of leaving them to pay themselves at the expense of the people. Nothing was really saved, for the debts would have eventually to be paid, and paid with interest—while meanwhile the 'inhabitants of the Pale were growing hostile to the English rule.'[1]

The danger to the State could hardly be exaggerated. M'Guyre had come into Dublin, with his last cottage in ashes, and his last cow driven over the hills into Shan's country; Argyle, with the whole disposable force of the Western Isles, was expected in person in Ulster in the summer.

Elizabeth's irritation had been unable to wait till she had received Knolles's letters. She made herself a judge of Sidney's projects; she listened to Sussex who told her that they were wild and impossible. Whether Sussex was right or Sidney was right, she was called upon to spend money; and while she knew that she would have to do it, she continued to delay and make difficulties, and to vex Sidney with her letters.

His temper boiled over again.

'I testify to God, to her Highness, and to you,' he wrote on the 3rd of June to Cecil, 'that all the charge is lost that she is at with this manner of proceeding. O'Neil will be tyrant of all Ireland if he be not speedily

---

[1] Sir F. Knolles to Cecil, May 19.—*Irish MSS. Rolls House.*

withstood. He hath as I hear won the rest of O'Donnell's castles; he hath confederated with the Scots; he is now in M'Guyre's country. All this summer he will spend in Connaught; next winter in the English Pale. It may please the Queen to appoint some order for Munster—for it will be a mad Munster in haste else. I will give you all my land in Rutlandshire to get me leave to go into Hungary, and think myself bound to you while I live. I trust there to do my country some honour: here I do neither good to the Queen, to the country, nor myself. I take my leave in haste, as a thrall forced to live in loathsomeness of life.'[1]

The Council finding Sidney's views accepted, and endorsed by Knolles, united to recommend them; a schedule was drawn out of the men, money, and stores which would be required; a thousand of the best troops in Berwick, with eight hundred Irish, was the increase estimated as necessary for the army; and the wages of eighteen hundred men for six months would amount to ten thousand four hundred and eighty pounds. Sixteen thousand pounds was already due to the Irish garrison. The provisions, arms, clothes, and ammunition would cost four thousand five hundred pounds; and four thousand pounds in addition would be wanted for miscellaneous services.[2]

The reluctance of Elizabeth to engage in an Irish campaign was not diminished by a demand for thirty-four thousand nine hundred pounds. Sussex continued malignant and mischievous, and there was many a Catholic about the court who secretly wished O'Neil to

---

[1] Sidney to Cecil, June 3.—*Irish MSS. Rolls House.*
[2] Notes for the army in Ireland, May 30. In Cecil's hand.—*MS. Ibid.*

succeed. 'The Court,' wrote Cecil to Sidney, 'is not free from many troubles—amongst others none worse than emulations, disdains, backbitings, and such like, whereof I see small hope of diminution.'

The Queen at the beginning refused to allow more than six hundred men to be sent from England or more than four hundred to be raised in Ireland. To no purpose Cecil insisted; in vain Leicester challenged Sussex and implored his mistress to give way. 'Her Majesty was absolutely determined.' The Ormond business had created fresh exasperation. Sir Henry, though admiring and valuing the Earl of Ormond's high qualities, had persisted in declaring himself unable to decide the litigated questions between the house of Butler and the Desmonds. Archbishop Kirwan the Irish Chancellor, was old and incapable; the Deputy had begged for the assistance of some English lawyers; 'but such evil report had Ireland that no English lawyer would go there.'[1] The Queen flew off from the campaign to the less expensive question. Lawyer or no lawyer, she insisted that judgment should be given in Ormond's favour. She complained that the Deputy was partial to Desmond, and—especially wounding Sidney, whose chief success had been in the equity of his administration, and whose first object had been to check the tyrannical exactions of the Irish noblemen—she required him to make an exception in Ormond's favour, and permit 'coyn and livery,' the most mischievous of all the Irish imposts, to be continued in Kilkenny.

'I am extremely sorry,' Sidney replied to Cecil, when the order reached him; 'I am extremely sorry to receive her Majesty's command to permit the Earl of Ormond to exercise coyn and livery, which have been the curse of

---

[1] Cecil to Sidney, June 16.—*Irish MSS. Rolls House.*

this country, and which I hoped to have ended wholly. I would write more, if I did not hope to have my recall by the next east wind. Only weigh what I have said. Whatever becomes of me you will have as woeful a business here as you had in Calais if you do not look to it in time.'[1]

Elizabeth was not contented till she had written out her passion to Sidney with her own hand. She told him that she disapproved of all that he was doing. If he chose to persist, she would give him half the men that he required, and with those he might do what he could on his own responsibility.[2] It seemed however that she had relieved her feelings as soon as she had expressed them. A week later she yielded to all that was required of her. Cecil soothed Sidney's anger with a gracious message;[3] Sidney, since she was pleased to have it so, consented to remain and do his duty; and thus after two months had been consumed in quarrels, the preparations for the war began in earnest.

The troops from England were to go direct to Lough Foyle; to land at the head of the lake and to move up to Lifford, where they were to entrench themselves and wait for the Deputy, who would advance from the Pale to join them. The command was given to Colonel Edward Randolph, an extremely able officer who had served at Havre; and the men were marched as fast as they could be raised to Bristol, the port from which the expedition was to sail, while Sidney was setting a rare example in Dublin, and spending the time till he could take the field 'in hearing the people's causes.'

---

[1] Sidney to Cecil, June 24.—*Irish MSS. Rolls House.*
[2] Elizabeth to Sidney, June 15.—*MS. Ibid.*
[3] Cecil to Sidney, June 24.—*MS. Ibid.*

Shan O'Neil finding that no help was to be looked for from France and that mischief was seriously intended against him, tried a stroke of treachery. He wrote to Sidney to say that he wished to meet him, and a spot near Dundalk being chosen for a conference, he filled the woods in the neighbourhood with his people and intended to carry off the Deputy as a prize. Sir Henry was too wary to be caught. He came to the Border on the 25th of July; but he came in sufficient strength to defend himself; Shan did not appear, and waiting till Sidney had returned to Dublin, made a sudden attempt on the 29th to seize Dundalk. Young Fitzwilliam, who was in command of the English garrison there, was on the alert. The surprise failed. The Irish tried an assault but were beaten back, and eighteen heads were left behind to grin hideously over the gates. Shan himself drew back into Tyrone: to prevent a second occupation of Armagh Cathedral by an English garrison, he burnt it to the ground; and sent a swift messenger to Desmond to urge him to rise in Munster. 'Now was the time or never to set upon the enemies of Ireland. If Desmond failed or turned against his country, God would avenge it on him.'[1]

CHAP XI
1566 July
O'Neil attacks Dundalk, and fails.

Had Sidney allowed himself to be forced into the precipitate decision which Elizabeth had urged upon him, the Geraldines would have made common cause with O'Neil. But so long as the English Government was just, Desmond did not care to carve a throne for a Celtic chief; he replied with sending an offer to the Deputy 'to go against the rebel with all his power.' Still more opportunely the Earl of Murray at the last moment de-

Desmond refuses to join O'Neil.

---

[1] Commendation from O'Neil to John of Desmond, September 9.—*Irish MSS. Rolls House.*

tached Argyle from the pernicious and monstrous alliance into which he had been led by his vindictiveness against Elizabeth. The Scots of the Isles freed from the commands of their feudal sovereign resumed their old attitude of fear and hatred. Shan offered them all Antrim to join him, all the cattle in the country and the release of Surlyboy from captivity; but Antrim and its cattle they believed that they could recover for themselves, and James M'Connell had left a brother Allaster who was watching with eager eyes for an opportunity to revenge the death of his kinsman and the dishonour with which Shan had stained his race.

The Scots though still few in number hung as a cloud over the north-east. Dropping boat-loads of Highlanders from the Isles were guided to the coast by the beacon-fires which blazed nightly over the giant columns of Fairhead. Allaster M'Connell offered his services to Sidney as soon as the game should begin; and Shan after all instead of conquering Ireland might have enough to do to hold his own. The weather was unfavourable and the summer was wet and wild with westerly gales. Sir Edward Horsey who was sent with money from London was detained half August at Holyhead; Colonel Randolph and his thousand men were chafing for thirty days at Bristol, 'fearing that their enemies the winds would let them that they should not help Shan to gather his harvest;'[1] and Sidney as from time to time some fresh ungracious letter came from Elizabeth would break into a rage again and press Cecil 'for his recall from that accursed country.'[2] Otherwise however the prospects grew brighter with the autumn. In the second week in

---

[1] Edward Randolph to Cecil from Bristol, Sept. 3.—*Irish MSS. Rolls House.*
[2] Sidney to Cecil, September 10.—*MS. Ibid.*

September the Bristol transports were seen passing into the North Channel with a leading breeze. Horsey came over with the money; the troops of the Pale with the long due arrears paid up were ordered to Drogheda; and on the 17th, assured that by that time Randolph was in Lough Foyle, the Deputy accompanied by Kildare, the old O'Donnell, Shan M'Guyre, and another dispossessed chief O'Dogherty, took the field.

1566 September

Randolph lands at Lough Foyle.

Passing Armagh, which they found a mere heap of blackened stones, they reached the Blackwater on the 23rd. On an island in a lake near the river there stood one of those many robber castles which lend in their ruin such romantic beauty to the inland waters of Ireland. Report said that within its walls Shan had stored much of his treasure, and the troops were eager to take it. Sidney selected from among the many volunteers such only as were able to swim, and a bridge was extemporized with brushwood floated upon barrels. The army was without artillery; it had been found impracticable to carry a single cannon over roadless bog and mountain, and the storming party started with handgrenades to throw over the walls. The bridge proved too slight for its work; slipping and splashing through the water the men got over, but their 'fireworks' were wetted in the passage and they found themselves at the foot of thirty feet of solid masonry without ladders and with no weapons but their bows and battle-axes. 'The place was better defended and more strongly fortified' than Sidney had supposed. Several of the English were killed and many more were wounded; and the Deputy had the prudence to waste no more valuable lives or equally valuable days upon an enterprise which when accomplished would be barren of result. On the 24th the army crossed the river into Shan's own country.

Sidney continues his march.

The Irish hung on their skirts but did not venture to molest them, and they marched without obstruction to Benbrook, one of O'Neil's best and largest houses, which they found 'utterly burnt and razed to the ground.' From Benbrook they went on towards Clogher, through pleasant fields and villages 'so well inhabited as no Irish county in the realm was like it:' it was the very park or preserve into which the plunder of Ulster had been gathered; where the people enjoyed the profits of unlimited pillage from which till then they had been themselves exempt. The Bishop of Clogher was a 'rebel,' and was out with Shan in the field; his well-fattened flock were devoured by Sidney's men as by a flight of Egyptian locusts. 'There we stayed,' said Sidney, 'to destroy the corn; we burned the country for twenty-four miles' compass, and we found by experience that now was the time of the year to do the rebel most hurt.' Here died M'Guyre at the monastery of Omagh within sight of the home to which he was returning by the pleasant shores of Lough Erne. Here too the Earl of Kildare nearly escaped being taken prisoner: he was surprised with a small party in a wood, attacked with 'harquebusses and Scottish arrows,' and hardly cut his way through.

Detained longer than he intended by foul weather, Sidney broke up from Omagh on the 2nd of October, crossed 'the dangerous and swift river there,' 'and rested that night on a neck of land near a broken castle of Tirlogh Lenogh, called the Salmon Castle.' On the 3rd he was over the Derry, and by the evening he had reached Lifford, where he expected to find Randolph and the English army.

At Lifford however no English were to be discovered, but only news of them.

Randolph, to whose discretion the ultimate choice of his quarters had been committed, had been struck as he came up Lough Foyle with the situation of Derry. Nothing then stood on the site of the present city save a decrepit and deserted monastery of Augustine monks, which was said to have been built in the time of St. Columba; but the eye of the English commander saw in the form of the ground, in the magnificent lake, and the splendid tide river, a site for the foundation of a powerful colony suited alike for a military station and a commercial and agricultural town. There therefore Colonel Randolph had landed his men, and there Sidney joined him, and after a careful survey entirely approved his judgment. The monastery with a few sheds attached to it provided shelter. The English troops had not been idle and had already entrenched themselves 'in a very warlike manner.' O'Donnell, O'Dogherty and the other friends of England 'agreed all of them that it was the very best spot in the northern counties to build a city.'

At all events for present purposes the northern force was to remain there during the winter. Sidney stayed a few days at Derry, and then leaving Randolph with 650 men, 350 pioneers and provisions for two months, continued his own march. His object was to replace O'Donnell in possession of his own country and castles, restore O'Dogherty and the other chiefs and commit them to the protection of Randolph while he himself would sweep through the whole northern province, encourage the loyal clans to return to their allegiance and show the people generally that there was no part of Ireland to which the arm of the Deputy could not reach to reward the faithful and punish the rebellious.

Donegal was his next point after leaving Lough Foyle—once a thriving town inhabited by English colonists—at the time of Sidney's arrival a pile of ruins, in the midst of which, like a wild beast's den strewed round with mangled bones, rose 'the largest and strongest castle which he had seen in Ireland.' It was held by one of O'Donnell's kinsmen, to whom Shan—to attach him to his cause—had given his sister for a wife. At the appearance of the old chief with the English army it was immediately surrendered. O'Donnell was at last rewarded for his fidelity and sufferings, and the whole tribe with eager protestations of allegiance gave sureties for their future loyalty.

Leaving O'Donnell in possession and scarcely pausing to rest his troops Sidney again went forward. On the 19th he was at Ballyshannon; on the 22nd at Sligo; on the 24th he passed over the bogs and mountains of Mayo into Roscommon; and then 'leaving behind them as fruitful a country as was in England or Ireland all utterly waste,' the army turned their faces homewards, swam the Shannon at Athlone for lack of a bridge on the 26th, and so back to the Pale. Twenty castles had been taken as they went along and left in hands that could be trusted. 'In all that long and painful journey' Sidney was able to say that 'there had not died of sickness but three persons;' men and horses were brought back in full health and strength, while 'her Majesty's honour was re-established among the Irishry and grown to no small veneration'[1]—an expedition 'comparable only to Alexander's journey into Bactria,' wrote an admirer of Sidney to Cecil—revealing what to Irish eyes appeared the magnitude of the difficulty, and forming a measure of the effect which it produced. The English

---

[1] Sir H. Sidney and the Earl of Kildare to Elizabeth, November 12.—*Irish MSS. Rolls House.*

Deputy had bearded Shan in his stronghold, burnt his houses, pillaged his people, and had fastened a body of police in the midst of them to keep them waking in the winter nights. He had penetrated the hitherto impregnable fortresses of mountain and morass. The Irish who had been faithful to England were again in safe possession of their lands and homes. The weakest maddest and wildest Celts were made aware that when the English were once roused to effort they could crush them as the lion crushes the jackal.

Meantime Lord Ormond had carried his complaints to London, and the letter which Sidney found waiting his return was not what a successful commander might have expected from his sovereign. Before he started he had repeated his refusal to determine a cause which he did not understand without the help of lawyers. There was no one in Ireland of whom he thought more highly than of Lord Ormond; there was none that he would more gladly help; but disputed and complicated titles to estates were questions which he was unable to enter into. He could do nothing till the cause had been properly heard; and in the existing humour of the country it would have been mere madness to have led Desmond to doubt the equity of the English Government. But Sidney's modest and firm defence found no favour with Elizabeth. While he was absent in the North she wrote to Sir Edward Horsey desiring him to tell the Deputy that she was ill satisfied with his proceedings; he had allowed himself to be guided by Irish advisers; he had been partial to Desmond; 'he that had least deserved favour had been most borne withal.' While in fact he had done more for Ireland in the eight months of his government than any English ruler since Sir Edward Bellingham, the Queen insisted that he had attended to none of her wishes and had occupied himself wholly with matters of no importance.

Most likely she did not believe what she said; but Sidney was costing her money and she relieved herself by finding fault.

'My good Lord,' Cecil was obliged to write to him to prevent an explosion, 'next to my most hearty commendations I do with all my heart condole and take part of sorrow to see your burden of government so great and your comfort from hence so uncertain. I feel by myself—being also here wrapped in miseries and tossed with my small vessel of wit and means in a sea swelling with storms of envy, malice, disdain and suspicion—what discomfort they commonly have that mean to deserve best of their country. And though I confess myself unable to give you advice, and being almost desperate myself of well-doing, yet for the present I think it best for you to run still an even course in government, with indifferency in case of justice to all persons, and in case of favour, to let them which do well find their comfort by you; and in other causes in your choice to prefer them whom you find the Prince most disposed to have favoured. My Lord of Ormond doth take this commodity by being here to declare his own griefs; I see the Queen's Majesty so much misliking of the Earl of Desmond as surely I think it needful for you to be very circumspect in ordering of the complaints exhibited against him.'[1]

It must be admitted that Elizabeth's letter to Horsey was written at the crisis of the succession quarrel in Par-

---

[1] Cecil to Sidney, October 20.—*Irish MSS. Rolls House.*

liament, and that her not unprovoked ill-humour was merely venting itself upon the first object which came across her: nor had she at that time heard of Sidney's successes in Ulster and probably she despaired of ever hearing of successes. Yet when she did hear, the tone of her letters was scarcely altered; she alluded to his services only to reiterate her complaints; and she would not have gone through the form of thanking him had not Cecil inserted a few words of acknowledgment in the draft of her despatch.[1] Sidney's patience was exhausted. Copies of the Queen's disparaging letters were circulated privately in Dublin, obtained he knew not how, but with fatal effect upon his influence. He had borne Elizabeth's caprices long enough. 'For God's sake,' he wrote angrily on the 15th of November in answer to Cecil's letter, 'for God's sake get my recall; the people here know what the Queen thinks of me, and I can do no good.'[2]

From these unprofitable bickerings the story must return to Colonel Randolph and the garrison of Derry. For some weeks after Sidney's departure all had gone on prosperously. The country people, though well paid for everything, were slow to bring in provisions; the bread ran short; and the men had been sent out poorly provided with shoes or tools or clothes. But foraging parties drove in sufficient beef to keep them in fresh meat. Randolph who seems to have been a man of fine foresight had sent to the English Pale for a supply of forage before the winter set in; he had written to England 'for shirts, kerseys, canvas, and leather;' he kept Cecil constantly informed of the welfare and wants of

---

[1] The words 'for which we are bound to thank you' are inserted in Cecil's hand.—*The Queen to Sidney*, November, 1566.
[2] *Irish MSS. Rolls House.*

the troops;[1] and for some time they were healthy and in high spirits, and either worked steadily at the fortress or were doing good service in the field.

While Sidney was in Connaught, Shan who had followed him to Lifford turned back upon the Pale, expecting to find it undefended. He was encountered by Sir Warham St. Leger, lost two hundred men and was at first hunted back over the Border. He again returned however with 'a main army,' burnt several villages and in a second fight with St. Leger was more successful; the English were obliged to retire 'for lack of more aid;' but they held together in good order, and Shan with the Derry garrison in his rear durst not follow far from home in pursuit. Before he could revenge himself on Sidney, before he could stir against the Scots, before he could strike a blow at O'Donnell, he must pluck out the barbed dart which was fastened in his unguarded side.

Defeat of O'Neil and death of Randolph.

Knowing that he would find it no easy task, he was hovering cautiously in the neighbourhood of Lough Foyle, when Randolph fell upon him by surprise on the 12th of November. The O'Neils fled after a short, sharp action. O'Dogherty with his Irish horse chased the flying crowd, killing every man he caught, and Shan recovered himself to find he had lost four hundred men of the bravest of his followers. More fatal overthrow neither he nor any other Irish chief had yet received at English hands. But the success was dearly bought; Colonel Randolph himself leading the pursuit was struck by a random shot and fell dead from his horse. The Irish had fortunately suffered too severely to profit by his loss. Shan's motley army, held together as it was by the hope of easily-bought plunder, scattered when the

---

[1] Edward Randolph to Cecil, October 27.—*Irish MSS. Rolls House.*

service became dangerous. Sidney allowing him no rest struck in again beyond Dundalk, burning his farms and capturing his castles.[1] The Scots came in over the Bann, wasting the country all along the river side. Allaster M'Connell like some chief of Sioux Indians sent to the Captain of Knockfergus an account of the cattle that he had driven, and 'the wives and bairns' that he had slain.[2] Like swarms of angry hornets these avenging savages drove their stings into the now maddened and desperate Shan, on every point where they could fasten; while in December the old O'Donnell came out over the mountains from Donegal, and paid back O'Neil with interest for his stolen wife, his pillaged country, and his own long imprisonment and exile. The tide of fortune had turned too late for his own revenge: worn out with his long sufferings he fell from his horse at the head of his people with the stroke of death upon him; but before he died he called his kinsmen about him and prayed them to be true to England and their Queen, and Hugh O'Donnell who succeeded to his father's command went straight to Derry and swore allegiance to the English crown.

Tyrone was now smitten in all its borders. Magennis was the last powerful chief who still adhered to Shan's fortunes; the last week in the year Sidney carried fire and sword through his country and left him not a hoof remaining. It was to no purpose that Shan, bewildered by the rapidity with which disasters were piling themselves upon him, cried out now for pardon and peace,

---

[1] Sidney to the Lords of the Council, December 12.—*Irish MSS. Rolls House.*
[2] Allaster M'Connell to the Captain of Knockfergus; enclosed in a letter of R. Piers to Sir H. Sidney, December 15.—*MS. Ibid.*

the Deputy would not answer his letter, and 'nothing was talked of but his extirpation by war only.'[1]

A singular tragedy interrupted for a time the tide of English success, although the first blows had been struck by so strong a hand that Shan could not rally from them. The death of Randolph had left the garrison at Derry as—in the words of one of them—a headless people.[2] Food and clothing fell short, and there was no longer foresight to anticipate or authority to remedy the common wants of troops on active service. Sickness set in. By the middle of November 'the flux was reigning among them wonderfully.'[3] Strong men soon after were struck suddenly dead by a mysterious disorder which no medicine would cure and no precaution would prevent. It appeared at last that either in ignorance or carelessness they had built their sleeping quarters over the burial ground of the Abbey, and the clammy vapour had stolen into their lungs and poisoned them. As soon as their distress was known, supplies in abundance were sent from England; but the vices of modern administration had already infected the public service, and a cargo of meal destined for the garrison of Derry went astray to Florida. No subordinate officer ventured to take the vacant command. 'Many of our best men,' Captain Vaughan wrote a few days before Christmas, 'go away because there is none to stay them; many have died; God comfort us!'[4]

Colonel St. Loo came at last in the beginning of the new year. The pestilence for a time abated, and the

---

[1] Sidney to the English Council, January 18.—*Irish MSS. Rolls House.*
[2] Geoffrey Vaughan to Admiral Winter, December 18.—*MS. Ibid.*
[3] Wilfred to Cecil, November 15.—*MS. Ibid.*
[4] Vaughan to Winter, December 18.—*MS. Ibid.*

spirits of the men revived. St. Loo, to quicken their blood, let them at once into the enemy's country; they returned after a foray of a few days driving before them seven hundred horses and a thousand cattle;[1] and the Colonel wrote to Sidney to say that with three hundred additional men 'he could so hunt the rebel that ere May was past he should not show his face in Ulster.'[2]

Harder pressed than ever, Shan O'Neil, about the time when the Queen of Scots was bringing her matrimonial difficulties to their last settlement, made one more effort to gain allies in France. This time he wrote, not to the King, but to the Cardinals of Lorraine and Guise, imploring them in the name of their great brother the Duke, who had raised the cross out of the dust where the unbelieving Huguenots were trampling it, to bring the fleur-de-lys to the rescue of Ireland from the grasp of the ungodly English. 'Help us!' he cried, blending— Irish like—flattery with entreaty. 'When I was in England I saw your noble brother the Marquis d'Elbœuf transfix two stags with a single arrow. If the Most Christian King will not help us, move the Pope to help us. I alone in this land sustain his cause.'[3]

As the ship laboured in the gale the unprofitable cargo was thrown overboard. Terence Daniel relieved of his crozier went back to his place among the troopers; Creagh was accepted in his place, and taken into confidence and into Shan's household; all was done to deserve favour in earth and heaven, but all was useless. The Pope sat silent, or muttering his anathemas with bated breath; the Guises had too much work on hand at home

---

[1] St. Loo in his despatch says 10,000. He must have added one cipher at least.—*St. Loo to Sidney, February* 8.—*Irish MSS. Rolls House.*
[2] Ibid.
[3] Shan O'Neil to the Cardinals of Lorraine and Guise, 1567.—*MS. Ibid.*

to heed the Irish wolf, whom the English having in vain attempted to trap or poison, were driving to bay with more lawful weapons.

Success or failure however was alike to the doomed garrison of Derry. The black death came back among them after a brief respite, and to the reeking vapour of the charnel-house it was indifferent whether its victims returned in triumph from a stricken field, or were cooped within their walls by hordes of savage enemies. By the middle of March there were left out of eleven hundred men but three hundred available to fight. Reinforcements had been raised at Liverpool, but they were countermanded when on the point of sailing: it was thought idle to send them to inevitable death. The English council was discussing the propriety of removing the colony to the Bann, when accident finished the work which the plague had begun, and spared them the trouble of deliberation. The huts and sheds round the monastery had been huddled together for the convenience of fortification. At the end of April, probably after a drying east wind, a fire broke out in a blacksmith's forge, which spread irresistibly through the entire range of buildings. The flames at last reached the powder magazine; thirty men were blown in pieces by the explosion; and the rest paralyzed by this last addition to their misfortunes made no more effort to extinguish the conflagration. St. Loo, with all that remained of that ill-fated party, watched from their provision boats in the river the utter destruction of the settlement which had begun so happily, and then sailed drearily away to find a refuge in Knockfergus.

Such was the fate of the first effort for the building of Londonderry; and below its later glories, as so often happens in this world, lay the bones of many a hundred gallant men who lost their lives in laying its foundations. Elizabeth, who in the immediate pressure of calamity resumed at once her nobler nature, 'perceiving the misfortune not to come of treason but of God's ordinance, bore it well;' 'she was willing to do that which should be wanting to repair the loss;'[1] and Cecil was able to write cheerfully to Sidney, telling him to make the best of the accident and let it stimulate him to fresh exertions.[2]

Happily the essential work had been done already, and the ruin of Derry came too late to profit Shan. His own people, divided and dispirited, were mutinying against a leader who no longer commanded success. In May a joint movement was concerted between Sidney and the O'Donnells, and while the Deputy with the light horse of the Pale overran Tyrone and carried off three thousand cattle, Hugh O'Donnell came down on Shan on the river which runs into Lough Foyle. The spot where the supremacy of Ulster was snatched decisively from the ambition of the O'Neils, is called in the despatches Gaviston. The situation is now difficult to identify. It was somewhere perhaps between Lifford and Londonderry, on the west side of the river.

Conscious that he was playing his last card, Shan had gathered together the whole of his remaining force, and had still nearly three thousand men with him. The O'Donnells were fewer in number; but victory, as generally happens, followed the tide in which events were setting. After a brief fight the O'Neils broke and fled; the enemy was behind them, the river was in front; and when the Irish battle-cries had died away over moor and

---

[1] Cecil to Leicester, May, 1567.—*Irish MSS. Rolls House.*
[2] 'Et contra audentior Ito.'—*Cecil to Sidney, May 13. MS. Ibid.*

CHAP XI
1567
March

The settlement at Derry finally ruined.

to heed the Irish wolf, whom the English having in vain attempted to trap or poison, were driving to bay with more lawful weapons.

Success or failure however was alike to the doomed garrison of Derry. The black death came back among them after a brief respite, and to the reeking vapour of the charnel-house it was indifferent whether its victims returned in triumph from a stricken field, or were cooped within their walls by hordes of savage enemies. By the middle of March there were left out of eleven hundred men but three hundred available to fight. Reinforcements had been raised at Liverpool, but they were countermanded when on the point of sailing: it was thought idle to send them to inevitable death. The English council was discussing the propriety of removing the colony to the Bann, when accident finished the work which the plague had begun, and spared them the trouble of deliberation. The huts and sheds round the monastery had been huddled together for the convenience of fortification. At the end of April, probably after a drying east wind, a fire broke out in a blacksmith's forge, which spread irresistibly through the entire range of buildings. The flames at last reached the powder magazine; thirty men were blown in pieces by the explosion; and the rest paralyzed by this last addition to their misfortunes made no more effort to extinguish the conflagration. St. Loo, with all that remained of that ill-fated party, watched from their provision boats in the river the utter destruction of the settlement which had begun so happily, and then sailed drearily away to find a refuge in Knockfergus.

Such was the fate of the first effort for the building of Londonderry; and below its later glories, as so often happens in this world, lay the bones of many a hundred gallant men who lost their lives in laying its foundations. Elizabeth, who in the immediate pressure of calamity resumed at once her nobler nature, 'perceiving the misfortune not to come of treason but of God's ordinance, bore it well;' 'she was willing to do that which should be wanting to repair the loss;'[1] and Cecil was able to write cheerfully to Sidney, telling him to make the best of the accident and let it stimulate him to fresh exertions.[2]

Happily the essential work had been done already, and the ruin of Derry came too late to profit Shan. His own people, divided and dispirited, were mutinying against a leader who no longer commanded success. In May a joint movement was concerted between Sidney and the O'Donnells, and while the Deputy with the light horse of the Pale overran Tyrone and carried off three thousand cattle, Hugh O'Donnell came down on Shan on the river which runs into Lough Foyle. The spot where the supremacy of Ulster was snatched decisively from the ambition of the O'Neils, is called in the despatches Caviston. The situation is now difficult to identify. It was somewhere perhaps between Lifford and Londonderry, on the west side of the river.

Conscious that he was playing his last card, Shan had gathered together the whole of his remaining force, and had still nearly three thousand men with him. The O'Donnells were fewer in number; but victory, as generally happens, followed the tide in which events were setting. After a brief fight the O'Neils broke and fled; the enemy was behind them, the river was in front; and when the Irish battle-cries had died away over moor and

---

[1] Cecil to Leicester, May, 1567.—*Irish MSS. Rolls House.*
[2] 'Et contra sudentior Ito.'—*Cecil to Sidney, May 13. MS. Ibid.*

mountain, but two hundred survived of those fierce troopers who were to have cleared Ireland for ever from the presence of the Saxons. For the rest, the wolves were snarling over their bodies, and the sea-gulls wheeling over them with scream and cry as they floated down to their last resting-place beneath the quiet waters of Lough Foyle. Shan's 'foster brethren,' faithful to the last, were all killed; he himself, with half a dozen comrades, rode for his life, pursued by the avenging furies; his first desperate intention was to throw himself at Sidney's feet, with a slave's collar upon his neck; but his secretary, Neil M'Kevin, persuaded him that his cause was not yet absolutely without hope.

Surlyboy was still a prisoner in the castle at Lough Neagh; 'the Countess of Argyle' had remained with her ravisher through his shifting fortunes, had continued to bear him children, and notwithstanding his many infidelities was still attached to him. M'Kevin told him that for their sakes, or at their intercession, he might find shelter and perhaps help among the kindred of the M'Connells.[1]

In the far extremity of Antrim, beside the falls of Isnalcara, where the black valley of Glenariff opens out into Red Bay, sheltered among the hills and close upon the sea, lay the camp of Allaster M'Connell and his nephew Gillespie. Here on Saturday, the last of May, appeared Shan O'Neil, with M'Kevin and some fifty men. He had brought the Countess and his prisoner as peace offerings: he alighted at Allaster's tent, and threw himself on his hospitality; and though the blood of the M'Connells was fresh on his hands he was received 'with dissembled gratulatory words.' The feud seemed to be

---

[1] Attainder of Shan O'Neil.—*Irish Statute Book*, 11 ELIZ.

buried in the restoration of Surlyboy; an alliance was again talked of, and for two days all went well. But the death of their leaders in the field was not the only wrong which Shan had offered to the Western Islanders: he had divorced James M'Connell's daughter; he had kept a high-born Scottish lady with him as his mistress; and last of all, after killing M'Connell he had asked Argyle to give him M'Connell's widow for a wife. The lady herself, to escape the dishonour, had remained in concealment in Edinburgh; but the mention of it had been taken as a mortal insult by her family.

The third evening, Monday the 2nd of June, after supper, when the wine and the whisky had gone freely round, and the blood in Shan's veins had warmed again, Gillespie M'Connell, who had watched him from the first with an ill-boding eye, turned round upon M'Kevin and asked scornfully 'whether it was he who had bruited abroad that the lady his aunt did offer to come from Scotland to Ireland to marry with his master?'

M'Kevin, meeting scorn with scorn, said 'that if his aunt was Queen of Scotland she might be proud to match the O'Neil.'

'It is false!' the fierce Scot shouted; 'my aunt is too honest a woman to match with her husband's murderer.'

Shan, who was perhaps drunk, heard the words; and forgetting where he was, flung back the lie in Gillespie's throat. Gillespie sprung to his feet, ran out of the tent, and raised the slogan of the Isles. A hundred dirks flashed into the moonlight, and the Irish wherever they could be found were struck down and stabbed. Some two or three found their horses and escaped; all the rest were murdered; and Shan himself, gashed with fifty wounds, was 'wrapped in a kern's old shirt' and flung into a pit dug hastily among the ruined arches of Glenarm.

Even there what was left of him was not allowed to rest; four days later Piers, the captain of Knockfergus, hacked the head from the body, and carried it on a spear's point through Drogheda to Dublin, where staked upon a spike it bleached on the battlements of the castle, a symbol to the Irish world of the fate of Celtic heroes.[1]

So died Shan O'Neil, one of those champions of Irish nationality, who under varying features have repeated themselves in the history of that country with periodic regularity. At once a drunken ruffian and a keen and fiery patriot, the representative in his birth of the line of the ancient kings, the ideal in his character of all which Irishmen most admired, regardless in his actions of the laws of God and man, yet the devoted subject in his creed of the Holy Catholic Church; with an eye which could see far beyond the limits of his own island, and a tongue which could touch the most passionate chords of the Irish heart; the like of him has been seen many times in that island, and the like of him may be seen many times again, 'till the Ethiopian has changed his skin and the leopard his spots.'

Many of his letters remain, to the Queen, to Sussex, to Sidney, to Cecil, and to foreign princes; far-reaching, full of pleasant flattery and promises which cost him nothing; but showing true ability and insight. Sinner though he was, he too in his turn was sinned against; in the stained page of Irish misrule there is no second instance in which an English ruler stooped to treachery or to the infamy of attempted assassination; and it is not to be forgotten that Lord Sussex, who has left under his own hand the evidence of his own baseness, continued a trusted and favoured councillor of Elizabeth, while Sidney,

---

[1] Sir William Fitzwilliam to Cecil, June 10.—*Irish MSS. Rolls House.*

who fought Shan and conquered him in the open field, found only suspicion and hard words.

How just Sidney's calculations had been, how ably his plans were conceived, how bravely they were carried out, was proved by their entire success, notwithstanding the unforeseen and unlikely calamity at Londonderry. In one season Ireland was reduced for the first time to universal peace and submission. While the world was full of Sidney's praises Elizabeth persevered in writing letters to him which Cecil in his own name and the name of the Council was obliged to disclaim. But at last the Queen too became gradually gracious; she condescended to acknowledge that he had recovered Ireland for her Crown, and thanked him for his services.

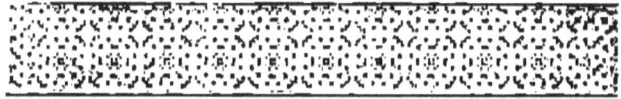

CHAPTER XII.

Chap XII

IT is the purpose of this chapter to trace the first movements of the struggle which transferred from Spain to England the sovereignty of the seas; the first beginnings of that proud power which, rising out of the heart of the people, has planted the saplings of the English race in every quarter of the globe, has covered the ocean with its merchant fleets, and flaunts its flag in easy supremacy among the nations of the earth.

In the English nature there were and are two antagonistic tendencies—visible alike in our laws, in our institutions, in our religion, in our families, in the thoughts and actions of our greatest men: a disposition on the one hand to live by rule and precedent, to distrust novelties, to hold the experience of the past as a surer guide than the keenest conclusions of logic, and to maintain with loving reverence the customs, the convictions, and traditions which have come down to us from other generations: on the other hand, a restless impetuous energy, inventing, expanding, pressing forward into the future, regarding what has been already achieved only as a step or landing-place leading upwards and onwards to higher conquests—a mode of thought which in the half-educated takes the form of a rash disdain of earlier ages, which in the best and wisest creates a sense that we

shall be unworthy of our ancestors if we do not eclipse
them in all that they touched, if we do not draw larger
circles round the compass of their knowledge, and
extend our power over nature, over the world, and over
ourselves.

In healthy ages as in healthy persons the two tendencies coexist, and produce that even progress, that strong vitality at once so vigorous and so composed, which is legible everywhere in the pages of English history. Under the accidental pressure of special causes one or other disposition has for a time become predominant, and intervals of torpor and inactivity have been followed by a burst of licence, when in one direction or another law and order have become powerless; when the people, shaking themselves free from custom, have hurried forward in the energy of their individual impulses, and new thoughts and new inclinations, like a rush of pent-up waters, have swept all before them.

Through the century and a half which intervened between the death of Edward the Third and the fall of Wolsey the English sea-going population with but few exceptions had moved in a groove, in which they lived and worked from day to day and year to year with unerring uniformity. The wine brigs made their annual voyages to Bordeaux and Cadiz; the hoys plied with such regularity as the winds allowed them between the Scheldt and the Thames; summer after summer the 'Iceland fleet' went north for the cod and ling which were the food of the winter fasting days; the boats of Yarmouth and Rye, Southampton, Poole, Brixham, Dartmouth, Plymouth, and Fowic fished the Channel. The people themselves, though hardy and industrious, and though as much at home upon the ocean as their Scandinavian forefathers or their descendants in modern

England, were yet contented to live in an unchanging round from which they neither attempted nor desired to extricate themselves. The number of fishermen who found employment remained stationary; the produce of their labour supported their families in such comforts as they considered necessary. The officials of the London companies ruled despotically in every English harbour; not a vessel cleared for a foreign port, not a smack went out for the herring season, without the official licence; and the sale of every bale of goods or every hundredweight of fish was carried on under the eyes of the authorities, and at prices fixed by Act of Parliament.

To men contented to be so employed and so rewarded, it was in vain that Columbus held out as a temptation the discovery of a New World; it was in vain that foreigners guided English ships across the Atlantic and opened out the road before their eyes. In 1497 John Cabot, the Venetian, with his son Sebastian—then a little boy—sailed from Bristol for 'the Islands of Cathay.' He struck the American continent at Nova Scotia, sailed up into the Greenland seas till he was blocked by the ice, then coasted back to Florida, and returned with the news of another continent waiting to be occupied. The English mariners turned away with indifference; their own soil and their own seas had been sufficient for the wants of their fathers; 'their fathers had more wit and wisdom than they;' and it was left to Spain, in that grand burst of energy which followed on the expulsion of the Moors and the union of the Crowns, to add a hemisphere to the globe and found empires in lands beyond the sunset.

Strange indeed was the contrast between the two races, and stranger still the interchange of character, as we look back over three hundred years. Before the sixteenth century had measured half its course the shadow of Spain already stretched beyond the Andes; from the mines of Peru and the custom-houses of Antwerp the golden rivers streamed into her imperial treasury; the crowns of Arragon and Castile, of Burgundy, Milan, Naples, and Sicily, clustered on the brow of her sovereigns; and the Spaniards themselves, before their national liberties were broken, were beyond comparison the noblest, grandest, and most enlightened people in the known world.

Greatness of Spain in the sixteenth century.

The spiritual earthquake shook Europe: the choice of the ways was offered to the nations; on the one side liberty, with the untried possibilities of anarchy and social dissolution; on the other the reinvigoration of the creeds and customs of ten centuries, in which Christendom had grown to its present stature.

The Reformation.

Fools and dreamers might follow their ignis fatuus till it led them to perdition: the wise Spaniard took his stand on the old ways. He too would have his reformation, with an inspired Santa Teresa for a prophetess, an army of ascetics to combat with prayer the legions of the evil one, a most holy Inquisition to put away the enemies of God with sword and dungeon, stake and fire. That was the Spaniard's choice, and his intellect shrivelled in his brain, and the sinews shrank in his self-bandaged limbs; and only now at last, with such imperfect deliverance as they have found in French civilisation and Voltairian philosophy, is the life-blood stealing again into the veins of the descendants of the conquerors of Granada.

Meanwhile a vast intellectual revolution, of which the religious reformation was rather a sign than a cause, was making its way in the English mind. The discovery of the form of the earth and of its place in the planetary system, was producing an effect on the imagination which long familiarity with the truth renders it hard for us now to realize. The very heaven itself had been rolled up like a scroll, laying bare the illimitable abyss of space; the solid frame of the earth had become a transparent ball, and in a hemisphere below their feet men saw the sunny Palm Isles and the golden glories of the tropic seas. Long impassive, long unable from the very toughness of their natures to apprehend these novel wonders, indifferent to them, even hating them as at first they hated the doctrines of Luther, the English opened their eyes at last. In the convulsions which rent England from the Papacy a thousand superstitions were blown away, a thousand new thoughts rushed in, bringing with them their train of new desires and new emotions; and when the fire was once kindled, the dry wood burnt fiercely in the wind.

First expansion of the English navy.

Having thrown down the gauntlet to the Pope, Henry the Eighth had to look to the defences of the kingdom; and knowing that his best security lay in the command of the 'broad ditch,' as he called it, which cut him off from Europe, he turned his mind with instant sagacity to the development of the navy. Long before indeed, when Anne Boleyn was a child, and Wolsey was in the zenith of his greatness, and Henry was the Pope's 'Defender of the Faith,' he had quickened his slumbering dockyards into life, studied naval architecture, built ships on new models, and cast unheard-of cannon. Giustiniani in 1518 found him practising at Southampton with his new brass artillery. The 'Great Harry' was the wonder of Northern Europe; and the fleet afterwards collected at Spithead, when D'Annebault brought his sixty thousand Frenchmen to the Isle of Wight, and the 'Mary Rose' went down under Henry's eyes, was the strongest, proudest, and best formed which had yet floated in English waters. The mariners and merchants had caught the impulse of the time. In 1530, when the divorce question was in its early stages, Mr. William Hawkins of Plymouth, 'a man for his wisdom, valour, experience, and skill of sea causes much esteemed and beloved of King Henry the Eighth,' 'armed out a tall and goodly ship,' sailed for the coast of Guinea, where he first trafficked with the negroes for gold dust and ivory, and then crossed the Atlantic to Brazil, 'where he behaved himself so wisely with the savage people' that 'the King of Brazil' came back with him to see the wonders of England, and was introduced to Henry at Whitehall. The year after Hawkins went back again, and 'the King' with him; the King on the passage home died of change of air, bad diet, and confinement; and there were fears for the Englishmen who had been left as hostages among the Indians. But they were satisfied that there had been no foul play; they welcomed Englishmen as cordially as they hated the Spaniards; and a trade was opened which was continued chiefly by the merchants of Southampton.

In 1549 Sebastian Cabot, who in his late manhood had returned to Bristol, was appointed by Edward the Sixth Grand Pilot of England; and as enterprise expanded with freedom and with the cracking up of superstition, the merchant adventurers who had started up in London on principles of free trade, and who were to the established guilds as the Protestants to the Catholic bishops, sent their ships up the Straits to the Levant, explored the Baltic, and had their factors at Novgorod. In 1552 Captain Windham of Norfolk followed William Hawkins to the coast of Guinea, and again in 1553, with Antonio Pintendo, he led a second expedition to the Bight of Benin and up the river to the court of the King. The same year the noble Sir Hugh Willoughby, enchanted like John Cabot with visions of 'the Islands of Cathay,' sailed in search of them into the Arctic circle, turned eastward into the frozen seas, and perished in the ice.

But neither the 'frost giants' of the north nor the deadly vapours of the African rivers could quell the spirit which had been at last aroused. Windham and Pintcado died of fever in the Benin waters; and of a hundred and forty mariners who sailed with them, forty only ever saw Ramhead and Plymouth Sound again; but the year following John Lok was tempted to the same shores by the ivory and gold dust; and he—first of Englishmen—discovering that the negroes 'were a people of beastly living, without God, law, religion, or commonwealth,' gave some of them the opportunity of a lift in creation, and carried off five as slaves.

It is noticeable that on their first appearance on the west coast of Africa, the English visitors were received by the natives with marked cordiality. The slave trade hitherto had been a monopoly of the Spaniards and Portuguese; it had been established in concert with the native chiefs, as a means of relieving the tribes of bad subjects, who would otherwise have been hanged. Thieves, murderers, and such like, were taken down to the depôts and sold to the West Indian traders.[1] But the theory, as was inevitable, soon ceased to correspond

---

[1] 'When they (the negroes of the Rio Grande) sit in council in the consultation-house, the king or captain sitteth in the midst and the elders upon the floor by him (for they give reverence to their elders), and the common sort sit round about them. There they sit to examine matters of theft, which if a man be taken with, to steal but a Portugal cloth from another, he is sold to the Portugal for a slave.'—HAKLUYT, vol. iii. p. 599.

with the practice; to be able-bodied and helpless became
a sufficient crime to justify deportation; the Portuguese
stations became institutions for an organized kidnapping; and when the English vessels appeared they were
welcomed by the smaller negro tribes as more harmless
specimens of the dangerous white race. But the theft of
the five men made them fear that the new comers were
no better than the rest; the alarm was spread all along
the coast, and Towrson, a London merchant, found his
voyage the next year made unprofitable through their
unwillingness to trade. The injury was so considerable,
and the value of the slaves in England so trifling, that
they were sent back; and the captain who took them
home was touched at the passionate joy with which the
poor creatures were welcomed.

Thus it was that the accession of Elizabeth found commerce leaving its old channels and stretching in a thousand
new directions. While the fishing trade was ruined by the
change of creed, a taste came in for luxuries undreamt of
in the simpler days which were passing away. Statesmen accustomed to rule the habits of private life with
sumptuary laws, and to measure the imports of the realm
by their own conceptions of the necessities of the people,
took alarm at the inroads upon established ways and
usages, and could see only 'a most lamentable spoil to
the realm, in the over quantity of unnecessary wares
brought into the port of London.'[1]

From India came perfumes, spices, rice, cotton, indigo,
and precious stones; from Persia and Turkey carpets,
velvets, satins, damasks, cloth of gold, and silk robes

---

[1] List of articles entered from abroad in the Port of London in the second year of Queen Elizabeth.—*Domestic MSS. Rolls House.* Note of commodities brought into the realm in the year 1564.—*MS. Ibid.*

'wrought in divers colours.'[1] Russia gave its ermines and sables, its wolf and bear skins, its tallow, flax, and hemp, its steel and iron, its ropes, cables, pitch, tar, masts for ships, and even deal boards. The New World sent over sugar, rare woods, gold, silver, and pearls; and these, with the pomegranates, lemons, and oranges, the silks and satins, the scented soaps and oils, and the fanciful variety of ornaments which was imported from the south of Europe, shocked the austere sense of the race of Englishmen who had been bred up in an age when heaven was of more importance than earthly pleasure. Fathers were filled with panic for the morals of their children, and statesmen trembled before the imminent ruin of the realm.[2]

To pay for these new introductions England had little to spare except its wool, its woollen cloths, and fustians. It was true that the demand which was opened out abroad for these things quickened production at home, and the English woollen manufacturers grew with the foreign trade; but Cecil found no comfort in a partial prosperity which withdrew labour from agriculture, and tended to bring back or to support the great grazing farms, which it was a passion with English statesmen to limit or break up: he was disturbed to observe that

---

[1] The Eastern trade was carried on either through Russia and Poland or else through Turkey and the Levant.

[2] It appears from the customs entries that the heaviest foreign trade was in canvas, linen, cloth, wood, oil, and wines. The total value of the wine entered at the Port of London alone, in the year 1559, was 64,000*l.*; the retail selling price being then on an average sevenpence a gallon. The iron trade with Sweden, Russia, and Spain was considerable; and strange to say, the English then depended on foreign manufacturers for their knives, their nails, their buttons, and even their pins and needles. Hops stand at a large figure, and so does sugar. Among miscellaneous articles are found dolls, tennis-balls, cabbages, turnips, tape and thread, glasses, hats, laces, marmalade, baskets, and rods for baskets.—*Domestic MSS. Rolls House.*

London was importing corn; and in a paper of notes on the phenomena which he saw around him, he added as a fact to be remarked and remembered, 'that those who depend upon the making of cloths are of worse condition to be quietly governed than the husbandmen.'[1] He dreaded, further, the supposed fatal effect of an export of gold, as the necessary consequence of an over-rapid growth of commerce; and he could see no remedy save to 'abridge' by Act of Parliament 'the use of such foreign commodities as were not necessary,' 'whereof the excess of silks was one,' 'excess of wine and spices another.' The great consumption of wine especially 'enriched France, whose power England ought not to increase;' 'the multiplying of taverns was an evident cause of disorder amongst the vulgar, who wasted there the fruits of their daily labour, and committed all evils which accompany drunkenness.' Anticipating the language of the modern Protectionist, Cecil thought it was an ill policy to encourage manufactures at the expense of tillage, when war might at any time throw the country back upon its own resources.

Another strange fact, at first sight utterly inexplicable, perplexed Elizabeth's ministers. Along with the increase of the foreign trade the 'port towns of the realm had been steadily decaying;' harbours, which at the beginning of the century 'had been well furnished with ships and mariners,' were left with but a few boats and barges. 'It needeth no proof,' wrote Cecil in 1566,[2] 'that more wine is drunk now than in former times; let men that keep households remember whether commonly they spend not more wines than their grand-

---

[1] Notes on the state of trade, October, 1564. In Cecil's hand.—*Domestic MSS. Rolls House.*

[2] Trade notes.—*Domestic MSS.* Eliz. vol. xli. *Rolls House.*

fathers, yea, percase, than themselves within twelve years; let all noblemen compare their household books with their ancestors', and it will be as manifest as can be that England spendeth more wines in one year than it did in antient times in four years.'

Other imports from foreign countries had increased almost in the same proportion; and yet the ports were sinking and the navy dwindling away.

There were several causes. Much of the common carrying trade was done by the French and Flemings; English enterprise was engaged in expeditions of a different kind, to which I shall presently refer. Another immediate and most important occasion was the cessation of the demand for fish.

'In old time,' (I again quote from Sir William Cecil,)[1] 'no flesh at all was eaten on fish days; even the King could not have licence; which was occasion of eating so much fish as now is eaten in flesh upon fish days.' In the recoil from the involuntary asceticism, beef and mutton reigned exclusively on all tables; and 'to detest fish' in all shapes and forms had become a 'note' of Protestantism. The Act of Edward,[2] prescribing 'due and godly abstinence as a means to virtue to subdue men's bodies to their soul and spirit,' had been laughed at and trampled on; and thus it was that the men who used to live 'by the trade and mystery of fishing' had to seek some other calling. Instead of the Iceland fleet of Englishmen which used to supply Normandy and Brittany as well as England, 'five hundred French vessels,[3] with from thirty to forty men in each of them,' went annually to Newfoundland, and even the home

---

[1] Notes upon an Act for the increase of the navy, 1563.—*Domestic MSS. Rolls House.*
[2] 2 & 3 Edward VI. cap. 19. [3] Sic.

fisheries fell equally into the hands of strangers. The Yarmouth waters were 'occupied by Flemings and Frenchmen,' 'the narrow seas by the French,' 'the western fishing for hake and pilchard by a great navy of French within kenning of the English shores.' 'The north parts of Ireland, and especially the Bann, within ten years, was in farm of the merchants of Chester; and now both the herring and salmon fishing was in the hands of the Scots;' 'the south part of Ireland was yearly fished by the Spaniards;' 'so that England was besieged round about with foreigners, and deprived of the substance of the sea fishing, being as it appeared by God's ordinance peculiarly given to the same; and more regard had how to entice merchants and mariners to a further trade to employ themselves to carry treasure into France, and from that to overburden the realm with wines, rather than to recover their antient natural possession of their own seas and at their own doors, in which kind of trade men were made meeter to abide storms and become common mariners than by sailing of ships to Rouen or Bourdeaulx.'[1]

So wrote the most farsighted of English statesmen; and knowing that the safety of England depended upon its fleet, and that 'to build ships without men to man them was to set armour upon stakes on the sea shore,'[2] of 'means to encourage mariners' he could see but three.

First, 'Merchandise;'

Second, 'Fishing;'

And thirdly, 'The exercise of piracy, which was detestable and could not last.'[3]

---

[1] Trade notes.—*Domestic MSS.* ELIZ. vol. xll. *Rolls House.*
[2] Ibid.
[3] Ibid.

It will be seen that 'piracy' could last; that buccaneering in some irregular combination with trade and religion, not only would be one among other means, but the very source and seed-vessel from which the naval power of England was about to rise.

But Cecil, who believed in God in a commonplace manner, and had been bred up in old-fashioned objections to 'the water-thieves,' could not persuade himself that good would come of them. Trade was already overgrown, and so far as he could judge was on the way to become entirely ruinous. The only remedies therefore which he could think of were, first, 'a navigation law,' laying foreign vessels under disabilities; and secondly, to force once more 'a politic ordinance on fish eating' through an unwilling and contemptuous House of Commons. In the Parliament of 1562-3 he brought in a Bill[1] to make the eating of fish on Fridays and Saturdays a misdemeanour, punishable by a fine of three pounds or three months' imprisonment; and, as if this was not enough, adding Wednesday as a subsidiary half-fish day, on which 'one dish of flesh might be allowed, provided there were served at the same table and at the same meal three full competent usual dishes of sea fish of sundry kinds, fresh or salt.'

'The House of Commons,' Cecil admitted, 'was very earnest against him;' he carried his measure only by arguing that if the Bill was passed it would be almost inoperative: 'labourers and poor householders could not observe it,' he said, 'and the rest by licence or without licence would do as they would;[2]' while to satisfy the

---

[1] 5 Eliz. cap 4, 5.
[2] Arguments in the House of Commons, February, 1562-3. Cecil's hand.— *Domestic MSS. Eliz.* vol. xxvii.

Puritans he was obliged to add the ludicrous provision that, 'because no person should misjudge the intent of the statute, which was politicly meant only for the increase of fishermen and mariners, and not for any superstition for choice of meats, whoever should preach or teach that eating of fish or forbearing of flesh was for the saving of the soul of man or for the service of God, should be punished as the spreader of false news.'[1]

How powerless such an Act must have been to stem the stream of popular tendency it is needless to say. Cecil however had at all events shown an honourable detestation of the wild piratical doings which were fast spreading; and if events proved too strong for him, he had delivered his own soul.

According to some persons the notion of property is a conventional creation of human society. The beast of prey refuses to the fat sweet juicy animal which cannot defend itself a right of property in its own flesh; among savages there is no right but of strength; in more advanced stages of civilization the true believer, Israelite or Mahometan, spoils the heathen without remorse, of lands, goods, liberty, and life. Ulysses, a high-bred gentleman, the friend of the gods, roves the seas with his mariners, sacks unguarded towns, and kills the unlucky owners who dare to defend themselves: Rob Roy lives on Lowland cattle-lifting without forfeiting romantic sympathy. The more advanced philosophers indeed maintain that property itself is the only true theft, and that the right of man 'to call anything his own' will disappear again as the wheel comes full round, in the light of a more finished cultivation.

---

[1] Clause to be added to the Fisheries Act, 5 ELIZ. cap. 4, 5. In Cecil's hand.—*Domestic MSS.* ELIZ. vol. xxvii.

'The ancient Greeks,' says Thucydides, 'even those not lowest in rank among them, when they first crossed the seas betook themselves to piracy. Falling on unprotected towns or villages they plundered them at their pleasure, and from this resource they derived their chief means of maintenance. The employment carried no disgrace with it, but rather glory and honour; and in the tales of our poets, when mariners touch anywhere, the common question is whether they are pirates—neither those who are thus addressed being ashamed of their calling, nor those who inquire meaning it as a reproach.'

In the dissolution of the ancient order of Europe, and the spiritual anarchy which had reduced religion to a quarrel of opinions, the primitive tendencies of human nature for a time asserted themselves, and the English gentlemen of the sixteenth century passed into a condition which, with many differences, yet had many analogies with that of the Grecian chiefs. With the restlessness of new thoughts, new hopes and prospects, with a constitutional enjoyment of enterprise and adventure, with a legitimate hatred of oppression, and a determination to revenge their countrymen who from day to day were tortured and murdered by the Inquisition, most of all perhaps, with a sense that it was the mission of a Protestant Englishman to spoil the Amalekites, in other words the gold ships from Panama, or the richly-laden Flemish traders, the merchants at the sea-ports, the gentlemen whose estates touched upon the creeks and rivers, and to whom the sea from childhood had been a natural home, fitted out their vessels under the name of traders, and sent them forth armed to the teeth with vague commissions, to take their chance of what the gods might send.

Already in this history I have had occasion to describe how in the unsettled state of England, young Catholics or Protestants, flying alternately from the despotism of Edward and Mary, had hung about the French harbours, or the creeks and bays which indent the Irish coast, where they had gathered about them rough wild crews who cared nothing for creeds, but formed a motley and mixed community living upon plunder. Emerging when England was at war into commissioned privateers, on the return of peace they were disavowed and censured; but they were secured from effective pursuit by the weakness of the Government, and by the certainty that at no distant time their services would again be required. The 'vain-glorious' Sir Thomas Seymour, finding too little scope at home for his soaring ambition, had dreamed of a pirate sovereignty among the labyrinths of Scilly. During the Marian persecution, Carews, Killigrews, Tremaynes, Strangways, Throgmortons, Horseys, Cobhams—men belonging to the best families in England, became roving chiefs. On Elizabeth's accession most of them came back to the service of the Crown: Strangways, the Red Rover of the Channel, was killed on a sandbank in the Seine, leading volunteers to the defence of Rouen; 'Ned Horsey,' the ruffling cavalier of Arundel's, who had sung the catch of evil omen to priests and prelates, became Sir Edward Horsey, Governor of the Isle of Wight; the younger Tremayne was killed doing service at Havre; and Henry Killigrew became a confidential servant of Elizabeth, and one of her most trusted agents. But the lawless spirit had spread like a contagion, especially through the western counties; and the vast numbers of fishermen whose calling had become profitless had to seek some new employment. Though their leaders had

CHAP XII left them, the pirate crews remained at their old trade; and gradually it came about that, as the modern gentleman keeps his yacht, so Elizabeth's loyal burghers, squires, or knights, whose inclination lay that way, kept their ambiguous cruisers, and levied war on their own account when the Government lagged behind its duty.

A fast Flemish trader has sailed from Antwerp to Cadiz; something happens to her on the way, and she never reaches her destination. At midnight carts and horses run down to the sea and over the sands at Lowestoft; the black hull and spars of a vessel are seen outside the breakers, dimly riding in the gloom; and a boat shoots through the surf loaded to the gunwale. The bales and tubs are swiftly shot into the carts; the horses drag back their loads, which before daybreak are safe in the cellars of some quiet manor-house; the boat sweeps off; the sails drop from the mysterious vessel's yards, and she glides away into the darkness to look for a fresh victim.[1]

Another rich trader has run the gauntlet of the Channel; she is off the Land's End, and believes her danger is past. A low black lugger slips out from among the rocks, runs alongside, and grapples her bulwarks; the buccaneers swarm upon her decks—English, French—'twenty wild kernes with long skeens and targets,' 'very desperate and unruly persons without any kind of mercy;'[2] the ship is sent to Kinsale or Berehaven, or to the bottom of the sea, as she sails fast or ill; the crew if they escape murder are thrust on shore at the nearest point of the coast of France.[3]

---

[1] Piracy at Lowestoft, April, 1561.—*Domestic MSS.* ELIZ. vol. xvi.

[2] Piracy at the Land's End.—*MSS. Ibid.* vol. xl.

[3] Illustrating these scenes, we find a petition to the Crown in 1563 from the mayor and bailiff of Cork for artillery and powder, 'their harbour being so beset with pirates, rovers, and other malefactors, whom they had no strength to beat off.'—*Irish MSS. Rolls House.*

The rovers were already venturing into lower latitudes in search of richer prizes. In May 1563 a galleon was waylaid and plundered at Cape St. Vincent by two small evil-looking vessels, recognized as English by the flights of arrows which drove the Spaniards from the decks;[1] while again the Spanish ships of war provoked a repetition of such outrages by their clumsy and awkward reprisals.

About the same time the Indian fleet coming into the Azores found five brigs from Bristol and Barnstaple loading with wood. The Englishmen were getting under weigh as the Spanish Admiral, Pedro Melendez, entered the harbour. They neglected to salute, and in half insolence carried the St. George's cross at the main. Melendez instantly gave chase. 'Down with your flags, ye English dogs! ye thieves and pirates!' he shouted, as he ran into the midst of them, firing right and left. The crews were thrown into irons; the ships and cargoes were taken into Cadiz and confiscated. The English ambassador appealed to Philip; the case was inquired into, and the innocent character of the vessels was perfectly established. But when the owners applied to have their property restored to them, Melendez had made it over to the Inquisition: the Inquisition had sold it; and the crews were at last glad to depart with their empty vessels, having suffered nothing worse than six months' imprisonment on bread and water in the gaol at Seville.[2]

The Inquisition had the management of the Spanish harbours, and the Englishman was to be considered for-

---

[1] 'The mariners say plainly that they were Englishmen, for that they shot so many arrows that they were not able to look out.'—*Hugh Tipton to Sir T. Chaloner*, June 1, 1563. *Spanish MSS. Rolls House.*

[2] *MS. Ibid.*

tunate who extricated himself alive from their hands. Though the English rovers were often common plunderers, yet there was a noble spirit at work at the bottom of their proceedings, which raised many of them into the wild ministers of a righteous revenge.

In August 1561 Thomas Nicholls, an English merchant resident in the Canaries, wrote thus to Elizabeth's ambassador at the court of Philip the Second:—

'Please your lordship to consider that I was taken prisoner by them of the Inquisition about twenty months past, and put into a little dark house about two paces long, laden with irons, without sight of sun or moon all the said time of twenty months.

'When I was arraigned they laid to my charge that I should say our mass to be as good or better than theirs; also that I went not to mass; also that I should say I had rather give my money to the poor than to buy bulls of Rome with it; with other paltry inventions. I answered, proving the allegations untrue with many witnesses. Then they put me again in prison for a certain space, and alleged anew against me six or seven articles against our Queen's grace, saying her Majesty was enemy to the faith, and her Grace was preached to be the antichrist, and that her Grace did maintain 'circumcision' and the Jewish law; and also a friar shaked off the dust of his shoes against her and the city of London, with such abominable and untrue sayings. Then stood I to the defence of the Queen's Majesty's cause, proving the infamies to be most untrue. Then was I put in Little Ease again till the end of twenty months finished, protesting mine innocent blood against the judge to be demanded before Christ.'[1]

---

[1] Spanish MSS. Rolls House.

In the year 1563 the following petition was addressed to the Lords of Elizabeth's Council:—

'In most lamentable wise sheweth unto your honours your humble orator Dorothy Seeley, of the city of Bristol, wife to Thomas Seeley, of the Queen's Majesty's guard, that where her said husband upon most vile, slanderous, spiteful, malicious, and most villanous words spoken against the Queen's Majesty's own person by a certain subject of the King of Spain—here not to be uttered— not being able to suffer the same did flee upon the same slanderous person and gave him a blow—so it is most honourable Lords, that hereupon my said husband, no other offence in respect of their religion then committed, was secretly accused to the Inquisition of the Holy House, and so committed to most vile prison, and there hath remained now three whole years in miserable state with cruel torments. For redress whereof, and for the Queen's Majesty's letter to the King of Spain, your said suppliant was heretofore a humble suitor to the Queen's Majesty at Bristol in that progress; and her Majesty then promised to write and see redress. But whether her Majesty did by letter or by ambassadors after sent into Spain deal with the said King for redress I know not; but certain it is that my said husband, with divers others the Queen's subjects, remain yet in prison, without hope, without your honours' help to be delivered.[1]

---

[1] In the list of captains who accompanied Drake to the West Indies in his famous voyage of 1585-6, I find the name of Thomas Seeley in command of the 'Minion.' Perhaps it was the same man. It is more likely however that the husband of Dorothy Seeley was one of the many hundred English sailors who rotted away in the dungeons of the Inquisition, or were burnt to please the rabble of Valladolid, and that Drake's companion was a son bred up by his mother in deadly hatred of the Spanish race.

CHAP XII
1563

In tender consideration whereof and of the daily common tormenting of the Queen's Majesty's subjects, it may please your honours to grant your favourable earnest letters herein to the King of Spain—or rather to permit and suffer the friends of such her Majesty's subjects as be there imprisoned, afflicted and tormented against all reason, to make out certain ships to the sea at their own proper charges, and to take such Inquisitors or other such Papistical subjects to the King of Spain as they can take by sea or land, and them to retain in prison in England with such torments and diet as her Majesty's subjects be kept with in Spain; and that it may please the Queen's Majesty withal, upon complaint to be made thereupon by the King of Spain or his subjects, to make such like answer as the King of Spain now maketh to her Majesty or her ambassador suing for her subjects imprisoned by force of the Inquisition.

'Or that it may please her Majesty to grant unto the Archbishop of Canterbury and other bishops, the like commission in all points for foreign Papists as the Inquisitors have in Spain for the Protestants, that thereby they may be forced not to trouble her subjects repairing to Spain, or that there may be hereupon an interchange of delivery of prisoners—of Protestants for the Papists; that the Queen's Majesty's subjects may be assured hereby that they have a Prince with such honourable Council that cannot nor will not longer endure such spoils and torments of her natural subjects, and such daily pitiful complaints hereabout; and that the Spaniard have not cause by the Queen's Majesty's long sufferance to triumph, or to think that this noble realm dare not seek the revenge of such importable wrongs daily done to this realm by daily spoiling her Majesty of the lives and goods of her good subjects; and consequently spoiling the realm of great force and strength. And your poor supplicant, with many others the Queen's Majesty's subjects, shall daily pray for your honours in health and felicity long to continue.'[1]

Either as the afterthought of the writer, or as the comment of some person in authority, the following singular note was appended to Dorothy Seeley's petition:—

'Long peace such as it is, by force of the Spanish Inquisition becometh to England more hurtful than open war. It is the secret and determined policy of Spain to destroy the English fleet and pilots, masters and sailors, by means of the Inquisition. The Spanish King pretends that he dare not offend the Holy House, while it is said in England, we may not proclaim war against Spain for the revenge of a few, forgetting that a good war might end all these mischiefs. Not long since the Spanish Inquisition executed sixty persons of St. Malo in France, notwithstanding entreaty to the King of Spain to stay them. Whereupon the Frenchmen armed and manned forth their pinnaces, and lay for the Spaniards, and took a hundred and beheaded them, sending the Spanish ships to the shore with the heads, leaving in each ship but one only man to render the cause of revenge; since which time the Spanish Inquisition has never meddled with those of St. Malo.'[2]

The theology of English sailors was not usually of a very rigid character. Out of seventy-one of Sir John Hawkins's men who were taken by the Spaniards in 1567, three only held out against rack and scourge with sufficient firmness to earn martyrdom; yet on the 10th

[1] Petition of Dorothy Seeley, 1563. *Spanish MSS. Rolls House.*
[2] Ibid.

of January 1563 Sir William Cecil stated that in the one year then last past, twenty-six English subjects had been burnt to death in different parts of Spain.[1]

But the stake was but one of many forms of judicial murder. The following story indicates with some detail both the careless audacity of the English and the treatment to which they were exposed:—During the war between England and France, on the 15th of November 1563, a fleet of eight English merchantmen, homeward bound from the Levant, were lying in the harbour of Gibraltar, when a French privateer full of men and heavily armed, came in and anchored within speaking distance of them. The sailors on both sides were amusing themselves with exchanging the usual discourtesies in word and gesture, when the vicar of the Holy Office, with a boatload of priests came off to the Frenchman; and whether it was that the presence of their natural foe excited the English, or that they did not know what those black figures were, and intended merely to make a prize of an enemy's vessel, three or four of the ships slipped their cables, opened fire, and attempted to run the Frenchman down.

The Spaniards, indignant at the breach of the peace of the harbour, and the insult to the Inquisition, began to fire from the castle; the holy men fled terrified; a party of English who were on shore were arrested, and the alcalde sent a body of harbour police to arrest others who were hanging in their boats about the French vessel. The police on coming up were received with a shower of arrows; the officer in command was wounded; and they were carried off as prisoners to the English

---

[1] At the beginning of 1563, foreigners residing in London were forbidden to hear mass in their private houses. The Bishop of Aquila remonstrated, and Cecil answered, 'Quo en España han quemado este año veinte y seis Ingleses.—*De Quadra to Philip*, January, 1563. MS. Simancas.

ships, where they were detained till their comrades on shore were restored.

The next morning a second effort to seize or sink the Frenchman was prevented by the guns of the fortress. The English had given up the game and were sailing out of the bay, when Alvarez de Vasar happened to come round with a strong force from Cadiz. The ships, after a fruitless attempt at flight, were seized and confiscated; the ensigns were torn down and trailed reversed over the Spanish admiral's stern; and the captains and men, two hundred and forty in all, were condemned as galley slaves.[1] They forwarded a memorial to Chaloner at Madrid, telling their own story, and praying him to intercede for them.

'Ye served some angry saint,' Chaloner wrote in answer, 'so unadvisedly to take such an enterprise in hand in these parts where our nation findeth so short courtesy; and ye played the part of wavering inconstant heads, having once begun a matter to suffer yourselves so vilely to be taken, which if ye had held together I think ye needed not. Most of all I accuse the wonted fault of all merchants of our nation who go about every man to shift for himself, and care not for their fellows so they make sure work for themselves.'[2]

'Although the treatment of our people,' the ambassador wrote in relating the matter to Elizabeth, 'has been most cruel and rigorous, yet I must say that a great part thereof has proceeded of the counterdealing of our adventurers, or rather pirates, during these wars, having spoiled and misruled the King's subjects very

---

[1] Hugh Tipton to Sir Thomas Chaloner, December 8, 1563.—*Spanish MSS.*
[2] Sir T. Chaloner to the merchants and mariners taken at Gibraltar, March 3, 1564.—*Spanish MSS. Rolls House.*

much. These men would not have remained by the heels had not other English adventurers by force broken the jurisdiction of this King's ports, and taken Frenchmen out of their havens; so at last when they chanced to catch any such in their gripe, they determined to make them an example for the rest.'[1]

An example they did make of them, or rather of their own wilful cruelty. England and Spain were nominally at peace; and the fault of the eight ships in those lawless times had a thousand precedents to bespeak lenient punishment. The ambassador interceded, entreated, explained; Philip and Alva listened with grave courtesy; and a commission was appointed to examine into the circumstances at Gibraltar. But the investigation was studiously deliberate while the treatment of the prisoners was as studiously cruel. Nine months after the capture there were but eighty survivors out of the two hundred and forty; the rest had died of cold, hunger, and hard labour. Then at last, after humiliating apologies from Chaloner, with excuses founded 'on the barbarous nature of sailors, occasioned by their lives on so barbarous an element as the sea,' the famished wretches that were left alive were allowed to return to England.[2]

The King of Spain had been already warned of the danger of provoking the spirit of English sailors. 'Our mariners,' said Sir Thomas Chamberlain to him, on his first return from the Netherlands, 'have no want of stomach to remember a wrong offered to them, which if

---

[1] Chaloner to the Queen, June 18, 1564.—*Spanish MSS. Rolls House*.

[2] 'Se debe considerar la poca discrecion que ordinariamente suelen tener hombres marineros, los quales por la mas parte platicando con un elemento tan barbaro como es la Mar, suelen á ser tan bien de costumbres barbaras y inquietos, no guardando aquellos respetos que suelen tener otros hombres mas politicos.'—*Chaloner to Philip, Oct. 1564.—MS. Ibid.*

they shall hereafter seek to revenge with recompensing one wrong with another when the matter should least be thought of, the Queen of England must be held excused;'[1] As the scene at Gibraltar was but one of many like it; as the cruel treatment of the crews was but a specimen of the manner in which the Holy Office thought proper to deal with Englishmen in every port in Spain, so is the following illustration of Chamberlain's warning to Philip but a specimen also of the deadly hate which was growing between the rivals for the sovereignty of the ocean.

The sons of Lord Cobham of Cowling Castle, who had first distinguished themselves in Wyatt's rebellion, had grown up after the type of their boyhood, irregular lawless Protestants; and one of them, Thomas Cobham, was at this time roving the seas, half pirate, half knight-errant of the Reformation, doing battle on his own account with the enemies of the truth, wherever the service to God was likely to be repaid with plunder. He was one of a thousand whom Elizabeth was forced for decency's sake to condemn and disclaim in proclamations, and whom she was as powerless as she was probably unwilling to interfere with in practice. What Cobham was, and what his kind were, may be seen in the story about to be told.

A Spanish ship was freighted in Flanders for Bilbao; the cargo was valued at 80,000 ducats, and there were on board also forty prisoners condemned, as the Spanish accounts say, 'for heavy offences worthy of chastisement,'[2] who were going to Spain to serve in the galleys. Young Cobham, cruising in the Channel, caught sight of the vessel, chased her down into the Bay of Biscay, fired

---

[1] Chamberlain to Elizabeth, November 15, 1561.—*Spanish MSS. Rolls House.*

[2] 'Por graves delitos dignos de punicion y castigo.'

into her, killed her captain's brother and a number of men, and then boarding when all resistance had ceased, sewed up the captain himself and the survivors of the crew in their own sails and flung them overboard. The fate of the prisoners is not related; it seems they perished with the rest. The ship was scuttled; and Cobham made off with booty, which the English themselves admitted to be worth 50,000 ducats, to his pirate's nest in the south of Ireland. Eighteen drowned bodies, with the mainsail for their winding-sheet, were washed up upon the Spanish shores—'cruelty without example, of which but to hear was enough to break the heart.'[1]

English hearts in like manner had been broken with the news of brothers, sons, or husbands wasting to skeletons in the Cadiz dungeons, or burning to ashes in the Plaza of Valladolid. But this fierce deed of young Cobham was no dream of Spanish slander: the English factor at Bilbao was obliged to reply to Chaloner's eager inquiries that the story in its essential features was true, and he added another instance of English audacity. A Spanish vessel had been cut out of the harbour at Santander by an Anglo-Irish pirate, and carried off to sea. The captain, more merciful than Cobham, saved the crew alive, kept them prisoners, and was driven into another Spanish port for shelter, having them at the time confined under his hatches. They were discovered; the pirates were seized and died—it is needless to inquire how; but so it came about that 'what with losing their goods, and divers slain having no war, and again for

---

[1] 'Tomáron á todos los que dentro iban, y los cosiéron en las velas, y los echáron á la mar, y en una de las velas se habian hallado 18 hombres abogados en la costa de España. Cruelidad nunca vista, y que en solo oyrlo quiebra el corazon.'—*Lovis Romano to Cardinal Granvelle, February 20, 1564. MS. Simancas.*

religion, the Spaniards thought that for the hurt they could do to an Englishman they got heaven by it.'[1]

Cobham was tried for piracy the next year at the indignant requisition of Spain. He refused to plead to his indictment, and the dreadful sentence was passed upon him of the *peine forte et dure*.[2] His relations, de Silva said, strained their influence to prevent it from being carried into effect; and it seems that either they succeeded or that Cobham himself yielded to the terror, and consented to answer. At all events he escaped the death which he deserved, and was soon again abroad upon the seas.

When the Governments of Spain and England were tried alternately by outrages such as these, the chief matter of surprise is that peace should have been preserved so long. The instincts of the two nations outran the action of their sovereigns; and while Elizabeth was trusting to the traditions of the House of Burgundy, and Philip was expecting vainly that danger would compel Elizabeth to change her policy, their subjects encountered each other in every sea where the rival flags were floating, with the passions of instinctive hate. The impulse given to the English privateers on the occupation of

---

[1] Cureton to Chaloner, March 14, 1564.—*Spanish MSS. Rolls House.*

[2] 'The English judgment of penance for standing mute was as follows: that the prisoner be remanded to the prison from whence he came and put into a low dark chamber, and there be laid on his back on the bare floor naked; that there be placed upon his body as great a weight of iron as he could bear, and more; that he have no sustenance save only on the first day three morsels of the worst bread, and on the second day three draughts of standing water that should be nearest to the prison door; and in this situation this should be alternately his daily diet till he died, or, as anciently the judgement ran, till he answered.'—BLACKSTONE's *Commentaries*, book iv. chap. 25.

CHAP XII.
1563

Letters of marque to prey on Papists.

Havre and the breaking out of the war with France, almost brought matters to a crisis.

While Philip was openly assisting the Duke of Guise, and Condé was still the ally of England, letters of marque were issued in the joint names of the Huguenot Prince and the Earl of Warwick. Vessels manned by mixed crews of French and English, were sent out to prey on Spaniards, Portuguese, and all other 'Papists' with whom they might encounter; and although their commissions were not formally recognized by Elizabeth, yet the officers of the English ports were ordered to supply them privately with food, arms, stores, and anything which the service might require. In December 1562, one of these irregular rovers, commanded by Jacques le Clerc, called by the Spaniards Pié de Palo,[1] sailed out of Havre, captured a Portuguese vessel worth 40,000 ducats, then a Biscayan laden with wool and iron, and afterwards chased another Spanish ship into Falmouth, where they fired into her and drove her ashore. The captain of the Spaniard appealed for protection to the Governor of Pendennis; the Governor replied that the privateer was properly commissioned, and that without special orders from the Queen he could not interfere:[2]

---

[1] Timber leg.

[2] 'Le respondió que si la Reyna no se lo mandaba, que el no le podia hacer, por cuanto el Pié de Palo le habia monstrado un patente firmado del Principe de Condé y del Conde de Warwick General de los Ingleses en Havre de Grace, la cual contenia una comission de poder prender todos los navios y gente de Españoles, Portogueses, Bretones, y otros cuales quiera Papistas que encontrase, encargando á los ministros y oficiales de la Reyna de Inglaterra le favoreciesen ayudasen y vitualleen para su armada de todo lo necesario,' &c.—*Relacion de Nicolas de Landa Verde, January 20, 1563. MS. Simancas.* Landa Verde was the English captain.

A letter of De Quadra to Philip at the beginning of the month states that similar commissions were generally issued.—*De Quadra to Philip, January 10. MS. Ibid.*

Pié de Pâlo took possession of him as a prize, and then lying close under the shelter of Pendennis waited for further good fortune. Being midwinter, and the weather being as usual unsettled, five Portuguese ships a few days later were driven in for shelter. Finding the neighbourhood into which they had fallen, they attempted to escape to sea again; but Pié de Pâlo dashed after them, and two out of the five he clutched and brought back as prizes.[1]

Elizabeth herself at the same time, catching at the readiest and cheapest means to 'annoy the French,' had let loose the English privateers under the usual licence from the Crown. Their commissions of course empowered them only to make war upon the acknowledged enemy; but they were not particular. Captain Sorrey, Pié de Pâlo's consort, was blockading a fleet of rich Biscayans in Plymouth, and the Crown privateers were unwilling to be restricted to less lucrative game. If Sir Thomas Chaloner was rightly informed four hundred of these lawless adventurers were sweeping the Channel in the summer of 1563.[2] In a few months they had taken six or seven hundred French prizes; but the time-honoured dispute on the nature of munitions of war, and the liability of neutral ships engaged in an enemy's carrying trade, made an excuse for seizing Flemings and Spaniards; and the scenes which followed in the Channel

---

[1] 'Dice que saliendo del puerto de Falmouth cinco navios Portugueses juntos vió que salió Pié de Pâlo tras ellos, y tornó dos naos de las dichas cinco, y las otras se salvaron á la vela; loqual todo dice en cargo de su conciencia ser verdad.'—*Relacion de Nicolas de Landa Verde. MS. Ibid.*

[2] Of all historical statements those involving numbers must be received with greatest caution. Chaloner wrote from the official statement sent in at Madrid.

Chaloner to the Queen, June 11, 1564.—*Spanish MSS. Rolls House.*

and out of it were such as it would be hard to credit, were they not in large measure confessed and regretted in the English State Papers.

Plunder of Spanish subjects.

A list, with notes in Cecil's hand, of 'depredations committed at sea during the war on the subjects of Philip,' contains sixty-one cases of piracy,[1] of which the following are illustrative examples:—

The 'Maria,' from St. Sebastian, with a cargo of saffron, valued at 4000 ducats, was taken by Captain Sorrey and brought in as a prize to the Isle of Wight.

The 'Crow,' from Zealand, was robbed of twenty-three last of herring by boats from Foy and Plymouth.

The 'Flying Spirit,' from Andalusia, with a rich cargo of cochineal, was plundered by Martin Frobisher.

The 'Tiger,' from Andalusia to Antwerp, with cochineal, silk, wool, gold, silver, pearls, and precious stones, was taken by Captain Corbet and Captain Hewet.

Such a stormy petrel as Stukely of course was busy at such a time. Stukely, in June 1563, took a Zealand ship called the 'Holy Trinity,' with 3,000*l*. worth of linen and tapestry; and then joining a small fleet of west countrymen, fourteen sail in all, he lay off Ushant, watching professedly for the wine fleet from Bordeaux, but picking up gratefully whatever the gods might send. No less a person than the Mayor of Dover himself was the owner of one of these seahawks.[2] Wretched Spaniards flying from their talons were dashed upon the rocks and perished. If a Fleming was caught by mistake, it was an easy thing with an end of loose rope and

---

[1] *Flanders MSS. Rolls House.* The Paper is dated May 27, 1565.
[2] Ibid.

a tourniquet to squeeze out a confession that made him a lawful prize.

The baser order of marauders were not slow to imitate their betters, and the Thames was no safer than the Channel. Much of the richest merchandise which reached London was imported in coasters from Antwerp, and the water thieves which hung about the mouth of the river made a handsome harvest.

'Bartholomew Panselfen, mariner of Antwerp, age twenty-four years or thereabouts,[1] deposed and declared on oath that about Christmas last past he was plying to London in company with other vessels, and that coming to Margate Roads he found there eight or nine English merchant ships lying at anchor. The said Bartholomew passing them by upon his course, the sailors in the said ships did cry out to him—"Heave to, heave to, filz du putain Flameng!"—of the which when he took no heed but pursued his way they did shoot their cannon at him, cutting the rigging and striking the hull of deponent's vessel; and moreover did fire upon him flights of innumerable arrows. He nevertheless keeping all sail, they could not overtake him, and for that time he escaped from pillage.'

'Being asked whether at any other time he had been so attacked, the said Bartholomew declared that about a twelvemonth passed, certain Englishmen boarded his ship, and took from him two pieces of artillery, with powder, shot, the money which his passengers had on their persons, with their bread, cheese, and meat.'

---

[1] This and the following depositions are taken from a report of a commission appointed in 1565 by the Regent of the Low Countries, to inquire into these outrages.—*Flanders MSS. Rolls House.*

'Adrian Peterson, mariner of Antwerp, deposed that being on his way to London in the January of that year, an hour after sunset, he was boarded off Margate by eight or ten armed men in masks whom by their voices he knew to be Englishmen. He himself fled from them into the hold, where he lay concealed; but they beat his servant, and took from the ship more than two hundred pounds' worth of goods.'

'Bartholomew Cornelius deposed that for the whole year past he has never made the voyage to England without suffering some outrage, being robbed of victuals, shirt, coat, and all the goods he has had on board. Even in the river at Greenwich, under the very windows of the palace, and the very eyes of the Queen, he had been fired into four or five times, and his sails shot through.'

Among the worst sufferers from these manner piracies were the poor Dutch fishermen. The English who had ceased to fish for themselves, resented the intrusion of foreigners into their home waters. They robbed their boats of the fish which they had taken; they took away their sails, masts and cordage, nets, lines, food, beds, cushions, money; they even stripped the men themselves of their clothes, and left them naked and destitute on the water. As one specimen of a class of outrages which were frightfully numerous—

'Francis Bertram, of Dunkirk, said and deposed that he had been herring fishing in the north of the Channel. He had had great success and was going home, when an English vessel came down upon him, with forty armed men—took from him ten last of herrings, stripped his boat bare—to the very ropes and anchor—and sailed away, leaving him to perish of hunger. The hull of the vessel when he was attacked by her was painted white

and yellow; three days later she was seen elsewhere
painted black, and the crew with blacked faces after the
manner of Ethiopians.'¹

Nor were these depredations confined to privateers or
pirates. On the 19th of December 1563, Margaret of
Parma complained to Elizabeth of the daily thefts and
robberies of the subjects of the King of Spain committed
on the coast of England—not only by persons unknown,
but by ships belonging to the Queen's own navy.

'One of your subjects named Thomas Cotton,' said the
Regent, 'commanding your ship the "Phœnix," lately
seized a vessel off Boulogne belonging to a merchant of
Antwerp, and sent her with a foreign crew into England.
The "Phœnix" came afterwards into Flushing, and the
owner of the vessel sent a water-bailiff to arrest Captain
Cotton, and make him restore his capture or else pay for
the injury. Captain Cotton however refused to submit
to our laws. He spoke insolently of the King's Majesty
our Sovereign, resisted the arrest, and sailed away in
contempt. Madam, these insolences, these spoils and
larcenies of the King's subjects cannot continue thus
without redress. It is provided in the treaties of intercourse between us, that the perpetrators of violent acts
shall be arrested and kept in ward till they have made
satisfaction, and shall be punished according to their
demerits. I beseech you, Madam, to take order in these
matters, and inflict some signal chastisement as an
example to all other evil doers. I require that the losses
of our merchants be made good—being as they are

---

¹ Petition of the Burgomasters of Newport and Dunkirk, September 24, 1565.—*Flanders MSS. Rolls House.*

molested and troubled on so many sides by the subjects of your Majesty. These, Madam, are things that can no longer be endured.'[1]

Had Philip been satisfied with the state of affairs in France he would probably have now made common cause with Catherine de Medici, declared war against Elizabeth, and proclaimed Mary Stuart Queen of England. But the break up of the Catholic league on the death of the Duke of Guise, the return of Montmorency to power, and his reconciliation with Condé, had reinstated in Catherine's cabinet the old French party which was most jealous of Spain, and was most disposed to temporize with the Protestants. Philip felt his early fears revive that Mary Stuart's allegiance to France might prove stronger than her gratitude to himself, and he hesitated to take a step which might cripple his predominance in Europe. He was uneasy at the increasing disaffection of the United Provinces, which a war with England would inevitably aggravate; and though again and again on the verge of a rupture with his sister-in-law, he drew back at the last moment, feeling 'that the apple was not ripe.'[2] Determined however to check the audacity of the privateers, and those darker cruelties of Cobham and his friends, he issued a sudden order in January 1564 for the arrest of every English ship in the Spanish harbours, with their crews and owners. Thirty large vessels were seized; a thousand sailors and merchants were locked up in Spanish prisons, and English traders were excluded by a general order from the ports of the Low Countries.

---

[1] Margaret of Parma to Elizabeth, December 19, 1563.—*Flanders MSS. Rolls House.*
[2] Chaloner to Elizabeth, January 22, 1564.—*Spanish MSS. Ibid.*

An estimate was made of the collective damage inflicted by the English cruisers, and a bill was presented to Sir Thomas Chaloner for a million and a half of ducats, for which the imprisoned crews would be held as securities.[1]

'Long ago I foretold this,' wrote Chaloner, 'but I was regarded as a Cassandra. For the present I travail chiefly that our men may be in courteous prison, a great number of whom shall else die of cold and hunger.'

With the French war still upon her hands, Elizabeth was obliged to endure the affront and durst not retaliate. With the Catholic party so powerful, a war with Spain and the contingencies which might arise from it, was too formidable to be encountered. She wrote humbly to Philip entreating that the innocent should not be made to suffer for the guilty; the wrong which she admitted might have been done she attributed to the confusion of the times; she protested that she had herself given neither sanction nor encouragement to her subjects' lawless doings; she would do her utmost to suppress the pirates; and if her merchants and sailors were set at liberty she would listen to any proposal which Philip might be pleased to make.[2]

As an earnest of the good intentions of the Government,

---

[1] Chaloner to Elizabeth, Jan. 20.—*Spanish MSS. Rolls House.*

[2] Elizabeth to Philip, March 17.—*MS. Ibid.*
Her subjects themselves were not so submissive. 'One insolence,' wrote Chaloner, 'sundry of the council here have much complained of to me: that in Gallicia, upon occasion of certain of our merchants detained by the corregidor of a port town there, the same town was shot at with artillery out of the English ships, and four or five of the townsmen slain and hurt. This they term "combatir una tierra del Rey; y, Que es esto? y, Como se puede sufrir?" Sure our men have been very outrageous. It was full time the piece took up, or else I ween they would yet have spoken louder.'— *Chaloner to Elizabeth, June 18, MS. Ibid.*

the English Prize Courts made large awards of restitution; and it was proposed that a joint commission should sit at Bruges to examine the items of the Spanish claim.

But Elizabeth saw that she must lose no time in settling her differences with France. Peace was hastily concluded; she amused Catherine and frightened Philip with the possibility of her accepting the hand of Charles the Ninth; and by the beginning of the summer which followed the close of the war, she was able to take a bolder tone. The trade with England was of vital moment to the Low Countries. The inhibition which the Regent had issued against English vessels had given the carrying trade to the Flemings; and the ships in Spain continuing unreleased, Elizabeth on her part at the beginning of May retaliated upon the Duchess of Parma by excluding Flemings from the English ports. The intercourse between the two countries was thus at an end. The Queen bade Chaloner say to Philip, that 'whatever injury might have been done to subjects of Spain, she had more to complain of than he; Spanish ships might have been robbed, but the offenders were but private persons; the banner of England had been trailed in the dirt by public officers of Castile, as if it had been taken in battle from the Turks; English subjects had been seized, imprisoned, flogged, tortured, famished, murdered, and buried like dogs in dungheaps; she too as well as he would bear these wrongs no longer.'[1]

To the letter of Margaret of Parma she replied with equal haughtiness.

'In the month of January last,' she wrote, 'we re-

---

[1] Memorial presented by Sir T. Chaloner to Philip II., June 4, 1564.—*Spanish MSS. Rolls House.*

ceived intelligence from our ambassador resident in Spain that all manner of our subjects there, with their ships and goods were laid under arrest, and that our subjects themselves had been used in such cruel sort by vile imprisonment, torture, and famine, as more extremity could not be showed to the greatest criminal. Nor were there any pretences alleged for this violence, save only that a ship on the way to that country from Flanders was robbed by certain English vessels of war—which indeed might be true, as hitherto we know not any certainty thereof; and yet no cause to make such a general arrest and imprisonment of so great a multitude of people; whereof none were nor could be charged with any evil fact, but were proved to have come thither only for merchandise. Wherefore being troubled with the miserable complaints of the wives, children, and friends of our subjects oppressed in Spain, and seeing on the one part you will neither by means of your edict permit our subjects to come thither with their cloths, nor to bring any commodity from thence, and on the other none of our subjects may come into any port of Spain but they are taken, imprisoned, and put in danger of death; we appeal to the judgment of any indifferent person, what we can less do but, until some redress made for these intolerable griefs, to prohibit that there be no such free resort of merchandise from thence, to the enriching only of a few merchants of those countries.'[1]

The English prisoners in Spain had suffered frightfully. Out of the two hundred and forty taken at Gibraltar only eighty, as has been already said, were alive at the end of nine months. The crew of the 'Mary Holway,'

---

[1] Elizabeth to Margaret of Parma, May 7, 1564.—*Flanders MSS. Rolls House*.

of Plymouth, numbered fifty-two when they went in January into the Castle of St. Sebastian. By the middle of May twenty-four were dead of ill-usage, and the remaining twenty-eight 'were like to die.'[1] Some notion may be formed from these two instances of the loss of life which had followed on the general arrest. Quite evidently the Spanish and English people wanted but a word from their sovereigns to fly like bull-dogs at each others' throats. But the peace with France and the eclipse of the ultra-Catholic faction at the French court had decided Philip that the time was not yet come; he listened to Chaloner's expostulations with returning moderation;[2] and Chaloner—though against his own interest, for his residence in Spain was a martyrdom to him, and a war would have restored him to England—advised Elizabeth to postpone her own resentment. The injuries after all had been as great on one side as the other; she would find every just complaint satisfied at last, 'but not so much by the lion as by the fox;' and 'for the avoiding of trouble in England' he recommended her to allow 'the traffic with the Low Countries to be redintegrate.'[3] He thought that there were

---

[1] The Lords of the English Council to Chaloner, June 1.—*Spanish MSS. Rolls House.*

[2] Chaloner's description of Philip is interesting, and agrees well with Titian's portraits.

'The King,' he said, 'heard us very quietly, making few and short but calm answers; which his nature to them that know it is not to be marvelled at, seeing to all ambassadors he useth the like; for as he hath great patience to hear at length and note what is said, receiving quietly what memorials or papers are presented to him, so hardly, for as much as I have hitherto perceived, shall a stranger to his countenance or words gather any great alteration of mind either to anger or rejoicement, but after the fashion of a certain still flood. Nevertheless both his looks and words unto me gave show of a certain manner of extraordinary contentation.'—*Chaloner to Elizabeth, June 11. MS. Ibid.*

[3] Ibid. Chaloner's lamentations over his residence at Madrid were piteous. 'Spain! rather pain,' he wrote to Sir John Mason in 1562.

symptoms of a revival of the old quarrels between France and Spain, when she might look for Philip's help to recover Calais; and by the autumn concessions were made on both sides. De Silva was sent to England to heal all wounds; the English ships and the surviving

CHAP XII
1564
Concessions on both sides.

Roads, food, lodging, about Madrid itself were scarcely tolerable, and elsewhere 'were past bearing.' The cost of living was four times greater than in England; and the Duke of Alva was the only person in whom he found 'wisdom and courteous usage.'

'Think with yourself,' he wrote in June, 1564, in the midst of his trouble, 'whether this alone is not to a free mind an importable burden; two years and three-quarters to bear my cross in Spain; a place and nation misliked of all others save themselves; driven here not only to forbear, but patiently like an ass to lay down mine ears at things of too, too much indignity.'

If his health failed at last, between the climate, the garlic diet, and his public worries.

'Surely I have had great wrong,' he said in a letter to Sir Ambrose Cave; 'but it is the old wont of our court never to think upon the training of a new servant till the old be worn to the stump. It is each man's part to serve their prince; but there is a just distributing, if subjects durst plead with kings. I have not much more to hope, having twenty years served four kings, now further from wealth or that staff of age which youth doth travail for, than I was eighteen years agone. Methinks I became a retrograde crab, and yet would gladly be at home with that that yet resteth, to pay my debts and live the rest of my life perhaps contentedly enough.'

Of the danger of trusting to Spanish physicians he had frightful evidence. In August this same year, 1564, Philip's Queen (Elizabeth of France) miscarried of twins. Fever followed. They bled her in both arms; they bled her in both feet; and when spasms and paroxysms came on they cupped her, and then gave her up and left her to die. 'She was houselled, and the King to comfort her was houselled also for company;' and at the moment when Chaloner was writing to England 'she was lying abandoned of her physicians to the mercy of God. The palace gates were shut; the lamentations in the court both of men and women very tender and piteous; the chapel was filled with noblemen all praying on their knees for her; and great and unfeigned moans on all parts.'

Nature eventually proved too strong even for Spanish doctors. She rallied; and they flew at her once more. 'At last by means of a strong purgative of agaricum that made her have twenty-two stools, given at a venture in so desperate a case to purge those gross humours, she was ever since amended.'—*Letter of Sir Thomas Chaloner. Spanish MSS. Rolls House.*

Chaloner himself was less fortunate. He was recalled after long entreaty, in 1565; but he died a few weeks after he landed in England.

sailors were released from the clutch of the Inquisition. After a correspondence between Cecil and Egmont the Flanders trade was reopened, and commissioners were appointed to sit at Bruges to hear all complaints and to settle terms of restitution. The letters of marque expired with the war, and 'the adventurers' had to look elsewhere to find a theatre for their exploits: some few continued to lurk in the western rivers; the more desperate, inoculated with a taste for lawless life, hung about their old haunts in the Irish creeks—whither Stukely, as was seen in the last chapter, after fitting out an expedition to Florida, found it more attractive to betake himself. Elizabeth consented to open her eyes to proceedings which were bringing a scandal upon her Government, and took measures at last, though of a feeble kind, to root out these pirates' nests.

On the 29th of September 1564 she wrote to Sir Peter Carew at Dartmouth, that 'whereas the coasts of Devonshire and Cornwall, the Land's End, and the Irish seas were by report much haunted with pirates and rovers,' she desired him to fit out an expedition with speed and secrecy to clear the seas of them.[1] She gave him discretionary powers to act in any way that he might think good; 'she would allow anything which he might put in execution,' and she 'would victual his ships out of the public stores.' Characteristically however she would give him no money; Sir Peter and his men might pay themselves out of whatever booty they could take; and the temptation of plunder would perhaps rouse them into an energy which might not otherwise be excessively vigorous.

---

[1] Elizabeth to Sir Peter Carew, September 29, 1564.—*Domestic MSS. Eliz.* vol. xxxiv.

Carew on these terms undertook the service; he armed three vessels, collected something under three hundred men from among the disbanded privateers, and in the spring of 1565 sent them out upon their cruise.

The result may be told in the words of his own report to the Council.

'Running along the west coast of England and finding nothing there meet for their purpose they sailed over into Ireland, where they found a hulk of Stukely's in Cork Haven, which they brought away, himself being before they arrived on shore with the Lord Barrymore, having left certain of his men in the hulk to guard her, who being shot unto rowed unto the shore in their longboat. From thence they went to Berehaven, where before their coming Haydon, Lysingham and Corbet, with other pirates their accomplices had withdrawn themselves into a castle belonging to O'Sullivan Bere, and also their vessels near the same, planting their ordnance on the shore and also in the castle so as our men were not able to annoy them. They mustered in sight of our men five hundred galloglasse and kernes besides their own soldiers, which were as they could judge a hundred and sixty at the least. Although our men had killed one of their captains with shot, which as I am informed was Lysingham, yet their own ships being shot through nor seeing otherwise how to prevail further, considering what force Haydon was, having married with O'Sullivan's sister who had committed the charge of the castle unto his custody, by which means he was like daily to be succoured by those kernes, thought best for fear of sinking after sundry shots between them both—which continued from ten o'clock in the morning to four o'clock in the afternoon—to depart, which service I for my part am sorry had no better success.'[1]

The Queen's attempt to get the work done cheap was not successful, especially as Carew's men having failed to obtain plunder clamoured to be paid. The pirates gathered fresh courage from the feebleness with which they had been assailed; and in the face of the escape of Cobham and the evident unwillingness of the Government to use severity on the rare occasions when a pirate was taken prisoner, it is plain that Elizabeth's Government was not as yet awake to the necessity of resolute dealing in the matter. In the beginning of August 1565 de Silva laid before Cecil a fresh list of outrages upon Spanish commerce. He demanded 'that the more noted pirates should be diligently inquired after,' and that when taken and convicted 'they should not be pardoned;' while cautiously but firmly he insisted that the Queen's officers in the western harbours should no longer allow them 'to take in stores and run in and out at their pleasure;' that 'their receivers and comforters should be punished to the example of others;' and that rewards should be offered for the discovery and conviction of the persons most engaged in these enterprises.[2]

These requests were certainly not excessive. It is remarkable that the last was distinctly refused on the plea that to assist justice with the offer of rewards was contrary to English usage.[3] Additional salaries however were given to the admiralty judges to quicken their

---

[1] Sir Peter Carew to the Council, April 17, 1565.—*Domestic MSS.* ELIZ. vol. xxxvi.
[2] De Silva to Cecil, August 5.—*Spanish MSS. Rolls House.*
[3] 'Haud hoc nostræ reipublicæ convenit, sed salaria a Reginâ nova dantur judicibus in bonc usum.'—*Cecil to De Silva, MSS. Ibid.*

movements; Queen's ships were sent to sea to prosecute the search more vigorously; and on the 12th of August 'the Council taking into consideration a complaint of the Spanish ambassador of spoils done upon Spanish subjects upon the seas,' directed inquiry to be made all along the English coast, with the immediate trial of all persons charged with piracy and their punishment on conviction; 'her Majesty being resolved to show to the world that she intended to deal honestly in that matter.'[1]

Nevertheless the energy of the Council was still unequal to their professions, and there was still large deficiency either of power or of will. In October a vessel going from Flanders to Spain 'with tapestry, household stuff, clocks,' and other curiosities, for Philip himself, was intercepted and plundered;[2] and this final audacity seems really to have created an alarm. Harbour commissioners at last were actually appointed; codes of harbour rules were drawn out for the detection and detention of ambiguous vessels; and as an evidence that the Government were in earnest they struck faintly at the root of the disease. The gentlemen on the coast 'were the chief maintainers of pirates;' and Sir William Godolphin of Scilly and the Killigrews of Pendennis were threatened with prosecution.[3]

Yet still no one was hanged. Pirates were taken and somehow or other were soon abroad again at their old trade. Godolphin and Killigrew suffered nothing worse than a short-lived alarm.

The commission met at Bruges after long delay in the beginning of the following year. England was repre-

---

[1] *Council Register*, August 12, 1565.
[2] Phayre to Cecil, October 12.—*Spanish MSS.*
[3] *Council Register*, November, 1565.

sented by Haddon, Sir A. Montague, and Doctor Wotton. The Spanish Government had given a proof of their desire to settle all differences quietly by appointing to meet them Count Montigny and Count Egmont—Montigny, murdered afterwards by Philip with such ingenious refinement at Simancas, and Egmont the best friend that Elizabeth had in the King of Spain's dominions.

Nevertheless even with these two the problem was almost beyond solution. The proceedings had scarcely opened when another and most audacious act of piracy was committed at the mouth of the Thames. The Flemish commissioners said they did not question the good will of the Queen of England, but her conduct was very strange. They challenged Wotton to name a single pirate who had yet been executed; and Wotton with all his eagerness to defend Elizabeth confessed himself unable to mention one. They said frankly that if the Queen's Government did not see to the safety of their own seas, 'another way must be taken' which would lead to war.

'For our part,' wrote Wotton in his report to Cecil, 'we must needs think our fortune very hard; our men in their offences are so far out of all order, and the cases so lamentable if the account be true, that we can scant tell how to open our mouths for any reasonable satisfaction therein.'[1]

Elizabeth could but answer that she had done her best, and either the story was exaggerated or 'else it was a matter impossible to be reformed.' She said however that she had sent special persons to every port in England with extraordinary powers, from whose exertions

---

[1] Wotton to Cecil, May 13, 1566.—*Flanders MSS.*

an effect might be looked for.¹ Philip fortunately was in a most unwarlike humour, and her excuses were accepted for more than they were worth. But the conference was suspended till her good intentions had been carried into acts; and the commissioners separated on the 17th of June still leaving all outstanding claims unsettled.

English Protestants it was too evident regarded the property of Papists as lawful prize wherever they could lay hands on it; and Protestantism stimulated by these inducements to conversion was especially strong in the sea-port towns. Exasperated by the murder of their comrades in the prisons of the Inquisition, the sailors and merchants looked on the robbery of Spaniards as at once the most lucrative and devout of occupations; and Elizabeth's Government was unable to cope with a tendency so deeply rooted. The destinies, beneficent or evil, however, which watched over the fortunes of the nation, provided a more distant field of lawless enterprise, which gradually attracted the more daring spirits to itself; and while it removed the struggle with Spain into a larger sphere, postponed for a few years longer the inevitable collision, and left the Channel in peace.

It has been seen how in the early days of the Guinea trade the English had half in play coquetted with the capture of negroes; how they stretched out their hands towards the forbidden fruit, touched it, clutched at it and let it go: the feeble scruples were giving way before familiarity with the temptation.

The European voyagers when they first visited the coasts of Western Africa found there for the most part a quiet, peaceable and contented people basking in the

---

¹ Elizabeth to the Commissioners at Bruges, June 1, 1566. Cecil's hand.—*Flanders MSS.*

sunshine in harmless idleness, unprovoked to make war upon one another because they had nothing to desire, and receiving strangers with the unsuspecting trustfulness which is observed in the birds and animals of new countries when for the first time they come in contact with man. Remorse for the desolation created by the first conquerors of the New World among the Indians of Mexico and the isles, had tempted the nobler Spaniards into a belief that in this innocent and docile people, might be found servants who if kindly treated would labour without repugnance; and thus the remnants of those races whose civilization had astonished their destroyers might be saved from the cruelty of the colonists. The proud and melancholy Indian pined like an eagle in captivity, refused to accept his servitude and died; the more tractable negro would domesticate like the horse or the ass, acquiesce in a life of useful bondage, and receive in return the reward of baptism and the promise of eternity.

Charles the Fifth had watched over the interests of the Indians, as soon as he became awake to their sufferings, with a father's anxiety. Indian slavery in the Spanish dominions was prohibited for ever; but that the colonists might not be left without labourers, and those splendid countries relapse into a wilderness, they were allowed to import negroes from Africa, whom as expensive servants it would be their interest to preserve. The Indians had cost them nothing; the Indians had been seized by force, chained in the mines or lashed into the fields; if millions perished there were millions more to recruit the gangs. The owner of a negro whom he had bought and bought dear, would have the same interest in him as in his horse or his cow; he would exact no more work from his slave than the slave could perform without injury to himself, and he would be the means of saving a soul from everlasting perdition.

Nor was the bondage of the negro intended to be perpetual, nor would the great Emperor trust him without reserve to men who had already abused their powers. The law secured to the slave a certain portion of every week when the time was his own; if he was industrious and frugal he could insist upon his freedom as soon as he could produce the price of it; he could become an owner of property on his own account; and evidence remains that in the sixteenth century, under the protecting laws of the mother country many a negro in the Spanish colonies was a free and prosperous settler who paid his taxes to the Crown.[1]

Negro slavery in theory was an invention of philanthropy—like the modern Coolie trade, an unobjectionable and useful substitute for the oppression of races to whom loss of freedom was death; yet with the fatal blot in the design that the consent of the negroes themselves, who were so largely interested in the transaction, was neither sought nor obtained. The original and innocent pretext which confined the purchase to those who had offended against the negro laws, melted swiftly before the increase of the demand; the beads, the scarlet cloaks and ribands which were fluttered in the eyes of the chiefs, were temptations which savage vanity was unable to resist; they sold their own people; they made war on one another to capture prisoners, which had become a valuable booty; and the river mouths and harbours where the Portuguese traders established their factories were envenomed centres from which a moral pestilence

---

[1] I need scarcely more than allude for my authority on this subject to the admirable book of Mr. Helps on the Spanish Conquest of America.

crept out among the African races. The European first converted the negro into a savage, and then made use of his brutality as an excuse for plunging him into slavery.

The English at first escaped the dread and detestation which were inspired by the slave dealers: they came as traders to barter for gold dust; they were fired upon whenever they approached the factories, and the natives welcomed as friends the enemies of the Portuguese and Spaniards. But the unfortunate people were themselves the richest part of their merchandise. The Spanish Government, aware perhaps after a time of the effect produced in Africa, and wishing to ensure the good treatment of the slaves by enhancing their value, had begun to set their faces against the slave trade. The Governors of the Spanish-American colonies were instructed to prevent the importation of negroes unless under a licence from the home administration, which was dearly bought and charily given. A duty of thirty ducats was laid on the sale of every slave; and thus while the demand for labour increased with the prosperity of the settlements, the price was enhanced, the supply was artificially kept down, and the English traders at the Azores and at Madeira came to understand that licence or no licence the market of the West Indies would be open to them. If slaves could be brought to their doors the colonists would eagerly buy them, and with discretion and courage the negro trade might be made a thriving business.

First slaving voyage of John Hawkins.

The first venture was made by John Hawkins of Plymouth, so famous afterwards in English naval annals, son of old William Hawkins who had brought over the Brazilian King. John Hawkins and Thomas Hampton, in October 1562, fitted out three vessels, the largest a hundred and twenty tons, and sailed with a hundred men for Sierra Leone.[1] After hanging some time about the coast, 'partly by the sword and partly by other means,' they collected three hundred negroes, and crossed the Atlantic to St. Domingo. Uncertain at first how he might be received, or not caring to avow the purpose of his voyage, Hawkins pretended on his arrival that he had been driven out of his course by stress of weather, that he was in want of food, and was without money to pay his men; he therefore requested permission to sell 'certain slaves which he had with him.' The opportunity was eagerly welcomed; the Governor, supposing apparently that his orders from home need not be construed too stringently, allowed two-thirds of the negroes to be sold; the remaining hundred, as it was uncertain what duty should be demanded on an unlicensed sale, were left as a deposit with the oidores or council of the island. Neither Hawkins nor the Governor anticipated any serious displeasure on the part of Philip. Hawkins invested his profits in a return cargo of hides, half of which he sent in Spanish vessels to Cadiz under the care of his partner, and he returned with the rest to England, as he supposed, 'with prosperous success and much gain to himself.'

Prosperous in point of money the voyage undoubtedly was, although the profits proved less than he anticipated. He had brought away with him a testimonial of good behaviour from the authorities at St. Domingo, who would gladly have seen him return on the same errand. The Spanish Government viewed the affair differently. Philip the Second, to whatever crimes he might be driven by religious bigotry, was not inclined to tolerate free trade in negroes, however large the duty which he

---

[1] First voyage of Mr. John Hawkins.—HAKLUYT, vol. iii. p. 594.

could exact upon them; and the intrusion of the English into his transatlantic dominions, his experience of them nearer home made him particularly anxious to prohibit. On Hampton's arrival at Cadiz his cargo was confiscated and sold, he himself narrowly escaping the clutches of the Inquisition;[1] the negroes left at St. Domingo were forfeited, and Hawkins saw snatched from him a full moiety of his hard-earned prize. He estimated his loss at forty thousand ducats; he cursed, threatened, and implored, with equal unsuccess; fearless of man or devil he thought at first of going in person to Madrid and of taking Philip by the beard in his own den; but Chaloner, to whom he wrote, told him with some sarcasm 'that he would do well not to come thither;' 'it was an ill time for obtaining any suit further than the right or justice of the cause would bear;' he advised him 'to attempt to obtain a part of the thing to be demanded, by procuring some favourite about the King to ask for the whole as a forfeit confiscate;' he might then perhaps recover some part of his loss by a private arrangement.[2]

Neither by this, however, nor by any other means could Hawkins obtain one penny for his lost hides and negroes; and the result of his demands was only the despatch of a peremptory order to the West Indies that no English vessel should be allowed under any pretence to trade there. Foreseeing that when the road had been once opened hundreds would rush into it, Philip said distinctly to the ambassador that if the English persisted in going thither evil would come of it; and so impressed was Chaloner with the feelings of the Spanish Govern-

---

[1] Hugh Tipton to Chaloner, December, 1563.—*Spanish MSS. Rolls House.*
[2] Chaloner to Hawkins, July 6, 1564.—*Spanish MSS.*

ment on the subject, that he entreated Elizabeth earnestly
to make her subjects respect their objections.[1]

The warning, if Elizabeth had possessed either power
or inclination to act upon it, was not unneeded. Traces
appear of more than one attempt to follow in Hawkins's
track before he himself moved again; and the African
tribes being now on their guard, the slave hunters had
been received with poisoned arrows, and had found a
difficulty in escaping with their lives.[2]

But Hawkins knew better what he was about; he *Second voyage with the sanction of Queen and Council.* understood how to catch negroes; he understood how to sell them to Spaniards, whatever Philip might please to say; he would not repeat the single mistake into which he had fallen; and the profits seemed so certain and promised to be so large, that Lord Pembroke and others of the Council were ready to take shares in a second adventure. Even the Queen herself had no objection to turn a little honest money; and contenting herself with requiring a promise from him that he would do no injury to the Spaniards, she left the rest to his discretion, and placed at his disposal one of the best ships in her service. Cecil alone, ever honourable, ever loathing cruelty and unrighteousness, though pressed to join with the rest, refused, 'having no liking for such proceedings.'[3]

Thus encouraged and supported, Hawkins sailed once

---

[1] 'Our folks must be narrowly looked to, and specially that they enterprise no trade or voyage to the Indies or islands of this king's navigation; which if they do, as already they have intelligence of some that do propose it, surely it will breed occasion of much matter of pick.'—*Chaloner to Elizabeth, June 18, 1564.—MS. Ibid.*

[2] See Robert Baker's *Metrical History of Two Voyages to Guinea in 1562 and 1563,* printed by HAKLUYT.

[3] 'El secretário Cecil me ha dicho que é el le ofreciéron quando partió Achines que le admitirian como á los demas; pero que el lo habia rehusado porque no le contentáron semejantes negocios.'—*De Silva to Philip, November 5, 1565. MS. Simancas.*

more from Plymouth on the 18th of October 1564 in the 'Jesus of Lubeck,' a ship of 700 tons, armed to the teeth, his old vessel the 'Solomon,' enlarged somewhat, perhaps with a more roomy hold, and two small sloops to run up the shallow creeks.

A rival expedition sailed at the same time and for the same purpose from the Thames, under David Carlet, to whom the Queen had also given a ship. Carlet had three vessels, the 'Minion,' Elizabeth's present, the 'John the Baptist,' and the 'Merlin.' The 'Merlin' had bad luck; she had the powder on board for the nigger hunt; fire got into the magazine, and she was blown in pieces. Carlet, therefore, for a time attached himself with his two remaining ships to Hawkins, and the six vessels run south together. Passing Teneriffe on the 29th of November, they touched first at the Cape de Verde Isles, where the natives 'being very gentle and loving and more civil than any others,' it was proposed to take in a store of them. Either, however, the two commanders could not agree, or Hawkins claimed the lion's share of the spoil; they quarrelled, and the 'Minion's' men being jealous gave the islanders to understand what was intended, 'so that they did avoid the snares laid for them.'

After so unworthy a proceeding the west countryman shook off his companion, and leaving Carlet to go his own way, went down the coast past the Rio Grande, storing his hold as he went along among the islands and rivers. On one occasion he was played a trick by some Portuguese which might have had bad consequences: they offered to guide him to a village where he would find a hundred unprotected women and children, and they betrayed him into ambuscade when his men, who were scattered in search of plunder, were set upon by two hundred negroes. Seven were killed and seven-and-twenty wounded, and in return for their loss they carried off but ten slaves. 'Thus,' reported one of the party, 'we returned back somewhat discomforted, although the captain in a singular wise carried himself with countenance very cheerful outwardly, although his heart was inwardly broken at the loss of his men.'

But this was the single interruption of otherwise unbroken success. Between purchases from the Portuguese and the spoils of his own right arm, Hawkins in a few weeks had swept up about four hundred slaves; his ships were inconveniently crowded, symptoms of fever began to show among the crew, and the shore was no longer safe, 'the natives having laid a plan to entrap and kill them.' 'God, however, who worketh all things for the best, would not have it so, and by Him they escaped danger, His name be praised.' The captain decided that he had done enough, and headed away for the West Indies. He was troubled at first with calms; he feared that the water might run short, and that part of his cargo might die, or have to be thrown overboard. 'Almighty God, however, who never suffers His elect to perish,'[1] 'sent a breeze in time, and the Indian islands were reached without the loss of a man. A second venture at St. Domingo was thought dangerous; Hawkins had arranged with the Council before he sailed 'not to send any ship or ships to any of those ports of the Indies that were privileged to any person or persons by the King of Spain;'[2] and precautions had probably been taken to make any further trade at the scene of his first visit

---

[1] *Narrative of the Second Voyage of Mr. John Hawkins*, by one of the party. Printed by HAKLUYT.
[2] *Council Register MS.*

impossible. He contented himself with touching there for water, and made as fast as he could for the mainland. His best chance to dispose of his wares was to choose some harbour where the inhibition was unlikely to be known, or where he would be able to force an entry if it was refused; and running on into Burbarotta,[1] he anchored close off the town and went on shore.

He at once learnt that the interdict had arrived: in reply to his proposal to trade he was informed that the King of Spain had forbidden the colonists under pain of death[2] to admit any foreign vessels there or have any dealings with them; and he was entreated to go his way. But the town was weak and Hawkins was strong; he repeated his old story that he was driven in by foul weather, that he had a large crew, and was in distress for food and money. He showed his commission from Elizabeth—'a confederate and friend of the King of Spain;' and he said that unless he was allowed to trade peaceably, his men would go on land, and might perhaps do some injury.

How Hawkins sold his negroes.

The inhabitants desired negroes; the menace was an excuse for the Governor to yield; but to save himself from some portion of the blame he insisted that Hawkins should at least pay the thirty ducats customs duty. The English commander, however, had no intention of contributing more than he could help to Philip's treasury. When some valuable time had been wasted in discussion, he cut the knot by landing a hundred men and two pieces of cannon; he put out a proclamation that seven and a half per cent. was a sufficient tax to be levied on

---

[1] Called Borbomata in the English accounts.
[2] 'Su pena de muerte,' according to the Spanish account at Simancas. The English story says 'upon penalty to forfeit their goods.'

any wares in any harbour, that his necessities were too
great to be trifled with, and that unless the people were
permitted to deal with him on these terms, he would not
answer for the consequences. The Governor allowed himself to be convinced by so effective an argument; the
planters in the neighbourhood swallowed their scruples; in
a few days half the cargo was happily disposed of, and
Hawkins sailed away with the rest, after first exacting
from the authorities, as before, a certificate of good
behaviour.[1]

From Barbarotta he went to Rio de la Hacha, where
the same scene was re-enacted with simple monotony.
The Governor, as before, protested that he was forbidden
by his master to let the English trade there; the English commander, as before, declared that he was in 'an
armada of the Queen of England sent about her other
affairs,' that he had been forced by contrary winds out of
his course, and that he expected hospitality. The authorities again refused, again Hawkins threatened violence,
and again there was a dispute over the customs duties.
Finally, with or without an understanding with the
Governor, a few boats' crews with cannon once more
opened the market; the remaining negroes were sold off,
and with the hard money in his hand, a second testimonial,

---

[1] De Silva said that the exhibition of force had been secretly concerted between Hawkins and the Governor.

' El Capitan respondió que la gente que el traia era mucho, y que no podia el contenerlos, para que no saltasen en tierra y hiciesen daño, si no tuviesen licencia para contratar; y assi vinó á platicar en segreto con el Gobernador, y entre ellos se habia concertado que otro dia se echase gente en tierra y començase á herer ir al lugar y hacer daño, y que el saldria, porque no lo hiciese, le dexarian hacer su contratacion; lo qual se hizó assi; y pasó en tierra docientos hombres y ciertas pieças de artilleria, las quales començáron á pelear, pero luego cesó, y por bien de paz le dexáron negociar, habiendo passado entre ellos algunas cosas por escrito de requerimiento como se habia entre ellos concertado.'—*De Silva to Philip*, *November 5, 1565. MS. Simancas.*

and the black pens below decks washed clear of pollution, the fortunate Hawkins put to sea in full triumph and high spirits. Instead of hastening home he spent the summer of 1565 cruising in the Caribbean Sea, surveying the islands, mapping down the shoals and currents, and perhaps on the look out for some lame duck or straggler out of the Spanish treasure fleet.[1]

Sailing round Cuba and running up the Bahama Channel, the English commander then turned north, felt his way along the coast of Florida, landing from time to time to examine the capabilities of the country, and visiting and relieving the French settlements there. Finally passing up to the Banks of Newfoundland, he fed his tired and famished crews with his fishing lines; and so in September came safely back with his golden spoils into Padstow Harbour, having lost in the whole voyage, including those who had been killed by the negroes, not more than twenty men.[2]

Lord Pembroke and the other contributors made sixty per cent. on their adventure; nor need it be supposed that Elizabeth went without her share for the ship. Hawkins on his arrival in London, was the hero of the

---

[1] 'Esperando la flota de la nueva España ó tierra firma, para ver si de paso podrian tomar algun navio della.'—*De Silva to Philip. MS. Simancas.*

[2] From Padstow, Hawkins wrote the following letter to Elizabeth:—

'Please your Majesty to be informed that this 20th day of September I arrived in a port of Cornwall called Padstow, with your Majesty's ship the 'Jesus' in good safety—thanks be to God—our voyage being reasonably well accomplished according to our pretence. Your Majesty's commandment at my departing from your Grace at Enfield I have accomplished, so as I doubt not but it shall be found honourable to your Highness, for I have always been a help to all Spaniards and Portugals that have come in my way without any form or prejudice by me offered to any of them, although many times in this tract they have been under my power; I have also discovered the coast of Florida in those parts where there is thought to be great wealth. Your Majesty's, &c.'—*Pepys's MSS. Magdalen College, Cambridge.*

hour, affecting the most unconscious frankness, and unable to conceive that he had done anything at which the King of Spain could take offence.

'I met him,' de Silva wrote, 'in the palace, and invited him to dine with me; he gave me a full account of his voyage, keeping back only the way in which he had contrived to trade at our ports. He assured me on the contrary that he had given the greatest satisfaction to all the Spaniards with whom he had had dealings, and had received full permission from the governors of the towns where he had been. The vast profit made by the voyage has excited other merchants to undertake similar expeditions. Hawkins himself is going out again next May; and the thing requires immediate attention. I might tell the Queen that by his own confession he has traded in ports prohibited by your Majesty, and require her to punish him; but I must request your Majesty to give me full and clear instructions what to do.'[1]

From this time, and until his mantle descended to his friend and pupil Francis Drake, Hawkins, or Achines as the Spaniards called him, troubled the dreams and perplexed the waking thoughts of Philip the Second. In every despatch in which the name is mentioned the sprawling asterisks in the margin remain to evidence the emotion which it produced. The report of that audacious voyage enhanced the warmth with which the cause of Mary Stuart was adopted at Madrid; and the King of Spain was haunted with a vague foreboding that the visits of these roving English would carry ruin to his colonies, and menace the safety of his gold fleets.

---

[1] De Silva to Philip, November.—MS. Simancas.

Chap XII
1566

It would be to misread history and to forget the change of times, to see in Hawkins and his successors mere commonplace buccaneers; to themselves they appeared as the elect to whom God had given the heathen for an inheritance; they were men of stern intellect and fanatical faith, who believing themselves the favourites of Providence, imitated the example and assumed the privileges of the chosen people; and for their wildest and worst acts they could claim the sanction of religious conviction. In seizing negroes or in pillaging galleons they were but entering into possession of the heritage of the saints; and England had to outgrow the theology of the Elizabethan Calvinists before it could understand that the Father of Heaven respected neither person nor colour, and that His arbitrary favour, if more than a dream of divines, was confined to spiritual privileges.

Again in the following year the slave fleet was fitted for the sea. It was at the crisis in Elizabeth's fortunes when the birth of James had given fatal strength to the party of the Queen of Scots, and to affront Philip was dangerous. When on the eve of sailing, Hawkins was called before the Council, in deference to the imperious remonstrances of de Silva, and was bound in securities not to approach the West Indies, or break the laws, or injure in any way the subjects of the King of Spain.

Third voyage.

Shackled by these commands he sent out his vessels without himself accompanying them: no English record remains to say whither the expedition went; only it was known that the ships returned loaded with gold and silver and rich skins, and whispered stories reached de Silva's ears that the Council's orders had not been too closely followed. Whether the crews again effected some negro smuggling, which they and those who dealt with them were alike interested in concealing, or whether the spoils which they brought back with them formed the freightage of some Spanish vessel which never reached its port, the silent ocean kept its secrets; and when the bold adventurers came back to Plymouth, the Netherlands were plunging into mutiny, the Catholics in England were shattered by the explosion at Kirk-a-Field, and Elizabeth could afford to be more careless of Philip's pleasure.

Her subjects might now exact restitution at their pleasure for their murdered comrades in Spain,[1] and in the very midst of de Silva's outcries, in the autumn of 1567, the 'Jesus' was again placed at Hawkins's disposal; four more ships, all powerfully armed, were equipped as her consorts; and the intention was scarcely concealed with the faintest affectation of denial, to dare the King of Spain to do his worst, and to carry slaves whether he would or not to the American colonies.

The two countries were thus drifting fast into undeclared war, and peace existed but in name. While the fleet was preparing for sea in Plymouth a Spanish ship

---

[1] Hakluyt seems to have known nothing of any voyage of Hawkins's men in 1566; but the entries in the Council books prove that some voyage or other was contemplated; and the following words of de Silva in October, 1567, refer distinctly to the year preceding.

'V. M⁴. mandó el año pasado á Fenaar y á John Achines quando enviaban sus navios que no partiesen sin primero dar fianças de que no irian á aquellas partes, ni tratasen mal los subditos de su M⁴. que topasen en el mar. Que segun soy avisado no lo cumpliéron, en especial John Achines, como es cosa sabida, y se entiende de sus marineros, y por el oro y plata y cueros que han traido. Sobre lo qual V. M⁴. sera servida mandar que se haga lo que conforme á razon y justicia se debe, como contra personas que han contravenido al mandamiento de V. M⁴.; que todo es materia de mala consequencia, y que los que cometen estos delitos ó los que los mandan hacer y los que no los han castigado deben desear que la buena amistad que hay entre V. M⁴. y el Rey m Señor no se conserve procurandolo con semejantes excessos y otros tales, unos robando por la mar á sus subditos, otros yendo adoles está prohibido,' &c.—*De Silva to Elizabeth, October 6, 1567, Spanish MSS. Rolls House.*

of war came into Catwater with the Castilian flag flying; she had prisoners on board from the Netherlands, probably insurgents; and Hawkins affecting to suppose that she was come in with bad intentions, at once fired upon her,[1] and forced her to lower her flag. The prisoners in the confusion escaped, took refuge on board the 'Jesus,' and a few days after were carried off in a Flemish vessel.

So violent an outrage could not be wholly overlooked; and Elizabeth sent to Plymouth to make inquiries; but Hawkins merely affected astonishment at her displeasure. He assumed that the Spaniard had intended to break the peace of the port, and claimed the thanks of his sovereign for having protected the honour of the realm.[2]

'Your mariners,' said the Spanish ambassador to Elizabeth, 'rob my master's subjects on the sea, and trade where they are forbidden to go; they plunder our people in the streets of your towns; they attack our vessels in your very harbours, and take our prisoners from them; your preachers insult my master from their pulpits; and when we apply for justice we are answered with threats.

'We have borne with these things, attributing them rather to passion or rudeness of manners than to any deliberate purpose of wrong; but seeing that there is no remedy and no end, I must now refer to my sovereign to learn what I am to do. I make however one concluding

---

[1] 'Hizo tirar desde una torre, y tan bien de los dichos navios seis ó siete canonagos, hasta dar dentro de mi navio con las balas, y por esta causa me fué forçado de quitar las banderas de V. M^d., lo qual nunca me ha socalido en ningun lugar de Inglatierra en avii ó xviii años que ha que tengo este cargo.'—*Copia de Capitulo de Cartes que M. de Wachen scrivió á su M^d. September 23. 1567.— MS. Simancas.*

[2] '*Copia de la Carta de Achines al Secretario Cecil.*'—*MS. Simancas.*

appeal to your Majesty; I entreat your Majesty to punish this last outrage at Plymouth, and to preserve the peace between the two nations.'[1]

Elizabeth gave a smooth answer; she affected—perhaps she felt—some real regret and displeasure; but Hawkins was allowed to sail, where the slow foot of justice at length came up with him.

---

[1] De Silva to Elizabeth, October 6, 1567.—*Spanish MSS. Rolls House.*